A Practical Guide to Patent Law

Second edition

Brian C. Reid

Barrister-at-Law, London

Sweet & Maxwell
1993

First Edition 1984
Second Edition 1993

ISBN 421 452 20 X

Published in 1993 by Sweet & Maxwell Limited, South Quay Plaza,
183 Marsh Wall, London E14 9FT

Printed in Great Britain by Short Run Press, Exeter
Typeset by Photo-graphics, Honiton

Contents

Chapter Four:
Acquisition of Patents *60*

Chapter Five:
Keeping and Losing of Patents *75*

Chapter Six:
Infringement of Patents (Law) *86*

Chapter Seven:
Infringement of Patents (Action)   *102*

Chapter Eight:
The Patents County Court   *119*

Chapter Nine:
Employee Inventions   *123*

Chapter Ten:
Licensing and Assignment *131*

Chapter Eleven:
Contest in the Patent Office *144*

Chapter Twelve:
International Patents *157*

Chapter Thirteen:
Patents in Relation to Other Forms of Intellectual Property *170*

Statutes *179*

Appendices *303*

Glossary *351*

General Bibliography *355*

Index *356*

Table of Cases

List of Abbreviations

Literature

AIPL	*Annual of Industrial Property Law* (1975–79)
BB	Chartered Institute of Patent Agents' *Guide to the Patents Act 1977* (the 'Black Book') (1st ed., 1980; 2nd ed., 1984; 3rd ed. 1990)
CIPA	*Journal of the Chartered Institute of Patent Agents* (1971 onwards)
CMLR	*Common Market Law Reports* (1962 onwards)
Cmnd.	Command Paper
ECR	*European Court of Justice Reports* (1954 onwards)
EIPR	*European Intellectual Property Review* (1979 onwards)
EPOR	*European Patent Office Reports* (1979–85; 1986 onwards)
F.Cas.	*Federal Cases* (United States) (1789–1880)
FSR	*Fleet Street Reports* (1963 onwards)
Gordon	*Monopolies by Patents* (1897)
Guidelines	*Guidelines for Examination in the European Patent Office* (1987)
Hare	*Hare's* [Vice-Chancellors' Court's] *Reports* (1841–1853)
IPD	*Intellectual Property Decisions* (1978 onwards)
JO	*Journal Officiel des Communautés Européennes*
JPOS	*Journal of the Patent Office Society* (Washington, DC, United States) (1919 onwards); now JPTOS
LJ Ch.	*Law Journal (Chancery) Reports* (1832–1949)
LQR	*Law Quarterly Review* (1885 onwards)
PLUK	*Patent Law of the United Kingdom* (Texts, Commentary and Notes on Practice by the Chartered Institute of Patent Agents) (the Blue Book) (1975)
RPC	*Reports of Patent Cases* (1883 onwards)
Transactions	*Transactions of the Chartered Institute of Patent Agents* (1883–1971)
SRIS	Science Reference and Information Service (of the British Library)

US   United States Supreme Court Reports
USPQ   *United States Patent Quarterly* (1929 onwards)
WLR   *Weekly Law Reports* (1953 onwards)
WPC   *Webster's Patent Cases*

Other

Commission Commission of the European Communities
CPC   Community Patent Convention
ECJ   European Court of Justice
EEC   European Economic Community
EPC   European Patent Convention
HMSO   Her Majesty's Stationery Office
PCT   Patent Co-operation Treaty
WIPO   World Intellectual Property Organization

Preface to the Second Edition

Since 1984, when the first edition of this work was published, there has been substantial advance in the pa ent law. The Copyright, Designs and Patent Act 1988 foreshadowed in 1977 has come into being. The important new litigation forum represented by the Patents County Court has been working highly successfully since 1990. The European Patent Office has broken much new ground in the life sciences field. The overall aim of the work remains, however, much as before. Although there may come a time in future when it will be possible to regard patent law as effectively starting with the European Patent Convention of 1973, and hence the main domestic provision (the 1977 Act), such point has not yet been reached. Pending the arrival of that golden age, it is hoped that the present second edition will continue to prove useful to those concerned to learn the mysteries of this unique branch of the law.

Brian C. Reid
Middle Temple
London
November 1992

1 History and Function of the Patent System

Introduction

Perhaps the most remarkable features of the patent system are its global persistence and pervasiveness. Nearly all major industrial countries, and the majority of minor ones, today make statutory provision for the protection of new inventions. Even a country like the USSR, which in the heady aftermath of the Bolshevik Revolution abolished the Tsarist patent law, subsequently found it expedient to reintroduce the patent system (albeit in a modified form). China remained for many years the only important exception, but eventually a formal patent law was enacted in 1984.

Many of such individual systems are of considerable antiquity. Individual monopoly grants dating back to the 13th and 14th centuries can be found in the records of various European territories. The first general statute is often reckoned to be that passed by the Venetian State in 1474;[1] the preamble and opening sentences of this statute set the scene:

> WE HAVE among us men of great genius, apt to invent and discover ingenious devices; and in view of the grandeur and virtue of our City, more such men come to us every day from diverse parts. Now, if provision were made for the works and devices discovered by such persons, so that others who may see them could not build them and take the inventor's honor away, more men would then apply their genius, would discover, and would build devices of great utility and benefit to our commonwealth. Therefore:

> BE IT ENACTED that, by the authority of this Council, every person who shall build any new and ingenious device in this City, not previously made in our Commonwealth, shall give notice of it to the office of our General Welfare Board when it has been reduced to perfection so that it can be used and operated. It being forbidden to every other person in any of our territories and towns to make any further device conforming with and similar to said one, without the consent and license of the author, for the term of 10 years . . .

Around one hundred patents are known to have been granted under this statute, in a wide variety of technical fields including windmills, mud excavation, brick-making, wood-sawing, keel-laying, glass-pouring and working intaglio in glass. It will be noted that even at this very early date in the history of technology, the requirements for novelty and non-obviousness of the new invention are enunciated ('. . . new and ingenious device . . . not previously made'); likewise there has to be utility ('. . . reduced to perfection . . .'). Infringement is prohibited, but the grantee can license others ('It being forbidden . . . without the consent and license of the author . . .').

In the United Kingdom, the effective foundation is generally assumed to be provided

---

1 JPOS Volume XXX (1948) at 176.

by the passing of the Statute of Monopolies[2] in 1624, although there are earlier precedents back to 1331. In the United States of America, the laws reflect the constitutional provision of 1787 that:

> The Congress shall have Power . . . To Promote the Progress of Science and useful Arts, by securing for limited Times to Authors and Inventors the exclusive Right to their respective Writings and Discoveries.[3]

The reason for such endurance of the patent system is not hard to find. It is simply that the patent system has in practice over the centuries been found to represent a unique and peculiarly effective means of encouraging the development of industry and technology. In the words of Abraham Lincoln (one of the few heads of state ever to have been a patentee himself): 'The Patent system added the fuel of interest to the fire of genius'.

On a more parochial note, it may be interesting to list a few of the more outstanding inventions of British origin in the 20th century. Many of these have served to create whole new industries since the end of World War II in 1945.

Jet engine[4]	Float glass[9]
Radar[5]	Polyester fibres[10]
Polyethylene[6]	Semi-synthetic penicillins (ampicillin, amoxycillin)[11]
Television[7]	Cephalosporin antibiotics[12]
Hovercraft[8]	Printed circuits[13]

Basic Theory

The basic theory of the patent system is very simple. It is that the state (or its personification) grants the inventor an exclusive monopoly for a limited time in his new invention in return for his disclosure of the invention so that the public at large will be able to practise the invention once the patent expires.

At one time, at least in the United Kingdom, the disclosure was by way of teaching apprentices the mystery of the craft. In the case of *Buck's Patent*,[14] granted in 1651 for the melting of iron and other metals by coal without charking thereof, there was for example a proviso:

2   21 Jac. 1 c.3.
3   Article 1, section 8.
4   Patents Nos. 347206 and 471368.
5   Patents Nos. 591130 and 593017.
6   Patent No. 471590.
7   Patent No. 222604.
8   Patent No. 854211.
9   Patent No. 769692.
10   Patent No. 578079.
11   Patents Nos. 873049, 902703, 1241844.
12   Patents Nos. 810196 and 953695.
13   Patent No. 639178.
14   1 WPC 35.

Provided also, that the said Jeremy Buck, and his assigns, after seven years of the term hereby granted, do and shall take apprentices, and teach them the knowledge and mystery of the said new invention.

Nowadays, in contrast, the teaching of the public is almost invariably provided for by the filing (formerly termed 'enrolling') of a written specification describing the new invention. Filing of such a specification in the Patent Office is a prerequisite for grant of the patent; the specification is a public document, open to public inspection.

The change in practice from disclosure by way of teaching apprentices to disclosure by way of a written publication started generally in the United Kingdom in 1711 with *Nasmith's Patent*[15] (for preparing and fermenting wash from sugar, molasses and grain, for distilling). By 1778 the change was complete. Lord Mansfield in that year, in *Liardet v Johnson*,[16] declared the function of the specification to be as follows:

> The law relative to patents requires, as a price the individual should pay the people for his monopoly, that he should enrol, to the very best of his knowledge and judgement, the fullest and most sufficient description of all the particulars on which the effect depended, that he was at the time able to do.

Although the theory of the patent system is straightforward and virtually universal, the practical details of its operation can still vary substantially from country to country. Consider, for example, the case where a given invention is made more or less contemporaneously by separate inventors working independently. This kind of situation occurs quite frequently in fields of technology which are advancing rapidly at the time – as was the manufacture of electric lamps at the end of the Victorian era, or as is biotechnology today. Who wins the patent race in such circumstances? In the United Kingdom, he who files his application first in the Patent Office wins. In the United States of America, it is, in contrast, the first to invent who succeeds.

Other important areas where national differences may still prevail include those of examination procedure, amendment of patents after grant, employee rights, shop rights, grace periods, renewal fees, criteria for assessment of infringement, intervention of third parties, compulsory licences – to name just a few of the topics discussed in succeeding chapters. Generally, there is a trend towards harmonisation of patent law on a global scale. But the road is littered with obstacles, and progress tends to be erratic.

Other Modes of Protection

It is important right from the beginning to understand the distinction between patents and other ways of protecting technological development. In the United Kingdom these other routes are:

(1) design registration;
(2) copyright (including unregistered design right); and
(3) as trade secrets.

15   Patent No. 387.
16   1 WPC 53.

Their interrelation with the patent system is discussed more fully in Chapter 13, but some preliminary comments are made here.

Design registration is covered by the Registered Designs Act 1949[17] (as amended by the Copyright, Designs and Patents Act 1988[18]), itself a statute building on a series of earlier Acts commencing (for practical purposes) with the Copyright of Designs Act 1839.[19] The law is concerned essentially with protecting a new appearance rather than a new mode of construction.

Copyright was governed (up to the recent Copyright, Designs and Patents Act 1988) by the Copyright Act 1956.[20] Its importance stemmed principally from the judicial recognition of engineering drawings as being capable of being ranked as 'artistic works' for the purposes of that Act. The 1988 Act effectively abolished this head of protection (transitional provisions apart) and substituted instead the new unregistered design right regime for the future.

The law of trade secrets (or 'confidential information' as it is often termed) is essentially a creature of the common law.

There is at present in the United Kingdom no system of utility model (petty patent) registration such as is encountered abroad in some countries, notably in Germany and Japan, for the protection of devices and articles which are a step forward in the art but not of sufficient intrinsic ingenuity to be regarded as proper inventions.

1624 to 1977 Era in the United Kingdom

The reign of Elizabeth I (1558–1603) had seen the gradual introduction of the practice of granting patents by the Crown for the encouragement of new trade and industry within the realm. Acontius' Patent,[21] granted in 1565 for the manufacture of machines for grinding, is often regarded as the first clear case of a grant for a new invention. Towards the end of Elizabeth's reign, abuses crept in. Monopolies were granted to court favourites and the like in respect of the right to sell staple commodities. There were vociferous complaints. D'Ewes' *Journal of the Parliament of 1601*[22] refers, for example, to the unwarranted behaviour of the patentee holding the monopoly in respect of the sale of aqua-vitae and vinegar in the town of Warwick.

The matter first came before the courts in the famous Case of Monopolies in 1602, *Darcy v Allein*.[23] This concerned the exclusive right to import, make and sell common playing cards. The grant was held void, as being contrary to both common law and divers Acts of Parliament.

Eventually, in 1624, the Statute of Monopolies was passed to curb the previous abuses and excesses and to regulate the whole matter. By section I of this Statute, all 'commissions graunts licences charters and letters patents . . . for the sole buyinge sellinge makinge workinge or usinge of any thinge within this Realme' were to be 'utterlie void and of none effecte, and in noe wise to be putt in use or execucion'.

17   12, 13 & 14 Geo.6 c.88.
18   1988 c.48.
19   2 Vict.c.13.
20   4 & 5 Eliz.2 c.74.
21   LQR Volume 12 (1896) at 148; [1983] 2 EIPR at 41.
22   Gordon, at 2.
23   1 WPC 1.

Section VI set out the all-important exception, in the following terms:

> Provided also and be it declared and enacted that any declaration before mentioned shall not extend to any letters patents and graunts of privilege for the tearme of fowerteen yeares or under, hereafter to be made of the sole workinge or makinge of any *manner of new manufactures* within this Realme, to the true and first inventor and inventors of such manufactures, which others at the tyme of makinge such letters patents and graunts shall not use, soe as alsoe they be not contrary to the laws nor mischievous to the State, by raisinge prices of commodities at home, or hurt of trade, or generally inconvenient
>
> . . . (*Emphasis added*)

'Manner of new manufacture' remained, right up to 1978 (when the present 1977 Patents Act[24] came into force), the definition of what constituted in principle the kind of subject-matter which constituted an 'invention' and hence could be patented.

From 1624 to 1835 the actual procedure for the grant and enforcement of patents remained entirely a matter for the common law. The gradual introduction of the requirement for a written specification, as already mentioned, represents an example of its development. In 1835, the first statute was passed, providing for disclaimers and prolongations of term. The first comprehensive statute, providing also for the establishment of the Patent Office, came in 1852 and the first modern statute was passed in 1883. This was followed by another comprehensive statute in 1907, with important amendments in 1932 codifying the grounds for invalidity of a patent, and finally came the last of the old statutes, the Patents Act 1949.[25] Various minor Acts were also passed. A comprehensive list of the relevant statutes (other than private Acts) is set out in Appendix 1.

Patents Act 1977

This Act represents a watershed in the development of United Kingdom patent law. Passage of the Act was necessary in order that the domestic law could be brought into harmony with the provisions of the European Patent Convention[26] of 1973, to which the United Kingdom now adhered. The procedures of the new European Patent Office, which that Convention set up, had to be accommodated; likewise the proposed new Community Patent had to be catered for. These latter subjects are discussed further in Chapter 12. Certain amendments of the 1977 Act, including in particular those relating to establishment of the Patents County Court and alteration of the compulsory licence provisions for old patents extended under the transitional provisions of that Act, were effected by the Copyright, Designs and Patents Act 1988.

The 1977 Act is thus a hybrid animal. Whereas previous Patents Acts had built steadily one upon the other, in the traditional British manner of statutory evolution rather than revolution, a number of distinct strands are woven into the new Act. In brief, there are:

(1) Provisions taken over wholly (or substantially so) from the 1949 Act, because they are unaffected by the terms of the European Patent Convention

---

24   1977 c.37.
25   12, 13 & 14 Geo.6 c.87.
26   Cmnd 5656.

and no other reason to change them was shown. An example is provided by the grounds on which a compulsory licence may be granted: section 48(3) lists virtually the same grounds as did section 37(2) of the 1949 Act.

(2) Provisions reflecting those of the European Patent Convention and which had no statutory counterpart under the 1949 Act. An important example is represented by the statutory criteria as regards interpretation of the scope of a patent – section 125 (1) and (3) of the 1977 Act together with the associated Protocol on the Interpretation of Article 69 of the Convention. Although section 4(3)(c) of the 1949 Act (calling for a specification to end with a claim or claims defining the scope of the invention claimed), taken with the form of Letters Patent prescribed by the then Rules, had previously between them produced under the case law an approach to interpretation not wholly dissimilar to that prescribed by section 125(1), yet there was no explicit statutory provision on the point. And section 125(3), with associated Protocol, are quite new.

(3) Provisions reflecting the terms of the European Patent Convention, but which did have pre-existing statutory counterparts in the 1949 Act. One example is provided by the provisions for amendment of patents, post-grant. The previous qualification, with its associated accretion of precedent dating back in part to practice under the Patents, Designs, and Trade Marks Act 1883,[27] was that amendment had to be by way of 'disclaimer, correction or explanation' and that (obvious mistake apart) the amendments would be refused if an amended claim did not fall wholly within the scope of an unamended claim, or if they served to claim or describe matter not in substance already present – see section 31(1) of the 1949 Act. The new provision, in section 76 of the 1977 Act, is simply that any amendment which 'extends' the scope of the protection conferred by the patent is precluded. The underlying intent is clearly similar. Case law so far under the 1977 Act indicates that the practice will be similar, even though notionally the new words do provide a completely clean slate upon which to work.

Another example, where the counterpart was by way of precedent under the 1949 Act (and earlier Acts) rather than any specific statutory provisions themselves, lies in the categories of inherently patentable subject-matter.

(4) Provisions which have no statutory counterpart under the 1949 Act (although they may reflect to some extent the existing common law outside that Act), and no counterpart either under the European Patent Convention. An example is provided by the new code for employee inventions contained in sections 39 to 43 of the 1977 Act.

(5) Provisions which have no statutory counterpart under the 1949 Act (although they may reflect the common law to some extent), but which can be identified with provisions of the 1975 Community Patent Convention.[28] The statutory provisions in section 60 of the 1977 Act concerning nature of infringing acts are, for example, clearly derived from the provisions of Articles 29 to 31 of the Community Convention.

(6) Pre-existing statutory provisions omitted in the 1977 Act because they would

---

27 46 & 47 Vict. c.57, section 18(1).
28 JO Volume 19 No.L17.

conflict with the terms of the European Patent Convention. One example is provided by the group of 1949 Act reasons for invalidating a patent claim on the so-called 'internal' grounds – ambiguity, inutility, unfair basis, and false suggestion or representation. Another example is provided by the traditional definition of 'invention' in terms of 'manner of . . . manufacture' (indeed the 1977 Act contains no formal definition of 'invention' as such, although it does specify the conditions which have to be fulfilled if a patent is to be granted for an invention).

Transition

The extent of the changes in the 1977 Act naturally led to transitional provisions of considerably greater complexity than was usual on the passing of a new Patents Act. These are contained overall in Schedules 1 to 6 of the 1977 Act (both as now amended). The scheme was not simply that old law (that is, the law of the 1949 Act) was retained for old patents (that is, patents granted under the 1949 Act and termed 'existing' patents by the 1977 Act), with new law (that is, the law of the 1977 Act) being introduced only for new patents (that is, patents granted under the 1977 Act), so as to effect a gradual replacement in the course of time as 'existing' patents expired and new patents arose. A more complicated line of division was set up. While new patents are governed virtually exclusively by the 1977 Act, 'existing' patents are governed partly by retained provisions of the 1949 Act and partly by the 1977 Act. Schedules 1 and 2, respectively, provide principally here. The term 'existing patent' is used generally in this book to denote a 1949 Act patent.

The question of infringement actions (with which there is almost invariably associated a counterclaim for revocation) under 'existing' patents merited particular attention. It was reasonably clear from the general plan of the transitional provisions that the intention of Parliament was that 'existing' patents should continue to have their validity judged by the 1949 criteria and new patents should have theirs judged by the 1977 criteria, with infringement (apart from a saving for pre-existing activities) being considered for both under the 1977 criteria alone. In *Therm-a-Stor v Weatherseal Windows*[29] the Court of Appeal affirmed that this intention had been effected by the transitional provisions, notwithstanding initial doubts in the meantime (because of the tortuous nature of the statutory wording) on the infringement point. The Court commented:

> . . . the Schedules are such a masterpiece of anfractuosity . . . One cannot help wondering, in fact, whether the drafting was not influenced by an unconscious desire to ensure that the administration of patents lived up to its Dickensian description (see *Little Dorrit*, Chap. 10).[30]

Other cases of interest in this area include *Convex Ltd's Patent*[31] (impact of the Interpretation Act 1978 in relation to accrued rights of restoration of a lapsed patent,

---

29 [1981] FSR 579.
30 At 590–591.
31 [1980] RPC 437.

under the 1949 Act), *Standard Oil Company (Fahrig's) Application*[32] (transitional opposition provisions under Schedule 4) and *Canon K.K.'s Application*[33] (certificate of validity following unsuccessful application for revocation under section 33 of the 1949 Act).

Although the impact of the transitional provisions will naturally fade during the forthcoming decade, as the remaining 'existing' patents gradually expire, it is still important in connection with any proceedings involving an 'existing' patent to check first as to exactly what statutory provisions or amalgam thereof apply. A striking example of the need to bear in mind at present both the 1949 and 1977 Act grounds for invalidity is provided by the recent decision in *Minnesota Mining & Manufacturing v Rennicks (UK)*,[34] involving a patent filed shortly before the 1977 Act came into force and due to expire (in the normal course of events) only in 1997.

Bibliography

P. Alexander, 'Russian Patents', *Transactions* Volume LXIV (1945–46) at 108.

R. Baker, *New and Improved – inventors and inventions that have changed the modern world*, British Museum Publications, 1976.

E. Churchill, 'Monopolies', LQR Volume 41 (1925) at 275.

N. Davenport, *The United Kingdom Patent System – A Brief History*, K. Mason, 1979.

'Venetian Patent Law', from Papers to Mark the 500th Anniversary of 1474 Law, IAPIP, A. Guiffre (ed.), Milan, 1974.

R. Hickman and M. Roos, 'Workmate', CIPA Volume 11 (1981–82) at 424.

J.J. Phillips, 'Charles Dickens and "The Poor Man's Tale of a Patent"' (1984).

D. Seabourne Davies, 'Early History of the Patent Specification', LQR Volume 50 (1934) at 86 and 260.

A. White, 'Transitional Provisions of the United Kingdom Patents Act 1977' [1983] EIPR 5.

E. Wyndham Hulme, 'The History of the Patent System under the Prerogative and at Common Law', LQR Volume 12 (1896) at 141.

E. Wyndham Hulme, 'The History of the Patent System under the Prerogative and at Common Law – A Sequel', LQR Volume 16 (1900) at 44.

E. Wyndham Hulme, 'History of Patent Law in the Seventeenth and Eighteenth Centuries', LQR Volume 18 (1902) at 280.

---

32   [1980] RPC 359.
33   [1982] RPC 549.
34   [1992] RPC 331.

2 Inherent Patentability

For a given item of new technology to be patentable, it must:

(i) be of a kind which is inherently patentable; and (ii) be distinct (to the limits required by the law) from the existing prior art in the field in question.

In the terms of the 1977 Act, a patent may be granted only for an invention which meets the following conditions:

(a) the invention is new;
(b) the invention involves an inventive step;
(c) the invention is capable of industrial application; and which
(d) is not otherwise excluded by the statutory exceptions to grant.

Inherent patentability (conditions (c) and (d)) is dealt with in this chapter, and patentability in face of the state of the art (conditions (a) and (b)) in the next chapter (Chapter 3).

All new technological processes (whether in the realm of chemistry, mechanical engineering or electrical engineering), machines, devices, articles, products and compositions are, generally speaking, of inherently patentable nature. Nevertheless, there are certain categories of excepted subject-matter. Prior to the 1977 Act, these categories had grown up on an *ad hoc* basis by means of the case law under the 'manner of manufacture' requirement of the parent Statute of Monopolies of 1624. The 1977 Act both codifies (largely) the exceptions and redefines them in terms corresponding to those of the European Patent Convention. The present list of exceptions is:

(1) A method of treatment of the human or animal body by surgery or therapy or of diagnosis practised on the human or animal body;
(2) A discovery, scientific theory or mathematical method;
(3) A literary, dramatic, musical or artistic work or any other aesthetic creation whatsoever;
(4) A scheme, rule or method for performing a mental act, playing a game or doing business, or a program for a computer;
(5) The presentation of information;
(6) Any invention the publication or exploitation of which would be generally expected to encourage offensive, immoral or anti-social behaviour;
(7) Any variety of animal or plant or any essentially biological process for the production of animals or plants, not being a microbiological process or the product of such a process.

The exclusions come formally under various different heads. Subject-matter under exception 1. is declared not to be capable of industrial application (section 4(2)). That under exceptions 2., 3., 4. and 5. is declared not to be an invention (section 1(2)). For that under exceptions 6. and 7. the Act just states that patents shall not be granted (section 1(3)). Each of these exclusions will now be considered in turn.

Exception 1. (Medical Treatment)

The 'medical treatment' exception (category 1. above) is traditional and can be traced back to 1914[1] at least. It is one of significant practical importance because progress in the medical field often arises from a finding that an existing known substance exerts – when administered to man – an unexpected physiological effect. The purpose of the exception was stated in *John Wyeth & Brother's Application; Schering's Application*[2] as being to ensure that:

> . . . the use in practice by practitioners of such methods of medical treatment in treating patients should not be subjected to possible restraint or restriction by reason of any patent monopoly.

The substance or composition or apparatus used for the treatment method (as the case may be) remains, however, unaffected by the exception.

The 1977 Act provides a somewhat different basis, as compared to the earlier law, for the rejection of medical methods. Previously, the philosophical basis appears to have been the vague notion that it was somehow unethical for any such monopoly to be granted. And because of the elasticity of the 'manner of manufacture' phraseology, there was little problem for the Patent Office in finding that it possessed the requisite legal power to refuse in such cases as it thought fit.

A side-effect of the old philosophy was that the arguments as to exactly what did (or did not) constitute medical treatment became finer and finer and generally took on an air of those bandied about amongst medieval theologians on the subject of angels dancing on the point of a pin. The judgments do not form the most impressive chapter of United Kingdom patent jurisprudence. Some idea of the degree of convolution can be gained from the following table of decisions:

Refused

> A method of extracting lead from the human body
> – *C & W's Application*[3]
> A method of inhibiting mitosis of malignant tumour cells
> – *U.S. Rubber's Application*[4]
> A method of extra-corporeal blood dialysis
> – *Calmic Engineering's Application*[5]
> A method of reducing sensibility to pain by applying sound waves
> – *Neva's Application*[6]
> A method of reducing gastric secretion
> – *Upjohn's (Robert's) Application*[7]
> A method of abortion
> – *Upjohn's (Kirton's) Application*[8]

1   *C & W's Application* 31 RPC 235.
2   [1985] RPC 545.
3   Above.
4   [1964] RPC 104.
5   [1973] RPC 684.
6   [1968] RPC 481.
7   [1977] RPC 94.
8   [1976] RPC 324.

A method of tooth cleaning
– *Oral Health Products' Application*[9]
A method of tooth filling
– *Lee Pharmaceutical's Application*[10]

Allowed

A method of hair-waving
– *Chamberlain's Application*[11]
A method of personal defence by injecting an irritant into an attacker
– *Palmer's Application*[12]
A method of hormonal contraception
– *Schering's Application*[13]
A method of testing for disease by means of radioactive tagged substances
operating on cell samples
– *Bio-Digital Science's Application*[14]
A method of making a wound dressing by polymerising *in situ*
– *Nolan's Application*[15]
A method of controlling ectoparasites or their ova by applying to a substrate
(which might include human skin) a given chemical compound
– *Stafford-Miller's Applications*[16]

Elsewhere (although by no means universally), a more realistic attitude was adopted.
In the United States, for example, the Patent Office has often granted medical-method
types of claims, although it may be true to say that convincing proof of efficacy will
be called for. And in *Dick v Lederle Antitoxin Laboratories*[17] the following Claim was
upheld by the Court:

> 7. The process of isolating hemolytic streptococci specific to scarlet fever, growing them
> in a suitable medium, obtaining a sterile toxin therefrom, and injecting the toxin into
> or through the skin of a human being.

There remains the question of where exactly the line will be drawn in future so far as
the United Kingdom is concerned. Although practice under the 1977 Act has not yet
settled down entirely, a number of points can legitimately now be made:

(i) Section 4(2) itself makes clear that methods for medical treatment of animals, as
well as humans, are now excluded. This represents a tightening-up of the previous law.
Although at one time veterinary methods were refused, as in *Canterbury Agricultural
College's Application*[18] (implantation of L-thyroxine or tri-iodothyronine into sheep to
increase wool yield), the practice changed in 1962 following the decision of the Divisional

  9 [1977] RPC 612.
 10 [1978] RPC 51.
 11 Unreported.
 12 [1970] RPC 597.
 13 [1971] RPC 337.
 14 [1973] RPC 668.
 15 [1977] FSR 425.
 16 [1984] FSR 258.
 17 6 USPQ 40.
 18 [1958] RPC 85.

Court in *Swift's Application*[19] (injection of enzyme into a living animal to improve tenderness of meat when the animal was subsequently slaughtered).

(ii) It appears from the decision in *Unilever's Application*[20] (use of oocysts, a form of bacteria, in immunising poultry against coccidiosis) that 'therapy' – the main head of wording actually used in section 4(2) – is likely to be construed broadly, as meaning both preventative or prophylactic, and curative, treatment.

(iii) The impact of section 2(6) has also to be taken into account. This sub-section is not concerned with the question of 'industrial application' as such, but instead with the question of novelty. It states in effect that an existing known substance or composition can still be regarded as novel, so far as its use for medical treatment is concerned, even though it was already known for other uses. The inference is that protection for a first (but not second) pharmaceutical usage may be validly obtainable provided that the claim is drafted in terms of 'substance (or composition) X when used for treatment of condition Y' even though a method claim directly to such treatment method is objectionable. Such inference is supported by decisions of the European Patent Office under corresponding provisions of the European Patent Convention, a typical example being provided by Case T128/82 *HOFFMAN-LA ROCHE/Pyrrolidine derivatives*[21] in which, *inter alia*, the following claim was allowed by the Technical Board of Appeal:

> Pyrrolidine derivatives having the general formula I as claimed in Claim 1 for use as active substances combatting cerebral insufficiency and improving intellectual ability.

A second pharmaceutical usage can, however, be protected by drafting the claims in so-called 'Swiss' form. This rule was laid down in *John Wyeth & Brother's Application; Schering's Application* where Claim 1 (in the *Schering* case) read:

> The use of an aromatase-inhibitor for the manufacture of a medicament for the therapeutic and/or prophylactic treatment of prostatic hyperplasia.

The 'Swiss' form of claim was pioneered in this context by the Swiss Patent Office and adopted by the European Patent Office in the decision of the Enlarged Board of Appeal in Case G05/83 *EISAI/Second medical indication.*[22] The Patents Court sitting *en banc* in *John Wyeth & Brother; Schering* in turn followed the European Patent Office, since the relevant sections of the 1977 had been framed so as to have, as nearly as practicable, the same effects in the United Kingdom as the corresponding provisions of the European Patent Convention do in the territories to which that Convention applies.

(iv) It seems clear that otherwise purely artificial forms of claim designed to circumvent the 'section 4(2)' and/or 'section 2(6)' limitations will be refused, just as they were when the 'manner of manufacture' rule applied in earlier times. Decisions here include *ICI's (Richardson's) Application*[23] involving a claim:

> A method of producing an anti-oestrogenic effect in warm blooded animals including man, which require such treatment, but excluding any method of treatment of the

19 [1962] RPC 37.
20 [1983] RPC 219.
21 [1979–85] EPOR Vol.B 591.
22 [1979–85] EPOR Vol.B 241.
23 [1981] FSR 609.

human or animal body by therapy, which comprises administering orally or parenterally to such a warm blooded animal an effective amount of (compound I).

(v) Lastly, the old pre-1977 Act decisions are still likely to be relied on as guidelines in suitable cases – even though they may no longer rank as strict precedents because of the change in the law. Thus, in *ICI's Application*[24] concerning a method of cleaning teeth for removal of dental plaque the previous decision in *Oral Health Products' Application* was followed, whereas in *Ciba-Geigy's Application*[25] concerning a method of treating intestinal helminths such as tapeworms *Stafford-Miller's Applications*[26] (control of ectoparasites (lice) on human beings) was distinguished.

Exceptions 2., 3., 4. and 5. (Not an Invention)

These exceptions are predicated on the basis that – industrial usefulness or not apart – such kinds of subject-matter are by definition not inventions for the purposes of the Act. The codification is not necessarily comprehensive. By virtue of the 'among other things' qualification in the preamble of section 1 (2) there is – notionally at least – an opportunity given for the specified exceptions in this group to be extended.

Discoveries and the like (exception 2.)

The scope of the 'scientific theory' and 'mathematical method' exclusions in this category is fairly self-evident. Newton could not have patented his law of gravitation, nor Einstein his theory of general relativity, nor Heisenberg his uncertainty principle. A more recent example relating to a theory of hereditary inheritance of significance in, *inter alia*, the prediction of sex of a child prior to performance of the relevant procreative act is, provided by *Simon's Application.*[27]

The 'discovery' exclusion is rather more difficult to grasp. What it means essentially is that there must be some kind of tangible embodiment to hand before a patent is obtainable and that mere discovery of new knowledge in the abstract – say, of some new physical or chemical effect – is not as such protectable. The standard example is that set out in the judgment of Lindley L.J. in *Lane-Fox v The Kensington and Knightsbridge Electric Lighting Company*:[28]

> When Volta discovered the effect of electric current from a battery on a frog's leg he made a great discovery, but no patentable invention.

Another well-known *dictum* is that of Buckley J. in *Reynolds v Herbert Smith*:[29]

> Discovery adds to the amount of human knowledge, but it does so only by lifting a veil and disclosing something which before had been unseen or dimly seen. Invention also adds to human knowledge, but not merely by disclosing. Invention necessarily involves also the suggestion of an act to be done, and it must be an act which results

---

24 SRIS 0/73/82.
25 IPD 8083.
26 [1984] FSR 258.
27 SRIS 0/139/86 and C/6/87.
28 9 RPC 413 at 416.
29 20 RPC 123 at 126.

in a new product, or a new result, or a new process or a new combination for producing an old product or an old result.

A similar approach is taken in the United States. In the famous 1862 case of *Morton v New York Eye Infirmary*,[30] involving the patent for the use of ordinary ether as an anaesthetic, it was stated:

> A discovery of a new principle, force, or law operating, or which can be made to operate, on matter, will not entitle the discoverer to a patent. It is only where the explorer has gone beyond the mere domain of discovery, and has laid hold of the new principle, force, or law and connected it with some particular medium or mechanical contrivance by which, or through which, it acts on the material world, that he can secure the exclusive control of it under the patent laws. He then controls his discovery through the means by which he has brought it into practical action, or their equivalent, and only through them.

For a fuller discussion, including a review of the authorities and of the impact of the final proviso in section 1(2) '. . . shall prevent . . . only to the extent that a patent or application . . . relates to that thing *as such*' (*emphasis added*), reference may be made to the three recent separate judgments of the Court of Appeal in the complex and difficult case of *Genentech Inc's Patent*.[31] The foundation of the patent here was the discovery of a novel DNA sequence which encoded t-PA.

Aesthetic creations (exception 3.)

Exception 3. of excluded subject-matter requires little comment. Subject-matter of these kinds is protected under copyright law. For a European Patent Office case of interest on the topic, under the corresponding Article 52(2) of the EPC, see *STERNHEIMER/Harmonic vibrations* (T366/87).[32]

Schemes and the like (exceptions 4. and 5.)

Exceptions 4. and 5. are best considered jointly; for practical purposes the line of distinction is between schemes and the like (including the presentation of information) and programs for computers.

Schemes and the like were, again, the subject of a considerable body of pre-1977 case law. This case law (as with the 'medical treatment' exclusion) is likely to carry weight for the future under the 1977 Act, even though it does not provide strict precedent in view of the formal statutory provision being new. In a book of this size, a comprehensive treatment is not possible but it may help to present a few contrasting cases.

Refused
> A camouflage painting method
> – *T's Application*[33]

---

30   17 F.Cas. 879.
31   [1989] RPC 147 at 208, 239, 269.
32   [1989] EPOR 131.
33   37 RPC 109.

A method of arranging buoys for navigational purposes
– *W's Application*[34]
A method of musical notation
– *C's Application*[35]
An installation for distribution of utilities services on a housing estate
– *Hiller's Application*[36]
A method of operating a jet engine so as to minimise noise
– *Rolls-Royce's Application*[37]
A method of speech instruction
– *Dixon's Application*[38]

Allowed

A blue squash ball
– *ITS Rubber's Application*[39]
A diamond topogram
– *De Beers' Consolidated Mines' Application*[40]
A new pack of cards for the game 'Canasta'
– *Cobianchi's Application*[41]
A ticket carrying information in duplicate so arranged that each half retained the information on either transverse or longitudinal bisection of the ticket
– *Fishburn's Application*[42]
A printed sheet carrying words printed according to the Pitman alphabet
– *Pitman's Application*[43]

Under the 1977 Act there may be mentioned the refusal of *Price's Application*[44] (trading stamp scheme for buying holidays), *Waring's Application*[45] (traffic violation ticket set), and of Claim 4 in *Furuno Electric's Application*[46] (method of locating shoals of fish by radar-location of flocks of birds).

Computer programs

The question of the extent to which improvements in computer science can be protected by patents is currently one of considerable industrial importance. Although, just as with the other exceptions to patentability, there is a body of pre-1977 Act case law, the relative significance of that case law is probably less. The reason is two-fold. Firstly, computer science only became a prominent field of industrial activity relatively shortly

34 31 RPC 141.
35 37 RPC 247.
36 [1969] RPC 267.
37 [1963] RPC 251.
38 [1978] RPC 687.
39 [1979] RPC 318.
40 [1979] FSR 72.
41 70 RPC 199.
42 57 RPC 245.
43 [1969] RPC 646.
44 SRIS 0/105/84.
45 IPD 13138.
46 IPD 14040.

before the 1977 Act; secondly, there is a greater volume of post-1977 law (including that in the European Patent Office). The pre-1977 Act case law is considered first, briefly, for the sake of completeness.

Pre-1977

Slee & Harris' Application (1965):[47] Claim to a method of operating a computer with a programme involving iterations, characterised in that succeeding iterations were initiated before completion of the previous iteration, rejected; claims to a computer programmed to produce this result, and to linear programming means for use in controlling data processing apparatus, were both allowed.

Badger's Application (1968):[48] Claims to a process of conditioning a known computer and a known associated plotter, for the production of piping drawings for chemical plant, and to the computer as arranged to produce a precursor sheet for the plotter, both allowed.

Gevers' Application (1969):[49] Claims to a data processor, and to its constituent controlling punched cards, for recording word trade marks (and hence facilitating trade mark searches) allowed, but claim to the underlying method involved refused.

Burroughs Corporation's (Perkins') Application (1973):[50] Claim to a method of controlling a computer (via the interruption by a slave computer of a central computer's routine operations) allowed.

International Business Machines' Patent (1978):[51] Claim to a programmed computer (for establishing prices of a given kind of fungible goods in an auction market) upheld.

Post-1977

In the broadest sense, the scope for protection in this field has been reduced by the 1977 Act. Although the formal prohibition of section 1(2)(c) is couched solely in terms of the program, a series of decisions of the Court of Appeal have made it clear that the question of patentability must be regarded realistically. Mere casting of a claim in terms of hardware will not suffice to evade the prohibition, if the subject-matter sought to be protected is intrinsically that of a program or other exception. The decisions are:

Genentech Inc's Patent[52] (*obiter*)

> It would be nonsense for the Act to forbid the patenting of a computer program, and yet permit the patenting of a floppy disc containing a computer program, or an ordinary computer when programmed with the program; it can well be said, as it seems to me, that a patent for a computer when programmed or for the disc containing the program is no more than a patent for the program as such.

Merrill Lynch's Application:[53] Claim to a data processing system for making a trading

47   [1966] RPC 194.
48   [1970] RPC 36.
49   [1970] RPC 91.
50   [1974] RPC 147.
51   [1980] FSR 564.
52   [1989] RPC 147 at 240.
53   [1989] RPC 561.

market in securities was involved. In carrying out the system a known computer system was used, controlled by a program coded in any known programming language. It was held that, although subject-matter excluded from patentability by section 1(2) could contribute to inventive step (in other words to the other requirements for patentability overall), nevertheless there must be present a new technical result which was not itself an excluded item. Such was the case here since the end result, making a trading market in securities, was in effect simply a method of doing business. The *International Business Machines* decision mentioned above was discounted, on the basis of it being a 1949 Act decision, notwithstanding the factual similarity.

Gale's Application:[54] The applicant here had discovered a method of calculating the square root of a number with the aid of a computer, which eliminated the prior art need for a division stage; the necessary instructions were put into a 'ROM'. The claim read:

> 1. Electronic circuitry, in the form known as 'ROM', to provide controlling means whereby four binary manipulative entities, of the type known as 'registers', shall derive the square root of an arbitrary number, and whereby such controlling shall so function that only such numbers shall be selected by the said controlling means, for use in deriving the square root, as shall eliminate recourse to the process of division, and shall further only perform the process of multiplication insofar as it is accomplished by the use of the binary operations of 'shift' and 'test', without the binary function of 'add', such as is usually required within the general form of multiplication of arbitrary numbers.

The claim was refused, the Court holding that it was right to strip away 'as a confusing irrelevance'[54a] the fact that it was drafted in terms of hardware; the claim was, in substance, a series of instructions which incorporated the improved method. It would equally be 'a nonsense',[54b] if a floppy disc containing a program should not be patentable (as *per* the *Genentech dictum*), but a ROM characterised only by the instructions in that program should be.

A leading European Patent Office decision, canvassed in all the Court of Appeal decisions mentioned above, is that of *VICOM/Computer-related invention* (T208/84).[55] Allowed Claim 1 here read:

> 1. A method of digitally processing images in the form of a two-dimensional data array having elements arranged in rows and columns in which an operator matrix of a size substantially smaller than the size of the data array is convolved with the data array, including sequentially scanning the elements of the data array with the operator matrix, characterised in that the method includes repeated cycles of sequentially scanning the entire data array with a small generating kernel operator matrix to generate a convolved array and then replacing the data array as a new data array; the small generating kernel remaining the same for any single scan of the entire data array and although comprising at least a multiplicity of elements, nevertheless being of a size substantially smaller than is required of a conventional operator matrix in which the operator matrix is convolved with the data array only once, and the cycle being repeated for each previous new data array by selecting the small generating kernel operator matrices and the number of cycles

54 [1991] RPC 305.
54a at 326.
54b at 325.
55 [1987] EPOR 74.

according to conventional error minimisation techniques until the last new data array generated is substantially the required convolution of the original data array with the conventional operator matrix.

The essential difference is that the process here was one of a fundamentally technical character.

Attention may be drawn here also to the trilogy of leading cases in the Supreme Court of the United States of America, *Gottschalk v Benson*,[56] *Parker v Flook*[57] and *Diamond v Diehr*.[58] Here again, there is a dividing line between the permitted and prohibited, although not drawn along quite the same path as in the United Kingdom, because of the different statute extant in the United States. This provides that:

> Whoever invents or discovers any new and useful process, machine, manufacture, or composition of matter, or any new and useful improvement thereof may obtain a patent therefor, subject to the conditions and requirements of this title.[59]

and as such is more akin to the manner of manufacture requirement of the United Kingdom than to the 1977 Act (and European Patent Convention).

In *Gottschalk v Benson* the Court held unpatentable a claim for an algorithm used to convert binary code decimal numbers to equivalent pure binary numbers, the sole practical application of the algorithm being in connection with the programming of a general purpose digital computer. In *Parker v Flook* the Court held unpatentable a claim for an improved method of calculation (of an alarm limit) even when tied to a specific end-use (the catalytic chemical conversion of hydrocarbons). In *Diamond v Diehr*, on the other hand, the Court held that a claim drawn to otherwise statutory subject-matter does not become non-statutory simply because it uses a mathematical formula, digital computer or computer program, and permitted a claim for a computer-controlled method of operating a rubber-moulding press; and since this decision is the most recent of the three, explaining and distinguishing the earlier two, it is clear that some substantial scope exists in the United States of America for the protection of inventions involving computers.

A completely separate head of protection for computer programs may arise under copyright law. Copyright as a whole is beyond the scope of this book, although its interface with patent law is discussed in part in Chapter 13.

Interlocutory decisions in the courts of the United Kingdom prior to the passage of the Copyright, Designs and Patents Act 1988[60] strongly suggested that copyright could subsist in computer programs, on the general basis that the program will possess originality and – being written down on paper or otherwise fixed at some point in its creation – can rank as a literary work. *Gates v Swift*,[61] concerning programs for a microcomputer, and *Sega Enterprises v Richards*,[62] concerning the assembly code program of the videogame 'Frogger', apply. And it is arguable generally that a similar

56   175 USPQ 673.
57   198 USPQ 193.
58   209 USPQ 1.
59   USC Title 35 section 101.
60   1988 c. 88.
61   [1982] RPC 337 at 339.
62   [1983] FSR 73.

position should apply in any country that adheres to the Berne Copyright Convention, in view of the definition in Article 2(1) of that Convention that:

> The term 'literary and artistic works' shall include every production in the literary, scientific and artistic domain, *whatever may be the mode or form of its expression* . . .
> *(Emphasis added)*

For the future, the United Kingdom position is now clarified since section 3 (1) of the 1988 Act specifically provides that 'literary work' includes a computer program.

Public order (exception 6.)

This represents the so-called 'public order' exception. The wording is somewhat vague and general. Its precise scope is inevitably somewhat uncertain and fluid, since notions and attitudes change in the course of time. But it is specifically provided that behaviour is not necessarily to be regarded as offensive, immoral or anti-social merely because it is prohibited by law. Thus, a new hallucinogenic pharmaceutical or opiate is not unpatentable merely because it could be misused, by addicts and/or those engaged in drug trafficking; their other proper medical uses might save them. A burglar's jemmy might well stand in the converse position, however. The European Patent Office, in *HARVARD/Onco-mouse* (T19/90)[63], has now accepted, at the stage of *ex parte* examination, under the corresponding provision (Article 53(a)) of the European Patent Convention the patentability of a biogenetically engineered mouse having enhanced susceptibility to carcinogenic susbtances (and hence making it useful for carcinogenicity testing purposes).

Biological inventions (exception 7.)

This exception concerns biological inventions. It is, like that of computers, of considerable current importance. The statutory provision in section 1(3)(b) is drafted in terms corresponding generally to Article 53(b) of the European Patent Convention.

Much of the current difficulty on the topic stems from the circumstance that Article 53(b) itself reflects Article 2(b) of the Strasbourg Convention of 1963 on the unification of certain points of substantive law on patents for invention. In 1963, modern biotechnology was in its infancy. The result, in short, is that Article 53(b), and hence section 1(3)(b), are not written in particularly apt terms for contemporary advances in this area. It is convenient for purposes of discussion to quote here the full terms of section 1(3)(b), namely that a patent shall not be granted:

> for any variety of animal or plant or any essentially biological process for the production of animals or plants, not being a microbiological process or the product of such a process.

Microbiological/biological

First of all, it is clear from the proviso to section 1(3)(b) that microbiological processes generally and their products are to be patentable; it is immaterial as to whether the

---

63 [1990] EPOR 501.

microbiological process involved produces something living (animal or plant) or something inanimate (say, a given chemical compound).

There is nothing particularly new here as compared to the earlier law. Industrial fermentation processes relying on micro-organisms, as for example those involved in brewing and baking, have always been regarded by the Patent Office as acceptable; even as far back as 1926, in *Commercial Solvents Corporation v Synthetic Products*,[64] a patent relating to the production of acetone and butyl alcohol by the bacterial fermentation of carbohydrates was upheld by the Court. In 1970, in *American Cyanamid (Dann's) Patent*, in relation to a patent claiming:

> 1. A method of producing an antibiotic designated porfiromycin which comprises subjecting a porfiromycin producing strain of *Streptomyces verticillatus* to aerobic fermentation in an aqueous nutrient medium containing assimilable sources of carbon, nitrogen and inorganic salts.

Lord Wilberforce said *obiter dicta* in the House of Lords:

> The priceless strain, being something living, found in nature, cannot be patented: the prosaic process, as applied to the strain, is capable of protection.[65]

The Patent Office was prepared to take the matter one stage further and to allow viral methods. A typical example of an accepted claim was:

> A process for the cultivation of a virus, in which the virus is cultivated in an embryonated quail egg or in a tissue culture of a quail embryo fibroblast.[66]

They would take a similarly wide view in relation to microbiological products, as evidenced by the following examples of accepted claims:

> Chicken kidney cells containing attenuated Marek's disease virus having the characteristics of the cells identified by No. LEV/16/AT held by the Central Veterinary Laboratory, Weybridge, Surrey, England.[67]

> A bacterium from the genus *Pseudomonas* containing therein at least two stable energy-generating plasmids, each of said plasmids providing a separate degradative hydrocarbon pathway (as hereinbefore defined).[68]

There would seem to be no particular reason for diverging under the 1977 Act from these practices, even though the statutory wording is fresh. The critical antithesis is between microbiological and essentially biological processes. Definitive pronouncement as to the location of the dividing line is, however, still awaited.

Where the process involved is, on the other hand, of 'macrobiological' kind then section 1(3)(b) does bite. Of course the mere fact that the process may be of use in commercial agriculture is not decisive. For purposes of the 'industrial application' test

---

64 43 RPC 185.
65 [1971] RPC 425 at 448.
66 Patent No. 1349362.
67 Patent No. 1292803.
68 Patent No. 1436573.

of section 1(1)(c), industry is defined in section 4(1) as including agriculture. And an agricultural method, even though it be of 'essentially biological' nature in that it is effective via interaction at biological level within the plant, may well not be one for the 'production' of plants. A method of controlling the growth of thistles among the corn by application of chemical X, or of controlling Colorado beetle among the potatoes by application of chemical Y should be allowable; a method of increasing the size (if not the flavour) of strawberries by application of chemical Z, on the other hand, might not.

The scope for patenting of animal methods of value in farming, if not agriculture strictly so-called, would seem to be rather less in any event; the specific extra exclusion of veterinary treatments methods under section 4(2) has already been mentioned. It is by no means clear as to whether inventions along the lines of that involved in the landmark 1949 Act case of *Swift's Application*, above, will continue to be protectable; it could be argued that the *Swift* process (of enzyme injection) was one for the 'production' of an animal (albeit one with meat of improved tenderness). This is not to suggest that there is no room at all for animal methods. *Prima facie*, for example, a method of sorting day-old chicks by optical scanning of a bald spot introduced into the heads of male chicks by suitable genetic breeding would appear to avoid the barriers of both section 1(3)(b) and section 4(2); neither production nor therapy is involved.

Animals

The primary view, expressed in the first edition of this book, was that section 1(3)(b) precluded the patenting of animals generally. This view was in line with the pre-1977 law also, since an animal could hardly be regarded as a manner of manufacture. Although there was no direct pre-1977 authority, the position was generally accepted to be that as stated in the *Manual of Patent Office Practice*:[69]

> New varieties of plants and animals *per se* appear to be unpatentable and objection is raised in such cases.

Accordingly, if the London Zoo managed to produce a new kind of sabre-toothed tiger with extra-long incisors, it was generally reckoned that neither that tiger *per se* nor the genetic breeding method involved in creating the tiger would be patentable (even before or after the 1977 Act).

The validity of this view has now been severely shaken by the decision of the European Patent Office in *HARVARD/Onco-mouse* above. The Technical Board of Appeal held here that corresponding Article 53(b) of the European Patent Convention provided no ban on the patenting of animals as a whole. There was a distinction between animal varieties and other animals. Only the former were excluded. On remittal, the Examining Division held that the animal involved here, defined in generic product Claim 17 as:

> 17. A transgenic non-human mammalian animal whose germ cells and somatic cells contain an activated oncogene sequence introduced into said animal, or an ancestor of

---

69 Paragraph 101,38 (2nd edition 1975 and 1978).

said animal, at a stage no later than the 8-cell stage, said oncogene optionally being further defined according to any one of Claims 3 to 10.

did not constitute an animal variety. The present situation in the United Kingdom is therefore uncertain, since it is to be expected that considerable attention will be paid by the Patent Office (and Court) to the eventual result in *HARVARD/Onco-mouse* once the anticipated oppositions (post-grant) in the European Patent Office have been heard and determined.

Plants

Similar to the position with animals, the primary view in the past has been that plants in general were excluded from patent protection. The black tulip or blue rose evolved by Kew Gardens would fail, just as the sabre-toothed tiger with extra-long incisors would fail. Alternative protection might well be available instead under the quite separate Plant Varieties and Seeds Act 1964[70] and 1983.[71] It was uncertain, however, as to whether the definition contained in section 38(1) of the 1964 Act in respect of 'plant variety' – namely, any clone, line, hybrid or genetic variant – would apply also to define the bounds of the exclusion of section 1(3)(b) in this respect.

The European Patent Office has again taken a hand in the matter. In *LUBRIZOL/ Hybrid plants*[72] (T320/87) the Technical Board held that product Claims 20, 21

20. Hybrid seed that yields plants that are phenotypically uniform, said seed having been produced by a process comprising:
   (a) selecting a heterozygous first parent plant and selecting a second parent plant;
   (b) crossing said first parent plant with said second parent plant to obtain original-parent-derived hybrids that are phenotypically uniform;
   (c) cloning said first parent plant to produce a first cloned parental line;
   (d) crossing plants of said first cloned parental line with said second parent plant or with a second parental line produced therefrom to obtain hybrid seeds which yield hybrids that are phenotypically uniform, provided that when said second parent plant is heterozygous and a second parental line produced therefrom is used in the crossing of step (d), said second parental line must be produced by cloning; and
   (e) repeating steps (c) and (d) as required to obtain hybrid seed that yields phenotypically uniform hybrid plants and, optionally, producing phenotypically uniform hybrid plants from the seed.
21. Phenotypically uniform hybrid plants produced from hybrid seed according to Claim 20.

did not come within the corresponding plant variety exclusion of Article 53(b) since they lacked, in view of the heterozygous nature of one of the parent plants, stability in some trait of the whole generation population. In the absence of stability, there was no 'variety'. The decision accordingly takes a fairly narrow view of the exclusion. The earlier decision in *CIBA-GEIGY/Propagating material*[73] (T49/83), allowing Claims to:

70   1964 c.14.
71   1983 c.17.
72   [1990] EPOR 173.
73   [1979–85] EPOR Vol.C 758.

13. Propagating material for cultivated plants, treated with an oxime derivative according to formula I in Claim 1.

14. Propagating material according to Claim 13, characterised in that it consists of seed.

is in similar vein.

In the circumstances it is therefore at present uncertain as to how widely the plant variety exception of section 1(3)(b) is likely to be construed in future. The narrower the exclusion the wider the potential scope for patentability, since section 1(3)(b) contains no overall prohibition of plants but only of plant varieties. Jurisprudential development in respect of both the patentability of plants and animals in the United Kingdom is therefore to be expected in the near future.

As for the position elsewhere, it is noteworthy that in the United States the Supreme Court in *Diamond v Chakrabarty*[74] has recently allowed a claim similar to that concerning the bacterium from the genus *Pseudomonas* quoted above (on page 20). The fact that in *Diamond v Chakrabarty* the product (the bacterium) was a live entity, animate as opposed to inanimate, was held immaterial since it resulted from the inventor's handiwork rather than nature's own. The outlook in the United States for workers in this area would therefore seem quite promising.

DNA

It would now seem reasonably clear that inventions relating to DNA sequences, fragments and the like are perfectly patentable from the standpoint of inherency, under the 1977 Act. Reference may be made, for example, to Claim 9 of Patent No. 2119804B, upheld in *Genentech Inc's Patent*,[75] and Claim 2 of Patent No. 2121048B, upheld in *Genentech Inc' (Human Growth Hormone) Patent*,[76] directed respectively to:

> 9. The plasmid pΔRIPA°) or pt-PAtrp12.

and

> 2. A plasmid according to Claim 1 whose human growth-encoding gene comprises in substantial proportion cDNA or a replication thereof.

A similar situation exists in the European Patent Office, working under the corresponding provisions of the European Patent Convention. Reference may be made here to *HOECHST/Plasmid pSG2* (T162/86),[77] where Claim 1 read:

> 1. Plasmid pSG2, obtainable from Streptomyces ghanaensis A ATCC 14672, characterised by a molecular weight of 9.2 megadaltons, a contour length of 4.58 μm and a molecular length of about 13.8 kb.

and to *BIOGEN/Recombinant DNA* (T301/87)[78] where granted Claim 6 read:

---

74   206 USPQ 193.
75   [1989] RPC 147.
76   [1989] RPC 613.
77   [1989] EPOR 107.
78   [1989] EPOR 109.

6. A recombinant DNA molecule according to any one of Claims 1 to 4, wherein said DNA sequence is selected from DNA sequence of the formula:

TTACTGGTGGCCCTCCTGGTGCTCAGCTGCAAGTCAAGCTGCTC
TGTGGGCTGTGATCTGCCTCAAACCCACAGCCTGGGTAGCAGGA
GGACCTTGATGCTCCTGGCACAGATGAGGAGAATCTCTCTTTTCT
CCTGCTTGAAGGATTACTGGTGGCCCTCCTGGTGCTCAGCTGCAA
GTCAAGCTGCTCTGTGGGCTGTGATCTGCCTCAAACCCACAGCCT
GGGTAGCAGGAGGACCTTGATGCTCCTGGCACAGATGAGGAGAA
TCTCTCTTTTCTCCTGCTTGAAGGACAGACAATGAACTTTGGATT
TCCCCAGGAGGAGTTTGGCAACCAGTTCCAAAAGGCTGAAACCA
TCCCTGTCCTCCATGAGATGATCCAGCAGATCCTTCAATCTCTTC
AGCACAAAGGACTCATCTGCTGCTTGGGAATGAGACCCTCCTAG
ACAAATTCTACACTGAACTCTACCAGCAGCTGAATGACCTGGAA
GCCTGTGTGATACAGGGGGTGGGGGTGACAGAGACTCCCCTGAT
GAAGGAGGACTCCATTCTGGCTGTGAGGAAATACTTCCAAAGAA
TCACTCTCTATCTCGAAAGAGAAGAAATATAGCCCTTGTGCCTG
GGAGGTTGTCAGAGCAGAAATCATGAGATCTTTTTCTTTGTCAAC
AAACTTGCAAGAAAGTTTAAGAAGTAAGGAA and TGTGATCTGC
CTCAAACCCACAGCCTGGGTAGCAGGAGGACCTTGATGCTCCTG
GCACAGATGAGGAGAATCTCTCTTTTCTCCTGCTTGAAGGACAG
CATGACTTTGGATTTCCCCAGGAGGAGTTTGGCAACCAGTTCCAA
AAGGCTGAAACCATCCCTGTCCTCCATGAGATGATCCAGCAGAT
CTTCAATCTCTTCAGCACAAAGGACTCATCTGCTGCTTGGGATGA
GACCCTCCTAGACAAATTCTACACTGAACTCTACCAGCAGCTGAA
TGACCTGGAAGCCTGTGTGATACAGGGGGTGGGGGTGACAGAGAC
TCCCCTGATGAAGGAGGACTCCATTCTGGCTGTGAGGAAATACTT
CCAAAGAATCACTCTCTATCTGAAAGAGAAGAAATACAGCCCTTG
TGCCTGGGAGGTTGTCAGAGCACAGAAATCATGAGATCTTTTTCTTG
TCAACAAACTTGCAAGAAAGTTTAAGAAGTAAGGAA

Bibliography

H. Aspden, 'Patentability of Computer Programs' in J. Kemp (ed.), *Patent Claim Drafting and Interpretation*, Oyez Longman, 1983.

S. Bent, 'Patent Protection for DNA Molecules', JPOS Volume 64 1982 at 60.

R. Braubach, 'Computer Software – International Protection' [1980] EIPR at 225.

R. Crespi, 'Biotechnology and Patents – Past and Future' [1981] 5 EIPR at 134.

R. Crespi, 'Innovation in Plant Biotechnology: The Legal Options' [1986] EIPR 262.

R.J. Hart, 'Application of Patents to Computer Technology – UK and the EPO Harmonisation' [1989] EIPR 42.

M. Kindermann, 'Computer Software and Copyright Conventions' [1981] 1 EIPR at 6.

R. Nott, 'Patent Protection for Plants and Animals' [1992] EIPR 107.

L. Perry, 'Computer Programs – Art or Science?' CIPA Volume 10 (1980–81) at 97.

R. Teschemacher, 'The Practice of the European Patent Office Regarding the Grant of Patents for Biotechnological Inventions' (1988) 19 IIC 18.

J. van Voorthuizen, 'Patentability of Computer Programs and Computer-Related Inventions under the European Patent Convention' (1987) 18 IIC 627.

H. Wegner, 'The *Chakrabarty* Decision – Patenting Products of Genetic Engineering' [1980] EIPR at 304.

A. White, 'Patentability of Medical Treatment' [1980] EIPR at 364.

A. White, 'Patentability of Medical Treatment Claims – the *Nimodipin* Cases' [1984] EIPR at 38.

S. Wright, 'Patentability of Plants and Animals', CIPA volume 18 (1988–89) at 323.

3 Patentability in Fact

PART I: PATENTABILITY IN FACE OF THE ART

Historically, it has always been regarded as improper to permit the re-patenting (and hence re-monopolisation) of subject-matter which lay already in the public domain. Indeed, that can be regarded as the very evil which the Statute of Monopolies[1] was intended to eradicate back in 1624. To encourage fresh industry, but yet not shackle existing industry, the manner of manufacture in question (for which the patent grant was sought) had to be 'new'.[2]

What has changed over the centuries (particularly over the last hundred years) in the United Kingdom, and what has in any event often differed abroad from country to country, is the concept of the extent of the public domain. In other words, what part(s) of the totality of the prior art (at the date of the patent) can be relied on by the Patent Office Examiner in the first place during prosecution and/or by the defendant attacking validity of the patent in subsequent proceedings in Court.

The position is now regulated, for patents granted under the 1977 Act, by the provisions of sections 2(2) and (3). They reflect the definition of 'state of the art' contained in the European Patent Convention[3] and provide a very substantial expansion as to what earlier prior art can be relied on. In particular, the previous restrictions as to geographical availability of the art in the United Kingdom, and chronological availability of the art within the past fifty years, have both been swept away for 'new' patents; 'existing' patents granted under the 1949 Act still enjoy their shelter, however. Although opinions may differ on the intrinsic desirability of the new provisions, there is no doubt but that it had by 1977 become highly artificial to exclude, say, a 1926-dated prior United Kingdom patent specification concerning the rolling of steel sheet just because it was one year too old: likewise, say, a 1966-dated article in the American technical press concerning synthetic rubber manufacture just because it had, fortuitously, failed to reach these shores.

Section 2(2) of the 1977 Act now defines the state of the art as being:

> The state of the art in the case of an invention shall be taken to comprise all matter (whether a product, a process, information about either, or anything else) which has at any time before the priority date of that invention been made available to the public (whether in the United Kingdom or elsewhere) by written or oral description, by use or in any other way.

Over such state of the art an invention must, in order to be patentable, be both new (section 1(1)(a) taken with section 2(1)) and non-obvious (section 1(1)(b) taken with section 3). Non-obviousness provides the statutory test for the existence of an inventive step; hence if obviousness is shown to exist there is a lack of inventive step.

The only exception arises where the prior art material was contained in another patent

1 21 Jac.1 c.3.
2 At section VI.
3 Articles 54(2) and (3).

application, already co-pending at the date when the application for the patent in suit was filed but published subsequent to that date. In this limited instance of contemporaneous (although not chronologically coincident) filing, novelty only is required (section 3 applies). This latter is generally termed the 'whole contents' test, to distinguish it from the 'prior claiming' test applied in comparable circumstances under the 1949 Act for existing patents.

Several matters arise in connection with this definition. First, the date at which novelty and obviousness has to be judged is that of the so-called 'priority date'. This priority date is either the date of filing the application in the Patent Office (not, it is to be noted, any earlier date such as that of first successful laboratory experimentation, first conception of the invention) or the earlier date of filing a corresponding application for the same invention in another country (provided it is a so-called 'convention' country) within the previous twelve months. The latter alternative reflects the international system of claiming priority, the so-called 'Paris Convention', which was first promulgated in 1883 and has proved since to be one of the key factors in promoting the growth of the patent system. It is discussed more fully in Chapter 12.

Secondly, there are the four kinds of anticipatory material:

(1) Written descriptions – for example, an article in the technical press;
(2) Oral descriptions – for example, delivery of a lecture at a research conference. This head can be important where the lecture comes before, but the subsequent printed version only after, the priority date.
(3) Use – for example, actual sales of the machine or product in question.
(4) Any other way – the potential width of this term is important. Although 1977 Act precedents are so far generally absent, it would certainly seem that the term is inherently capable of accommodating such items as photographs and engineering drawings. These were held in earlier cases under the 1907 and 1949 Acts (which lacked the statutory definition of the 1977 Act) to be capable of so ranking – in *Van der Lely v Bamfords*[4] and *Crowther's Application*[5] respectively. Moreover, it is apt to include matters of traditional common knowledge in a given trade, which have never been written down or of which previous oral disclosure (although it may well have occurred) cannot now be proven; an example might be that of some trick of the farrier's art in applying the molten shoe to the horse's hoof so that he does not immediately make a violent kick, passed down for generations from father to son. Another head, important for the future, is that of the modern alternative means of recording information. In the case of a magnetic tape, the information is present permanently in the form of electrical charge patterns, from which a visual image can be obtained by running the tape through a suitable reproducer. The charge pattern is hardly classifiable as writing; the visual representation may be in the form of writing symbols, but it is transitory. Among older recording means, there may be mentioned lecture-slides.

Thirdly, there is the question of 'made available to the public'. This is perhaps the

4 [1963] RPC 61.
5 51 RPC 72.

key phrase. As a general qualification to all the possible kinds of anticipatory material, it is fresh in the 1977 Act. Previously the phrase was only used in connection with the definition of the term 'published' in the 1949 Act, insofar as opposition on the ground of prior publication was concerned. The 1949 Act followed the 1919 Act in this respect, where the term was first introduced.

From the foregoing, it will be appreciated that the difficulty in determining the full scope of this phrase cannot be solved just by carrying over *in toto* the previous case law (over the 1919 to 1977 period) as to 'made available'. Nevertheless, it does seem likely that a court will still be guided where possible by that case law, and also by the still earlier pre-1919 precedents in this area generally. Under the earlier law it was clear, for example, that 'public' does not necessarily mean the populace at large. In the well-known Victorian case of *Humpherson v Syer* Bowen L.J. said:

> I . . . treat this as a question of whether there has been a prior publication; that is, in other words had this information been communicated to any member of the public who was free in law or equity to use it as he pleased.[6]

Both in this case and, for example, in the more recent case of *Bristol-Myers' Application*,[7] a single communicatee only was involved – an outside tradesman making WC waste water preventers, and a corporate patent department employee, respectively. The limitation to the communicatee being one under no obligation of confidence or the like is important; otherwise, it would be impossible for an inventor to have, for example, an experimental prototype made up by outside contractors prior to filing his patent application.

Conversely, it has been held in the past that where there has in fact been widespread dissemination of the relevant document among the relevant trade, a notional obligation of confidence on the part of each recipient may not save the patentee. Such was the situation in *Dalrymple's Application*,[8] wherein a 'private and confidential' research bulletin teaching the relevant subject-matter had been previously sent to all 1,079 members of the British Baking Industries Research Association. There is, of course, some inherent justification in regarding the trade public somewhat differently from the purely lay public. It is the former who are the ones primarily interested in actually using the information.

If the document is in an ordinary public library, it is undeniably available to the public. Availability in a trade or professional library, for example, that of the Royal Society of Medicine in the case of a medical journal or of the Chemical Society in the case of a chemical journal, is in practice normally also reckoned as enough. It remains to be seen as to how these rules will be applied in future under the more extreme circumstances which might arise from the 1977 Act – say, where the document is available only in a library in a foreign country effectively cut off (by censorship, prohibition of access or the like) from the outside world.

Reference may be made finally to the limited grace period (six months) provided by section 2(4) in respect of certain improper prior disclosures in breach of confidence and prior disclosure at certified international exhibitions. The further exception provided by

---

6   4 RPC 407 at 413.
7   [1969] RPC 146.
8   [1957] RPC 449.

section 51(2)(d) of the 1949 Act (six months grace period for disclosures in papers read before a learned society or published in transactions of the same) is no longer retained. The new law is in this respect harsher.

Cases where the assertedly anticipatory material is by way of a prior use can give rise to substantial problems. In the simple case of a machine or device invention, prior use via prior sale of that machine or device is effective because the purchaser is – notionally at least – at perfect liberty to take the machine to pieces and find out exactly how it works. As such, he is in the capacity of an ordinary member of the public already in possession of the invention; in other words, the invention is already in the public domain.

But more complicated situations are liable to exist in practice, along one or more of the following lines:

> (1) prior sale of a product made by a process the same as that of the patent, the product itself not revealing the process used;
> (2) actual use of the invention on private land, although no sale;
> (3) purely fortuitous prior use;
> (4) prior sale of an unanalysable product;
> (5) prior use of the invention on a purely experimental scale;
> (6) prior use of the invention on a commercial scale, under secrecy precautions;
> (7) prior gift.

It is not possible here to discuss comprehensively all the numerous (and sometimes conflicting) precedents on this topic. The topic provides one of the most difficult areas of patent law. The very fact that there are so many old precedents (in 19th century and earlier times there was both less printing of scientific material and less literacy, hence highlighting the importance of actual prior usage) has tended to cloud the matter. In the widest sense it is, however, legitimate to say that the Court has in the main been influenced by the two dominant considerations of:

> (1) the continued right to work – that is, no patent should be granted (or would be invalid if granted) which would have the effect of preventing any member of the public from continuing to do what he was already accustomed to do (even if he did not understand what he was doing – for example, the precise reaction mechanism of his bleaching process); of course, this consideration is inapplicable when the prior use being relied on is the patentee's own; and/or
> (2) the continuation of the public benefit – that is, if the public or any member thereof had already enjoyed the benefit of the invention then likewise no patent should be granted (or would be invalid if granted) that might serve to deprive the public of the continued enjoyment of that benefit; this consideration applies both to prior use by the patentee and by third parties.

The high-tide mark of this latter approach, prior to the 1977 Act can be seen in the case of *Bristol-Myers' (Johnson's) Application.*[9] A claim to ampicillin trihydrate *per se*, an improved form (slower loss of efficacy on storage and hence longer shelf-life) of the

9 [1975] RPC 127.

existing antibiotic ampicillin, was involved. All that the opponents could prove was that they had previously occasionally made (albeit quite unwittingly) ampicillin trihydrate in the course of their regular production of ampicillin, and (again quite unwittingly) had subsequently sold that ampicillin trihydrate in admixture with ordinary ampicillin; moreover, the presence of the trihydrate version in the mixture would, with the analytical techniques available at the time of sale, have been impossible to detect. Nevertheless, the House of Lords held that there had been an effective prior use. Some, at least, of the potential patient population needing treatment with ampicillin must have actually received the benefit of improved efficacy.

Whether the same lines of approach will be perpetuated in future under the new 1977 Act is perhaps uncertain. The new statute is drafted rather more stringently than the old; under the 1949 Act the requirement was simply that the invention should have been previously 'used'. The new requirement – that the invention should have been previously 'made available to the public' by virtue of the use – is couched in terms which would seem to be inherently narrower.

Moreover, the specific provision in the 1949 Act[10] concerning the inclusion of secret use as a species of prior use is not repeated in the new Act. Against that, it has to be borne in mind also that section 64 of the 1977 Act separately protects certain kinds of continued user by declaring that such user should not rank as an infringement of the patent (irrespective of whether or not the earlier use should suffice to invalidate the same); this 'franchise' approach is quite new to the law. Jurisprudence under section 64 is just beginning – see for example, *Helitune v Stewart Hughes*,[10a] where production of a prototype only (of a helicopter blade tracking system) was held to be inadequate to gain its shelter.

So far as 1977 Act/1949 Act (and earlier Acts) comparison is concerned, it is convenient here to elaborate also the whole contents/prior claiming distinction mentioned earlier in this Part. Prior claiming, as defined by sections 8(1), 14(1)(c) and 32(1)(a) of the 1949 Act for purposes of examination, opposition and revocation respectively, represented one of the most vexed areas of the earlier law. It was, naturally, virtually unknown for two overlapping applications to have claims couched in identical language; each individual draughtsman tends to use his own words. Yet if the wordings were different, how was the presence of prior claiming to be assessed? Moreover, one draughtsman may have claimed in terms of a process and another in terms of a machine for carrying out a process. The tests applied by the Patent Office and Court tended to fluctuate, but they can be regarded as culminating in the strict approach followed in *Daikin Kogyo (Shingu's) Application*[11] in 1973 by the Court of Appeal. For a full history and analysis, reference must be made to larger works. The new 'whole contents' test of the 1977 Act has largely now removed this problem for the future. Application of a strict approach has the significant practical disadvantage that there may then be in co-existence two separate patents covering very much the same underlying inventive idea.

10   Section 32(1)(l).
10a   [1991] FSR 171.
11   [1974] RPC 559.

PART II: INVENTION IN THE ROUND, AND INVENTION AS CLAIMED

If the alleged piece of prior art is, by reason of its nature, one that has to be taken into account, the next question is that of its application to the patented invention. The patented invention has to be compared against the prior art, to test whether the prior art deprives it of novelty or (if novelty does exist) the prior art is nevertheless sufficiently close to render it obvious. This comparison necessarily involves the ascertainment, in the first place, of exactly what the patented invention is.

Under the pre-1977 Act law (still applicable for existing patents), the position was clear. The patented invention was determined by the scope of the claim(s) of the patent, when correctly construed; usually, of course, a patent would have a principal Claim 1, defining the invention in its widest scope, followed by a series of subsidiary claims introducing successively features of importance of the invention. The purpose of such a claim structure is to provide the patentee with one or more narrower claims on which he can fall back if the wider claims are held bad.

Thus, section 32(1)(e) of the 1949 Act couched the lack of novelty ground in terms of:

> . . . that the invention, *so far as claimed in any claim of the complete specification*, is not new having regard to what was known or used, before the priority date of the claim, in the United Kingdom. *(Emphasis added)*

Section 32(1)(f), providing for the obviousness ground, was couched in comparable terms.

Under the new 1977 Act (applicable henceforth for new patents), the position is not quite so certain. The references to the 'invention as claimed' are gone; instead it is merely the 'invention' which has to be new and unobvious. And 'invention' is defined by section 125(1) as being:

> . . . that specified in a claim of the specification of the application or patent, as the case may be, as *interpreted* by the description and any drawings contained in that specification, and the extent of the protection conferred . . . shall be determined accordingly. *(Emphasis added)*

This is qualified further (via section 125(3)) by the Protocol on the Interpretation of Article 69 of the European Patent Convention. That Protocol provides that:

> Article 69 should not be interpreted in the sense that the extent of the protection conferred by a European patent is to be understood as that defined by the strict, literal meaning of the wording used in the claims, the description and drawings being employed only for the purpose of resolving an ambiguity found in the claims. Neither should it be interpreted in the sense that the claims serve only as a guideline and that the actual protection conferred may extend to what from a consideration of the description and drawings by a person skilled in the art, the patentee has contemplated. On the contrary, it is to be interpreted as defining a position between these extremes which combines a *fair protection for the patentee with a reasonable degree of certainty for third parties*. *(Emphasis added)*

Precisely what section 125(1) and the Protocol between them amount to is undoubtedly (at present) still open to some question. The House of Lords has still to pronounce upon the subject (which is discussed further in Chapter 6). But it would seem clear that the Court is henceforth entitled to take a somewhat less rigid view on construction if it so wishes and, in appropriate cases, make some amalgam of the claims and supporting description in enunciating what the patented invention is.

Once the patented invention has been determined, however, there is no reason to suppose that the Court's criteria as to what in fact actually constitutes lack of novelty or obviousness of the patented invention will change significantly from those applied heretofore. Both the 1949 and 1977 Acts employ (albeit in slightly different contexts) the same key adjectives – namely, 'new' and 'obvious'.

PART III: LACK OF NOVELTY

The test here is at present strict. After some vacillation in the Victorian and Edwardian eras (arising partly from the fact that at that time the two objections of lack of novelty and obviousness had not yet become quite separate, but tended to be lumped together to a certain extent as 'anticipation') it became established for pre-1977 Act patents that the prior art must come squarely within the boundary of the invention as claimed, in order to deprive the claim(s) in question of novelty. And it appears (as just indicated) that a test of similar severity will apply in the future for 1977 Act patents; the only change will then lie in the ground-rules for ascertaining exactly what is the location of the boundary, the ring-fence of the invention, within which the prior art must come if it is to succeed against the patent. The prior art may, of course, be of any of the various kinds statutorily allowed to be taken into account, for the patent in question.

Thus, in the leading modern authority of *General Tire & Rubber v Firestone Tyre & Rubber* it was declared by the Court of Appeal that:

> A signpost, however clear, upon the road to the patentee's invention will not suffice. The prior inventor must be clearly shown to have planted his flag at the *precise destination* before the patentee.[12]   (*Emphasis added*)

The 'flag' analogy used here pinpoints the difference between lack of novelty and obviousness. If the flag is poised vertically above the stretch of turf in question, with its sharp-pointed end directed to the vital spot, it is still only obviousness; for lack of novelty, that pointed end must be shown to have been actually thrust down into the ground.

Thus, a novelty attack will usually fail if the prior art teaching is itself capable of being interpreted in more than one way; this is what happened in the *General Tire* case itself. Claim 1 of the patent in suit related to a method of making a vulcanisable plastic rubber compound suitable for a rubbery tyre tread which comprised mixing a certain synthetic rubbery polymerisation product with a certain amount of a compatible hydrocarbon mineral oil plasticiser in such a way that:

> . . . the plasticiser is distributed through and uniformly absorbed by the polymerization product before it has been appreciably deteriorated by mastication . . .[13]

12   [1972] RPC 457 at 486.
13   At 486.

The Semperit (a) citation relied upon by the defendant as prior art suggested employing generally similar starting ingredients. As regards processing, it described two methods. For the first method, it mentioned: 'These substances are mixed with the other customary additives *in the usual way*.'[14] (*Emphasis added*). For the second, it said: '. . . is worked up *in the usual manner* in a kneader into a carbon black batch, and is then processed on a roller mill into the final compound'.[15] (*Emphasis added*). The novelty attack failed because these passages did not clearly teach mixing with minimal mastication. The usual way of carrying out these instructions (both at the date of the citation and at the date of the patent) would have been with conventional mastication; and the fact that the compounder might have found in practice, if he had carried the prior Semperit process out, that he could have obtained adequate mixing with minimal mastication only, was not enough.

Likewise, the novelty attack will probably fail if the prior art teaching is inadequate. In current phraseology, the prior art teaching must be an 'enabling disclosure'. That term itself is reckoned to be derived from United States jurisprudence, although the underlying concept can be traced back to one of the classic Victorian judgments, that of Lord Westbury in *Hills v Evans*[16] where he said:

> . . . the antecedent statement must be such that a person of ordinary knowledge of the subject would at once perceive and understand and be able practically to apply the discovery without the necessity of making further experiments . . . the information . . . given by the prior publication must, for the purposes of practical utility, be equal to that given by the subsequent patent.

This was rephrased a century later by Lord Reid in *Van der Lely v Bamfords*[17] as:

> There may be cases where the skilled man has to have the language of the publication translated for him or where he must get from a scientist the meaning of technical terms or ideas with which he is not familiar, but once he has got this he must be able to make the machine from what is disclosed by the prior publication.

The question of 'enabling disclosure' can be of significance in chemical cases and the like, in particular, on account of the intrinsically less certain nature of such sciences as compared to mechanical science. Moreover, it is simple for a chemist to speculate (on paper) as to formulae for new chemical compounds, without having any clear idea as to how they might be prepared in practice. Thus the doctrine was applied in *Genentech Inc's (Human Growth Hormone) Patent*[18] to rebut a novelty attack in a biotechnological case and similarly by the House of Lords in *Asahi Kasei's Application*,[19] involving human tumour necrosis factor, to disallow a priority claim for a chronologically overlapping application (and hence rebut a section 2(3) novelty attack). The doctrine has also been favoured by the European Patent Office (see Chapter 12).

Again, the attack will fail in the case of an apparatus cited as an anticipation of a process claim, if there is uncertainty as to whether the prior art positively teaches use

14   At 492.
15   At 492.
16   1862 31 LJ.Ch 457 at 463.
17   [1963] RPC 61 at 71.
18   [1989] RPC 613.
19   [1991] RPC 485.

of the apparatus in that manner. In another leading authority *Flour Oxidising v Carr,* Parker J. (as he then was) said on this topic:

> . . . it is not, in my opinion, enough to prove that an apparatus described in an earlier Specification could have been used to produce this or that result. It must also be shown that the Specification contains *clear and unmistakeable directions* so to use it.[20]
>
> *(Emphasis added)*

The patent claimed in this case:

> 1. In the process of conditioning flour and the like, passing the same with full exposure through an atmosphere containing a gaseous oxide of nitrogen or chlorine or bromine oxidising agent in the gaseous or vapourised state.[21]

Both the cited prior Frichot and Hogarth specifications were concerned with treating flour by spark discharge apparatus which would be capable, if adjusted and arranged in correct fashion, of producing oxide of nitrogen and hence of effecting the claimed process. Nevertheless, the attack failed because of absence of any positive instruction to do so. The quote from the judgment:

> In the case of Frichot's Fig.5 I think it quite certain that no one could have used it in the way suggested above without entirely disregarding the directions given in the Specification, and that it would never have occurred to anyone so to use it, but for the discovery which the Andrews made . . .[22]

and

> In the case of Hogarth's Fig.3, though there is nothing in his Specification absolutely inconsistent with its being used as it had been in the Defendants' experiments, there are certainly no clear directions which would lead to such user. I think it more than doubtful whether it would have occurred to anyone so to use it but for the discovery on which Andrews' Patent is based.[23]

But if in fact the prior art does come within the boundary of the claimed monopoly, it is immaterial that the earlier and later workers may have approached the matter from different standpoints, or used different language, in which to describe their respective contributions to the art; nor is it material that the later worker may himself have been ignorant, at the time, of the earlier art and hence may, subjectively, have made a novel step forward from still earlier work; nor does it assist if the monopoly claimed embraces, as well as the anticipated embodiment, other embodiments which are not anticipated. The test is, although stringent, entirely objective.

This objectivity is neatly illustrated in the well-known case of *Molins v Industrial Machinery.*[24] The patent involved related to high-speed cigarette-making machines of so-called 'continuous rod' type, in which the tobacco showered down vertically onto a

---

20   25 RPC 428 at 457.
21   At 431.
22   At 457.
23   At 458.
24   55 RPC 31.

moving paper web. To eliminate the known problem of 'piling up' of the tobacco on the web, the patentee had the idea of imparting to the falling tobacco a forward component of movement also, so that the tobacco met the web at an acute angle rather than at right angles. The prior art specification of Bonsack, dated some forty-eight years earlier, related only to low-speed machines of this type; in these machines, the piling up problem did not arise at all. Bonsack's machine did, however, contain an inclined trough which would have the incidental effect of imparting a forward component of motion. In these circumstances, it was held that Bonsack deprived Molins' Claim 1 as it stood of novelty even though Bonsack was not concerned in the slightest with the problem that Molins had solved; Molins' Claim 1 could only be saved by restricting it to high-speed machines, capable of producing nine hundred or more cigarettes per minute.

Another aspect of lack of novelty arises in the so-called 'inevitable result' cases. These occur mainly in the chemical field, for example in the instance when it can be shown that an allegedly new chemical product is in fact bound to be produced in the normal performance of some earlier known process, even though the description of that earlier process makes no mention of the fact. To take a somewhat fanciful (although not scientifically nonsensical) illustration, a Claim 1 as follows:

> Process for preparing a composition capable of inhibiting extra-epidermal excrescences, comprising reacting digitalin with an aliphatic dicarboxylic acid under elevated temperature for at least 24 hours in an aqueous medium in the presence of heavy metal ions as catalyst and then incorporating the residue with a conventional pharmaceutical excipient.

might well be capable of being anticipated by the publication of a traditional countryside recipe calling for maceration of rhubarb leaves and foxglove seeds together with virgin's water and stirring in ye olde copper cauldron on a fire of alder twigs until the moon has changed its phase and then poulticing up into a wart-removal charm.

But it is necessary that the result be obtained each time, in the normal course of events. In the ampicillin trihydrate case mentioned above (page 28), a separate attack along these lines failed because it was held, on the evidence adduced, that the fine colourless needles produced in the relevant Example of the earlier patent specification were just as likely to be monohydrate as trihydrate. Although an occasional failure might be overlooked, an obtention rate of 50 per cent only would not suffice.

PART IV: OBVIOUSNESS

Introduction

Obviousness is normally the most difficult, and important, issue as regards the validity of a patent. It only arises in the first place should the lack of novelty attack fall, because by definition it assumes that there is some gap present between the prior art (of the kinds permitted to be taken into account) and the invention as claimed (for 1949 Act patents) or patented invention (for 1977 Act patents). But whereas the patents practitioner can often form a reasonably confident view in advance of trial (or other proceedings) as regards lack of novelty, because of the very severity of the tests to be relied on in applying the ground, he is often much more uncertain as regards obviousness. Until the witnesses have given their evidence and been cross-examined concerning it – and all the other relevant facts elicited – it is often difficult to assess whether the difference between the invention and the prior art represents a mere exercise of routine skill by the worker in the field in question (in which case the patent is bad for obviousness) or, on the other hand, incorporates that 'impalpable something'[25] – to use the expressive phrase coined as long ago as 1891 – which is the hallmark of genuine invention (in which case the patent is good).

The importance of such evidence was admitted candidly by the Court in the 1977 case of *Lucas v Gaedor*, involving thin-walled polypropylene storage battery cases. Claim 1, as proposed to be amended, was directed to:

> 1. A case for a storage battery of the kind referred to said case being a single injection moulding composed of polypropylene and having partitions defining a plurality of cells for cell groups, the bottom, side walls, end walls and partitions of said case having thicknesses not in excess of 0.100 of an inch the case having a cover in the form of a single moulded polypropylene unit engaging the upper edges of the side walls, end walls and partitions there being a heat formed weld between the cover and the side edges.

Regarding the quantitative thickness dimension, the Court said:

> . . . when this case opened to me I felt the gravest doubts as to whether a claim to this dimensional limitation could possibly stand good. What was *done in practice* by so many experts *on the evidence* before me has indeed convinced me that the step taken leading to a battery with walls as thin as 0.10 or less was not an obvious one.[26]
>
> *(Emphasis added)*

As for the level of skill and knowledge to be expected of the notional worker in the field, by whose standards obviousness is to be judged, this is not (in the ordinary case) too high. He is to be the unimaginative skilled technician rather than the leading expert. As expressed by Lord Moulton concerning the cited Butler Specification in his classic judgment in *Gillette Safety Razor v Anglo-American Trading*:

> In ascertaining its effect, the Court must consider what it would convey to the public to whom it was addressed, i.e. to mechanicians. I recognise that it would be most unfair to subsequent patentees if we tested this by what it would convey or suggest to a *mechanical genius*; but, on the other hand, it would be equally unjust to the public to take it as though it were read only by *mechanical idiots*.[27]
>
> *(Emphasis added)*

There may also be cases where the notional skilled man can reasonably be regarded as being constituted of a multidisciplinary team, for instance where the art in question necessarily involves a variety of expertise. Xerography and telecommunications cables represent typical examples of such arts.

The concept of the notional skilled man does also mean that the Court may discount to some extent evidence of obviousness from actual witnesses who may properly, in the circumstances, be treated as super-skilled rather than just regularly skilled. In

---

25 *McClain v Ortmayer* 141 US 419 at 427.
26 [1978] RPC 297 at 368.
27 30 RPC 465 at 481.

General Tire & Rubber v Firestone Tyre & Rubber (mentioned above, see page 31), this was the fate of the defendant's principal witness, Dr Duck, on account of his distinction (or misfortune for this purpose) of having something like fifty patents to his name. Conversely, of course, if even the leading experts can be shown (somewhat as in the *Lucas v Gaedor* case, mentioned above) actually to have missed the invention in the course of their own researches, it reinforces the argument that the notional ordinary worker would have done so also.

In the extra-ordinary case, of an art at the frontiers of a new technology, rather more can be expected. This is what happened in *Genentech Inc's Patent*,[28] involving the use of recombinant DNA technology for the synthetic production of human tissue plasminogen activator. It was said here:

> But where one is looking at the research team, one cannot treat them as dull plodders, for such people would not be members of the team at all, except as laboratory assistants. We have to envisage people who are *skilled*, and skilled *in the art*. Here we have a difficult art, in which the skill consists in a substantial degree of an ability to solve problems. It must, I consider, follow from this that the hypothetical skilled man must be credited with that particular ability in the appropriate degree.[29]

Dicta

Because obviousness is essentially a factual issue and because those facts are, by definition, unique in each particular case, it is difficult to extract too much by way of definitive legal guidelines from the extensive case law. There are, of course, a considerable number of well-known *dicta* on the subject. Some are couched in terms favourable to the patentee: others in terms favourable to the applicant for revocation: still others are paraphrastic in nature. But care must be taken in their application; it can prove unwise to try and extend them too far beyond factual situations of the same general kind as those involved in the parent cases in which they were first promulgated. Diplock L.J. (as he then was) put the point well in *Parks-Cramer v Thornton* when he said:

> 'Obviousness' is *not a concept which can be clarified by elaborate exegesis*, and we do not propose to cite the many cases to which we have been referred in which various judges at various times, both before and after the phrase 'is obvious and does not involve any inventive step' was first inserted in the Patents Acts, have expressed the concept of obviousness, or lack of subject-matter as it was previously called, *in various ways appropriate to the particular invention* whose validity was challenged on this ground.[30]
>
> (*Emphasis added*)

These *dicta* should nevertheless be known; they constitute the legal background against which the Court will work. Often a given *dictum* will enjoy a temporary popularity with the Court, then disappear from view and be resurrected some decades later when a new case having facts apt for its application comes before the Court again. They include (in chronological order) the following:

---

28   [1989] RPC 147.
29   At 279.
30   [1966] RPC 407 at 417.

Von Heyden v Neustadt (1880)

> We are of opinion, that if it requires this *mosaic* of extracts from annals and treatises, spread over a series of years, to prove the defendants' contention, that contention stands thereby self-condemned.[31]   (*Emphasis added*)

American Braided Wire v Thomson (1888)

> . . . if you see that the thing never was done in the memory of man down to a particular point, and at the moment it is done it is a great success . . . It is not conclusive of the question of ingenuity but it forces this reflection on one: unless there is some ingenuity . . . *why* was it never brought out before?[32]   (*Emphasis added*)

Gadd and Mason v Mayor of Manchester (1892)

> 1. A patent for the mere *new use of a known contrivance*, without any additional ingenuity in overcoming fresh difficulties, is bad, and cannot be supported. If the new use involves no ingenuity, but is in manner and purpose analogous to the old use, although not quite the same, there is no invention; no manner of new manufacture within the meaning of the Statute of James. 2. On the other hand, a patent for a new use of a known contrivance is good and can be supported if the new use involves practical difficulties which the patentee has been the first to see and overcome by some ingenuity of his own.[33]   (*Emphasis added*)

Hickton's Patent Syndicate v Patents and Machine Improvements (1909)

> To say that . . . simply because when you have once got the idea it is easy to carry it out, that that deprives it of the title of being a new invention according to our patent law, is, I think, an extremely dangerous principle and justified neither by reason, nor authority . . .
> In my opinion, invention may lie in the *idea*, and it may lie in the way in which *it is carried out*, and it may lie in the *combination of the two*; . . .[34]   (*Emphasis added*)

British Westinghouse v Braulik (1910)

> . . . I view with suspicion arguments to the effect that a new combination, bringing with it new and important consequences in the shape of practical machines, is not an invention, because, when it has once been established, it is easy to show how it might be arrived at by starting from something known, and taking a series of apparently easy steps. This *ex post facto* analysis of invention is unfair to the inventors and in my opinion it is not countenanced by English patent law.[35]

Gillette Safety Razor v Anglo-American Trading (1913)

> . . . it is important that this method of viewing their rights should not be overlooked. In practical life it is often the only safeguard to the manufacturer. It is impossible for an ordinary member of the public to keep watch on all the numerous Patents which are

31 50 LJ Ch. 126 at 128.
32 5 RPC 113 at 125.
33 9 RPC 516 at 524.
34 26 RPC 339 at 347 and 348.
35 27 RPC 209 at 230.

taken out and to ascertain the validity and scope of their claims. But he is entitled to feel secure if he knows that which he is *doing* differs from what has been *done before* only in non-patentable variations, such as the substitution of mechanical equivalents or changes of material shape or size.[36]   (*Emphasis added*)

British Thomson-Houston v Duram (1918)

A patentee requires, in order to establish the validity of his claim, to show that it provided at least some *useful addition* to the stock of human knowledge.[37]

(*Emphasis added*)

British Thomson-Houston v Metropolitan Vickers Electrical (1928)

Would a man who was grappling with Rosenberg's problem, without having seen Rosenberg's Patent, and who had Tesla's Specification in his hand, have said 'That gives me what I wish'?[38]

Parkes v Cocker (1929)

. . . once it had been found, as I find here, that the problem had awaited solution for many years, and that the device is in fact novel and superior to what had gone before, and has been widely used, and used in preference to alternative devices, it is I think practically impossible to say that there is not present that *scintilla* of invention necessary to support the Patent.[39]   (*Emphasis added*)

British Celanese v Courtaulds (1935)

. . . a mere placing side by side of old integers so that each performs its own proper function independently of any of the others is not a patentable combination, but that where the old integers when placed together have some working inter-relation producing a new or improved result then there is patentable subject-matter in the idea of the working inter-relation brought about by the *collocation* of the integers.[40]

(*Emphasis added*)

Cleveland Graphite v Glacier Metal (1949)

What is obvious to a reader must normally be obvious to the *writer*.[41]

(*Emphasis added*)

Parks-Cramer v Thornton (1966)

As in all other cases of obviousness, the question is one of degree. There may be an inventive step in *recognising that a problem exists at all*: but given a problem which is known to exist which it is the object of the invention to solve, the question always is: 'Is the solution claimed by the patentee one which would have occurred to everyone of

36   30 RPC 465 at 480.
37   35 RPC 161 at 184.
38   45 RPC 1 at 22.
39   46 RPC 241 at 248.
40   52 RPC 171 at 193.
41   66 RPC 157 at 175.

ordinary intelligence and acquaintance with the subject-matter of the patent who *gave his mind* to the problem?'[42]   (*Emphasis added*)

Johns-Manville Corporation's Patent (1967)

. . . it is enough that the person versed in the art would assess the likelihood of success as *sufficient to warrant actual trial.*[43]   (*Emphasis added*)

Technograph Printed Circuits v Mills & Rockley (Electronics) (1969)

. . . the proper question to ask was not, *could* the one be derived from the other, but *would* it be so derived?[44]   (*Emphasis added*)

Olin Mathieson v Biorex (1969)

Would the notional research group . . . in all the circumstances . . . directly be *led as a matter of course to try* the – CF_3 substitution . . .[45]   (*Emphasis added*)

General Tire & Rubber v Firestone Tyre & Rubber (1972)

'Obvious' is, after all, a much-used word and it does not seem to us that there is any need to go beyond the primary dictionary meaning of *'very plain'.*[46] (*Emphasis added*)

American Cyanamid v Ethicon (Interlocutory) (1973)

. . . the *history* of the matter, which is often the best evidence for or against obviousness . . .[47]   (*Emphasis added*)

American Cyanamid v Berk Pharmaceuticals (1973)

If a thing is obvious you go *straight to it.*   (*Emphasis added*)

and

A patient searcher is as much entitled to the benefits of a monopoly as someone who hits upon an invention by some lucky chance or an inspiration.[48]

Jamesigns' (Leeds) Application (1982)

What would have been significant in the Kampfer specification for the appropriately skilled technician was the *reason* which Kampfer gave for the advantages of his invention . . The *same reason* could, and would, have been applied to the use of ballatine sheeting under a transparent plate.[49]   (*Emphasis added*)

42 [1966] RPC 407 at 418.
43 [1967] RPC 479 at 494.
44 [1969] RPC 395 at 404.
45 [1970] RPC 157 at 187.
46 [1972] RPC 457 at 497.
47 [1975] RPC 513 at 517.
48 [1976] RPC 231 at 257.
49 [1983] RPC 68 at 74.

Windsurfing International v Tabur Marine (Great Britain) (1985)

> The hypothetical Skilled Man is, no doubt, (together with his cousins the Reasonable Man and the Officious Bystander) a useful concept as setting a standard and, in the instant case, as providing the touchstone by which the question of obviousness may be judged by the equally hypothetical Juror; but he must not be allowed to obscure the nature of the inquiry which the words of the statute require, and one cannot help feeling that his image may lead to confusion if one seeks to attribute to him human qualities either of constitutional idleness or of perception beyond the knowledge and skill in the field in which he is hypothetically supposed to operate.[50]

Van der Lely v Ruston's Engineering (1985)

> I do not for my part think that it is sufficient to repel an attack on grounds of obviousness to demonstrate that what is now claimed as an obvious solution is *not the first* solution that occurred to anyone.[51]   (*Emphasis added*)

Genentech Inc's Patent (1989)

> Another possibility is to fasten on the word "step", and to look at the steps which were actually taken by the inventor on the road to the first realisation of the invention: the first making of the product, the first working of the process. Yet this too is unsound, for the cases show that the history of the route by which the applicant arrived at the invention is not material to the validity of the patent, and may (and indeed probably should) be omitted from the specification. Furthermore, I believe that this interpretation places too much weight on the choice of the particular word "step", which in the context of a case such as the present must carry the meaning of "activity", as the other two texts of the Convention make plain.[51a]
>
> . . . .
>
> As to skill, one sees it in abundance. But this is not the same as inventiveness.[51b]

On a purely historical note, it should also be mentioned that in Victorian and Edwardian days, obviousness was sometimes denoted as 'lack of subject-matter'; conversely, 'subject-matter' denoted non-obviousness. The transition case, terminologically speaking, may conveniently be pinpointed as *British Celanese v Courtaulds*, above, where Lord Tomlin managed to discuss all three topics of lack of novelty, lack of subject-matter and obviousness quite separately.

Discussion of Dicta

To put the *dicta* above into their proper perspectives, it is useful to consider further the circumstances in which they arose. Working again in chronological order, the *Von Heyden v Neustadt* rule will be dealt with first.

It is essential to realise that *Von Heyden* does not preclude *in toto* any combination of prior art teachings. Indeed, it is well established that any prior art teaching is to be looked at through the eyes of the skilled person appraised of the common general

---

50   [1985] RPC 59 at 71.
51   [1985] RPC 461 at 484.
51a   [1989] RPC 147 at 275.
51b   At 286.

knowledge of the art; that common general knowledge may itself be found in some document (say, the standard textbook in the art). Alternatively, there may in the circumstances be some other good reason for combining two pieces of prior art together, as in *Allmanna Svenska Elektriska v Burntisland Shipping*[52] or *Dow Chemical's (Mildner's) Patent.*[53]

The latter case provides a particularly good example. The patent was concerned with an electric cable construction. Electric cables represent an art of 'mixed technology' kind – electrical, mechanical and chemical considerations all enter into the selection of materials for the individual components of the cable, and their assembly. Claim 1 called for:

> Electrical cable having a conductor core and a metallic shield wherein a plastics jacket is securely bonded to at least one of the surfaces of the metallic shield through an intermediate boundary layer of a thermoplastic polymer of a major proportion by weight of ethylene and a minor proportion of an ethylenically unsaturated carboxylic acid, the bond being substantially coextensive with the common surface of contact of the shield and the jacket.

This Claim was held obvious by the Court of Appeal, in belated opposition proceedings under the 1949 Act (where the benefit of the doubt would always be given in any event to the patentee), in face of one document disclosing a cable with all the features except the particular adhesive polymer specified and another quite separate second document disclosing the polymer and its usefulness as a plastics/metal adhesive (but not in the context of electric cables).

To cite from Scarman L.J.'s judgment:

> . . . the evidence establishes that the art of electric cable making is a highly developed technology which includes skills in the application of a number of different sciences to the problem of making a cable. Thus it comes that men experienced in the application of polymer science take part in this art and their skills must be imputed to the hypothetical uninventive skilled technician in the art.[54]

What *Von Heyden* does prohibit is the obviousness attack based on a patchwork quilt of a multiplicity of pieces of prior art – the making of a quite new pattern out of the pieces, that is – a proper 'mosaic', as opposed to their mere placement side-by-side. Thus, in *Von Heyden* itself, an unsuccessful attempt was made to invalidate a claim to a chemical process for the manufacture of salicylic acid by combining no less than seven different separate items of prior chemical knowledge.

American Braided Wire enunciates the rhetorical question – why not before? There may naturally be perfectly good answers to that question – previous unavailability of necessary raw materials at the right price, industry prejudice, difficulties in raising the necessary capital for exploitation, and the like. The force of the question is, of course, also much less when reliance is placed on recent prior art (say, one year before) than on much older art (say, twenty to thirty years ago).

Gadd and Mason involved, as the cited extract indicates, a patent employing a known

---

52   69 RPC 63.
53   [1975] RPC 165.
54   At 169.

device in a new context. A patent directed to a gasometer incorporating an anti-tilting and -jamming arrangement was held valid in face of earlier patents showing use of similar arrangements in floating docks and pontoons; the adaptation to gasometers involved difficulties, the overcoming of which required invention.

Hickton's Patent Syndicate involved an invention the subsequent realisation of which was simple once the original conception had been made by the inventor. It was concerned with lace manufacture, and the facts are of some complexity. A simpler example was given in the leading judgment itself, namely that of Watt's invention of the separate condenser in the steam engine. Given the idea, said the judge (at 347), 'It could be done in a thousand ways and by any competent engineer . . .'.

A successful contemporary application of the *Hickton* principle is to be found in *Mutoh Industries' Application*,[55] concerning application of the well-known effect of magnetic repulsion to reduction of friction as between the moving parts of an otherwise known architect's drawing device. The fact that there would be no difficulty in knowing where to put the pairs of repulsive magnets, once in possession of the idea of using the effect, did not suffice to render the claimed inventions obvious.

British Westinghouse represents the classic denunciation of the hindsight view. Milton in *Paradise Lost* (Book VI, lines 498 to 501) also had something to say back in the 17th century along the same lines, in relation to Satan's invention of gunpowder:

> Th'invention all admir'd, and each, how hee
> To be th'inventor miss'd, so easy it seem'd
> Once found, which yet unfound most would have thought
> Impossible . . .

Gillette Safety Razor represents the equally classic enunciation of the 'right to work' principle. If the alleged infringement is, as a matter of technology, itself obvious over the cited prior art, then the defendant cannot be stopped. The plaintiff must lose either on invalidity (if his patent is construed sufficiently broadly so as to embrace the infringement) or on non-infringement (if his patent is construed sufficiently narrowly as to avoid the impact of the prior art). He is impaled on the horns of a dilemma.

It should be noted that the judgment goes on to put the point as: 'The defence that "the alleged infringement was not novel at the date of the plaintiff's Letters Patent" is a good defence in law . . .'. This has since become widely known as the 'Gillette Defence'. But the use here of the word 'novel' can, to the modern reader, prove a little misleading. At the date of the judgment, lack of novelty and obviousness had not yet become disentangled completely from each other as grounds of objection. Lack of novelty could exist then in situations which today, because of the strictness of the contemporary test, would rank as situations of obviousness only. The facts in *Gillette Safety Razor*, as well as in the *dictum* quoted earlier, make this clear.

Thus, the Gillette Patent related to the now conventional safety razor employing a thin double-edged blade. The prior Butler Specification showed a similar arrangement generally, but using a single-edged blade of approximately isosceles triangular cross-section similar to that of a cut-throat razor. Other prior art showed use of thin sheet steel blades in razors. The Court was prepared in the circumstances to aggregate these

55   [1984] RPC 35.

teachings, but even so Claim 1 was good because it required also, on its true construction, the requirement for the blade to be flexible and hence to be capable of adopting a lengthwise curved (slightly) configuration in its holder. Consequentially, the defendants' razor did not infringe, since it lacked any capacity for adjustment by curvature of the blade; the backing and guard, between which the blade was clamped, were both flat.

The defence should, therefore, be more accurately defined today as: 'The defence that "the alleged infringement was obvious at the date of the plaintiff's Letters Patent" is a good defence in law . . .'. And an enunciation to this effect was eventually, and recently, made in the Court of Appeal in *Windsurfing International v Tabur Marine (Great Britain)*.[56] No doubt the lengthy interim delay arose from the special position occupied by Lord Moulton in the pantheon of patent lawyers.

In *British Thomson-Houston v Duram* (see page 38 above) there was a wide Claim 1, for:

> The method of working tungsten, which consists in subjecting the metal in a coherent form to the action of heat whilst it is being operated on or manipulated.

Although the patentee's specific process (for making tungsten electric light filaments) had been successful, it was held that the Claim as it stood provided no contribution to the art; being so wide, it would have the effect of preventing others from generally availing themselves of the common tools and routine of the metal worker for the purpose of making use of a property inherent in the metal tungsten itself. The decision clearly echoes the *Gillette* principle.

Parkes v Cocker involved a gadget (a clip for holding labels, tickets and the like in position). The *dictum* provides a convenient peg for a Court wishing to find in favour of a patentee; it naturally tends to be relied on heavily in argument by that class. But it can hardly be right if taken to its full literal extent, inasmuch that it seems to suggest that non-obviousness is composed of novelty + success alone.

In *British Celanese*, the patent was concerned with the dry spinning of cellulose acetate and the like into textile filaments. Four integers (features) were used, all individually old in themselves, and the combination was recited in both the process and apparatus claims. These were (1) downward extrusion, (2) an enclosing casing, (3) a counter-current of hot air, and (4) outside winding. It was held, on the facts, that there was no interrelated working in the sense of any one of the individual integers doing, in the combination, something which it could not do without the presence of one or more of the others. They each just performed their own intrinsic function, but no more.

Cleveland Graphite draws attention to another relevant factor: what kind of document is the prior publication relied upon? Is it a prior patent specification? A straight scientific paper? A brief communication in *Nature* revealing a significant breakthrough? An article in the popular technical press? A review-type article discussing at length recent progress and still outstanding problems in a given field? A manufacturer's advertisement?

The reaction of the notional skilled man, by whose standards obviousness has to be judged, may vary in each case. He would not expect, for example, to find many remarks in a patent specification as to possible commercial significance of the taught subject-matter.

56 Above, at 77.

For the scientific paper, he would at least expect that the specific examples (in a chemical case) were a report of what had actually been done in the laboratory as opposed to the armchair. The brief communication in a scientific journal concerned to provide early news of important developments would naturally be sparse in detail but might well spur him to immediate further investigation – it would be a 'hot' piece of prior art whereas the patent specification residing untouched for many years on the shelves of the Patent Office Library would be 'cold'. He might well think that the popular article, being written by a journalist rather than a scientist, might contain errors and/or exaggerations. The review article would be likely to be taken seriously. The manufacturer's advertisement would perhaps be taken with a pinch of salt.

In *Cleveland Graphite*, the patent involved a thin-wall bearing intended for heavy-duty use, for example the journaling of crankshafts of internal combustion engines. The prior art was an article in a United States periodical *Automotive Industries* discussing the forthcoming new Chevrolet motor car, and published a few days before the Convention date of the patent. In the words of Greene M.R. (at 169):

> . . . the article is quite clearly of an advertising character and has a title expressed in the worst possible style of publicity, such as to discourage the serious reader . . . one of the ostensibly scientific statements which it contains is so absurd as to excite the derision of the initiated.

Notwithstanding it defects, however, the article had to be taken into proper account.

Parks-Cramer makes the point that there is not always an apparent technological problem requiring solution. Of course, there often is – good examples are provided by the piling-up problem in cigarette manufacture solved by the Molins' Patent or the thread loss problem in lace-making machines solved by the Hickton Patent. But this is not always so. Those engaged in the art may be already (although wrongly) satisfied with its state of advancement, quite overlooking the possibility of further improvement in one or other of its respects. Alternatively, an invention can break quite new technological ground – as in the case of the hovercraft or transistor or even the windsurfer, where it was pointed out in *Windsurfing International* that:

> The instant case is not one of which it can be said that there was an existing problem for which the sailing-boat or leisure industries had been searching for a solution . . .[57]

If so, there is only a problem requiring solution in the most general sense – the improvement of mass or individual means for transportation over water, or of means for influencing flow of electric currents, respectively. The significance of this point for purposes of assessing obviousness is that, absent a problem, there may be less incentive for the skilled man in the first place to experiment and improve.

In *Johns-Manville*, the prior art was a recent manufacturer's advertising pamphlet entitled 'Polyacrylamide – a new, synthetic, water-soluble gum'. It recommended the new agent in general terms as having a wide application for flocculation of suspensions. This recommendation was held to render obvious a later patent directed to use of the same agent in one particular flocculation context – the manufacture of shaped

57 Above at 70.

asbestos-cement articles. This was not surprising; as it stood, the pamphlet constituted a positive invitation to experiment.

In *Technograph Printed Circuits*, on the other hand, the prior art was a document (a patent specification) of quite opposite kind. It was discouraging in tone, and quite old. The relevant part consisted in the description of an alternative (to the main method) way of making the electrostatic shield in question; this alternative was described as providing an expensive and messy operation. It was not even embraced by the claims of the prior patent. Hence, although the gap between this alternative method and the patent in suit (the basic patent on printed circuits) was small, there was no reason to bridge it. The could/would distinction was, in the circumstances, particularly apt.

Olin Mathieson was a chemical case, concerned with new compounds having a certain therapeutic (tranquillising) activity. The approach is of value in such cases, because until the compound(s) has (have) been made and tested it is often impossible to know whether it has the desired activity; there is an inherent degree of uncertainty in chemical science.

General Tire & Rubber and the two *American Cyanamid* decisions provide a trio of *dicta* popular in their decade, the 1970s. They emphasise the importance of looking at the question of obviousness from a practical standpoint, and no doubt reflect the zeitgeist of that era – just as, to converse effect, *British Celanese* reflected the spirit of the Courts in the 1930s. Such standpoint, although superficially attractive, is not immune from criticism. For if the state of the art is to be defined objectively, rather than subjectively in terms of what the inventor actually knew at the time of making his invention, artificiality (that is, a non-practical standpoint) is inevitably present. Nor in any event does such a standpoint necessarily always favour the patentee. In the recent *Jamesigns' (Leeds)* case, for example, the Court of Appeal upheld an obviousness attack based upon a 38-year old prior patent. Notwithstanding its age, and absence of any evidence as to it ever having been put into practice, it taught the fundamental idea on which the new patent was based; the fact that the material used by the new patent (for reflective vehicle registration plates) was unknown in 1934 was immaterial. Essentially, the case was merely one of old art brought up to date, or, more colloquially, one of 'new wine in old bottles'. *Windsurfing International, Van der Lely*, and *Genentech* complete the chronology

Commercial Success

It is important to note that commercial success of the invention is unlikely to be decisive in itself in favour of non-obviousness. There may be other explanations, beyond that of inventive ingenuity, for such success – better marketing, availability of new raw material, raising of statutory controls, and the like. Thus, when stainless steel and nylon first became available as new materials it was no invention to make from them table-knives and stockings respectively; bearing in mind the inherent needs of such articles, it was obvious that the materials would be suitable therefor. Conversely, lack of commercial success is unlikely to be decisive in favour of obviousness. It may well be possible to explain the lack away – particularly if the patent comes into dispute at an early stage of its life. Where the degree of commercial success is outstanding, the position may be rather different – particularly if the success is coupled with extensive copying by competitors and the cited prior art is some years old. An inference arises in such circumstances that a real technical contribution to the art, in turn suggestive of an inventive step, has been made.

Contemporary Climate

The *dicta* and other considerations discussed above (and, of course, the list is not complete) provide a somewhat bewildering assembly of possible guidelines for Court to follow in any obviousness dispute. How is it possible to forecast which will be followed in the case in issue, and hence what will be likely to be the result? This is not the simplest of questions to answer. In one of its most recent decisions *Minnesota Mining and Manufacturing v Rennicks* (UK),[57a] the court has followed an enunciation given in the *Windsurfing International*[57b] case.

> There are, we think, four steps which require to be taken in answering the jury question. The first is to identify the inventive concept embodied in the patent in suit. Thereafter, the court has to assume the mantle of the normally skilled but unimaginative addressee in the art at the priority date and to input to him what was, at that date, common general knowledge in the art in question. The third step is to identify what, if any, differences exist between the matter cited as being 'known or used' and the alleged invention. Finally, the court has to ask itself whether, viewed without any knowledge of the alleged invention, those differences constitute steps which would have been obvious to the skilled man or whether they require any degree of invention.

But fashions may change.

It is suggested that a useful first approach step is always to consider – what is the kind of situation presented by the technical facts of the invention? Not all the *dicta* are always potentially applicable. The *British Celanese dictum* concerning combination patents is, for example, inherently unsuitable for application to a case involving patentability of new chemical compounds – but quite possibly inherently suitable for a case involving the patentability of a complicated piece of machinery, say, an automatic sewing machine or a biscuit-packaging apparatus.

A second step is to consider the type of surrounding facts involved (so far as already known, or expected to be shown at trial). Is, for example, the prior document (or indeed use if that be relied on) of inherently discouraging (*Technograph*) or encouraging (*Johns-Manville*) kind? And there are the consequential questions of whether there was any actual usage of the prior art and if so, with what result; if not, how was the prior art actually received (at the time or later) by those working in the art? And how does the background common general knowledge in the art influence the matter? Again the situation may (or may not) be one of potential 'mosaicing' type.

As a third and final approach step, it may then be useful to bear in mind that there are (at least today) certain individual factors which seem to be particularly cogent to the eventual determination of an obviousness issue.

Among these, the initial one is the angle of the judicial pendulum. In recent times (in a broad sense) this has undoubtedly swung towards the patentee end of its arc. This was not always so. In the 1930s it used to be jocularly asserted in the United States

57a   [1992] RPC 331 at 350.
57b   at 73.

that the only valid patent was one which the Supreme Court had not got its hands on yet; a similar remark would have been largely true for the United Kingdom also.

The turning point is often taken as the speech of Salmon L.J. (as he then was) in *Ethyl Corporation's Patent* in 1969; although that case was concerned with amendment, and not obviousness, his remarks are quite general:

> From 1883 until after the end of the last war, the courts tended to regard patent monopolies with some disfavour as being generally contrary to the public interest. Since, at any rate, 1949, the climate of opinion had changed. It is now generally recognised that it is *in the public interest* to encourage inventive genius. Accordingly the modern tendency of the courts has been to *regard patent claims with considerably more favour than formerly.*[58]   (*Emphasis added*)

The 'before' and 'after' attitudes are neatly contrasted by the judicial approaches displayed in two decisions of the House of Lords, in, respectively, *Rado v Tye*[59] (1968 – plastic sachet patent held invalid for obviousness) and *Technograph Printed Circuits* (1971 – printed circuit patent held non-obvious and valid). In both cases, an extensive assortment of prior art documents (some quite old and of relevance not easy to discern) was brought forward; in the first, it was aggregated together – virtually in true 'mosaic' form – to defeat the claim; in the second, the great majority were unceremoniously tossed aside.

It is to be expected that the pendulum may in the course of the next decade or so start swinging back towards the opponent end, and incipient signs of such reversal can be detected in contemporary decisions of the Court of Appeal. Attention may be drawn, for example, to their treatment of the Darby citation in *Windsurfing International*,[60] or their re-affirmation in *Hallen v Brabantia*[61] of the principle that the attainment of an added benefit (bonus effect), however great, would not render the patent valid if the claimed invention was obvious for another purpose.

Another factor is the considerable emphasis on the guidance given by contemporaneous events. Evidence of unsuccessful attempts by other workers in the field at the time (date of the patent) to solve the problem in fact solved by the patentee is powerfully persuasive in his favour; so is evidence of disbelief by other workers when the invention first comes out, or evidence that other workers had in fact already had the invention in their hands in the privacy of their laboratories, but had failed to perceive the gold lying within the muddy outside surface of the nugget.

In the case when the prior art resides in a prior document rather than in a prior use another factor may lie in the so-called 'circumstances of publication'. This is a relatively new doctrine, and likely to prove of increasing significance in the future with the 1977 Act expansion of what constitutes the state of the art (and hence range of citable documents). It is a doctrine which reflects the realisation by the Court of the fact that with the recent (say, since 1945) increase in the amount of scientific literature published it may well be impossible in practice for the skilled person to keep himself up to date; some documents are inherently more accessible and/or well known than others.

---

58   [1972] RPC 169 at 193.
59   [1968] FSR 563.
60   At 73–74.
61   [1991] RPC 195 at 216.

In 1969 in *Woven Plastic Products v British Ropes*[62] the traditional, and objective, approach was followed – under protest – by the Court of Appeal. The specifications of four Japanese Utility Models relating to woven floor mats were relied on to invalidate the patent even though there was no evidence that their disclosures had ever come to the notice of anyone in the industry in Great Britain; the documents had been confined strictly, so it appeared, to the vaults of the Patent Office Library. In 1971 in the *Technograph Printed Circuits* case the House of Lords introduced the concept of the 'diligent searcher'. This was accepted in the immediately following *General Tire & Rubber* case, where two war-time Austrian patent specifications (the Semperit(a) document previously mentioned, and Semperit(c), available only on microfilm in cardboard boxes in the basement of the Patent Office along with some 146,000 others and arranged only by division into 89 classes of technical subject-matter, appear to have had their undoubtedly considerable relevance so far as obviousness was concerned somewhat discounted because of the asserted difficulty (a likely 'enormous fee' for the search) in finding them. In 1977, in *ICI's (Pointer's) Application*[63] the phrase itself was coined by the Patents Appeal Tribunal, to provide an alternative reason for rejecting an obviousness attack based on a trade pamphlet available only in the private libraries of two companies neither of which was commercially concerned with the problem solved by the later patent.

Claimed Matter

One final point remains to be emphasised. This is that – at least under traditional law – obviousness has to be tested (just as lack of novelty has to be) in relation to the invention as claimed. The invention as claimed may (or may not) reflect the inventor's actual inventive step (if any). He may have claimed too narrowly or, rather more likely in real life, too widely.

Hence, if the boundary of the monopoly claimed embraces a number of separate embodiments, one or more of which is obvious while the remainder are non-obvious, then the claim is bad as it stands until the offending embodiment has been excised by amendment. The position is comparable to that which may arise in respect of an attack based on lack of novelty. Thus, in *Woodrow v Long Humphreys* (1933), manhole covers of a certain type might, when shaped in rectangular or higher polygonal form, have possessed 'subject-matter' (to use the then contemporary phraseology to denote non-obviousness); the claim as drafted, however, covered triangular ones as well and these certainly did not possess 'subject-matter'; the claim was accordingly bad. As stated by Romer L.J.:

> But I cannot agree that a claim in its totality has subject-matter if it includes, as this one does, something that has none.[64]

Another enunciation of the same principle is found in the slightly later (1943) case of *Non-Drip Measure v Strangers* (concerning devices for dispensing measured quantities of whisky and the like) where Greene M.R. said: 'Now this is a wide and comprehensive

62   [1970] FSR 47.
63   [1977] FSR 434.
64   51 RPC 25 at 34.

claim. If in one of its embodiments the invention as claimed lacks subject-matter, the whole claim is necessarily bad.'[65]

Of course, it does not follow that all claims can be dissected in this fashion into good and bad embodiments, with consequential opportunity for amendment. Much depends on the inherent nature of the invention, and the manner in which the claim is drafted. It may well be the case that a particular claim is in the circumstances either wholly good or wholly bad.

This same principle is likely to be followed in future for patents granted under the 1977 Act, although in relation to the invention as 'interpreted' (overtly by specification and claim jointly) as distinct simply from the invention as claimed. The possible change, as compared to the traditional law, made by the 1977 Act has already been discussed in Part II of this chapter.

PART V: SELECTION PATENTS AND CHEMICAL PATENTS

As aptly put by the Superintending Examiner in *Snam's Application*:

> A 'selection patent' by its very nature must lie in the *penumbra* between the shadow of an unambiguous anticipation on the one hand and obviousness and clear lack of inventive step on the other.[66] (*Emphasis added*)

The selection position arises where the earlier prior art discloses a class, and the later patentee finds that a particular individually novel member(s) of that class possesses (possess) an unexpected advantage. The situation is liable to arise primarily in the chemical field, although it is not a doctrine peculiar to chemistry and in fact was first promulgated in a mechanical case *Clyde Nail v Russell*[67] (selection of particular shape for nail blank). To take a simple example, if the prior art teaches the use of a metal in a particular catalytic process, there is the possibility of making a selection invention by choosing manganese as the particular metal provided, of course, that the prior document does not explicitly teach the use of manganese. Another example, in the electro-mechanical field, would be where the prior art teaches the use of a brush with synthetic fibre bristles for cleaning residual toner off the web of an electrostatic copying machine, and the later worker finds that polytetrafluoroethylene (PTFE) fibres are particularly effective because of their lubricant qualities.

The classic enunciation of the requirements for a selection patent is contained in the judgment of Maugham J. (as he then was) in *IG Farbenindustrie AG's Patents* (reactant combinations for azo-dyestuffs):

> First, a selection patent to be valid must be based on some substantial advantage to be secured by the use of the selected members. (That phrase will be understood to include the case of a substantial disadvantage to be thereby avoided.) Secondly, the whole of the selected members must possess the advantage in question. Thirdly, the selection must be in respect of a quality of a special character which can fairly be said to be peculiar to the selected group.[68]

65 59 RPC 1 at 23.
66 [1970] FSR 425 at 429.
67 33 RPC 291.
68 47 RPC 269 at 322.

Notwithstanding its age, this decision is still the leading case on the subject – note the remarks to this effect in the 1990 decision of the Court of Appeal in *Hallen v Brabantia*, above.

Where difficulty often arises in practice in selection cases is in instances where the class out of which the selection is made is itself small, since the smaller the parent class the more difficult it may be to assert that the selected compound or the like is itself novel in the first place. What might be termed 'bare novelty' is usually still necessary; the selection rules (if fulfilled) can be regarded as providing a defence to an attack of obviousness based on the standpoint that disclosure of a class of whatever scientific kind suggests, to say the least, all the individual members of the class.

This latter issue is the subject of the 1982, and still controversial, decision of the House of Lords in *Du Pont de Nemours' (Witsiepe's) Application*[69] concerning terephthalate copolyesters; this decision indicates that novelty is only destroyed on proof that there had been both disclosure, and actual manufacture also, of the relevant prior art compounds. It remains to be seen as to how widely this view will be followed in future chemical cases, with their own necessarily different individual facts. Certainly, it would be unprecedented in the field of mechanical or electrical patents to suggest that an earlier description and/or drawing could not be relied on unless it had also been proven that the article or circuit in question had been constructed.

It follows that a patentee who wishes to rely on the attainment of surprising effect in support of validity may well wish to argue that his patent can be treated as a selection patent. But he may find himself blocked in this endeavour (as did the patentee in *Hallen v Brabantia* above, involving a PTFE-coated corkscrew) if his specification was not drafted in the first place as relating to such a kind of invention.

More generally, the problems with chemical patents in our law largely spring – perhaps – from the peculiar nature of chemical science as compared to its mechanical and physical sisters. Given a lead compound, say a new semi-synthetic penicillin characterised by the presence of a particular heterocyclic ring structure in its side-chain, any organic chemist worth his salt can probably envisage almost immediately a vast array of new related compounds – homologues, analogues, isomeric forms and/or substituted versions of the parent. They are immediately 'structurally obvious' compounds. Should such mental process suffice to defeat a later claim to one of the related compounds *per se*, when it is subsequently prepared and found to possess some valuable unexpected activity? After all it is the activity, rather than the mere compound, that provides the contribution to the art.

English law tends to follow a somewhat artificial approach in order to find a solution of this problem in favour of the later patentee – who undoubtedly has the merits on his side. The point is taken that – although the possible existence of the related compound may well, as a mental abstraction, be clear – the notional skilled man (by whose standards obviousness must be judged) would not in practice have any incentive actually to make it until he was aware of the valuable properties, and by definition he could not be aware of those properties until the later invention had been made.

The United States Patent Office (at least) tends in contrast to take a much more robust and sensible attitude, to reach a similar end. In the famous 1963 case of *In re Papesch*, involving a homologue of the prior art compound and possessing anti-

69 [1982] FSR 303.

inflammatory activity quite absent in the former, Judge Giles Rich enunciated the 'inseparability' doctrine as follows:

> From the standpoint of patent law, a *compound and all of the properties are inseparable*; they are one and the same thing. The graphic formulae, the chemical nomenclature, the systems of classification and study such as the concepts of homology, isomerism, etc., are mere symbols by which compounds can be identified, classified and compared. But a *formula is not a compound* and while it may serve in a claim to identify what is being patented, as the metes and bounds of a deed identify a plot of land, the *thing that is patented is not the formula but the compound identified by it*. And the patentability of the thing does not depend on the similarity of its formula to that of another compound but on the similarity of the former compound to the latter. There is no basis in law for ignoring any property in making such a comparison. An assumed similarity based on a comparison of formulae must give way to evidence that the assumption is erroneous.[70]
>
> *(Emphasis added)*

Granted that this decision was under United States law (the wording of which differs from that of the 1949 and 1977 United Kingdom Acts), nevertheless it is to be hoped that its refreshing breeze will eventually reach the United Kingdom.

Alloy patents present special difficulties of their own since:

(1) often the particular metallurgical effect desired requires the presence of a combination of alloying ingredients; and
(2) the effect can often be influenced markedly by the addition of other incidental ingredients to the alloy base.

The principles as to the drafting and scope of claims in such cases are discussed in *Mond Nickel's Application (Alloys)*.[71]

PART VI: PATENTABILITY WITHIN THE FOUR CORNERS OF THE SPECIFICATION

As far as patentability in face of the art is concerned, the patentee is not his own master. If the prior art is of a kind which is intrinsically citable, it must be taken into account quite irrespective of whether or not the patentee was aware of it at the time of making his invention and/or having his patent specification drafted. If the prior art in fact deprives the relevant patent claims of novelty, or renders them obvious, then they are bad; that is the end of the matter.

In contrast stand the intrinsic legal requirements for the specification and claims themselves. Hence, the patentee is his own master; if his drafting is defective, he has only himself to blame.

Hence, the distinction has grown up between the requirements for so-called 'external' validity (in relation to the prior art) and 'internal' validity (in relation to inherent contents of the specification).

---

70   137 USPQ 43 at 51.
71   65 RPC 123.

Insufficiency

The most important of these 'internal' requirements is, and always has been, that of sufficiency. The need for sufficiency derives from the fundamental nature of the patent system; in return for the limited monopoly, the patentee must teach the public what his invention is. Hence the specification must be 'sufficient' for that purpose. If it is not, there is 'insufficiency' and the patent is bad.

The point is put forcefully in some of the earliest *dicta* on the subject:

> . . . the end and meaning of the specification is, to teach the public, after the term for which the patent is granted, what the art is; and it must put the public in possession of the secret in as *ample and beneficial* a way as the patentee himself uses it.[72]
>
> *(Emphasis added)*

(*R v Arkwright*, in 1785, concerning a machine for preparing silk, cotton, flax and wool for spinning; the Specification was very abbreviated in form, especially in relation to the spinning rollers, and evidence was given to the effect that it had been deliberately drafted 'to be as obscure as the nature of the case would admit'.)

> . . . if he makes the article, for which the patent is granted, with cheaper materials than those which he has enumerated, though the latter will answer the purpose equally well, the patent is void because he does not put the public in possession of his invention, or enable them to derive the *same benefit* which he himself does.[73]   *(Emphasis added)*

(*Turner v Winter*, in 1787, involving a Specification for the manufacture of a yellow lead pigment.)
Liardet v Johnson[74] in 1778, already cited in Chapter 1 (page 3) and concerning cement compositions, is to the same effect. In more recent (relatively) times, the same vein was followed in *Vidal Dyes Syndicate v Levinstein* (1912). It was said here that:

> It is settled law that a patentee must act towards the public *uberrima fide*, and must give the best information in his power as to how to carry out the invention.[75]

It is, of course, unnecessary that the patentee should describe all ways known to him of carrying out the invention; specifications of absurdly great length would arise if that were so, but it is not. A specification may also be perfectly sufficient even though the reader has to perform experiments of routine kind to obtain a successful result; it all depends on the nature of the invention in question. The inadequacy of the disclosure must also be looked at as a matter of substance. If there are, for example, some errors in the drawings which the skilled engineer in the field in question would immediately perceive and know how to correct, then the deficiency is not necessarily fatal. The opposite applies, of course, if the remedy is not self-apparent.

This latter point is well illustrated by the classic 'iron autoclave' case, *Badische Anilin*

---

72   1 WPC 64 at 66.
73   1 WPC 77 at 81.
74   1 WPC 53.
75   29 RPC 245 at 269.

und Soda Fabrik v Société Chimique (1898).[76] Relevant Example 2 of the patentees' specification described the heating of dyestuff components (diethyl rhodamine hydrochlorate and methyl or ethyl alcohol) in 'an autoclave'. In fact, the dyestuff would only be produced satisfactorily if the autoclave was made of iron (to absorb the hydrochloric acid produced); autoclaves made of other materials, including the more expensive and better class of enamel-lined autoclaves, would not suffice. The omission to specify iron was apparently unintentional; the patentees had used iron autoclaves in their original experiments and had no reason at that time to suspect that its presence was in reality critical. Nevertheless, the patent was held bad for insufficiency because of omission to state the requirement.

Another standard case, *Valensi v British Radio Corporation* (1972)[77] (involving one of the basic patents on colour television), makes a similar point. The facts are complex, and can only be given in part. A number of embodiments were described in the specification and objection was taken in respect of the following four matters:

(a) the arrangement in the first embodiment, illustrated in figure 2, for deriving the signal T from (t_1-t_3);

(b) the crest of the luminous curve and the nature of the striped screen in the second embodiment;

(c) the question of 'normalising' in the third embodiment;

(d) the modified form of receiver described at page 11, line 57.

The remarks in the unanimous Court of Appeal judgment on these four matters are illuminating:

As to (a), . . . it was shown by the evidence that *some modification* of what was described by Valensi would be needed to make the system work. Dr White . . . and Mr Bedford . . . differed as to whether the description was sufficient to enable a reasonably competent man to get it to work. We think this is a borderline case and, the *onus being on the defendants*, do not find that they have established insufficiency.

As to (b), . . . We cannot read the specification as indicating anything other than that the crest of the curve would produce a signal based on a single section of the striped screen, and we cannot read it as suggesting voltages in any other than a linear relationship. We consider that here were *two definite errors and that devising means of surmounting each of them would involve inventive steps*. We therefore hold that here the description was insufficient.

As to (c), it is common ground that in the third embodiment the signals required to be normalised . . . In our view, the right conclusion from the evidence is that while a man skilled in the art would probably have realised that Valensi had made a mistake in not providing for normalising, he would have been likely to have had great difficulty in learning how normalising was to be effected . . . Mr Bedford was accepted (like all the other witnesses) as completely honest, and there was no doubt of his *high standing in the art. If he would have found difficulty in knowing how to divide, and so to normalise, it was, in our view, asking for too much of the notional addressee* to expect him to be able to devise a way of doing it. We conclude that the description of this embodiment was insufficient.

As to (d), the receiver described at page 11, line 57, is an important part of the invention because no other type of receiver is suggested which can achieve the high

76   15 RPC 359.
77   [1973] RPC 373.

degree of fidelity put forward at page 1 as one of the alternative objects of the invention . . . One piece of equipment required for this receiver was a tube with a second control grid. This was *not an ordinary article of commerce* in 1939, the addressee might well not have known how to obtain or manufacture such a tube. See the evidence of . . . For these reasons we are of the opinion that the description of this receiver was insufficient.[78]

(Emphasis added)

Although an objection of insufficiency is normally founded on an inadequacy in the experimental instructions given in the specification (as the above examples illustrate), it can have – on occasions – a wider ambit. For example, there may be present in the specification some kind of contradiction between the specific experimental instructions and the more generalised part of the description, and/or within that description itself, which renders it difficult for the reader at the end of the day to determine exactly what the invention is. In the 1949 Act case of *Fuji Photo Film's (Kiritani's) Application*[79] there was no dispute concerning the specific Examples (of colour-former solutions for pressure-sensitive recording materials); but the general description called at one place for the solvents used to be liquid and at another place provided a list of suitable solvents only some of which were liquids with the remainder being solids. Insufficiency in opposition proceedings under section 14(1)(g) of the 1949 Act was found. In *Eastman Kodak's Application*,[80] section 14(1)(g) had been further extended to defeat an open-ended claim of speculative character to:

1. A solid, highly crystalline, polypropylene having a tensile strength at yield of *at least* 5,500 p.s.i., a stiffness of *at least* 180,000 p.s.i. and a limiting melting point as herein defined, of *at least* 180°C.   *(Emphasis added)*

founded on experimental details which led to a polypropylene having only a modest increase in limiting melting point and stiffness as compared to previous polypropylene.

Comment is necessary about the precise wording of the present statutory requirements on the subject of insufficiency. Under the 1949 Act (still applicable to 'existing' patents) there is emphasis on the need for the patentee to provide the 'best' information. The relevant section 32(1)(h) ground of invalidity reads as follows:

. . . that the complete specification does not sufficiently and fairly describe the invention and the method by which it is to be performed, or does not disclose the *best method* of performing it which was known to the applicant for the patent and for which he was entitled to claim protection . . .

(Emphasis added)

although it may be noted that the corresponding opposition ground was less strict, in omitting the adjective 'best' (see section 14(1)(g)).

Corresponding section 72(1)(c) of the 1977 Act, applicable both in Patent Office and Court revocation proceedings, omits the adjective 'best' entirely. It reads:

78   At 379 to 381.
79   [1978] RPC 413.
80   [1970] RPC 548.

. . . the specification of the Patent does not disclose the invention *clearly enough and completely enough* for it to be performed by a person skilled in the art.

(Emphasis added)

In this respect, it reflects the former opposition ground but not the former revocation ground. The inference is that the new law is relaxed as compared to the old law, in regard to this particular aspect of insufficiency. Whether this inference will be followed is still unsettled. Certainly, it would not be surprising if the courts proved reluctant to do so, bearing in mind that it cuts across the grain of the traditional law. If the patentee can get away with disclosing in his specification only his 'next but one' best method, whilst keeping the best method itself as a trade secret, the public at the end of the patent term is not capable of deriving exactly the same benefit as the patentee.

Likewise it is uncertain as to whether such decisions as *Fuji Photo Film (Kiritani's) Application, Eastman Kodak's Application* survive – notwithstanding their self-evident sense – the 1977 Act. It can be argued at the extreme that the requirement of section 72(1)(c) is fulfilled, strictly, merely by the inclusion in the description of one specific example (in a chemical case) or one drawing (in a mechanical case) coming within the scope of Claim 1, quite irrespective of what else might (or might not) be contained in the document as a whole. Such prospect is not wholly attractive.

Insufficiency, if established, can of course be a particularly deadly canker in a patent because, in contrast to the situation with a finding of novelty or obviousness, amendment may well be impossible. Amendment as a subject is considered more fully in Chapter 5. It is sufficient for present purposes to say that (apart from the special, and rarely occurring, 'obvious mistake' jurisdiction of the 1949 Act) any amendment of a granted patent under either the 1949 or 1977 Act must always be of a restrictive kind. Thus, if generic Claim 1 is held bad for obviousness, amendment by way of disclaimer down to narrower Claim 2 may well be permitted; but new material to overcome a defect in the disclosure of the specification cannot be added, since that would constitute 'new matter'. In the *Badische Anilin* case mentioned above (page 52), amendment of Example 2 so as to specify that the autoclave was made of iron would no doubt have been refused if it had been applied for.

Additional Grounds under 1949 Act

The 1949 Act (but not the 1977 Act) provided a further clutch of 'internal' grounds of objection; because of the continued existence for some years ahead of 'existing' patents, these grounds require consideration. They are:

(1) inutility (section 32(1)(g));
(2) ambiguity (section 32(1)(i));
(3) unfair basis (section 32(1)(i)); and
(4) false suggestion or representation (section 32(1)(j)).

and will now be dealt with in turn.

Inutility arises when the patentee includes in his claim embodiments of the invention which are not useful for the purposes of the invention. It is to be distinguished as a matter of law from insufficiency, although the same set of facts can give rise to both objections. The difference between the two was defined in *Tetra Molectric's Application* as:

> If you cannot achieve the promised result because of deficiencies in the information given in the specification, there is insufficiency. But if, following that information and having achieved mechanically that which the specification promises you will achieve by so following it, the end product will not of itself achieve that promise, then that is inutility.[81]

The patent application in *Tetra Molectric's Application* related to automatic cigarette lighters. Substantially complete concealment and protection for the igniting mechanism within the casing was promised. It was clear from Figures 3 and 4 of the drawings, nevertheless, that in one of the embodiments described the hole from which the flame emerged was always open; hence there was no substantially complete concealment. But because there was substantially complete concealment in other embodiments specifically described there was no insufficiency; a lighter with such advantages and as defined in the Claims, could be obtained. Hence the defect in the Figures 3,4 embodiment (when constructed) went to inutility rather than insufficiency.

The objection could be of particular significance in chemical cases where the patentee has, on the basis of slender initial experimentation, claimed a huge class of chemical compounds only a fraction of which later turn out to have the promised activity. This was the situation in *May and Baker v Boots Pure Drug*,[82] concerning anti-bacterial sulphonamide drugs; Claim 1 covered the production of over 93 million compounds (on all permutations of substituent groups) yet only two (sulphathiazole – the well-known M & B 693 – and sulphamethylthiazole) were proven as truly effective.

However, it is only usefulness for the purposes promised by the patentee which has to be proven; commercial usefulness is not required, unless the patentee has specifically asserted such. And although courts are now somewhat unwilling to trip a patentee up on captious objections, the ground cannot be ignored in a clear case. A recent example where inutility was found in the mechanical field is provided by *Horville Engineering v Clares (Engineering)*,[83] concerning pallets; the claim attacked in this case covered mechanical constructions in which the side walls could not be attached to the pallet when loaded, directly *contra* to the patentee's promise.

Ambiguity is also an objection which is only effective nowadays to a limited extent. Again this is partly due to the more favourable attitude of the Courts towards patentees today as compared to, say, 50 years ago; but the tendency over recent decades to increased precision in claim-drafting in the first place has also assisted.

The mere fact that plaintiff and defendant can reasonably argue for different constructions of the claim does not in itself lead to ambiguity. For instance, in *Ransburg v Aerostyle*,[84] Claim 1 of the patent in suit used the phrase 'under the influence of' in the context of atomising paint into particles for an electrostatic paint-coating process. Three meanings of the term were discussed by the various Courts, including the House of Lords. These were:

81   [1977] RPC 290 at 297.
82   67 RPC 23.
83   [1976] RPC 411.
84   [1968] RPC 287.

(1) formed into particles by atomisation conducted within the influence of electrostatic forces (for example, by a mechanical spray gun discharging into an electrostatic field);

(2) formed into particles by influence of electrostatic forces as the sole cause;

(3) formed into particles by influence of electrostatic forces as a contributory (that is, partial) cause.

But there was no finding (or even serious suggestion) anywhere of ambiguity just by reason of the range of possibilities; each successive Court found itself quite able to choose, albeit differently, between them. Nor is the fact that intellectually interesting puzzles as to potential infringement at the borderline of the claim can be set, enough to establish the ground.

For the objection to succeed, the position must rather be that the Court finds itself, for some reason or another, incapable of coming to any definite view at all as to the scope of the claim; it should be remembered that the Court is not compelled to reach a view. Such impossibility can arise in instances of inherently muddled claim phraseology; sometimes also where the Court is confronted with a choice of meanings, of substantial equal credibility yet with totally different significance, as in the case of the term 'alkaline xanthate' in *Minerals Separation v Noranda Mines*.[85] 'Alkaline xanthate' could mean either a xanthate of an alkali metal or an alkaline solution of any xanthate; chemically, there is little common ground between the two.

Unfair basis is an objection which can occasionally be properly raised when the claim, although directed to novel and non-obvious subject-matter, is nevertheless disproportionately wide as compared to the extent of the patentee's teaching. As expressed recently in *American Cyanamid v Berk Pharmaceuticals*:

> . . . while it is vital to give inventors the fullest possible protection in respect of the contribution which they have made it must be, to my mind, wrong to give them a monopoly which will cover something to which they have really made no genuine contribution at all.[86]

The ground represents a statutory recognition of the 'Mullard' principle, hallowed in the annals of patent law. *Mullard Radio Valve v Philco Radio & Television*,[87] decided in 1936, related to the screened pentode valve. Claim 1 covered a circuit arrangement, but Claim 2 (in issue) was drafted in wider terms to the valve construction *per se*. It read:

> 2. A discharge tube having at least three auxiliary electrodes between the cathode and the anode characterised in that the auxiliary electrode nearest to the anode is directly connected to the cathode so as to be maintained continuously at the cathode potential.

Yet the desired electrical advantage (avoiding an increase in screening grid current at the expense of anode current), which constituted the whole point of the invention, was obtained only when the two other auxiliary electrodes were employed in a certain

85   69 RPC 81.
86   [1976] RPC 231 at 259.
87   53 RPC 323.

electrical fashion unspecified in Claim 2. The Claim was held bad, because it extended beyond the subject-matter of the invention. Lord Macmillan put the point in the following words:

> It is undoubtedly the case that a claim may be too wide, in the sense that it claims protection for that for which the patentee is not entitled to protection, or that it gives him a wider protection than his discovery entitles him to receive. In the present instance the Patentee has claimed a monopoly of all valves with a certain feature of construction although the merit of his invention does not lie in the feature but in the utilisation in a particular and limited way of a valve containing that feature of construction. In so doing he has in my opinion overreached himself and his claim is wider than the law will support.[88]

It is important to note, finally, that although unfair basis (and ambiguity) can in effect be raised under the 1977 Act by the Patent Office at the prosecution stage (under section 14(5)(b) requirement that the claim 'be clear and concise' – and the section 14(5)(c) requirement that it 'be supported by the description' respectively) no corresponding grounds for invalidity are so specified. No doubt this omisison was due to the need to follow the European Patent Convention (where no opposition ground corresponding to Article 84 subsists). But the omission is to be regretted. In *Genentech Inc.'s Patent*[89] a classic state of facts for an unfair basis type of objection was present. Claims 1 to 3 read:

> (1) Recombinant human tissue plasminogen activator essentially free of other proteins of human origin.
> (2) Human tissue plasminogen activator unaccompanied by associated native glycosylation.
> (3) Human tissue plasminogen activator as produced by recombinant DNA technology.

and as such were far too wide having regard to the inventor's actual contribution to the art. They could be regarded as covering any synthetically made t-PA (human tissue plasminogen activator), t-PA itself being a natural product produced in small quantities in normal human tissue. The Patents Court, acutely aware of the realities of the situation, attempted in effect to re-introduce the unfair basis objection into the 1977 Act by a side-wind (arguing that the specification in such circumstances could not be directed in the first place to a patentable invention). But its worthy attempt was unceremoniously denounced on appeal.[90] What is needed is a revision of the European Patent Convention, enabling in turn a revision of section 72(1) of the 1977 Act, so as to include this ground of revocation.

False suggestion or representation is a rare objection. It can, *inter alia*, cover matters like deliberate impropriety in the completion of the patent application documents, or misleading the Patent Office during prosecution of the patent application – for example, as to the true purpose of a widening amendment to a claim. But it does not necessarily

---

88 At 347.
89 HC [1987] RPC 553.
90 CA [1989] RPC 147.

connote fraud or the like. A suggestion in a patent specification can be, scientifically, quite untrue but yet have been inserted originally in perfect good faith.

Bibliography

Part I:

J. Bailey, 'Prior User – Public, Private and Secret' (1956–57) *Transactions* Volume LXXX C 51.

B. Reid, 'The Meaning of Accident', JPOS Volume 56 (1974) 687.

A. White, 'The Patentability of Naturally Occurring Products', [1980] EIPR 37.

Part II:

J. Beton and K. Heimbach, 'Claim Drafting and Significance – An Anglo-German Industrial View', and P. Graham, 'The Interpretation and Drafting of Claims – A British Appreciation' in J. Kemp (ed.), *Patent Claim Drafting and Interpretation*, Oyez Longman, 1983.

Part III:

J. Ellis, 'Novelty in the EPO', CIPA Volume 18 (1988–89) 3.

A. White, 'Prior Secret Publication', *Transactions* Volume LXXXVII (1968–69) C 59.

A. White, 'The Novelty-destroying Disclosure: Some Recent Decisions' [1990] EIPR 315.

Part IV:

J. Bochnovic, 'The Inventive Step: Its Evolution in Canada, the United Kingdom and the United States' (Max Planck Institute, Munich 1982).

S. Gratwick, 'Having regard to What was Known or Used', LQR Volume 88 (1972) 341.

S. Gratwick, 'Having regard to What was Known or Used – Revisited', LQR Volume 102 (1986) 403.

H. Merwin, *The Patentability of Inventions*, Little, Brown & Co. (Boston, USA), 1883, page 59 to 72.

G. Szabo, 'The Problem and Solution Approach to Inventive Step' [1986] EIPR 293.

A. White and J. Warden, 'The British Approach to Obviousness' [1977] AIPL at 447.

E. Williamson, 'The Invention', *Transactions* Volume LIX (1940–41) at 90.

E. Williamson, 'The Linguistic Basis of Patent Law', *Transactions* Volume LXI (1942–43) at 82.

E. Williamson, 'Invention and Inventive Level', CIPA Volume 2 (1972–73) at 123.

Part V:

J. Jeffs, 'Selection Patents' [1988] EIPR 291.

R. Kelly, 'Markush Claims', JPOS Volume 37 (1955) at 164.

R. Mathys, 'Some Thoughts on Selection Patents', *Transactions* Volume LXVII (1948–49) at 62.

P. May, 'Chemical Inventions and their Protection', *Transactions* Volume LXII (1943–44) at 90.

M.F. Vivian, 'Novelty and Selection Inventions' [1989] 20 IIC 303.

A. von Füner, 'Problems of Patenting in Eastern European Countries, especially in the Field of Chemistry', CIPA Volume 7 (1977–78) at 217.

A. White, 'The Patentability of Naturally Occurring Products', [1980] EIPR at 37.

Part VI:

G. Everington and P. Ford, 'Utility', *Transactions* Volume LXXIX (1960–61) at C 45.

C. Gholz, 'Best Mode – Intent to Conceal', JPOS Volume 65 (1983) at 436.

4 Acquisition of Patents

This chapter will be confined to the acquisition of United Kingdom patents by the ordinary filing in the United Kingdom Patent Office of a patent application. Acquisition of United Kingdom patents via the European Patent Office, with the United Kingdom being a designated country, is considered in Chapter 12, as is also the acquisition of foreign patents by United Kingdom applicants. Since all patent applications henceforth will be governed by the 1977 Act, the rather different procedures called for by the 1949 Act will be considered only in bare outline, as a preliminary. However, they do still have some residual significance – for example, in providing a backcloth against which the new 1977 Act procedure can be viewed more acutely, and in relation to validity of existing patents granted under the 1949 Act. Certain countries abroad, which have in the past followed the United Kingdom patent system, still retain aspects of the former procedure.

1949 ACT PROCEDURE

The 1949 Act provided for the filing of separate so-called 'provisional' and 'complete' specifications, a distinction which had itself persisted ever since the early 1852 Act. The provisional specification had to furnish – as its name implies – a tentative description of the invention. The complete specification, which normally had to be filed within twelve months from the date of filing of the provisional specification, had particularly to describe the invention and the best method by which it was to be performed; it had to include a claim(s) which was (were) fairly based on the matter disclosed in the complete specification, related to a single invention, was (were) clear and succinct, and defined the scope of the invention claimed. Provided that a given claim was 'fairly based' on the matter described in the provisional specification it could be accorded, as priority date, the provisional specification's date of filing.

Alternatively, an application could be filed with a complete specification in the first instance. In the case of an invention originating abroad, a so-called 'convention application' could be filed, with a complete specification only, within twelve months of the foreign filing. Provided that the claim(s) was (were) fairly based on the foreign disclosure, priority would again be accorded, from the filing date of the foreign application.

Once a complete specification had been filed, it was in due course examined. Examination was carried out both as to form and as to substance. Examination as to form covered what might be regarded the procedural requirements of the 1949 Act – the need for a complete specification to end with a claim defining the scope of the invention as claimed (section 4(3)(c)), formal requirements as to drawings and the like. Examination as to substance covered both statutory requirements – for example, the need for the claims to relate to a single invention (section 4(4)), the prohibition against claims to substances capable of being used as food or medicine which were mere mixtures of known ingredients possessing only the aggregate of the known properties of the ingredients (section 10(1)(c) – and also search for anticipation by prior publication (section 7) and prior claim (section 8). There was no examination for obviousness; this omission attracted considerable criticism, for it enabled patent applications of trivial nature (possessing bare novelty over the art cited by the Examiner) to get through, and has been rectified since by the 1977 Act.

If the examination stage was successfully passed, the application was accepted and subsequently published. Opposition could be entered within three months of publication, on any of the grounds specified in section 14 of the 1949 Act. These included obviousness, to a limited extent. The ground was couched in terms of:

> (e) that the invention, so far as claimed in any claim of the complete specification, is obvious and *clearly* does not involve any inventive step having regard to . . .
>
> *(Emphasis added)*

whereas in the corresponding revocation ground (section 32(1)(f)) (and also in the corresponding provision in section 1(1)(b) taken with 3 of the 1977 Act) 'clearly' was omitted. The interposition of 'clearly', although no doubt well intended at the time when the 1949 Act was passed, led to unfortunate results. It was never quite clear as to exactly what it meant. Was it included to enable the Patent Office to return a 'not proven' type of verdict? Or did it mean that there were now two kinds of obviousness – striking obviousness and ordinary obviousness? In practice, it tended to mean that the attack could be repulsed whenever the patent applicant could show that there was some significant doubt. It encouraged an indecisiveness on the part of the Patent Office which can be seen, in retrospect, hardly to have been to the overall benefit of the patent system in the United Kingdom.

If there was no opposition (or if opposition was successfully overcome), the patent could be granted. For one year after grant the patent lay open to so-called 'belated opposition' – that is, to an application for revocation in the Patent Office on any of the grounds available in regular opposition. Revocation in the Court was, of course, also possible during this period (as well as during the regular term of the patent); the Court proceedings generally (although not necessarily) would take precedence in case both kinds of proceedings were started.

1977 ACT PROCEDURE

General

The 1977 Act has done away with the terms 'provisional specification', 'complete specification' and 'Convention application'. The distinction now is as between an original application and an 'earlier relevant application'; the latter can itself be either an earlier United Kingdom application or an application in a Convention country. Priority is possible within the twelve-month period, provided that the invention (as opposed to claim) is 'supported by' (as opposed to 'fairly based on') the matter disclosed in the earlier application (section 5(2)(a)).

From the practical standpoint, therefore, the position is much as before; in particular, the 1977 Act retains the previous facility (if desired) for a relatively cheap first filing in the United Kingdom of a patent application and deferment of any substantial expenditure for twelve months while the inventor develops his invention and looks for a backer.

Of course, it is not compulsory to invoke the priority claim procedure; an application can be filed in the first instance with the substantive specification.

Pitfalls may arise if it is desired to alter significantly the terms of the specification and/or claims as compared to those of the earlier application being relied upon for priority, particularly in instances of widening out. It now appears that the phrase 'supported by' will be interpreted by the Patent Office and the Court in similar fashion to the interpretation of 'fairly based' under the old Act, in such cases as *Mond Nickel's Application*[1] and its string of successors. *Mond Nickel* itself, involving a claim to priority from a provisional specification, called for a three-fold test to be fulfilled, namely:

> (1) Is the alleged invention broadly described in the provisional specification?
> (2) Is there anything in the provisional specification which is inconsistent with the alleged invention now claimed?
> (3) Does the claim include as a characteristic of the invention a feature as to which the provisional specification is wholly silent?

The point can be important in practice because frequently events during the twelve-month grace period (either the extent of the inventor's own further development and/or knowledge of competitors' activities) may cause the inventor to regard his initial disclosure in a very different light at the end of the period as compared to the beginning. He may, for example, find that he has made an incautious remark in the initial disclosure as to what is essential to success, and wish to renege therefrom.

Further pitfalls may arise where there are two or more earlier relevant applications. To begin with, it is, of course, perfectly permissible to claim priority from two or more such applications provided both were filed during the preceding twelve months; this is the so-called standard 'multiple priority' claim. But if one was filed more than twelve months ago, and the other during the twelve months period, priority cannot be claimed from the first; and priority will be allowed from the second only if the first has become effectively dead for all purposes (by unconditional withdrawal or the like) by the time the second was filed. This provision (which reflects again the position under the 1949 Act) may cause particularly acute problems in the case of inventions emanating from the United States of America, on account of the practice permitted by the United States Patent Office of filing continuation-in-part applications.

The 1977 Act will now be considered in more detail.

Entitlement

Although any person can apply for a United Kingdom patent, a valid patent can be granted only to a person who is formally entitled. Three classes of person only are so entitled:

> (1) The inventor, or joint inventors; this is the primary class, that is, the class entitled in the first instance.
> (2) Persons who are by operation of law or agreement entitled in preference to

---

1   [1956] RPC 189 at 194.

the inventor(s) to the whole property in the invention; a mere equitable interest is not enough.

(3) Successors in title of either class (1) or (2) persons.

Actual inventors (joint or sole, category (1) above) and their successors in title (category (3)) normally provide straightforward situations, although it should be remembered that there is a distinction between helping or assisting and co-inventing. For example, in the case of a new catalyst for the liquid-phase oxidation of p-xylene to terephthalic acid, the inventor is likely to be the chemist who thought up the new catalyst in the first place; the laboratory technician who merely performs the initial run under the chemist's direction is unlikely to be so regarded. Likewise with the electrical engineer who sketches a new form of construction of an optical fibre telecommunications cable and the workshop assistant who builds and tests the prototype.

It is the class (2) category which is more complex. This category covers, so far as domestic inventions are concerned, the important cases of inventions made by scientific employees, that is, those who are employed to *inter alia* invent, and inventions made by employees having fiduciary positions towards their companies; these topics are dealt with more fully in Chapter 9. The class also covers, for example, arrangements made by a lender to an independent professional inventor under which the inventor is financed for research work in return for, say, the legal title (with back royalty to the inventor) to any invention so made; conversely, if the relationship is such that the lender can only be regarded as having a beneficial interest in any invention so made.

Informal co-operative arrangements may, however, give rise to problems in this respect. In *Viziball's Application*[2] there was dispute between two squash players as to whether or not one party had made any contribution to the essential elements of the invention. In *James Industries' Patent*,[3] the communications between the parties were held to be adequate to render them partners in a joint commercial venture (and hence render a certain letter and sketches confidential and not a prior publication) but inadequate to create a contractual patent-sharing agreement.

The Act provides machinery (sections 8 to 12) for having disputes as to entitlement settled by the Patent Office, either before or after grant of the patent. This can include, in certain instances, power to enable a defrauded applicant to make a back-dated fresh application for the invention in dispute. If the Patent Office considers, however, that the dispute involves matters which would be more properly dealt with by the Court, it may decline to act.

It also appears from the Act that the Patent Office has some jurisdiction, at least, in connection with disputes as to property in patent applications or granted patents beyond the question of original entitlement. Section 8(1)(a) distinguishes, at the application stage, between the two categories of persons who (1) are entitled to be granted the patent and those (2) who would have any right in or under the patent. Section 37(2)(c), applicable to granted patents, covers the case of *inter alia* persons claiming to be licensees. The precise extent of the jurisdiction is not entirely clear, however. This may not matter too much in practice (financial costs apart – the Patent Office normally

---

2 [1988] RPC 213.
3 [1987] RPC 235.

being the cheaper forum), since the Court always has power in any event to settle any dispute.

Application Procedure

The 1977 Act envisages a five-step procedure for acquisition of a patent. The five steps are:

(1) Filing of the application
(2) Publication of the application
(3) Preliminary examination and search
(4) Substantive examination
(5) Grant

The step-wise procedure provides the applicant with an opportunity to withdraw his application during pendency and even (if withdrawal is effected before publication) of maintaining secrecy of the contents of the application. This procedure is frequently of benefit to the applicant; it means that he is not committed, right at the beginning, to the full expense of obtaining a granted patent. An invention which appeared initially to be sufficiently promising to justify the filing of a patent application may subsequently, a year or two after filing, prove not to be worth continuing. It will be recalled that, generally, the decision to file has to be taken at an early stage in the invention's life, before any dissemination of its subject-matter by the inventor (or other applicant) has taken place. Delaying filing also means that the risk of a competitor making a similar invention in the meantime, and filing a corresponding application of earlier date, has to be run.

The step-wise procedure necessarily also requires that the applicant attend to the various steps involved on his side within the specified time limits, and pay the appropriate fees. The Patent Office has power under the Act to set the fees; they naturally tend to change (generally in upward direction) from time to time. The latest edition of the Patents Rules[4] has to be consulted. As for time limits, the Act generally refers to a 'prescribed time period'. This again serves to give the Patent Office power to set the period in question and/or any possible extension thereof; these also may change from time to time, so rendering it inadvisable to provide here details of the currently available periods.

The question of what remedy (if any) is available to an applicant in an instance where he fails to take a given step and/or pay a given fee in time under the 1977 Act is a vexed question. The Patent Office is given, by section 123(2)(b), power to make rules 'authorizing the rectification of irregularities of procedure', and, by section 123(2)(h), the power to prescribe time limits and provide for alteration of the same.

Under these provisions, and the corresponding Rules 100 and 110 of the Patents Rules 1978, *Fater's Application*[5] (involving a failure to request preliminary examination and search in time) had initially suggested that the Patent Office had a very wide dispensing power. The Rules were accordingly then tightened up via the Patents

---

4 Currently, the Patents Rules 1990 (1990 No. 2384).
5 [1979] FSR 647.

(Amendment No. 4) Rules 1980, reflected in the subsequent Patents Rules 1982, so as to provide for limited extensions of time in some cases (under current Rule 110(3)) but no extension in other cases (under Rule 110(2)); only where the irregularity is attributable wholly or in part to an error, default or omission on the part of the Patent Office does the general power remain (under Rule 100). The Patent Rules 1990 do however continue a modest amelioration, originally introduced in the Patents (Amendment) Rules 1987. By present Rule 110(4), a further extension of Rule 110(3) period may be obtainable provided that suitable evidence verifying the grounds for the request is filed.

On the general issue, however, it was unequivocally declared by the House of Lords in *Energy Conversion Devices' Application*,[6] a case involving a failure to pay a filing fee on time for an application under the Patent Cooperation Treaty (dealt with later in Chapter 12), that the specific provisions of such rules override any purported general dispensing power under section 123. The fact that the provisions might lead to conflict with the United Kingdom's international obligations under the Treaty was irrelevant, in view of the clear wording of the rules.

While the legal reasoning behind their Lordships' decision may be impeccable, the conclusion is harsh on the patentee. The greater complexity of the application procedure(s) under the 1977 Act, as compared to the 1949 Act, means that there is substantially increased room for procedural errors to occur in the first place.

Step (1): Filing the application

The application for the patent must contain (section 14(2)) a formal request, a specification and claim(s) and abstract. The claim(s) and abstract can be filed late as can (on payment of fee) any drawing forming part of the specification. The purpose of the abstract is to assist the so-called 'information function' of patents; they are the current equivalent of the previous patent abridgement series which date back (in various classification systems) to 1852, and even earlier in other arrangements thanks to the energy and persistence of Bennet Woodcroft, the great Comptroller-General of the Patent Office in Victorian days.

The Act requires by section 14(3) that the specification disclose the invention:

> . . . in a manner which is clear enough and complete enough for the invention to be performed by a person skilled in the art.

It echoes in this respect the wording of the insufficiency ground of revocation set out in section 72(1)(c).

By section 14(5) the claim or claims shall:

    (i)   define the matter for which the applicant seeks protection;
    (ii) be clear and concise;
    (iii) be supported by the description; and
    (iv) relate to one invention or to a group of inventions which are so linked as to form a single inventive concept.

---

6 [1983] RPC 231.

The statutory language here is very like that found in the 1949 Act (sections 4(3) and (4)); much of the previous Patent Office practice in this area therefore continues.

Drafting of specification and claims

It follows that the drafting of the specification and claims continues to be, as it always has been, at once the most important and most difficult aspect of applying for a patent. Normally, it is advisable to have the specification and claims prepared by a chartered patent agent at least generally familiar (although he need not be expert) with the technology of the kind involved in the art in question; but this is not essential. A prolific individual inventor may well acquire such expertise in the art(s) in which he works as to be capable of preparing his own specifications. The Patent Office is quite happy to deal helpfully with unrepresented applicants.

The contents of a specification and claim(s) need not follow any set pattern, provided of course that the statutory requirements are met. Naturally, the degree of detail varies according to the kind of invention involved. In the case of a minor improvement to a well-known existing machine, only the improvement need, generally speaking, be described fully; the well-known machine can be brought in by cross-reference to standard textbooks, or to relevant earlier patent specifications, possibly supplemented by a brief summary. In the case of a fundamentally fresh or pioneer invention, fuller detail may, however, be necessary since the reader of the specification will often have little, if any, existing background against which to set the new idea. An applicant is cursory here at his peril, as demonstrated in the *Valensi v British Radio Corporation*[7] colour television case (already discussed in Chapter 3 at pages 53 to 54 and the *Anxionnaz v Rolls Royce*[8] jet engine case. The facts in *Anxionnaz* were again complex; a partial summary only will be provided here.

The main Anxionnaz Patent related to a jet reaction propulsion unit for aircraft travelling at speeds in the vicinity of Mach 1 (speed of sound). Claim 1 required, *inter alia*, that the inlet passage to the casing be designed in such manner that the velocity of the air at its entrance into the compressor be reduced with respect to the relative velocity of the aircraft with reference to the atmosphere. The description on this point in the specification was brief and couched in functional terms; the drawings were diagrammatic only; no precise quantitative parameters were given anywhere. Sir Frank Whittle ('father' of the jet engine) gave evidence to the effect that, as the air velocity at compressor entry is determined by the engine characteristics, the shape of the inlet passage cannot and does not affect it. It was held that the position was therefore one in which the instructed reader would be unable to find a way of meeting this characteristic requirement of the invention, and accordingly that there was insufficiency.

Perpetual motion devices can ground on the same rock. In the European Patent Office decision T05/86 (*NEWMAN/Perpetual motion*),[9] an application directed to various means for producing usable electrical energy characterised in that the amount of electrical energy generated was greater than any external energy input was rejected under corresponding Article 83 of the European Patent Convention on the basis that:

---

7 [1972] RPC 373.
8 [1967] RPC 419.
9 [1988] EPOR 301.

. . . the concepts involved are so revolutionary that a person of average skill in the art would not be able to fill in the missing details of the commutator and current retarding means on the basis of his own knowledge or as the result of a reasonable amount of trial and error.

A patent specification is often arranged in the following order:

(1) *Introduction* – specifying the art to which the invention relates.
(2) *Prior art* – acknowledgement of the nearest earlier proposals or usage in that art, together with reference to any problems encountered with them but solved by the new invention.
(3) *Statements of invention* – corresponding to Claim 1 and principal subsidiary claims.
(4) *General description.*
(5) *Specific description (with reference to drawings), of at least one detailed embodiment* – in chemical cases, presentation of a fair number of specific preparative examples is often desirable.
(6) *Claims.*

It is usual to present a wide principal (or generic) claim, Claim 1, representing a resumé of the essential features of the invention, followed by a series of narrower dependent subsidiary claims introducing, successively, important (but not essential) features. To a certain extent, these subsidiary claims can be drafted in independent form if preferred.

Claim 1 has substantial, although not necessarily controlling, influence on the scope accorded to the patent by the Court in relation to infringement, a subject dealt with more fully in Chapters 6 and 7. The subsidiary claims represent backstops. If it is later found that Claim 1 is too wide – say, in view of some subsequently unearthed prior art – amendment down to one or other may be allowed. The draftsman has always to steer – inevitably – between the Scylla of unnecessary narrowness and the Charybdis of excessive width.

It is also possible to present different sets of claims to different aspects of one invention, or to inventions separate as such but linked by a unifying underlying concept. Examples here include the case of a new machine or apparatus and the mechanical process achieved by the same; of a new chemical process and compounds (and compositions derived therefrom) produced by the process; a combination of elements and sub-combination of the same (for example, a new oil-feeding device for a furnace, and resulting furnace incorporating the same); associated inventions (for example, a new kind of padlock and the corresponding new shape of key therefor). If non-unity is nevertheless found to exist by the Patent Office Examiner during prosecution of the application, then the Act (section 15(4)) makes provision for the filing of a suitable divisional patent application(s), retaining the original filing date or priority date as the case may be. These latter provisions can also be relied on by the applicant for the purpose of making a voluntary divisional application if he thinks fit, provided that he makes such divisional application during pendency of the parent application. Post-grant, neither compulsory nor voluntary division is possible, but it is provided (section 26) that a granted patent shall not have its validity impugned on this basis. Some further discussion on the topic is provided at the end of this chapter.

A useful test for the draftsman is for him to ask the inventor the following triple-barrelled catechism:

(1) Tell me why you think you've been so clever.
(2) Tell me what you need to make it work.
(3) Tell me what you want to stop the other person from doing.

The answer to Question (1) assists the draftsman to identify the inventive step forward; that to Question (2) enables him to ensure that the invention is properly described in the specification; that to Question (3) assists him in his claim-drafting strategy.

The following represents a typical set of claims:

> 1. A method of producing the conductive metal portions of an electric circuit component, being a network of conductors by which other circuit components are connected together and the metal of which is continuous over substantial lengths or areas in position upon an insulating backing, which consists in making an imprint upon the metal of a composite material consisting of metal foil upon an insulating backing, in an ink which serves as a resist, and thereafter so treating the foil, in part protected by the imprint, as finally to leave upon the insulating backing a conductive pattern constituting the network.
> 2. A method according to claim 1 which consists in making a positive imprint upon the metal foil on the insulating backing in an ink which serves as a resist, and thereafter removing by etching the foil not protected by the imprint.
> 3. An electric circuit component being a network of conductors by which other circuit components are connected together comprising a backing of impregnated paper on which the conductive pattern has been produced by the method of claim 1.
> 4. A method according to claim 2 including the additional step of punching out large areas of unprotected foil prior to etching away the remainder of the unprotected foil.

(From Patent No. 639178, as amended – litigated in *Technograph Printed Circuits v Mills & Rockley (Electronics)*[10] the printed circuit case)

Other examples of Claims 1, taken from classic litigated patents of the past, are as follows:

> 1. A sapphire stylus for sound reproduction, having a tapered conical portion subtending a vertex angle in the range of from *25 to 90* degrees and a flat ground on the point of a diameter of from *0.001 to 0.005 inches* so that the point enters a standard record sound groove and only makes substantially point contact with the inclined side walls of the sound groove. *(Emphasis added)*

(From Patent No. 603606, litigated in *Killick v Pye*,[11] the case of the flat-bottomed gramophone needle)

> 1. An incandescent electric lamp having a filament of tungsten or other refractory metal of *large* diameter or cross-section or of concentrated form and a gas or vapour of low heat conductivity at relatively high pressure, the combination being such that the filament may be raised to a much higher temperature than is practicable in a vacuum lamp without prohibitive vaporisation or deterioration or excessive shortening of useful life, substantially as set forth. *(Emphasis added)*

10 [1972] RPC 346.
11 [1958] RPC 366.

(From Patent No. 10918/1913, litigated in *British Thomson-Houston v Corona Lamp Works*,[12] the case of the half-watt lamp)

1. An ash receptacle which without the use of movable parts retains the smoke rising from objects thrown into it, characterised by the fact that it consists of a closed container (1, 2) into which extends a shaft (3) of substantially constant cross section, the sides of which with the sides of the receptacle form a trapped space closed above whilst wholly beneath the shaft is provided a deflecting member (4) which deflects objects thrown in wholly to one side of the lower mouth of the shaft, the *dimensions of the shaft and of the deflecting member being so chosen* relatively to one another and to the sides of the closed container that the smoke rising from objects thrown into the container is collected entirely in the trapped space, and after cooling is thrown down again without being able during this movement to pass the lower mouth of the shaft.   (*Emphasis added*)

(From Patent No. 253518, litigated in *No-Fume v Frank Pitchford*,[13] the case of the smokeless ashtray)

Contemporary examples include:

1. A security alarm device comprising a housing containing an audible alarm means and a visual alarm means, at least a portion of said housing being translucent, and means for operating each of said audible alarm means and said visual warning means.

(From Patent No. 2064190, litigated in *CQR Security Systems' Patent*[14])

1. An electrically powered depilatory device comprising: a hand held portable housing (2); motor means (4, 4') disposed in said housing; and a helical spring (24) comprising a plurality of adjacent windings arranged to be driven by said motor means in rotational sliding motion relative to skin bearing hair to be removed, said helical spring (24) including an arcuate hair engaging portion arranged to define a convex side whereat the windings are spread apart and a concave side corresponding thereto whereat the windings are pressed together, the rotational motion of the helical spring (24) producing continuous motion of the windings from a spread apart orientation at the convex side to a pressed together orientation on the concave side and for the engagement and plucking of hair from the skin of the subject, whereby the surface velocities of the windings relative to the skin greatly exceed the surface velocity of the housing relative thereto.

(From European Patent (UK) No. 0101656, litigated in *Improver Corporation v Remington Consumer Products*,[15] the 'Epilady' case)

To take these examples in turn, the *Technograph* series of claims shows a principal method Claim 1 with subsidiary Claim 2 directed to treating the foil by etching and subsidiary Claim 4 (dependent to the method defined by the combination of Claims 1 and 2) introducing the additional method step of punching out prior to etching; interpolated Claim 3 covers the product of the method. The *Killick* Claim 1 illustrates the use of quantitatively defined parameters, in relation to vertex angle and flat ground diameter. The *British Thomson-Houston* Claim 1 illustrates in contrast the successful use of a qualitative adjective – 'large' – in order to avoid being pinned down to an

12   39 RPC 49.
13   52 RPC 231.
14   [1992] FSR 303.
15   [1990] FSR 181.

arbitrary quantitative range (for filament diameter) such as might provide an infringer's charter. The *No-Fume* Claim 1 shows successful use of a functional type of definition (to specify the mutual form and interrelation of shaft and deflecting member). The employment of reference numerals in the claim was (at the date involved), and is today, somewhat unusual; it probably arose from the German origin of the patent, use of reference numerals in the claims having always been a standard practice there. The *CQR* Claim 1 illustrates the continuity of practice under the 1977 Act. The full text of the patent is provided in Appendix 2, as an example of contemporary drafting style.

Special provisions apply in the case of an invention involving use of a micro-organism, for example, a fermentation process for production of an antibiotic. Deposit of a specimen of the micro-organism in a recognised public culture collection is required, and deposit details have to be given in the specification. Schedule 2 of the Patents Rules 1990 sets out the precise provisions as they stand at the moment, being made under the relevant authorising section 14(4) and (8) of the 1977 Act.

One final point which has to be made under this head concerns the drafting of the specification and claims for foreign equivalents of a domestic patent, or for European patents. What might be termed the 'United Kingdom' style of drafting is by no means universally accepted. An introduction to the subject is provided in Appendix 3.

Step (2): Publication of the application

Publication of the application under section 16 (1) is undertaken by the Patent Office, as soon as possible after the end of the prescribed period. Currently, the prescribed period is eighteen months from the date of filing the patent application (if no priority is being claimed from an earlier foreign or United Kingdom application) or eighteen months from the date of the priority application (if priority is being so claimed). If the applicant wishes to withdraw he must do so before the Patent Office has completed its preparations for publication.

Publication means, essentially, the laying-out of the specification and claims open for public inspection. Thus, a published application has been made available to the public, and ranks as prior art as from its date of actual publication.

Special provisions (section 22) apply where the specification and claims contain information the further promulgation of which might be prejudicial to the defence of the realm or to the safety of the public; this umbrella includes inventions relating to atomic energy. The details of these are beyond the scope of this book, but it is important to note that the Patent Office may not only withhold publication by itself of the invention but may also prohibit the applicant (on pain of possible imprisonment if convicted on indictment) from himself publishing the invention. In similar vein are the provisions (section 23) prohibiting an applicant resident in the United Kingdom from making a foreign application on an invention that is the subject of an existing United Kingdom application until at least six weeks after the latter's filing; this interval gives the Patent Office time to inspect the contents of the application, to check whether the secrecy procedures should be brought into operation.

Step (3): Preliminary examination and search

It is up to the applicant (section 17(1)) to request preliminary examination of the application and search for relevant prior art, on payment of the prescribed fee and within the prescribed period.

Preliminary examination means that the Patent Office examine the patent application for compliance with the formal requirements of the Act, and unity of invention.

The Patent Office search the prior literature for relevant prior art, to the best of their ability. The search is, inevitably, limited to prior written material (excluding, for example, prior uses or prior oral descriptions, for example, lectures at professional conferences unless they have themselves been described in written material); moreover, it is limited to material accessible to the Examiner (in practice this normally means that it must be located in the Patent Office search files or other material in libraries open to the Examiner) and which he manages to find. There is no guarantee of completeness of search. Thus, the statutory requirement (section 17(4)) is phrased:

> . . . the examiner shall make such investigation as *in his opinion* is *reasonably practicable and necessary* for him to identify the *documents* which he thinks will be needed to decide, on a substantive examination under section 18 below whether the invention for which a patent is sought is new and involves an inventive step.   (*Emphasis added*)

There is also, quite separate from the Examiner's search, an informer procedure (section 21), which is discussed later in the chapter.

Step (4): Substantive examination

This has to be requested by the applicant (section 18(1)), and the fee paid, within the prescribed period. The Examiner has to consider whether the application meets the requirements of the Act, both for presence of patentable invention and generally. He writes an official letter to the applicant giving his report. If objections are raised the applicant has an opportunity to present argument and/or to amend his application so as to meet them. In particular, the applicant may be called on to restrict the scope of his Claim 1 in face of the prior art found on the search. The application may go backwards and forwards between the applicant and the Examiner a number of times in the course of such prosecution. Nothing that extends the disclosure of the specification may be done, however.

Prosecution cannot be prolonged indefinitely. It must be completed, unless an appeal to the Patents Court from the Patent Office on a maintained objection has been filed, within the prescribed period from filing of the application. In the normal case this is currently four years six months from filing or, in the case of a Convention application, from the foreign priority date; but the period is liable to change, on periodic reissue of the Patents Rules.

Although the Patent Office has been empowered to reject for novelty since 1905, its obviousness jurisdiction is fresh – so far as examination is concerned – in the 1977 Act. A fair body of case law has now emerged, on the practice, although clearly more time needs to elapse before it can be said to be fully mature. Generally speaking, it appears that the objection will only be pressed (or succeed if pressed) in a reasonably clear case; the *Mutoh Industries* (reduced-friction drawing boards)[16] case, discussed in Chapter 3 (see page 42), can be instructively compared with, say, *PCUK's Application* (flocculating agent in paper-making process)[17] or *Furuno Electric's Application* (locating shoals of

16   [1984] RPC 35.
17   [1984] RPC 482.

fish).[18] But it does not necessarily follow that an applicant is wise to press for an excessively wide claim even if the Patent Office can be persuaded to grant it. It may not be to his long-term advantage to be saddled with a patent incapable of surviving the more piercing scrutiny of the court.

Step (5): Grant

Once all objections raised during examination have been overcome, the final step of grant of a patent on the application (section 24) is performed by the Patent Office. A formal Certificate of Grant, as distinct from the Letters Patent under seal of the 1949 Act and earlier law, is sent to the patentee, and the fact of grant entered on the Patent Office Register. The grantee will be the official registered proprietor.

Appendix 4 provides a flow chart showing in diagrammatic form the processing of a patent application through the Patent Office, under the 1977 Act, up to the state of grant.

Informer Procedure

Mention should be made of the section 21 procedure, often called 'informer procedure'. Under section 21 third parties are allowed to make observations in writing to the Patent Office as to the patentability of the invention of a given application, once that application has been published but not yet granted. This can be a useful option for a third party where, for example, he is aware of a particular piece of prior art otherwise unlikely to come to the Examiner's attention, or considers that some head of inherent unpatentability applies. Its disadvantage is that the third party does not thereby become a formal party to any proceedings in the Patent Office concerning the patent application. He has no opportunity of pressing his case orally; such lack could be important if the precise significance of a piece of prior art involved was not immediately clear.

The informer procedure should be distinguished from the separate limited powers of the Patent Office, under section 73, to revoke granted patents on its own initiative. These powers are discussed in succeeding Chapter 5.

Division

This subject has already been mentioned briefly but merits further comment on account of its practical importance, arising mainly from the feature of back-dating.

It might at first sight be thought that the concept of division inherently implies that the matter split out, the subject of the divisional application, represents some mere fraction only of the matter of the parent application; a parent/child relation might be envisaged. But this is not necessarily so. The paradoxical result can arise that the divisional application, by being limited to just one or more of the individual features of the parent application, may have a wider claim than that of the parent application and hence dominate it. Two contrasting decisions involving voluntary division (as distinct from division following a unity objection by the Examiner) illustrate this point.

In *Glatt's Application*,[19] the invention lay in the field of conditioning fabrics for

18   IPD 14040.
19   [1983] RPC 122.

laundry driers; the fabric contained a conditioning composition, which was to be carried off from the fabric into the clothes being dried as tumbling took place. Claim 1 of the parent application called for the conditioning composition to be coated over a part only of the fabric surface, so necessarily rendering it air-permeable. Claim 1 of the requested divisional application was restricted, however, only by the requirements that the conditioning composition be applied in certain relative amounts and in such uneven fashion as to create a visual contrast between successive areas of the fabric – that is, without any limitation as to air-permeability. Divisional Claim 1 was refused, on the basis that the divisional specification (the same as the parent specification) taught that air-permeability was essential and hence that a Claim 1 lacking that feature was not properly supported by the description.

In the earlier 1949 Act case of *Formulast Corporation's Application*[20] the parent Claim 1 called for a sequence of shoe-making steps (for leather shoe uppers) of moistening + lasting + force-drying. Divisional Claim 1, however, required only that force-drying be carried out on a moist upper. As such, it dominated not only the parent Claim 1 sequence but also the opponent's rival sequence of lasting + moistening + force-drying – that is, the sequence in which the first two steps of the process were interchanged. The opponent had communicated his sequence to the patentee prior to the filing of the divisional application, but his objection as to obtaining (section 14(1)(a) of the 1949 Act) failed, the Patents Appeal Tribunal holding (rather surprisingly, on the facts) that the divisional Claim 1 was fairly based on the disclosure of the original United States Convention application from which priority was being claimed. The circumstance that it took the opponent's communication to draw the patentee's attention to the wider latent invention present in his original document (but unappreciated up till then) apparently did not matter.

The tightening-up of practice under the 1977 Act as compared to the 1949 Act may well be due to the fact that under the 1949 Act the Patent Office still possessed an ultimate discretion as to whether ante-dating of a purported divisional application should be granted whereas under the 1977 Act an applicant has a statutory right to ante-dating provided that the relevant statutory criteria are met. This distinction is discussed in *Van der Lely's Application*.[21]

Complex issues as to entitlement can also arise in the instance of voluntary widening divisional applications, indeed also in claim-widening during regular prosecution but without division, as discussed next. But detailed treatment of the matter is beyond the scope of this book.

Claim Widening

This issue is analogous to the issues of widening out over an earlier application from which priority is being claimed, or widening out by filing or a voluntary division, discussed earlier in this chapter. Again, the motivations may be similar – an appreciation that the application could have been drafted more broadly initially, the impact of the applicant's own further research and development, the sight of the competitor's product.

It should be made clear at once that there is no prohibition *in toto* against

---

20 [1970] RPC 243.
21 [1987] RPC 61.

claim-widening during prosecution. The position is opposite in this respect to that which arises post-grant, and discussed in Chapter 5. But the applicant does need to overcome the two hurdles represented by (a) the requirement that the claims be supported by the description in the specification (section 14(5)(c)) and (b) the prohibition against additional matter being introduced into the application (section 76(2)). In practice, of course, these hurdles tend to merge into each other.

The hurdles may accordingly be difficult to surmount. If the terms of Claim 1 as originally drafted are clearly narrower than the terms of the description then there may be little problem. But this is not the common situation. The more usual situation is that of an application with a mutually self-consistent description and claims, in respect of which it is now desired to broaden Claim 1. And such request is liable to be refused, as in *Protoned's Application*[22] where, in the case of an invention relating to chairs, amendment of the term 'mechanical compression spring' in Claim 1 to 'mechanical spring' was refused. Although the amendment purported to be by way of deletion (the opposite of addition), it in fact added notionally to the text the idea of using a whole range of other types of mechanical spring, of non-compression type. Such approach of 'implied added subject-matter' is similar to that relied on under the 1949 Act in respect of pre-acceptance widening amendment, even though the relevant statutory provisions of that Act were different. The 1949 Act case law, exemplified in *Garrod's Application*[23] (record sleeves – widening of Claim 1 so as to require presence of two flaps only, when description and drawings showed three flaps, refused) and its successor decisions, is therefore still of relevance in this connection.

Bibliography

J. Bushell, 'Drafting a Complete Specification', *Transactions* Volume LXXVII (1958–59) at C 25.
S. Crespi, 'Biotechnology Patents – A Case of Special Pleading?' [1985] EIPR 190.
J. Dunlop, 'Draft a Set of Claims', *Transactions* Volume LXXV (1956–57) at C 1.
G. Dworkin, 'Implied Added Subject-matter' CIPA Volume 23 (1990–91) 340.
P. Ford (His Honour Judge Ford), 'Functional Claims' [1985] IIC 325.
J. Kemp, 'Claim Drafting: An Historical Survey' in J. Kemp (ed.), *Patent Claim Drafting and Interpretation*, Oyez Longman, 1983.

22   [1983] FSR 110.
23   [1968] RPC 314.

5 Keeping and Losing of Patents

Term and Renewal

Under the 1977 Act as presently standing, the maximum life of a patent granted under the 1977 Act is twenty years from the date of filing the patent application. Renewal fees have to be paid, however, for each year beginning with the fifth year; these fees are generally on a scale increasing upwardly with the years passed, in order to try to discourage unworked patents from remaining on the Register and hampering industry. The rationale is that if a patentee is not working his invention for any reason, then it is proper that the invention should enter the public domain at an earlier time than might otherwise have normally been expected.

The twenty-year term reflects the corresponding provision of the European Patent Convention[1] and constitutes a welcome increase compared to the previous sixteen-year normal maximum term for patents granted under the 1949 Act. Such 1949 Act patents were split up into two groups for purposes of the extra term provided by the new Act. Patents dated on or prior to 1 June 1967 ('old existing patents' in the statutory phraseology) could be extended (if the facts justified) under the inadequate remuneration jurisdiction of section 23 of the 1949 Act, up to a maximum of four years; this provision has now become spent in the passage of time. Patents dated subsequent to 1 June 1967 ('new existing patents' in the statutory phraseology) can be extended as of right for the extra four years provided that appropriate renewal fees are paid and the patents endorsed 'licences of right'. Many such patents are of course still in force. In the special instance of a pharmaceutical patent where marketing has been delayed by the need for regulatory approval, the forthcoming 'supplementary protection certificate' procedure recently enunciated by the European Commission[1a] (reflecting an earlier similar dispensation in United States law) may permit a limited (up to five years) extension of protection.

The Patent Office does not issue advance reminders as to the due date for a renewal fee. What it is required to do, however, under section 25(5) (via Rule 39(4)) is to send the patentee (or other person registered as proprietor) a notification that payment is overdue. Such notification gives the patentee a chance to take advantage of the belated payment provisions (involving in effect a fine) of the Act. The patent is, on strict analysis of applicable section 25(4), restored from the dead even though the procedure is commonly termed one of mere late payment.

Restoration

The section 28 procedure commonly termed 'restoration' can be invoked once the first six month deadline has passed. But conditions have to be met. There is no automatic right to restore. Under the 1977 Act as originally promulgated the conditions were severe. The Patent Office had to be satisfied (under section 28(3)) that:

1   Article 63(1).
1a   EC Regulation No. 1768/92.

> (a) the proprietor of the patent took *reasonable care* to see that any renewal fee was paid within the prescribed period or that that fee and any prescribed additional fee were paid within the six months immediately following the end of that period, and
> (b) those fees were not so paid because of *circumstances beyond his control* . . .
>
> *(Emphasis added)*

The amendment of section 28(3) by the 1988 Act alleviated the patentee's plight to some extent, inasmuch that condition (b) was excised. The application to restore previously had also to be filed within the second six-month period (that is, within one year from actual date of lapse). But under the 1988 amendment the one year period was changed to the 'prescribed period', and the present prescribed period (under Rule 41 of the 1990 Rules) is 19 months. Third parties who have already, in reliance of the lapse, started to infringe and/or made in good faith effective and serious preparations to infringe are also protected; they cannot be precluded from continuing such activities. Any back renewal fees due also have to be paid.

In addition to the overdue reminder the Patent Office also sends a notice of lapsing once the first six-month period has elapsed. This is required by Rule 42. The patentee is therefore in effect reminded twice – once as to payment being overdue and then subsequently as to possible restoration.

The restoration conditions themselves, both as originally specified in the 1977 Act and as amended by the 1988 Act, provide a substantial change as compared to the 1949 Act and its antecedents, under which restoration was normally possible up to three years from expiration and under somewhat different criteria as to cause of lapsing. The key wording, under section 27(1) of the 1949 Act, was that the patentee had to show that the failure to pay the renewal fee(s) was 'unintentional' and that no 'undue delay' had occurred in applying to restore. Much of that former case law on the topic is, therefore, now irrelevant.

There has, nevertheless, been much case law under section 28 itself – although that relating to the 'circumstances beyond his control' condition is now of lesser significance in view of the 1988 Act change. This shows, broadly speaking, a distinction between individual and corporate patentees. Thus for the former class, restoration was granted in *Mead's Patent*[2] (where an individual patentee was ill), *Frazer's Patent*[3] (where an individual patentee relied upon a negligent solicitor), *Ling's Patent*[4] (where reliance on the Patent Office overdue notification alone, to the exclusion of any advance system, was held to be reasonable). But the latter class may be looked at more strictly. In *Cement and Concrete Association's Patent*,[5] for example, restoration was refused because the patentee's renewal system was inherently inadequate to deal with licensees' interests. The leading case on corporate patentees, although decided prior to the 1988 Act amendment, is however the decision of the House of Lords in *Textron's Patent*.[6] This involved, *inter alia*, the inexplicable failure of a legal assistant to the chief legal counsel to follow clear instructions as regards the action to be taken on receipt of the overdue reminder. A distinction was drawn between failure on the part of a person sufficiently high in the corporate hierarchy as to be capable of being regarded as the directing mind

2   [1980] RPC 146.
3   [1981] RPC 53.
4   [1981] RPC 85.
5   [1984] RPC 131.
6   [1989] RPC 441.

of the company, and failure on the part of a mere employee given a task by such directing mind; restoration was granted.

Amendment — Introduction

To maintain the validity of a patent, it may be necessary to apply at some time, post-grant, for amendment. Particularly in the case of a patent of substantial commercial importance, it is by no means uncommon for competitors to unearth at a later stage in the patent's life some piece of prior art that was missed by the Examiner or some defect in drafting of the specification and/or claims. To cure the defect now extant, amendment (if possible) may be essential.

Amendment (1977 Act)

Under section 76(3), no amendment of a specification of a patent granted under the 1977 Act – that is, a 'new' patent – will be allowed if it:

(1) results in the specification disclosing additional matter, or
(2) extends the protection conferred by the patent.

Section 76(3) itself was introduced only by the 1988 Act, but is generally comparable to the wording used in previously applicable 76(2) of the 1977 Act. So far as the prohibition against disclosure of additional matter is concerned, the rule is similar to that applicable during original prosecution of the patent application and discussed in preceding Chapter 4. The statutory wording here is fresh, although (as mentioned in Chapter 1) it is in generally similar vein to that employed in the 1949 Act and earlier Acts under which a considerable body of case law had grown up. Precisely how much of that case law is applicable to 1977 Act amendments is therefore uncertain, although it naturally does still apply to amendments of patents originally granted under the 1949 Act. There is still a paucity of authority on the new provisions; perhaps the most interesting decision to date has been that in *Philips Electronic and Associated Industries Patent,*[7] where the deletion of reference numerals from Claim 1 and the addition of an omnibus Claim 6 to:

> An accumulation-made charge-coupled device substantially as described with reference to Figures 1 and 2 of the drawings.

were allowed. But it would seem that:

(1) amendments which serve to add fresh description, drawings or preparative examples (in a chemical case) will normally continue to be refused;
(2) amendments by way of disclaimer, for example, restriction of Claim 1 by incorporation therein of the additional feature(s) of Claim 2, will normally continue to be allowed in keeping with the principles evolved under the 1949 and earlier Acts under this head, as to which see the next section – in *Hallen*

---

7 [1987] RPC 244.

v Brabantia[8] (PTFE-coated corkscrew of self-pulling type) the permitted amendment was to a combination of Claim 1 with Claims 8, 9 and 10;
(3) cancellation or alteration of remarks in the general description as to what constitute essential or important features of the invention or as to how the invention works or as to why the previous efforts to solve the problem now triumphantly overcome by the invention failed, are in a more delicate state; they may be refused. The point (new to the 1977 Act) is that it is now statutorily laid down that the claims are not conclusive of the scope of the patent but are only one parameter (albeit major) in such determination. Hence, adjustment of such remarks may indirectly serve to extend the scope of protection, which extension is forbidden.

The additional jurisdiction under section 117 and Rule 91 for correction of errors/mistakes in patent documents generally has also to be borne in mind. The scope of these provisions is not yet entirely clear. Their terms as they stand suggest an intermediate position between the separate 'clerical error'[9] and 'obvious mistake'[10] jurisdictions of the 1949 Act. Two contrasting recent decisions involving patent applications are *Antiphon's Application*[11] (where an application was filed with a duplicate of the first sheet of drawings in place of the intended second sheet) and *Dukhovskoi's Applications*[12] (where alteration of the word 'carbon tetrafluoride' to the generic term 'fluorocarbon' was involved). *Antiphon*'s amendment was refused, but *Dukhovskoi*'s amendment was allowed (as a translation error).

Amendment (1949 Act)

Under the 1949 Act provisions, which still apply in any event to 'existing' patents, that is, patents granted under the 1949 Act, any amendment had to be by way of 'disclaimer, correction or explanation' and, 'except for the purpose of correcting an obvious mistake', no amendment was allowed:

> . . . the effect of which would be that the specification as amended would claim or describe matter not in substance disclosed in the specification before the amendment, or that any claim of the specification as amended would not fall within the scope of a claim of the specification before the amendment. (section 31(1))

There is a plenitude of case law under the 1949 Act provisions and their antecedents; the triple-head of disclaimer, correction or explanation is found in the Patents Designs and Trade Marks Act of 1883 and the jurisdiction as a whole goes back to the Act of 1835. Apart from the omission of the 'obvious mistake' head, it would seem unlikely that Parliament intended to alter the law too much in 1977. The 1977 Act phraseology necessarily had to differ from before, in order to adapt the United Kingdom law in keeping with corresponding provisions of the European Patent Convention.[13] This is

---

8   [1991] RPC 195.
9   Section 76(1).
10   Section 31(1).
11   [1984] RPC 1.
12   [1985] RPC 8.
13   Articles 123(2) and (3).

in contrast to the position on restoration, where almost certainly Parliament did intend a statutory tightening-up.

The 1949 Act provisions are by no means defunct yet. There will continue to be existing patents until the middle of the present decade at least. Those that are renewed until the end of their life are likely to be ones of commercial importance, and hence more likely to be involved in litigation with the attendant risk of amendment being needed if the defendant's counterclaim for revocation succeeds in part. For these various reasons, therefore, an exposition of the old law (in relation particularly to 'disclaimer') is useful.

Disclaimer

'Disclaimer' means primarily the restriction of a claim; normally Claim 1 is involved. Thus, it was held by Lord Denning in the leading case of *Amp v Hellermann*[14] that:

> . . . a disclaimer takes place whenever the patentee reduces the ambit of his monopoly; for he thereby renounces his previous claim in its fullest scope and limits it to a narrower scope.

Disclaimer is normally carried out by incorporating into the claim in question either a feature (or features) of an existing subsidiary claim(s) or a feature (or features) disclosed in the specification but not already claimed. In *Amp* itself the patentee was accordingly permitted to limit his Claim 1 (to a crimping tool for crimping electrical connectors onto electrical conductors) by incorporation of a stop feature recited in original Claim 11. The fact that use of a stop (although described and illustrated in the drawings) was in no way put forward in the original specification as forming part of the patentee's invention (that is, inventive contribution to the art) did not matter. The fact of disclosure was enough in itself. In *Thomson's Patent*[15] the patentee was even allowed to introduce into Claim 1 a feature (coaxiality of the driving and driven members) not mentioned at all in the specification; it was shown only in the drawings attached to the specification.

Sometimes a new numerical limitation not explicitly disclosed before is allowed, as in *Ethyl Corporation's Patent*[16] (where insertion in a chemical case of a certain range for ingredients ratio, derived partly from specific individual ratios in the Examples and partly from an end-point recited in an existing claim, was allowed) or *Molins v Industrial Machinery*[17] (where limitation to cigarette-making machines producing nine hundred or more cigarettes a minute in order to overcome a prior document was allowed).

But other kinds of fresh intermediate generalisation are liable to be refused, as in *Rose Bros' Application*[18] (where limitation to use of a feeler member controlling a vibrating feed device of any type was refused since the disclosure in the specification and existing Claim 19 were both restricted to control of vibrating feed devices of electromagnetic type; the requested amendment would hence clearly serve to embrace

14   [1962] RPC 55.
15   51 RPC 241.
16   [1972] RPC 169.
17   55 RPC 31.
18   [1960] RPC 247.

use of feed devices of, for example, mechanical or pneumatically operated kind, of which the patentee had originally given no hint).

A straightforward 'bite' type of disclaimer, leaving a so-called 'n-1' type of claim, may also be permitted, particularly in the case when the amendment is necessary purely to avoid incidental overlap with the prior art. A good example is in *Holliday's Application*,[19] where the following 'n-2' restriction was allowed:

> We are aware of an offer for sale in the United Kingdom in Du Pont Technical Bulletin D147 entitled 'Dyeing and Finishing of Dacron Polyester Staple' of 2-component dyestuff compositions under the trade names 'Latyl Violet BN' and 'Latyl Blue 4R'. Latyl Violet BN consists of substantially 91% of 1-hydroxy-4-anilinoanthraquinone and substantially 9% of 1,4-dianilino-anthraquinone. Latyl Blue 4R consists of substantially 93% of 1-hydroxy-4-*p*-anisidino anthraquinone and substantially 7% of 1,4-di-*p*-anisidino anthraquinone. We make no claim to either of these compositions.
>
> We are also aware of U.S. patent specification No. 2,342,191 which discloses a mixture of 1-amino-4-(*p*-hydroxyphenyl)-aminoanthraquinone and 1,4-di-(phenylamino)-anthraquinone. We make no claim to this latter mixture, in any proportions.
>
> Subject to the foregoing disclaimers . . .

But the line of bite must be clear in itself; if it is not, the resulting claim may be bad for ambiguity, as pointed in *British Celanese v Courtaulds*,[20] a case involving an attempt by the patentee of an invention relating to the spinning of synthetic fibres to disclaim the entirety of the teaching of a rather vague earlier patent in terms of: 'We are aware of a Specification of A.M. Clark No. 2695 of 1887 and we make no claim to what is therein contained'. And although ambiguity no longer constitutes a ground for revocation, for a 1977 Act patent, it is to be expected that the Court in its discretion would continue to refuse an amendment which created ambiguity, having regard to the requirement for clarity of claim at the time of original examination. A claim subject to a disclaimer can be regarded as a new form of claim, as compared to a claim derived simply, by combining together the features (and hence words) of existing claims, and as such should be subject to a similar test.

Alteration in the species of claim may be permitted in appropriate cases, as in *Farbwerke Hoechst's Application*[21] (alteration from a fungicidal/bactericidal preparation to a fungicidal/bactericidal method of use) and in *Beecham Group's (Amoxycillin) Application*[22] (alteration from chemical compound *per se* to pharmaceutical composition containing the compound).

The head 'disclaimer' is also capable of embracing the renunciation or watering-down of some assertion in the specification, that is, a disclaimer in a popular sense as distinct from a technical sense (*American Cyanamid v Ethicon*).[23] The patentee in this case (in respect of an invention relating to absorbable surgical sutures) was allowed to delete from his Specification the sentence, 'The present sutures are stable in physiological saline for at least one month at 37°C', this comment not being particularly germane either to production of the sutures or to their use (since in the body enzymatic hydrolysis would come into play).

19 [1978] RPC 27 at 46.
20 52 RPC 171 at 176.
21 [1972] RPC 703.
22 [1980] RPC 261.
23 [1979] RPC 215 at 272.

The same decision makes the useful further point that the three heads, disclaimer, correction and explanation, are not mutually exclusive; a given amendment can come under one or more heads.

Correction and explanation

The heads 'correction' and 'explanation' provide more of a rag-bag. If the desired amendment cannot be classified on any view as 'disclaimer', the patentee tries here instead. Inconsistencies between the specification and claims can sometimes be cleared up, as in *Polymer Corporation's Patent*.[24] In *Plastic S.A.'s Patent*,[25] a statement of advantages in a patent relating to the manufacture of blown hollow bodies from plastic material – to the effect that the invention permitted use of materials having a restricted zone of plasticity as the lateral walls are formed quickly and further that it was unnecessary to heat the walls of the mould – was allowed to be deleted. Ambiguous terms may also at times be clarified. Thus, in *Johnson's Application*[26] a patentee was allowed to explain that by 'soda' he meant soda ash and not washing soda crystals; and in *General Tire's Patent*[27] 'dihydroxy-terminated' was changed to 'having at least two terminal hydroxy groups'. But the circumscribing prohibition against addition of new matter necessarily provides a strong fetter on the patentee's freedom of action. Subsequent correction of claimed structural chemical formulae may in particular prove difficult as in *Zambon's Patent*[28] (change from 5-hydroxymethyl-1-(5'-nitrofurfurylidenamino)-hydantoin to the corresponding 3-hydroxy-methyl-1-(5'-nitrofurfurylidenamino) compound refused) although a more lenient view was taken in *NRDC's Application*[29] (change from

allowed).

Obvious mistake

The 'obvious mistake' approach is often sought because the limitations against addition of new matter or expansion of the claims no longer apply. But the mistake must be 'obvious', that is, plain on the face of the document. Thus, in *Farmhand v Spadework*[30] Claim 1 had been wrongly drafted; it recited a sequence of events which was in the context (moving bales of hay in a hay bale accumulator) clearly mechanically impossible, and hence at total variance with what was described. Amendment was allowed. Amendment was similarly allowed in the subsequent

24 [1972] RPC 39.
25 [1970] RPC 22.
26 26 RPC 780.
27 [1974] RPC 207.
28 [1971] RPC 95.
29 [1957] RPC 344.
30 [1975] RPC 617.

House of Lords decision in *Holtite v Jost*,[31] now the leading authority. The patent related to twist locks for securing freight containers to transporters, and there was a self-evident inconsistency between the drawings and description of the preferred embodiment on the one hand and Claim 1 on the other. As it was put by Lord Diplock:

> . . . a reader of the specification would most readily understand what the invention really was by studying the drawings and description of the device said to be constructed in accordance with the invention. Anyone who had done this and then looked at Claim 1 must have realised something had gone wrong. It cannot matter tuppence to the usefulness of the invention if something projects below the bottom of the housing when the twist-lock head is in the retracted position. No one has suggested how it can.[32]

A suitable amendment, eliminating any need for there to be nothing projecting below the bottom surface of the housing in retracted position, was allowed; the decision made it clear, moreover, that a mistake did not fail to be 'obvious' merely because there was more than one way of expressing the necessary correction.

Amendment (Procedure and Discretion)

Procedurally, amendment applications under both Acts can be made to either the Patent Office or the Court. If the patent is already involved in Court proceedings at the time, for example, infringement proceedings, an amendment application naturally has to be instituted there. Third parties can also come in as opponents, in either forum and under both Acts.

The jurisdiction is, moreover, discretionary under both Acts. While there is always a right to apply for amendment, it does not necessarily follow that every amendment that fulfils the literal terms of the statute will necessarily be allowed. It was well established under the 1949 Act that amendment will be refused where there has been excessive delay in applying to amend once the patentee has become aware of the defect in his patent, for example, as in *Western Electric v Racal-Milgo*[33] (seven-year delay); this consideration is all the stronger if the patentee has in the interval tried to take advantage of his patent notwithstanding the defect, as in *Bentley Engineering's Patent*.[34] Failure to disclose the complete story as to the history of the patent and origin of the defect may also be fatal – see *Chevron Research's Patent*[35] and *Du Pont de Nemours (Robert's) Patent*.[36] The fact that the specification and claims if remaining unamended might provide an embarrassment to the patentee is not in itself enough to have the discretion exercised in his favour as in *Union Carbide (Bailey & O'Connor's) Application*[37] (deletion of passages in specification inferring perhaps an improper priority claim refused). Claims tenaciously fought all the way up to the House of Lords may also be disallowed amendment, for example, as in *Raleigh v Miller*,[38] although *contra* where

31   [1979] RPC 81.
32   At 93 and 94.
33   [1981] RPC 253.
34   [1981] RPC 361.
35   [1976] RPC 580.
36   [1972] RPC 545.
37   [1972] RPC 854.
38   67 RPC 226.

only excision of invalid claims is requested, for example, as in *Van der Lely v Bamfords* (amendment).[39]

It is reasonable to suppose that these principles will continue to apply under the 1977 Act. For example, amendment was refused in discretion in *Autoliv Development AB's Patent*,[40] where there had been a four-year delay in seeking amendment once the patentee had learnt of the relevant prior art, compounded by the patentee's action in continuing to brandish the unamended specification in front of manufacturers even after an internal decision to amend had been taken.

Revocation

A patentee may also face an application for revocation; if so, distinction has to be drawn again between 'new' patents granted under the 1977 Act and 'existing' patents granted under the 1949 Act.

For 'new' patents, such an application can be made either to the Patent Office or to the Court, at any time during the life of the patent. Where the application arises by way of counter-claim in an existing action for infringement it naturally has to go ahead in the Court. But where the revocation proceedings have already been started in the Patent Office before the infringement action is instituted in the Court, it does not necessarily follow that the whole matter will be transferred to the Court. The Court may, if the circumstances warrant, order a stay of the Court proceedings in favour of the existing Patent Office proceedings.

A pair of recent decisions involving existing patents are relevant here. In *Hawker Siddeley Dynamics v Real Time Developments*[41] where there was evidence of a cost ratio of around 10:1 (as between Court and Patent Office proceedings) and the applicant for revocation argued that he could afford the one but not the other, a stay was ordered. But in *Ferro v Escol*,[42] where there was a sharp conflict of evidence as to the likely cost ratio, a stay was refused; this decision can, in retrospect, be seen to be regrettable on account of the encouragement which it provides to the 'deep pocket' party.

Section 72(5) of the 1977 Act is another important provision. This declares that any decision of the Patent Office (either at first instance or on appeal) shall not estop any party in subsequent civil proceedings in which infringement is in issue from alleging invalidity again (on the grounds available). This in turn means that the Patent Office will be likely, just as it did in connection with opposition or belated opposition (revocation) proceedings with 'existing' patents under the 1949 Act, to err on the side of the patentee if it feels any doubt as to whether invalidity is established. Contentious procedure in the Patent Office is discussed more fully as such in Chapter 11.

The grounds available for revocation of a 'new' patent are formally limited to:

    (1) not a patentable invention – section 72(1)(a) (Chapter 2);
    (2) non-entitlement – section 72(1)(b) (Chapter 4);
    (3) insufficiency of the specification – section 72(1)(c) (Chapter 3);
    (4) existence of impermissible amendment – section 72(1)(d)and (e) (Chapter 5).

39 [1964] RPC 54.
40 [1988] RPC 425.
41 [1983] RPC 395.
42 [1990] RPC 651.

These topics have been severally discussed already, as indicated above. For an interesting instance of invalidity flowing from impermissible amendment under the 1977 Act see *Bonzel v Intervention (No. 3)*[43] (dilatation catheters), where the court laid down the approach as:

> (1) To ascertain through the eyes of the skilled addressee what is disclosed, both explicitly and implicitly in the application.
> (2) To do the same in respect of the patent as granted.
> (3) To compare the two disclosures and decide whether any subject matter relevant to the invention has been added whether by deletion or addition. The comparison is strict in the sense that subject matter will be added unless such matter is clearly and unambiguously disclosed in the application either explicitly or implicitly.

Finally, reference should be made again to the limited powers (fresh in the 1977 Act and revised by the 1988 Act) which the Patent Office has under section 73 to revoke patents on its own initiative; the patentee has to be given an opportunity of being heard first, and possibly amending his patent, before such action is finally taken. Put shortly, the powers are limited to instances of 'whole contents' objection under section 2(3) or double patenting as between a regular United Kingdom patent and corresponding European patent (UK).

For 'existing' patents, revocation proceedings can also now be instituted in the Patent Office or the Court at any time during the lifetime of the patent. The previous limitation as regards institution in the Patent Office to the period of twelve months from grant has been removed by the transitional provisions of the 1977 Act. This change represents an important step forward for those less able to bear the higher costs of Court proceedings.

For such patents the grounds available in the Patent Office and Court are again now identical (although different when the 1949 Act alone held sway), being defined by section 32(1) to (3) of the 1949 Act; this expansion of grounds is also valuable. The comparison between these 1949 Act grounds, and those of section 72(1) of the 1977 Act, has been mentioned earlier, in Chapter 3. In some respects, for example, in the limitation to prior art available in the United Kingdom at the date of the patent, the grounds are narrower; in other respects, for example, in respect of possible defects in the drafting of the specification and claims, the grounds are wider; a full analysis is beyond the scope of this book.

Surrender

Both 'new' and 'existing' patents can be formally surrendered under the procedure of section 29 of the 1977 Act, if desired, subject to opposition by third parties. Such procedure is occasionally invoked, for example, as a term in connection with settlement of infringement actions outside the Court.

---

43 [1991] RPC 553.

Bibliography

G. Aggus, 'The Equities of Amendment', CIPA Volume 10 (1980–81) at 389.
BB Commentary on section 28.
R. Whaite and N. Jones, 'Pharmaceutical Patent Term Restoration: The European Commission's Regulation' [1992] EIPR 324.

6 Infringement of Patents (Law)

Introduction

The ultimate accolade for a patentee is to prosecute successfully an action for infringement against a competitor who has copied his invention, in face of a counterclaim for revocation on the basis that the patent is invalid. Revocation and the grounds therefor has already been considered (in Chapter 3 and 5, pages 83 to 84); accordingly, the next two chapters are devoted to the substantive (Chapter 6) and procedural (Chapter 7) aspects of the law of infringement.

Patent infringement is a tort; previously, when the scope of the patent was determined by the traditional (and in many places archaic) words of the Letters Patent grant as interpreted by the case law since the Statute of Monopolies, it ranked as a common-law tort. Now, under the 1977 Act, it has become a statutory tort. The Act contains a formal definition of what constitutes an infringing act. Moreover, the 1977 Act applies in this respect to infringements of both 'existing' (granted under the 1949 Act) and 'new' (granted under the 1977 Act) patents (in contradistinction to the position on validity); there is a saving proviso[1] to the effect that an act which did not constitute an infringement under the earlier law, but does fall foul of the wider terms (in some respects) of the 1977 Act, shall be permitted to continue if started before the 1977 Act came into force.

Two fundamental questions arise in any action for infringement, namely:

(1) Is the act complained of one capable of inherently ranking as infringement ?; and

(2) If so, does the patent cover the infringement in fact ?

The patentee must convince the Court on both points, to the normal civil standard of balance of probability, if he is to succeed on infringement; the onus is on him. The onus of proof as regards invalidity lies, of course, with the defendant, should he decide to make such an attack; in the case of a pioneer invention, the defendant may well so abstain, since a 'footling' attack is liable just to irritate the Court.

INFRINGING ACTS

The main definition of infringing acts is contained in section 60(1) of the 1977 Act. This provides that a person (unless authorised by the patentee) infringes a United Kingdom patent if, while the patent is in force, he does any of the following things:

(a) where the invention is a product, he makes, disposes of, offers to dispose of, uses or imports the product or keeps it whether for disposal or otherwise;

(b) where the invention is a process, he uses the process or he offers it for use

1 Schedule 4, Article 3(3).

in the United Kingdom when he knows, or it is obvious to a reasonable person in the circumstances, that its use there without the consent of the proprietor would be an infringement of the patent;

(c) where the invention is a process, he disposes of, offers to dispose of, uses or imports any product obtained directly by means of that process or keeps any such product whether for disposal or otherwise.

It will be appreciated at once that these words are apt to include all the standard commercial activities whereby an infringer might make inroad on the benefit of the patentee's monopoly; in the case of a product invention, 'disposes of' in section 60(1)(a) covers sale, while 'makes' covers the original manufacture. In the case of a process invention, both performance of the process and susbequent commercial dealings with the product of the process are covered, by 'uses' in section 60(1)(b) and section 60(1)(c) respectively; in addition, the latter is covered by 'disposes of' in section 60(1)(c). Offering the prohibited subject-matter is also covered to a substantial extent, in each of the three sub-sections.

The precise bounds of some of the words are uncertain, however – especially those of 'keep' and 'dispose of', 'disposal'. All these are quite new in the 1977 Act, as compared to the earlier form of grant.

This previous form, in its latest pre-1977 version, gave the patentee the exclusive right to:

> make, use, exercise and vend the said invention

and commanded Her Majesty's subjects that:

> they do not at any time . . . either directly or indirectly make use of or put in practice the said invention, nor in anywise imitate the same

to the end that:

> the patentee may have and enjoy the sole use and exercise and the full benefit of the said invention.

The contrast between the archaic and circumlocutory language used here, and that in the new section 60(1), is self-evident. The full text of this earlier form is provided in Appendix 5.

It would seem, however, that the courts will move cautiously in extending the previous frontiers. Thus, in *Smith Kline & French Laboratories v Harbottle (Mercantile)*[2] the Court refused to regard 'keeps it for disposal or otherwise' as capable of including the activities of a mere warehouseman; a mere carrier or warehouseman never came within the prohibition in earlier times, for the very good reason that by carrying or warehousing he was hardly deriving benefit for himself out of the invention. His charges would normally be the same irrespective of whether or not the goods were patented.

One significant area in which section 60(1) of the new Act may have narrowed the earlier common law lies in the importation of goods produced abroad with the assistance

2   [1979] FSR 55.

of processes patented in the United Kingdom. Section 60(1)(c) now limits the protection to the instance when the goods have been obtained 'directly' by means of that process. It is certainly arguable that the effect of this term is to preclude protection where the patented process has been employed only at a beginning or intermediate stage of production abroad. Under the earlier common law, as first expounded in *Saccharin Corporation v Anglo-Continental Chemical Works*,[3] infringement might nevertheless be held in such circumstances provided that the earlier steps were sufficiently significant in the process as a whole. The point is often of considerable importance in connection with multi-step chemical syntheses, where the foreign producer can devise an alternative final step or steps.

CONTRIBUTORY INFRINGEMENT

Section 60(2), on the other hand, now adds to the patentee's net by providing for so-called 'contributory infringement', in certain instances. Specifically, there is infringement also if an unauthorised person supplies or offers to supply:

> . . . any of the *means*, relating to an *essential element* of the invention, for putting the invention into effect when he *knows*, or *it is obvious to a reasonable person in the circumstances*, that those means are suitable for putting, *and* are intended to put, the invention into effect in the United Kingdom.   (*Emphasis added*)

This provision represents an important step forward in the law as far as the patentee is concerned. Previously, it was generally believed (although the point was never satisfactorily fully settled one way or the other) that under the common law there was no such tort as contributory infringement. For example, in the well-known case of *Dunlop v Moseley*[4] sale of wheel rims 'ready for wires' (which wires, when added, would complete an infringing article) was held to escape. The precise extent of the provision is, however, by no means entirely clear. There is some difficulty, in particular, regarding the interpretation of the phrase '. . . means, relating to an essential element . . .'. Relevant case law is so far sparse. In the Malaysian case of *Rhône Poulenc v Dikloride Herbicides*,[5] involving United Kingdom patents registered in Malaysia and to which section 60 applied by virtue of the local Malaysian Patents Act, it was clear from the evidence that the defendants had induced planters to commit infringement of claims directed to the use of 2-chloroethyl phosphonic acid (ethephon) in the treatment of rubber trees. Inducement can show intention, whilst actual use shows suitability.

Exceptions

Section 60(3) provides that there shall be no contributory infringement in respect of supply, or offer to supply of a staple commercial product. Section 60(4) precludes infringement in respect of exhausted rights under the Community Patent Convention

3   17 RPC 307.
4   21 RPC 274.
5   [1988] FSR 282.

(see Chapter 12). Section 60(5) also exempts certain specific acts, which may be summarised under the heads of:

(1) private non-commercial acts;
(2) experimental acts;
(3) pharmaceutical prescriptions;
(4) acts arising in or from the transient passage through the United Kingdom of ships, vehicles, aircraft and hovercraft.

Some further analysis of sections 60(3) and (5) is provided below.

Section 60(3) is, like section 60(2), a new departure for the law and the meaning of 'staple commercial product' is as yet judicially untested. Although it has been criticised as inherently vague,[6] nevertheless it is an expressive term and will probably not create too many problems in practice for the courts.

In the United States, the long-standing equivalent exception in the law (from which the 1977 Act exception may have been ultimately derived) is couched in terms of: '. . . and not a staple article or commodity of commerce suitable for substantial non-infringing use',[7] and has proved quite workable. The status of the article or commodity is treated as a question of fact on which the parties can lead evidence. It may be easier to show staple quality if the article or commodity ('product' in the United Kingdom provision) is by way of being an ingredient (where the composition is constant) rather than an article (say, a kind of valve) where dimensions and construction may vary from one manufacturer to another. But the mere fact that a product is in the public domain does not make it a staple item; there has to be some degree of pre-existing commercial availability. Thus, in *Dawson v Rohm & Haas*,[8] a 1980 United States case involving a patent directed to the use of propanil as a herbicide, the fact that propanil as a chemical compound had been impliedly revealed in the art back in 1902 failed to assist the defendant. And in *Milton Hodosh v Block Drug*[9] in 1987, a toothpaste containing potassium nitrate (for desensitising purposes) was held not to be a staple product even though potassium nitrate itself (as a chemical compound) and also toothpaste (as a generic product) clearly were staple.

The section 60(5) exemptions, on the other hand, largely reflect the previous law. They are intrinsically quite reasonable. The experimental use exemption, for example, can be traced right back to the 1876 decision in *Frearson v Loe*.[10] But there can be dispute as to the exact bounds of the exemptions for private and experimental use. In *Monsanto v Stauffer Chemical*[11] field trials of a herbicide with a view to obtaining regulatory clearances were held to be outside the exemption. In *SKF Laboratories v Evans Medical*[12] experiments on a massive scale (using over 30 kg of the relevant material, the drug cimetidine) had been performed by the opponent to an application by the patentee for amendment of his patent, in support of an attack of anticipation by

---

6 [1979] EIPR at 91.
7 USC Title 35, section 271(c).
8 206 USPQ 385.
9 4 USPQ 2d 1935.
10 9 Ch.D 48.
11 [1985] RPC 515.
12 [1989] FSR 513.

way of inevitable result of an earlier process. Summary judgment was refused, and the Court discussed the distinction between the two heads.

As for more complex circumstances – for example, individual liability of directors of an infringing company, aiding and abetting infringement,[13] warranties under sale of goods legislation,[14] repair of patented articles (normally mere repair is excluded, although repair amounting to re-building may be caught),[15] joint tort feasorship as between domestic and foreign parties acting according to a common design[16] – reference should be made to larger works.

Mention should be made finally of section 64, which provides a personal (albeit devolvable) right of continued user in face of a new patent to a third party who had already been practising the invention before the date of the patent. Such a 'shop-right', as it may be termed, is new to the 1977 Act.

INFRINGEMENT IN FACT

The question of how the scope of protection (sometimes called the 'ambit of monopoly') afforded by a patent is to be determined, that is, how the position of the boundary fence is to be found, is one of the most difficult in patent law. It is a matter which in the end can only be settled finally by the Court, once it has heard the rival parties' contentions as to construction of the patent. There are very few cases where the scope is crystal-clear on the face of patent document itself; it is equally rare for the alleged infringement to be a carbon copy of anything specifically described or illustrated in the patentee's specification.

In practice, the plaintiff will often be urging a wide construction of the patent, so as to catch the infringement, and the defendant *vice versa*, so as to show that he falls outside. The use in the claims of qualitative words like 'large', 'flexible', 'U-shaped' positively invites argument; mathematically quantitative terms like 'having a vertex angle in the range of from 25 to 90 degrees' or other scientifically precise definitions like 'a C_1–C_4 alkyl group', on the other hand, discourage argument.

It must be remembered, moreover, that a patent claim must be given the same construction for both infringement and validity purposes. This elementary proposition often tends to be overlooked, although it dates back to early days of patent jurisprudence. In 1884, we find Grove J. directing the jury in *Young v Rosenthal* (seam arrangements in stays and corsets) to the effect:

> If the Patentees have a right to claim as substantially their invention, slightly curved lines, then slightly curved lines made and used before this patent would be an anticipation of the invention. They *cannot have it both ways.*[17]   (*Emphasis added*)

Hence, a patentee who urges a wide construction may (if his construction is accepted by the court) find that he has thereby simultaneously opened the door to an attack on ground of lack of novelty or obviousness. Conversely, a defendant who urges a narrow

13   *Dow Chemical v Spence Bryson* [1982] FSR 598.
14   *Microbeads v Vinhurst* [1976] RPC 19.
15   *Solar Thompson Engineering v Barton* [1977] RPC 537.
16   *Unilever v Gillette (UK)* [1989] RPC 583.
17   1 RPC 29 at 33.

construction may (if his construction is accepted instead) find that his counterclaim for invalidity fails. In short, there can arise what is often termed an infringement/validity 'squeeze'. For a contemporary example of a successful such squeeze, see *Prout v British Gas*[17a] (securing brackets for lamps around gas excavations).

A further point of theoretical difficulty, at least, arises from the 1977 Act. This Act is stated, as previously mentioned, to apply to both 'new' patents (that is, those granted under the 1977 Act) and 'existing' patents (that is, those granted under the 1949 Act). So far as kinds of infringing activity are concerned, this provides essentially no problem. But as regards infringement in fact, the 1977 Act excludes the operation of section 125(1) and (3), and their associated Protocol on Interpretation of Article 69 of the European Patent Convention, from 'existing' patents. And since section 125(1) and (3) provide on their face for a somewhat more liberal approach to interpretation of claims, as compared to earlier traditional approaches, the position might notionally arise that there would in future be two systems of construction applicable according to the type of patent involved.

In the first edition of this book, it was speculated that the courts might nevertheless try to converge towards a common standard. This has now happened, although it is fair to mention that the House of Lords has not yet pronounced definitively on the subject. The jurisprudence is at Court of Appeal level only. In the interlocutory proceedings on *Improver Corporation v Remington Consumer Products*[17b] it was stated explicitly:

> So far as the development of English law is concerned, the latest decision is the decision of the House of Lords in *Catnic Components Ltd v Hill & Smith Ltd.*, 1982 RPC 183. It seems to me, if I may say so with respect, that the well-known speech of Lord Diplock in that case correctly indicates the same approach to construction as is indicated in the Protocol.

The *Catnic* decision is discussed more fully later in this chapter. Notwithstanding its 1982 date, the decision in fact involved a 1949 Act patent and 1949 Act law. It is possible to argue that the courts, in equating 1977 Act law with *Catnic*, have in truth sacrificed the law at the altar of expediency, alternatively of chauvinism.

Since construction is probably the most important single topic in patent law, a degree of historical perspective does not come amiss. In order to provide such perspective, the following set of guidelines is presented. Some of course are today more important than others, and to some extent also they overlap with each other. Currently, Guideline 4 (the *Catnic* decision) dominates. But times and fashions may change again. And knowledge of the earlier cases (and the principles derived therefrom) is essential for a thorough understanding.

Guideline 1

The words of the claim (when themselves correctly construed) provide the *prima facie* boundary of protection.

17a   [1992] FSR 478 at 487.
17b   [1989] RPC 69 at 76.

The statutory root for this can be found in the requirement of section 4(3)(c) of the 1949 Act that a complete specification:

> shall end with a claim or claims defining the scope of the invention claimed.

Although section 4 is concerned only with the contents of a specification, and not with infringement, the formal Letters Patent granted under the 1949 Act would contain (as before) a prohibition against use by others of the invention. Taking the statutory requirement and the form of grant together, as pointed out in Lord Diplock's speech in *Beecham Group v Bristol Laboratories*[18] (where the alleged infringement was a precursor form of a particular semi-synthetic penicillin), the rule is then reached.

Jurisprudentially, the emphasis to be attached to the actual words of the claim is made clear in the well-known speech of Lord Russell in 1938 in *EMI v Lissen* (variable mu valves):

> The function of the claims is to define clearly and with precision the monopoly claimed, so that others may know the exact boundaries of the area within which they will be trespassers. Their primary object is to limit and not to extend the monopoly. What *is not claimed is disclaimed.*[19]   *(Emphasis added)*
>
> . . .
>
> But I know of no canon or principle which will justify one in departing from the unambiguous and grammatical meaning of a claim and narrowing or extending its scope by reading into it words which are not in it; or which will justify one in using *stray phrases* in the body of a Specification for the purpose of narrowing or widening the boundaries of the monopoly fixed by the plain words of a claim.[20]   *(Emphasis added)*

The rebuke was indeed justified on the facts of the case. In order to avoid the impact of the prior art, the patentee was putting forward an audaciously narrower construction of his Claim 1. To quote further from Lord Russell:

> I cannot assent to this suggestion. It looks to me like throwing scientific dust in the eyes of the Court. To my mind, this is a plain case of plain English . . . [21]

Guideline 2

The boundary of protection must be determined in the first place from the patent alone, without an eye to the alleged infringement or alleged anticipation. The purpose of this guideline is clear; the court must not twist the construction of the patent so as to try to catch an infringer who might be considered to be acting in a morally reprehensible way. The matter must be approached objectively; it is after all the patentee who in the first place is able to choose the words he uses for his specification and claims. In the more picturesque language of nearly a century ago:

---

18   [1978] RPC 153 at 198.
19   56 RPC 23 at 39.
20   At 41.
21   At 43.

Therefore, in construing this patent, one has no right to do what Mr Moulton so often invited us to do, to construe the patent by considering what the Defendant has done. I abjure that altogether, and I say we are bound to construe the patent as if we had to construe it before the Defendant was born, if the patent was before that time.[22]

The importance of this guideline has more recently been emphasised in *American Cyanamid v Berk Pharmaceuticals*[23] and *Horville Engineering v Clares (Engineering)*.[24]

Guideline 3

The court can receive expert evidence as to the meaning of technical terms (individual or composite) in the claims, but must not surrender its role to the expert witnesses; the eventual ascertainment of the boundary of the claim remains a task for the court alone.

One of the latest authorities here is *American Cyanamid v Ethicon*.[25] Claim 1 called for:

> 1. A sterile article for the surgical repair or replacement of living tissue, the article being readily absorbable by living tissue and being formed from a polyhydroxyacetic ester.

The question was whether this Claim was limited to homopolymeric materials or whether it covered copolymeric materials also; the defendants were proposing to use a 90 : 10 copolymer of hydroxyacetic acid units and lactic acid units. The Court pointed out that polymer chemistry was a field in which the meaning of many technical terms may be entirely dependent on the context in which they are used, and found useful the evidence of experts as to how far substitution could take place on the constitutent methyl group of acetic acid without destroying its essential 'acetic' character.

It should not be thought that *American Cyanamid* was enunciating any drastically new principle. As the Court pointed out, a similar approach had been adopted over a century ago in the classic judgment of Lord Westbury in *Hills v Evans* (a case relating to purification of coal gas), where he said:

> It is undoubtedly true as a proposition of law that the construction of a specification, as the construction of all other written instruments, belongs to the court; but a specification of an invention contains most generally, if not always, some technical terms, some phrases of art, some processes, and requires generally the aid of the light derived from what are called surrounding circumstances. It is, therefore, an admitted rule of law that the explanation of the words or technical terms of art, the phrases used in commerce, and the proof and results of the processes which are described (and in a chemical patent the ascertainment of chemical equivalents), that all these are *matters of fact upon which evidence may be given*, contradictory testimony may be adduced, and upon which undoubtedly it is the province and right of a jury to decide.[26]
>
> *(Emphasis added)*

---

22 11 RPC 519 at 523 (1894, by the Master of the Rolls) in *Nobel v Anderson*.
23 [1976] RPC 231.
24 [1976] RPC 411.
25 [1979] RPC 215.
26 31 LJ Ch. 457 at 460.

The similarity of legal thought as between *Hills* (1862) and *American Cyanamid* (1978) is indeed an impressive monument to the continuity of United Kingdom patent law.

Naturally the role of the expert must not be taken too far. In a case involving simple subject-matter, say, children's building blocks, the court may (wisely or unwisely) come to the conclusion that no explanations at all are necessary. And it was in a case of fairly straightforward subject-matter (if not quite so simple as building blocks), that the well—known strictures as to the need to control the role accorded to expert witnesses were uttered. This was *British Celanese v Courtaulds* in 1935, concerning the manufacture of artificial silk by dry-spinning, where it appears that over nine thousand questions were asked at the trial, and Lord Tomlin on appeal to the House of Lords was moved to complain:

> The proceedings in the Trial Court provide an illustration of the licence which in these days in cases of this kind is enjoyed by expert witnesses and by Counsel examining them.
>
> In my judgment the time has come to curtail that licence whatever be the difficulties involved in doing so.
>
> The area of the territory in which in cases of this kind an expert witness may legitimately move is not doubtful. He is entitled to give evidence as to the state of the art at any given time. He is entitled to explain the meaning of any technical terms used in the art. He is entitled to say whether in his opinion that which is described in the specification on a given hypothesis as to its meaning is capable of being carried into effect by a skilled worker. He is entitled to say what at a given time to him as skilled in the art a given piece of apparatus or a given sentence on any given hypothesis as to its meaning would have taught or suggested to him. He is entitled to say whether in his opinion a particular operation in connexion with the art could be carried out and generally to give any explanation required as to facts of a scientific kind.
>
> He is *not entitled* to say nor is Counsel entitled to ask him *what the Specification means*, nor does the question become any more admissible if it takes the form of asking him what it means to him as an engineer or as a chemist.[27]   (*Emphasis added*)

The applicability of expert evidence on the *Catnic* approach to construction is discussed under succeeding Guideline 4.

Guideline 4

A claim must be given a 'purposive construction'.

This guideline is based on the speech of Lord Diplock in *Catnic Components v Hill & Smith*, where he said:

> A patent specification should be given a *purposive construction* rather than a purely literal one derived from applying to it the kind of meticulous verbal analysis in which lawyers are too often tempted by their training to indulge. The question in each case is: whether persons with practical knowledge and experience of the kind of work in which the invention was intended to be used would understand that strict compliance with a particular descriptive word or phrase appearing in a claim was intended by the patentee to be an *essential* requirement of the invention so that *any* variant would fall outside the monopoly claimed even though it could have no material effect on the way the invention worked.

27   52 RPC 171 at 195 and 196.

The question, of course, does not arise where the variant would in fact have a material effect upon the way the invention worked. Nor does it arise unless at the date of publication of the specification it would be obvious to the informed reader that this was so. Where it is not obvious, in the light of then-existing knowledge, the reader is entitled to assume that the patentee thought at the time of the specification that he had good reason for limiting his monopoly so strictly and had intended to do so, even though subsequent work by him or others in the field of the invention might show the limitation to have been unnecessary. It is to be answered in the negative only when it would be apparent to any reader skilled in the art that a particular descriptive word or phrase used in a claim cannot have been intended by a patentee, who was also skilled in the art, to exclude minor variants which, to the knowledge of both him and the readers to whom the patent was addressed, could have no material effect upon the way in which the invention worked.[28]   (*Emphasis added*)

Whether by 'purposive construction' the late Lord Diplock really meant anything much more than 'sensible view' is open to doubt; 'purposive construction' happened to be a phrase currently favoured by their Lordships (particularly in relation to the interpretation of statutes) and *Catnic* was the first instance where it had been applied by them in a patent context. Lord Diplock, in particular, had a predilection towards the long word and convoluted phrase. His utterances include, in the intellectual property area generally:

> This was not an *encomium* calculated to encourage the reader to adapt this alternative method to the manufacture of a wholly different and much more complicated kind of electrical device . . .[29]

> Conspiracy to injure a person in his trade or business is one, slander of goods is another, but most *protean* is that which is generally and nowadays, perhaps misleadingly, described as 'passing off'.

and

> In seeking to formulate general propositions of English law, however, one must be particularly careful to beware of the logical fallacy of the *undistributed middle*.[30]

> . . . and if the extent of the *uncompensatable disadvantage* to each party would not differ widely, it may not be improper to take into account in tipping the balance the relative strength of each party's case as revealed by the evidence adduced on the hearing of the application.[31]

Thus in *Codex Corporation v Racal-Milgo*,[32] also involving a 1949 Act patent, the Court of Appeal after referring to Lord Diplock's speech as providing: 'the clear and authoritative summary of the relevant law',[33] continued:

28   [1982] RPC 183 at 243.
29   [1972] RPC 346 at 362 (*Technograph Printed Circuits v Mills & Rockley* – patent infringement/validity).
30   [1980] RPC 31 at 91, 93 (*Ervin Warnink v J. Townend* – passing-off).
31   [1975] RPC 513 at 543 (*American Cyanamid v Ethicon* – interlocutory injunction in patent infringement).
32   [1983] RPC 369.
33   At 380.

> The question to be asked is one of construction, but of purposive *or realistic* construction through the eyes and with the learning of a person skilled in the art.[34]
>
> (*Emphasis added*)

Certainly, the facts in *Catnic* provided an ideal example for application of the guideline. A claim directed to a building lintel contained the word 'vertically'; if construed in a strict geometric sense of 90° to the horizontal, it meant that the claim had an extraordinarily narrow scope and left the patentee with a virtually worthless grant. If construed more widely as 'substantially vertically', so as to include both the exact 90° direction and also directions a few degrees each side thereof (but not so great as to lose the mechanical function flowing from the upright position of the lintel component in question), then the patentee received a reasonable scope of protection. In the context, the patent being directed to a device for use on a practical building site rather than in a scientific laboratory, it was held that the broader construction should prevail.

The *Catnic* question was usefully redefined in simpler terms by the Court in *Improver Corporation v Consumer Products*[35] at the substantive hearing of the action. The question was split up into three parts, each providing a successive hurdle which the patentee needed to vault over, for any instance where the claim could not on its primary or literal meaning be read onto the alleged infringement. It should be noted that this is a somewhat different situation as compared to that arising in *Catnic* itself, or in for example the later decision in *Société Nouvelle des Bennes Saphem v Edbro*.[36] In both those cases the Court could choose between giving a narrower or a wider meaning to a given term in the Claim ('vertically' and 'slide' respectively). In *Improver Corporation* on the other hand, the relevant term in the claim ('helical spring') could not possibly be interpreted as it stood so as to include the defendant's slitted rubber rod.

According to the redefinition, the Court should ask itself the following sub-questions:

> (1) Does the variant have a material effect upon the way the invention works ? If yes, the variant is outside the claim. If no –
> (2) Would this (i.e. that the variant had no material effect) have been obvious at the date of publication of the patent to a reader skilled in the art ? If no, the variant is outside the claim. If yes –
> (3) Would the reader skilled in the art nevertheless have understood from the language of the claim that the patentee intended that strict compliance with the primary meaning was an essential requirement of the invention ? If yes, the variant is outside the claim.
>
> On the other hand, a negative answer to the last question would lead to the conclusion that the patentee was intending the word or phrase to have not a literal but a figurative meaning (the figure being a form of synecdoche or metonymy) denoting a class of things which included the variant and the literal meaning, the latter being perhaps the most perfect, best-known or striking example of the class.[37]

Although the facts in *Improver Corporation* were complicated by the presence in the specification of an 'equivalents' clause, the decision does nevertheless show that the

---

34 At 381 to 382.
35 [1990] FSR 181.
36 [1983] RPC 345.
37 At 189.

Court will be prepared to receive expert evidence on the *Catnic* factors. The issues of material effect and obviousness (given the invention and the variant, is it obvious to the skilled person that both work in the same way ?), at least, are factual rather than legal in nature. Hence reliance upon evidence for their resolution is quite proper. Other post-*Catnic* cases like the interlocutory decision of the Court of Appeal in *Anchor Building Products v Redland Roof Tiles*[38] illustrate the same point.

The longer-term prospects for the *Catnic* decision may be more uncertain. The history of patent law generally suggests that a House of Lords decision has a vogue, but only until their Lordships restate the law again. And it is likely that in the not too distant future the House of Lords will have before them a case involving squarely the correlation of *Catnic* with sections 125(1) and (3) (including the Protocol on the Interpretation of Article 69 of the EPC) of the 1977 Act. At present, the authority for regarding the two approaches as identical is only at Court of Appeal level.

Guideline 5

The Court is entitled to distinguish between the essential and inessential features of an invention as claimed, and to regard the scope of protection as being circumscribed by the essential features alone.

This guideline is based on the enunciation by Lord Upjohn in 1968 in *Rodi & Wienenberger v Henry Showell*[39] of the latest (pre-1977 Act) form of the doctrine of infringement by equivalents – often in earlier times referred to also as the doctrine of 'pith and marrow'. The doctrine is one of long standing in patent law, although its force has swung to and fro over the decades – being perhaps at its zenith in Victorian and Edwardian days and at its nadir immediately after World War II. Prior to the advent of 'purposive construction', it was central in any situation where the claim could not textually be read onto the alleged infringement.

Thus, in *Benno Jaffe und Darmstadter Lanolin Fabrik v John Richardson*[40] in 1893, a Claim directed to a process for the manufacture of lanolin from wool fat and calling for a step in which waste wool liquors were treated in a centrifugal machine was held infringed by a process using a simple settling tank instead. In *Marconi v British Radio Telegraph & Telephone*[41] in 1911 substitution of an auto transformer for a two-coil transformer, in a patent relating to electric wave telegraphy, was likewise held to infringe. In contrast, in *Nobel v Anderson*[42] in 1895, the claim:

> 1. The manufacture from nitroglycerine and soluble nitrocellulose, of a horny or semi-horny explosive compound, susceptible of granulation, substantially as and for the purposes herein described.

was held not to be infringed by the use of insoluble nitrocellulose in place of soluble.

All three decisions involved the assessment, in their contexts, of the importance of

---

38 [1990] RPC 283.
39 [1969] RPC 367.
40 11 RPC 261.
41 28 RPC 181.
42 12 RPC 164.

the claimed feature not taken by the defendant. In the first two, the Court held in effect that it was not an essential feature whereas in the third it was.

Lord Upjohn's formulation in *Rodi & Wienenberger* was as follows:

> In considering the claim the court must ascertain what are the essential integers of the claim, this remains a question of construction and no general principles can be laid down.
>
> . . .
>
> Secondly, the essential integers having been ascertained, the infringing article must be considered. To constitute infringement the article must take each and every one of the *essential* integers of the claim. *Non-essential* integers may be omitted or replaced by *mechanical equivalents*; there will still be infringement. I believe that this states the whole substance of the 'pith and marrow' theory of infringement.[43] (*Emphasis added*)

Rodi & Wienenberger itself related to expansible watch bracelets. Claim 1 called specifically for pairs of 'U-shaped' bows in the connecting links of the bracelet. The infringer used single C-shaped bows instead; in other words, he extended each of a pair of the opposed U-arms until they met together and formed a single crossbar. It was held that the quality of U-shapedness (which led in turn to use of pairs of bows) was in the context essential, since this provided improved lateral flexibility of the bracelet. Accordingly, there was no infringement.

Another leading pre-1977 Act case is *Van der Lely v Bamfords*.[44] The relevant Claim 11 called for dismountability of the 'hindmost' rake wheels in an agricultural machine; 'hindmost' could not possibly be expanded as a term so as to include the converse arrangement wherein the dismountable rake wheels were 'foremost'. Hence, the patentee could only rely on the doctrine of equivalents and he failed here since the hindmostedness of the rake wheels was held to be an essential (since it was the only fresh novel) feature of the claim. A similar antithesis, as between soluble and insoluble nitrocellulose, arose in the *Nobel v Anderson* case mentioned above.

The correlation of *Catnic* with *Rodi & Wienenberger*, given that both cases were decided under the 1949 Act, is as yet unclarified. Lord Diplock in *Catnic* did not dissent from the enunciations as to law contained in *Rodi & Wienenberger*, *Van der Lely v Bamfords* (also that in the *Beecham Group v Bristol Laboratories*[45] decision of 1977 concerning hetacillin/ampicillin). The question may therefore reasonably be asked – if Lord Upjohn's enunciation was already correct and comprehensive, then why was it necessary for Lord Diplock to restate it at all ? Certainly, much time, effort and words on the part of patent practitioners generally could have been saved in the years since if Lord Diplock had refrained from making his restatement. It should be borne in mind of course that the question of correlation of *Catnic* with the *Rodi & Wienenberger* line of authority is quite separate from the question of correlation of *Catnic* with sections 125(1) and (3) of the 1977 Act.

43 At 391.
44 [1963] RPC 61.
45 [1978] RPC 153.

Guideline 6

The court will not artificially strain the construction of a claim so as to include in the scope of protection a variant (of some given feature or features of the claim) which has a material effect on the working of the patented invention.

This is derived formally from Lord Diplock's speech in *Catnic*, although its genesis is older. It is illustrated by *Catnic*, where the inclination of the vertical lintel back plates in the infringements (6°, 8°) led only to a marginal loss of load bearing capacity (0.6%, 1.2% respectively); also, conversely, by *Rodi & Wienenberger*, where the change from pairs of U-shaped bows to single C-shaped bows had a substantial impact on the functioning of the bracelet.

Guideline 7

In contrast the mere fact that the defendant's product or process, as the case may be, represents an improvement or, conversely, a worsening over the patented product or process does not in itself necessarily enable infringement to be avoided. What matters, even in the case of an improvement which represents such an advance in the art as to be independently patentable of its own accord, is whether or not it comes within the terms of the claim as correctly construed.

Some of the well-known traditional *dicta* in this connection include:

> The superadding of ingenuity to a robbery does not make the operation justifiable. The fact that that new lamp, which is the result of having taken the invention of another person, is an improvement upon that other person's idea does not excuse the person who borrows what is not his. (*Wenham Gas v Champion Gas Lamp*)[46]
> (Divided instead of single chamber, and no projecting burner nozzles)

> Such improvements may involve so much inventive ingenuity as to entitle them to the protection of a patent; but whether they do so or not, and whether they are patented or not, their author cannot use them without the licence of the original Patentee or his assigns during the currency of their Letters Patent.
> (*Gormully and Jeffrey Manufacturing v The North British Rubber Company*)[47]
> (Bicycle outer tire formed with additional flaps to fit under hook-shaped edge of metal rim)

> . . . you cannot avoid infringement by taking a patented machine and then making it work a little worse than it naturally would and then remedying that worseness by another device . . . (*British Thomson-Houston v Metropolitan-Vickers Electrical*)[48]

Claim 1 in *British Thomson-Houston* called for:

> 1. Arrangement for starting synchronous dynamo electric machines by means of an electric motor, in which a series or electrically equivalent connection is provided between the windings of the starting motor and the synchronous machine, for the purpose of effecting in one operation both the speeding up and the synchronising of the synchronous machine with the supply current.

46 9 RPC 49 at 56.
47 15 RPC 245 at 256.
48 45 RPC 1 at 25.

The defendant's machine incorporated an additional choke coil through which a current could be passed in shunt past the starting motor direct to the rotary, so requiring in turn a two-stage rather than a one-stage starting operation.

Although this guideline is ancient rather than modern it has, incidentally, been supported in the recent *Improver Corporation* decision. The Court, after considering the obviousness of the variant in question continued:

> An affirmative answer would not be inconsistent with the variant being an inventive step. For example, the choice of some material for the bendy rod which was *a priori* improbable (e.g. on account of its expense) but had been discovered to give some additional advantage (e.g. painless extraction) might be a variant which obviously worked in the same way as the invention and yet be an inventive step.[49]

Guideline 8

A claim will only be capable of including a variant (of some given feature or features as specified in the claim) which is itself of obviously equivalent function to the claimed feature at the date of publication of the patent.

Expressed in these terms, the guideline is again derived (like Guideline 6) from Lord Diplock's further remarks in *Catnic* as explained in *Improver Corporation*. But it can be regarded as springing from much older roots. *Heath v Unwin*,[50] a case which occupied much time in the Victorian courts of the 1840s and 1850s, culminating in a decision of the House of Lords in 1855, concerned a patent for the manufacture of cast steel using in the melting pot a small amount of manganese carburet. The defendant used instead a mixture of manganese oxide and coal tar; this was much cheaper than manganese carburet. It was proved that the mixture produced, in the high temperature conditions of the melting pot, manganese carburet. But because this was new knowledge, unavailable at the date of the patent, it was held that there was no infringement.

Guideline 9

The Court will not extend the scope of protection so as to include a variant of a feature or features as specified in any instance where the patentee has committed himself to the exclusion of variants.

This final guideline is derived also from *Catnic*, although not spelled out as such in these words. If the patentee has so committed himself, then he must clearly have intended to confine his Claim to its primary meaning. It is suggested that it obviously makes good sense.

Although such committal is relatively uncommon, it can nevertheless arise in a number of ways. The patentee may, for example, have said in his specification that 'by vertical, I mean vertical and not inclinations a little way either side of the perpendicular as well'. Alternatively, there may be an express negative limitation in his Claim 1, say, like:

> 1. A food processing oven suitable for baking biscuits or cookies and comprising . . .

49   At 192.
50   2 WPC 296.

(recitation of structural features) . . . the oven chamber having *no* fixed baffles separating the first, second and third stage zones but the baking trays serving, in operation of the oven, to inhibit migration of heat between the respective stage zones.[51]

maybe originally introduced by the patentee in an excess of caution in face of prior art, or because he then felt that the limitation reflected correctly the *modus operandi* of his invention.

A still further possibility is that he may during the course of initial prosecution of the patent, or in defence to an opposition or application for revocation in the Patent Office, have argued for some particular interpretation of a phrase in his Claim 1 so as to overcome a novelty or obviousness attack. If he has, then the court may be slow to let him subsequently change his tune even if there be no formal estoppel in law. The recent interlocutory decision in *Furr v C.D. Truline (Building Products)*[52] supports this view (claims limited during prosecution to double-flange wall-tying members, to the exclusion of single-flange members; defendant used single-flange members), although it is as yet premature to suggest that the United Kingdom has developed a full-blown doctrine of 'file wrapper estoppel'.

Bibliography

W. Hayhurst, '*Catnic v Hill* – A Commentary', CIPA Volume 12 (1982–83) at 191.
K. Hoffmann, 'Contributory or Indirect Infringement – A Review of the Legal Position in Selected Countries', CIPA Volume 6 (1976–77) at 371.
S. Levy, 'What Constitutes Infringement', *Transactions* Volume LXXXI (1962–63) at C 35.
M. Pendleton, '*Catnic* – Signpost to Where?' [1982] EIPR 79.
B. Sherman, 'Comment – Epilady United Kingdom II', IIC Volume 21 (1990) 866.
A. Walton, 'Purposive Construction' [1984] EIPR 93.

---

51 Patent No. 1525121.
52 [1985] FSR 553.

7 Infringement of Patents (Action)

Introduction

Full discussion of the procedure in a Patents Court action for infringement of a patent (with which is often combined the defendant's counterclaim for revocation of the patent) is beyond the scope of this book; the treatment given below is more by way of outline. Generally, of course, normal High Court procedure, as provided for by the Rules of the Supreme Court, is followed, but matters peculiar to patents are dealt with in comprehensive 0.104[1] of these Rules. Introduced in 1978 following the passing of the 1977 Act, 0.104 covers all proceedings under both the 1977 Act and residual provisions of the 1949 Act.

Since 1990, it has also been possible to sue for infringement (and counterclaim for revocation) in the County Court. This is a nascent jurisdiction, likely to become of increasing importance in future. Procedural aspects of the County Court (insofar as they differ from those of the High Court) and also the interrelation between the two, are discussed separately in succeeding Chapter 8. From the strict nomenclatural standpoint, the Patents Court is part of the Chancery Division of the High Court constituted under section 6(1)(a) of the Supreme Court Act 1981[2] whilst the Patents County Court is a county court designated for this purpose under section 287(1) of the Copyright, Designs and Patents Act 1988[3] (the '1988 Act').

Three stages are involved, essentially, in a patent infringement action in the Patents Court, often referred to more simply as the 'Court'. These are:

(1) Pleadings;
(2) Interlocutory steps;
(3) Trial.

These three stages will be considered first. The important practical topic of interlocutory relief is considered separately at the end of this chapter.

Pleadings

In a straightforward case, the successive pleadings steps are:

Writ
Statement of Claim, with associated Particulars of Infringement
Defence and Counterclaim, with associated Particulars of Objection
Reply and Defence to Counterclaim

Further and/or additional pleading steps can be interposed, for example, a Request

1   White Book 1991.
2   1981 c.54.
3   1988 c.48.

for Further and Better Particulars of the Statement of Claim and a Reply to the same. Amendment of the pleadings is also common, as where a defendant subsequently uncovers some fresh piece of prior art in support of his existing obviousness objection, or where he wishes to adduce an additional ground, for example, insufficiency.

Pleadings are normally rather barren documents, often couched in somewhat involved and/or alternative language, but they do serve to provide each party with the bones of the other party's case. They should contain the material assertions on which the party relies – for example, that Claim 1 is obvious over the teaching of prior Specification No. 123456 – as opposed to the evidential facts by which those assertions are to be subsequently proven at trial. Appendix 6 provides a typical set of Patents Court forms for use in a patent infringement action under the 1977 Act in respect of an 'existing' Patent.

Interlocutory Steps

Once the pleadings have closed, it is necessary to make arrangements for the multitude of further pre-trial steps which have to be undertaken before the action is tried.

Although there are naturally certain resemblances between the further interlocutory procedure in a patent action, and that in a civil action generally in the High Court, the differences are sufficiently substantial for 0.104 to provide virtually a procedural code in its own right. The chronological procedure contemplated by 0.104 is at present (following the changes introduced in 1986):

> Admissions
> Discovery of Documents
> Notice(s) of Experiments
> Summons for Directions

These stages will now be considered briefly in turn.

The purpose of requesting admissions of fact from the other party is to minimise the amount of evidence necessary subsequently, either by way of experimental evidence or by way of experts. At the extreme, a case can even be fought entirely on a statement of facts agreed between the parties, as in *American Cyanamid Company (Dann's) Patent*.[4] Thus a defendant may ask the plaintiff for admissions as to the state of the common general knowledge in the art at the priority date of the patent, whilst the plaintiff may ask the defendant for admissions as to the nature of his process or product – for example, as to whether a certain resinous component had been 'cured' under atmospheric conditions. But the requested admissions must be couched in specific factual terms.

Discovery is of course a standard procedure in the High Court. Each party has to provide discovery of:

> the documents which are or have been in their possession, custody or power relating to matters in question in the action.[5]

---

4   [1970] RPC 306 at 324.
5   O. 24 r.1(1).

In the leading case of over a century ago, this was held to require the disclosure of any document which, it is reasonable to suppose,

> contains information which may – not which must – either directly or indirectly enable the party requiring the affidavit either to advance his own case or to damage the case of his adversary.[6]

In short, therefore, a party must disclose both documents which are favourable to his case and those which are unfavourable.

The Court may often pay considerable attention to discovered documents so far as validity is concerned, since such documents tend to express the writer's spontaneous reaction at the time on the issue involved – long before any question of litigation has surfaced. A good example is provided by Document 10076 in the oil-extended rubber litigation, *General Tire & Rubber v Firestone Tyre & Rubber*.[7] Here, following announcement of the improvement enabled by the invention '20 per cent more rubber now', witness Greer, then an official in the Office of Rubber Reserve, had been asked to provide a summary of the possible methods which General Tire might have been using. Only one of his five suggestions (No. 4) came close to the patented process. His suggestion as to the most probable process (No. 5 on his list) was quite different.

There is however, often, considerable controversy between the parties as to exactly how wide the discovery net extends. In *Fuji Photo Film v Carr's Paper et al.*,[8] for example, discovery of indemnities given by one defendant to his customers was refused as being irrelevant to the question of obviousness of the patent.

Experiments may, again, go either to validity or infringement. A defendant may wish to show, for example, that the experimental directions given in one or more of the examples in the Specification are inadequate. The plaintiff may wish to put in experimental results as to the properties of the defendant's product. Each party's formal notice of experiments has to set out the facts alleged to be established by the experiments, and give full particulars of the technique used. The purpose of such particulars is to enable the other party to decide for himself whether or not to accept the results without forcing the first party to perform the otherwise normally required repetition of the experiment in his (the other party's) presence. Repetition of experiments clearly adds to a party's potential costs liability.

The hearing of the summons for directions takes place before the judge in the Patents Court. Its purpose, broadly, is two-fold. First, the Court will be asked to deal with disputes which may have arisen between the parties out of the preceding interlocutory stages – for example, in connection with the pleadings or requests for further discovery. Secondly, the Court has to make provisions concerning the conduct of the trial. Such matters as to the numbers and identities of the proposed expert witnesses on each side, advance exchange of expert witness statements, possible repetition of experiments and the like, reliance upon models and films, inspection of machinery or plant, appointment of scientific adviser to the Court, preparation of agreed primer, preparation of written resumés of argument, may all have to be considered.

It is important to remember in these connections that the practice of the Patents

---

6 *Compagnie Financière du Pacifique v Peruvian Guano* (1882) II QBD 55 at 63.
7 [1971] RPC 173 at 244.
8 [1989] RPC 713.

Court is, generally speaking, currently in a state of flux following a long period of stability. Complaints as to the costs of, and delay in, patent litigation are perennial. In the past, such complaints have tended to be shrugged aside. But in the last decade or so there has been an increasing realisation that such costs are, essentially, an obstruction to industrial progress. If disputes arising out of patents cannot be dealt with reasonably promptly and efficiently, then the patent system as a whole may wither away. The newly founded Patents County Court provides the Patents Court with a formidable competitor, since the more liberal rules of audience in the Court and its generally more flexible procedure should achieve substantial saving of expense.

Thus the Court will now normally order the exchange of expert witness statements, with cross-examination left until the trial. Such exchange is a *volte face* of the traditional wholly oral mode of giving evidence. It is not clear as to whether the practice of filing written resumés of argument, which can be taken as starting with *American Cyanamid v Ethicon*[9] in 1978 and was subsequently warmly approved in *Société Nouvelle des Bennes Saphem v Edbro*,[10] is likely to become a permanent feature. The Practice Direction of 1989[11] called for a 'reading guide' (preferably agreed) to be provided to the Court in advance of trial; this again is a wholly new development in procedure. An agreed technical primer is often useful in cases of scientific complexity, in order to reduce the volume of evidence. A sample of such a primer is printed in the report of *Olin Mathieson Chemical Corporation v Biorex Laboratories*.[12]

A final point concerns the restricted disclosure of material divulged at interlocutory stage. Each party may possess documents which are in principle discoverable but which contain material of confidential financial or technical nature. The defendant's alleged infringing process may amount in its own right to a highly valuable trade secret. Such material is therefore normally provided in the first place to the other party's professional advisers (counsel, solicitor, patent agent and the like) against suitable undertakings. If the other party then wishes to extend the circle of confidentiality, he may apply to the Court. But such permission is not lightly given. Thus, in *Warner-Lambert v Glaxo Laboratories*,[13] an attempt by the plaintiffs to have the discovery of the defendants' allegedly infringing process made unconditional or alternatively to have it extended so as to cover also (1) the plaintiffs' chief executive in the USA (2) their general counsel in the USA (3) their patent counsel in the USA and (4) an Italian scientist resident and employed by them in Italy was rejected, except for the chief executive (1). In *Roussel Uclaf v Imperial Chemical Industries*[14] disclosure had been made to the plaintiffs' independent expert, a distinguished British chemist, but an attempt to allow further disclosure in turn to the latter's nominee in France for the purpose of conducting consequential experiments on the defendants' process failed.

Trial

The trial will usually be held before one of the specialist patents judges of the High Court, sitting as the Patents Court. The normal order of events is:

9 [1979] RPC 215 at 227.
10 [1980] RPC 345 at 352.
11 [1990] FSR 216.
12 [1970] RPC 157 at 197.
13 [1975] RPC 354.
14 [1989] RPC 59.

Plaintiff's Speech

Plaintiff's Evidence – examination (unless previous written statements) + cross-examination + re-examination of witnesses

Defendant's Evidence – examination (unless previous written statements) + cross-examination + re-examination of witnesses

Defendant's Speech

Plaintiff's Speech-in-reply

Defendant's Speech-in-reply (only if Plaintiff in his speech-in-reply cites any fresh authority or raises any fresh point of law)

Provision is made under section 70(3) of the Supreme Court Act 1981,[15] replacing section 96(4) of the 1977 Act, for the appointment of a scientific adviser to assist the Court. It is usual for advantage to be taken of this facility only in cases of exceptional technical complexity, although the Court of Appeal (being normally composed of technically unqualified judges) tends to be more receptive to the possibility than does the Patents Court. One of the few instances in recent years has been that of *Western Electric v Racal-Milgo*[16] concerning patents for transmission of information between computers. In *Valensi v British Radio Corporation*,[17] concerning a colour television patent, a scientific adviser was first appointed in the Court of Appeal only, in response to a request by the defendant (infringer) and in face of a protest by the plaintiff (patentee) who had won below at the trial. In *Genentech's Patent*,[18] concerning recombinant DNA technology, both parties appear to have agreed to the appointment.

Although the trial is, at root, an oral procedure (in line with High Court civil procedure generally), there is in practice appreciable room for deployment of documentary materials of evidential nature – usually (although not necessarily always) by agreement between the parties. These are over and above the written expert statements, resumés of argument and/or primers already mentioned. Some examples include:

(1) an agreed drawing of the standard machine in the art – say, of the generally used furnace for making rockwool – only depicted in small and somewhat undecipherable scale in the standard textbook in the art;

(2) agreement between the parties that the results in a given scientific paper – say, a study of the effects of a given drug against sleeping sickness in Central Africa, undertaken by a doctor attached to a Nairobi hospital – were in fact observed and accurately recorded (although inferences therefrom could still be disputed); this avoids the need for the doctor to give evidence in person, which he might well be unable to do or otherwise prove excessively costly;

(3) a 'Simkins list'; this is essentially a list (often with abstracts attached) of all the previous unsuccessful proposals to solve the problem now overcome by the patented invention. It is named after Dr Simkins, a witness for the plaintiffs in *Olin Mathieson Chemical Corporation v Biorex Laboratories*.[19]

15   1981 c.54.
16   [1981] RPC 253.
17   [1971] FSR 403.
18   [1989] RPC 147.
19   [1970] RPC 157 at 187.

Selection of witnesses is important. So far as attesting to purely historical fact is concerned – say, the genesis and development of the invention within his own organisation – a patentee may have relatively little choice. But so far as outside expert witnesses are concerned, it has to be remembered that the primary function of evidence is to inform the Court; each party wishes to place before the Court the facts which he considers most relevant to the issues, in the manner most favourable to him. A careful balance may, therefore, have to be struck between retaining an expert who is of sufficient standing to be impressive but yet is not academically over-charged, or super-skilled, or too opinionated. The Court is not chary of making comments in its judgment as to its estimation of the various witnesses – particularly where the dispute has centred on obviousness.

Thus, in *American Cyanamid v Berk Pharmaceuticals*,[20] Whitford J spoke of Professor Locci:

> I may say I found Prof. Locci a most compelling witness – modest, content to deal with any question that was put to him, prepared to consider and give due weight to other people's views, and to give his answers with a detachment which was not perhaps quite so obvious in the evidence given by other witnesses.

But of Professor Shirling:

> Prof. Shirling, a delightful witness who has, unfortunately, on his own showing, been perhaps a little too ready in the past to give evidence on matters with which he was perhaps imperfectly acquainted, . . .

In such cases, any findings of fact based on the Court's preference as to witnesses may be impossible to upset on appeal; the Appeal Court will only have in front of it the transcript of the evidence and not the live witnesses themselves. The vital element of witness demeanour will be missing.

Judgment may be given immediately on conclusion of the proceedings or may be reserved. The latter course is naturally more common when the case involves matters of substantial legal or scientific complexity.

Remedies

If the patentee is successful, he will normally be entitled under section 61(1) of the 1977 Act to an injunction restraining the defendant against future infringement, an inquiry as to damages (or alternatively an account of profits) in respect of past infringement, an order for destruction or delivery up of any infringing articles which the defendant still retains, and also a declaration that the patent is valid and has been infringed.

The precise form, enforcement and possible staying of the injunction (either pending appeal or in other exceptional circumstances) constitute a specialist topic that will not be dealt with here. It is, of course, the injunction which a defendant often fears more than the prospect of paying damages, for the reason that breach of the injunction may expose him to proceedings for contempt of court.

---

20   [1976] RPC 231 at 282, 281.

Assessment of damages also represents a specialist topic. A present leading case is that of *General Tire & Rubber v Firestone Tyre & Rubber* (damages),[21] where Lord Wilberforce reviews the previous case law in depth. The main points in brief are:

> (1) Patent infringement being an 'economic' tort, the general rule is that the measure of damages is to be, so far as possible, that sum of money which will put the injured party (the patentee) in the same position as he would have been in if he had not sustained the wrong.
>
> (2) It follows that where the patentee is himself also manufacturing, damages may be assessed on a 'lost profit' basis – that is, the profit which the patentee would himself have made on the sales lost by him to the defendant as a result of the latter's infringement.
>
> (3) Where, on the other hand, the patentee exploits his invention by way of licence, then the measure is the amount of royalty which he would otherwise have had to pay if he had also taken a licence. Complications may, of course, arise here if other licences have been granted at varying rates, or for a mixture of lump sum + running royalty. This is what happened in *General Tire* itself, where the patentee was a United States Corporation which had settled litigation involving the invention on different bases in different countries.
>
> (4) In instances where neither of the touchstones (2) and (3) given above are available (say, where the infringement takes place early in the life of the patent, before the patentee has commenced any exploitation at all), damages may be assessed on a 'reasonable' notional royalty basis. Exactly what was 'reasonable' might depend on such factors as the standard royalty range (if any) in the trade in question, potential profitability, necessary development expenditure by the infringer and the like; the Court may take into account anything which it considers relevant in the circumstances of the case.

An 'account of profits' – the successful patentee's other alternative – means that he is awarded instead the profits made by the infringer out of his infringement. The proper accountancy basis for calculating the profits may provoke further dispute – particularly where the infringing article is only one item in the defendant's overall product range, and overhead costs have to be correctly apportioned. Generally, this option is disfavoured; it can be a chancy avenue for the patentee, particularly since he normally has to opt one way or another at a time (judgment in the trial) when he lacks full information as to the defendant's figures.

Costs are normally awarded to the successful party, as in accordance with normal civil procedure; apportionment may be made, however, in certain cases, say, where the plaintiff wins on infringement but fails on validity (so as to render him the overall loser) or *vice versa*, or where the plaintiff sues on two patents but only wins on one. There is special statutory provision (section 63) for the case where the plaintiff succeeds on the valid part of an only partially valid patent. Costs may be allowed here only if the plaintiff can show that the specification was originally framed in good faith and with reasonable skill and knowledge.

21   [1976] RPC 197.

Appendix 9 provides a typical example of an eventual Order of the Court, in the more complex type of case.

Ancillary Aspects

Attention up to now has been focused on the main topic: the straightforward patent infringement action in the Court. But in practice there are a considerable number of ancillary matters which may also arise and which need review. These matters, constituting rather a mixed bag, will now be dealt with in turn in the order in which they appear in the 1977 Act itself:

Patent Office jurisdiction

If, but only if, both parties agree (and the Patent Office considers the case suitable for its determination), the infringement action can be heard by the Patent Office instead of the Court (section 61(3) of the Act). The potential benefits of this course should not be overlooked. The Patent Office Hearing Officer will normally be much more familiar with the art in question already as compared even to one of the Patents Judges, and hence the proceedings can be shortened and thereby rendered less expensive. Patent Office procedure is, moreover, inherently less cumbersome than that of the High Court, thereby simplifying the interlocutory stages also.

The Patent Office is somewhat restricted, on the other hand, as regards the relief it can grant. Only relief by way of damages (although there is no limit to their amount) and/or declaration of patent validity and infringement is available. Injunctive relief, orders for delivery up or destruction on oath, and an account of profits (as an alternative to damages) can only be granted by the Court; whether or not the absence of these other potential remedies matters – and in any event a defendant who just repeats his infringing activities obviously does so at peril of a second similar action – is up to the parties themselves to decide in the case in question.

Innocent infringement

Damages (or an account of profits) in respect of past infringements may be refused (section 62(1) of the Act) if the infringer can show that he acted in innocence of the patent in suit. This may not be easy for him to establish, particularly if both parties are working in a generally patent-conscious industry; excessive naïveté is liable to be scrutinised carefully by the Court, as in *Lancer Boss v Henley Forklift*.[22] Certainly it is normally wise for a patentee to mark his own products with their patent number; it is statutorily laid down in section 62(1) that mere general marking of 'patent' or 'patented' may not necessarily suffice to impute knowledge and destroy innocence.

Partially valid patent

Many a patent (particularly in the case of 1949 Act patents granted under a more lax examination system) will be partially valid only; Claim 1 may be invalid for lack of novelty or obviousness, while the later narrower dependent claims survive. Relief may

---

22 [1975] RPC 307 at 318 and 319.

be granted in such cases (section 63) in respect of the valid part of the patent, but it may be subject to the condition that the patentee attends to any necessary amendment. And damages in respect of past infringement will only be allowed if the patentee can show that the original patent specification was framed 'in good faith and with reasonable skill and knowledge'.

The proviso can raise interesting questions. In *Page v Brent Toy Products*[23] (toy building blocks) the hurdle was overcome on evidence by the patent agent who had originally drafted the claim that it was a modification of a 'fairly broad claim' which he had originally written deliberately in order to 'draw the Patent Office search report'. In *Ronson Products v Lewis (Westminster)*,[24] on the other hand, evidence that a patent agent had misinterpreted his clients' instructions as to the mode of operation of a valve mechanism in a smoker's lighter was fatal. It can accordingly be risky for a patentee not to check the specification prepared by his patent agent. More recently, in *Hallen v Brabantia (UK)*,[25] good faith was found on the strength of the evidence of the United Kingdom patent agent alone, to the exclusion of that of the United States attorney in charge of the priority United States application and also of the United States inventor.

Continued user

There is a limited third party right (section 64(1)) as mentioned in Chapter 6 (see page 90). The section was reworded, in clearer form, by the 1988 Act. Under the provision, a person who can show that before the priority date of a patent he had done either a putative infringing act, or had likewise made effective and serious preparations to do such act, may be permitted to continue that act. But variants are not provided for. So if he had made a putatively infringing prototype, he could continue to make and sell that prototype but probably not any improved version. Of course, if his pre-patent activities were of such nature and conducted in such circumstances as to rank as a proper prior use, then the patent would be invalid (until amended if possible) in any event and he need not rely on these provisions.

Certificate of contested validity

If a patent successfully survives a validity attack, then a certificate of contested validity may be obtainable under section 65(1). The advantage of this is that it empowers the patentee, in the next infringement suit on the patent, to obtain (if he wins again) costs on the higher 'solicitor and own client' scale (section 65(2); this is now reckoned, following the 1986 revision in High Court costs rules generally, to amount to the indemnity basis of O.62 r.15.

Co-owners and the like

Each co-patentee can sue for infringement in his own name (section 66). So can assignees and exclusive licensees (section 67) (but not mere ordinary licensees), provided that damages (or an account of profits) may be refused here if the relevant instrument

---

23   67 RPC 4 at 21.
24   [1963] RPC 103 at 137 and 138.
25   [1990] FSR 134 at 142 to 144.

whereby title was acquired was not entered timeously on the Patent Office Register (section 68).

Past damages

The normal limitation period of six years applies. This period can, however, in certain circumstances commence with the date on which the patent application was published (as distinct from the date of subsequent grant) even though action cannot actually be brought until grant has taken place (sections 69(2) and (3)). The principal requirement is that there should have been infringement of the patent in its published format (that is, assuming it to have been notionally granted at that time) as well as in its later actually granted format.

Threats

The 1977 Act continues to provide remedies against groundless threats of infringement proceedings (section 70), although the scope of such remedies is substantially less than it was under the 1949 Act (section 65) since groundless threats against manufacturers and importers of a product, users of a process, are now excluded under section 70(4). Customers are accordingly still included, however, and this is often an important category for commercial purposes in any event. A manufacturer may well be willing to run the risk of infringement for himself; many a customer of his, on the other hand, will automatically shy away and take his business away the moment he hears from a third party that he may be involved in a patent action. As put picturesquely by Lord Esher M.R. as long ago as 1892 in *Ungar v Sugg*:

> . . . a man had better have . . . anything happen to him in this world, short of losing all his family by influenza, than have a dispute about a patent.[26]

In the recent case of *Johnson Electric Industrial Manufactory v Mabuchi-Motor*,[27] for example, the threat was in respect of subsequent use of the patented electric motor components, in electrically powered equipment such as vacuum cleaners, hedge-cutters and the like. Since this was not use of a process, section 70(4) provided no shield.

If a threat is made, it is open to the threats action defendant (normally the patentee) to justify his threat by showing that the device, apparatus or process in question constituted an infringement of a valid patent. It is also open to him to argue, alternatively or in addition, that the communication in question (circular, letter, advertisement, spoken words, as the case may be) did not in the first place constitute a formal threat. There is here, naturally, a delicate tightrope to be walked; thus, in *Berkeley & Young v Stillwell, Derby* a letter to a customer containing the sentence:

> In our opinion, this device is copied from our Vibralux sign for which we hold all British Patents, and we are applying for an injunction against the makers to stop the manufacture of these machines . . . [28]

26 9 RPC 113 at 117.
27 [1986] FSR 280.
28 57 RPC 291 at 302.

was held to be a threat, whereas in *Surridge's Patents v Trico-Folberth*,[29] words spoken by the defendants' travellers along the lines 'There is an action going on' (and implying that 'you may therefore have difficulty in getting a further supply of blades') escaped.

Moreover, a mere general warning to the trade, or mere general advice to the trade as to the progress of an existing infringement action, need not necessarily constitute a threat. An instructive case on the topic is *Alpi Pietro v John Wright*,[30] where the proposed notice to be issued to the trade was in the terms:

> Take note that John Wright & Sons (Veneers) Limited and Aaronson Brothers Limited (Plaintiffs) intent on protecting their rights in the manufacture and importation of straight grain veneers, have begun an action in the Chancery Division of the High Court to restrain Avalon Furniture Limited (Defendants) from infringing letters patent No. 835, 075 granted in respect of an invention entitled 'Methods of Producing Veneers and Resulting Products' . . .

and relief (at the interlocutory stage) was refused. The Court held that the evidence was unsatisfactory to show that a specific warning finger was being pointed by the warning at the threats plaintiff.

It is also statutorily provided (section 70(5)) that in any event a mere notification of the existence of a patent does not constitute a threat. Such notification letters can, therefore, still safely be sent to customers of the possible infringer as well as to the infringer himself.

Declaration of non-infringement

This procedure (section 71) enables a person who fears that he may infringe to clarify his position before commencing manufacture, or the like, in earnest. If he has already unsuccessfully applied to the patentee for an acknowledgement that his manufacture or the like does not infringe, full details having been provided, then he may apply to the Court or the Patent Office for a formal declaration of non-infringement instead.

Interlocutory Injunction

The prospect of obtaining interlocutory injunctive relief against a defendant is often attractive to the plaintiff in a patent infringement action. By obtaining an injunction in advance of trial, that is, at the 'interlocutory' stage, the plaintiff can keep the defendant off the market for an appreciable interval in the meantime. Such interval may be for some one and a half to two years, since an interlocutory injunction will normally have to be applied for shortly after commencement of the infringement proceedings and the period between writ and trial is generally reckoned as being at least two years in the Patents Court (although it should be less in the Patents County Court). There are the further attractions (1) that the procedure is often relatively cheaper than a full trial, since the evidence on infringement and validity need not be complete (a matter discussed further below) and is generally given in written (affidavit) not oral form, and (2) that an injuncted defendant may in any event then decide to abandon his activities entirely and switch to an alternative product or process, as the case may be; in the latter

29   53 RPC 420 at 429.
30   [1972] RPC 125 at 133.

instance, the defendant may not re-emerge as a competitor even if the plaintiff is later unsuccessful at the trial.

It is, of course, necessary that the plaintiff give a cross-undertaking in damages, as a condition of being granted injunctive relief, in case he should lose at the eventual trial. And if there is doubt as to the reliability of the cross-undertaking, the plaintiff may be required to provide supporting security at the interlocutory stage. In *Improver Corporation v Remington Consumer Products*[31] the plaintiff had to provide a bank guarantee of £5.5 million – although this was an exceptional case.

Nevertheless, the grant of interlocutory relief is by no means automatic; it remains, at the end of the day, an exceptional remedy – given at the Court's discretion – for which exceptional cause has to be shown. The leading modern decision in this area of the law generally, *American Cyanamid v Ethicon* (Interlocutory),[32] was in fact enunciated in a patent dispute in 1974.

Lord Diplock's judgment in *American Cyanamid* enunciated the need for the Court to take a step-wise approach to the matter, in the given set of circumstances. To summarise his somewhat intricate language, the steps are:

(1) Does P (plaintiff) have an arguable case ? If the answer is 'no', P fails *in limine*. But if the answer is 'yes', proceed to step (2).

(2) Assuming that P was to win at trial, can he be adequately compensated by damages ? If the answer is 'yes', then no injunction. But if the answer is 'no', proceed to step (3).

(3) Assuming, conversely, that D (defendant) was to win at trial, could D be adequately compensated for his interim exclusion from the market by P's cross-undertaking in damages? If the answer is 'no', then no injunction. But if the answer is 'yes', then such adequacy provides in itself no ground to refuse injunction; this conclusion is not tantamount to finding that an injunction should be granted, since other reasons for refusal may still exist. So then (as well as in any case where 'adequacy' of damages in step (2) or (3) is – on the evidence adduced – doubtful) proceed to step (4).

(4) Where lies the balance of convenience generally ? If the balance is tilted neither way, then proceed to step (5).

(5) Where lies the *status quo* ? This should be preserved, as far as possible. But if this test still fails to tip the scales one way or the other, then proceed to the final step (6).

(6) Which party has the apparently stronger case on the evidence adduced ? Decide in favour of the stronger party, provided that there is a clear disproportionation in relative strength.

The *American Cyanamid* approach can be approximated – albeit rather crudely – to that of a boxing match lasting six rounds. Either plaintiff or defendant can gain a knock-out win in rounds before the final bell goes; but if neither is knocked out, the plaintiff only obtains his interlocutory injunction if he is, at the final bell, decisively ahead on points. A draw or thereabouts must inevitably lead to refusal of the injunction.

31   IPD 12067.
32   [1975] RPC 513 at 541 and 542.

Some of the phraseology employed in *American Cyanamid* has been clarified by subsequent case law. It now appears fairly certain that 'arguable' (in step (1)) means something (maybe not very much) more than non-frivolous; there should be some reasonable prospect of success. 'Adequacy' in steps (2) and (3) has to be looked at both from the standpoints of inherent adequacy and actual adequacy – that is to say, of inherent suitability of the damages remedy in the circumstances of the case and actual ability (of the plaintiff or defendant as it may be) to pay those likely damages. He may be a man of straw and/or doubtful probity. 'Balance of convenience' in step (4) is described more correctly, although less elegantly, as 'balance of the risk of doing an injustice'.[33] '*Status quo*' in step (5) means normally (although not always) the state of affairs at date of writ rather than at date of hearing. *Potters Ballotini v Weston Baker*[34] illustrates the exception; this was a case where the Court of Appeal was influenced by the fact that by the date of hearing in that Court (the Court of first instance having refused the injunction) the defendant's factory for making ballotini, erected with the aid of the allegedly confidential information of the plaintiff, was already in operation. Maintenance of the *status quo* means also that if the application for interlocutory relief is launched *quia timet*, that is in advance of any actual potential infringing act, or immediately on commencement, such celerity may favour the patentee; *contra*, if the patentee has waited until the defendant has acquired a distinct foothold in the market.

A further point concerns the interrelation of the steps, of steps (2), (3) and (4) in particular. There may be overlap since a given commercial circumstance may be relevant under one or more. For example, if the grant of the injunction would force the defendant to lay off workers and threaten him with bankruptcy, both adequacy of damages (step (2)) and balance of convenience generally (step (4)) may be affected – the former because a bankrupt defendant would be incapable of paying damages and the latter because the creation of unemployment may well be regarded as *contra* to the public interest.

From a practical standpoint, the balance of convenience often dominates. There is no set list of constituent factors for such balance. Rather, it covers the whole bundle of the applicable economic and commercial circumstances. Some of the considerations often canvassed are as follows:

> (1) *Relative size of parties.* If the contest is one between commercial giants, each perfectly capable of looking after itself and of self-evident financial substance, then the Court may be slow to grant any injunction. This was the position in *Polaroid v Eastman Kodak*.[35] If the parties are of unequal size, then the Court may be sympathetic to the patentee if he is the smaller of the two – particularly if the defendant can be portrayed as deliberately trying to 'muscle in' on a market for a new product which the patentee has carefully built up under the protective umbrella of his patent, and is undercutting in price – so as to have the possible effect of driving the patentee out of business. Cases here include *Corruplast v George Harrison*[36] and *E.A.R. Corporation v Protector*

---

33 *Fleming Fabrications v Albion Cylinders* [1989] RPC 47 at 54.
34 [1977] RPC 202.
35 [1977] RPC 379.
36 [1978] RPC 761.

Safety Products.[37] *Contra*, if the defendant is smaller and capable of making only a small dent at best in the plaintiff's market. Is the defendant's bite that of a crocodile or a gnat?

(2) *Bridgehead.* If the patent has only a short period to run before expiry or possible compulsory licensing (in case of a new existing patent granted under the 1949 Act), the Court may be reluctant to provide the defendant with a flying start at that time. This is what the defendant would have, to the detriment of the patentee and other more law-abiding potential competitors, if an injunction were refused. In *Monsanto v Stauffer Chemical*[38] (three years to run before compulsory licence date), this consideration defeated the usual 'large Co.' presumption against injunctive relief just mentioned above.

(3) *'Snowball' effect.* This can be regarded as a variation of the 'bridgehead' factor (2). The Court may be more prepared to grant an injunction if it can be persuaded by the plaintiff's evidence that refusal would lead to a flood of other infringers entering the market also. This factor can be particularly pertinent if the product is likely in any event to enjoy only a brief period of commercial success – say, if it is a new kind of toy robot.

(4) *Stultification of investment.* If the defendant has invested heavily in new equipment the Court may be slow to let it remain idle pending trial of the action. Similarly, if he has invested in a distributorship or the like which he would be bound to lose permanently if injuncted now.

(5) *Loss of employment.* This consideration has already been mentioned. It can, of course, cut both ways. The defendant's activities may be likely to cause diminution, or even cessation, of the plaintiff's trade or *vice versa*. If either or both parties import, as opposed to manufacture, then the quantum of possible loss may be much less in any event, and hence become a less significant factor.

(6) *Public interest.* In the case where, for example, the defendant's alleged infringement consists of a unique and medically valuable drug, the Court may be reluctant to grant any kind of injunction (interlocutory or permanent) but leave a plaintiff to a remedy in damages. A case here is *Roussel-Uclaf v G. D. Searle*,[39] concerning the cardiac drug known as disopyramide. A similar approach (at least so far as interlocutory relief is concerned) may apply if the patentee has never up to now actually exercised his patent, so as to leave the market supplied by the defendant only.

(7) *Delay.* This has always been relevant. A patentee must act promptly once he is aware of the infringement, if he is to obtain interlocutory relief, although there is no set time limit. A rule of thumb is that action should preferably be taken within three months from the start of the defendant's activities. Beyond this sort of time a patentee may be hard-pressed to find any excuse for his delay; and, of course, the longer he delays the stronger the defendant's argument that it would now be unreasonable to stop him becomes. In *Carroll v Tomado*,[40] an interregnum of around five months was permitted, the defendants having delayed advertising their product so that the plaintiffs only first heard of it

37 [1980] FSR 574.
38 [1984] FSR 574.
39 [1977] FSR 125.
40 [1971] RPC 401.

some three months late. In *Minnesota Mining and Manufacturing v Johnson & Johnson*,[41] on the other hand, an unexplained gap of eight months in the plaintiff's handling of the matter was fatal against them.

(8) *Product quality.* If the defendant's product is of markedly inferior quality to the patentee's, and hence likely to lead to a degree of permanent harm to the patentee, incalculable simply from defendant's sales achieved by trial, then the Court may well be more willing to grant relief than in the case of comparable quality. *Contra*, perhaps, if the defendant (although arguably working within the patent) is nevertheless supplying a quite different sector of the market – say, carburettors for cars in the £10,000 as opposed to £100,000 price bracket.

The underlying motivation of the Court in deciding such applications is often described as one of seeking the best form of temporary peace-keeping. The following *dictum* puts the point well:

> . . . seeking to find a way which will best preserve the position in the meantime and secure the *minimum harm* to any person who, in the end, turns out to have been *wrongly* granted or *wrongly* refused interim relief.   (*Emphasis added*)
> (*per* Goff L.J. in *Netlon v Bridport-Gundry*)[42]

It is also inherent in the presently favoured re-definition of 'balance of convenience' as 'balance of the risk of doing an injustice', already mentioned.[43] In particular, the Court will not allow the *American Cyanamid* approach (which in principle is quite favourable to the patentee) to become by over-rigid application an engine of oppression. This is highlighted by the decision of the Court of Appeal in *Brupat v Sandford Marine Products*,[44] where a defendant of extremely modest financial standing (normally a good reason for grant of relief since it gives rise to doubt as to their eventual capacity to pay damages if infringement is found at the trial) was allowed to continue provided that he pay in the interim into an escrow account a reasonable royalty.

As an alternative to grant of interlocutory relief, the Court may order a speedy trial; indeed, often the main purpose of an application for an interlocutory relief is to obtain such an order.

Appeal

There is an appeal as of right from any decision of the Court (now the Patents Court) as to patent infringement (and associated counterclaim for revocation if any) to the Court of Appeal. The position where infringement proceedings are taken in the first place in the Patent Office instead of the Court (either under section 61(3) by agreement of the parties or under section 71 by way of application for declaration of non-infringement) is dealt with in Chapter 11.

The appeal can be in respect of issues of law (for example, does 'keeps' in section 60(1)(a) of the Act include 'warehousing' ?) and/or fact (for example, is it obvious to

41 [1971] FSR Supp (1) at 623.
42 [1979] FSR 530 at 535.
43 At page 113.
44 [1983] RPC 61.

the notional skilled man in the art to replace upward spinning in the given textile machine by downward spinning ?). The appeal is also, strictly, by way of rehearing – that is to say, the Court of Appeal approaches the issues *de novo* and is perfectly entitled to differ from the Court if it comes to opposite conclusions.

But the concept of there being a rehearing is not taken to extremes. The evidence is normally the same as that below; the witnesses are not reheard, reliance being placed instead on the transcript. Permission to adduce fresh evidence is difficult to obtain; the usual triad of conditions laid down in *Ladd v Marshall*[45] for civil cases generally (previous diligence + importance of the new evidence + credibility of the same) may have to be fulfilled. It follows that the Court of Appeal may be reluctant to overrule the trial judge's conclusions as to fact insofar as they are influenced by his views (as stated in the judgment) as to witness demeanour and the like. The Court of Appeal will generally have only the cold print, not the living person, in front of them. Sometimes a distinction can be drawn as between findings of primary fact (for example as to what was the state of common general knowledge in the field involved at the relevant date) and inferences drawn from such findings (for example does such common general knowledge taken together with the disclosure of document X render the subject-matter of Claim 1 obvious?).

Furthermore, the Court of Appeal is always interested as to why the appellant considers the decision below to be wrong; grounds of appeal have to be defined. They may also be reluctant to overthrow the exercise of a discretion by the High Court – for example, refusal of permission to amend a patent on ground of unreasonable delay. On a practical note, there has been introduced in more recent times the requirement for the parties to file skeleton arguments in advance of trial; their purpose is more to identify the points in issue than to provide complete expositions on those points, and hence to expedite hearing of the appeal.

From the Court of Appeal there is a further appeal with leave (either of the Court of Appeal or, if refusal there, of the House of Lords) to the House of Lords itself. Generally, it is necessary to show that an issue of law of general public importance is involved; an issue of fact is usually not enough, however great the commercial significance of the dispute to the parties. This is exemplified in the contrasting cases of *Beecham Group v Bristol Laboratories*[46] (involving, in relation to a comparatively unimportant antibiotic, the question of whether the early 1900 'Saccharin' doctrine as to infringing importation still held sway in 1973) with *Beecham Group's (Amoxycillin) Application*[47] involving an obviousness dispute in relation to an antibiotic of infinitely greater importance. A typical modern example under the 1977 Act is provided by the Court of Appeal's grant of leave in *Allen & Hanburys v Generics*[48] involving, *inter alia*, the issue of whether a compulsory licence under the transitional provisions of the 1977 Act would run from the date of application for the licence or, instead, from date of grant only.

45 1954 1 WLR 1489.
46 [1978] RPC 153.
47 [1980] RPC 261.
48 [1986] RPC 203.

Bibliography

J. Bailey, 'Teaching the Court', CIPA Volume 1 (1971–72) at 343.
G. Cooke, 'Discovery in Actions for the Infringement of Patent', *Transactions* Volume LXXXI (1962–63) at C 1.
M. Hoyle, 'Interlocutory injunctions in intellectual property disputes' [1988] EIPR 112.
B. Reid, 'Agents in Court', CIPA Volume 10 (1980–81) at 222.

8 The Patents County Court

History and Background

The creation of the Patents County Court in 1990, under the enabling provisions[1] of the Copyright, Designs and Patents Act 1988, represents the first serious attempt on the part of the legislature to deal with the high cost of patent litigation. An initial effort in the 1949 Act, under which the Patent Office had rights to adjudicate upon infringement/validity disputes, had essentially failed because of the inbuilt limitations of relevant section 67 (necessity for the parties to agree to use the Patent Office as forum; damages awards to be restricted to a maximum of £1000) coupled with the mishandling (by the parties) of the first case under the jurisdiction.[2] Somewhat wider powers were accorded to the Patent Office under the later 1977 Act. But the reluctance of the Court to stay its own jurisdiction in favour of the Patent Office (unless wholly exceptional circumstances, as in the 'very unusual'[3] case of *Hawker Siddeley Dynamics Engineering v Real Time Developments*,[4] were present) meant that in practice the situation was little ameliorated.

The reasons for the high cost are multiple. Probably the most important in the past have been the traditional Court requirement for evidence to be wholly oral (although that requirement has very recently been modified by the practice of exchanging witness statements) taken with the archaic demarcation rules governing representation of the parties (which have typically resulted in the presence in Court at trial of no less than four professional persons on each side – solicitor + patent agent + QC + junior counsel – even though only one is speaking at any given time). Implementation of the Courts and Legal Services Act 1990[5] may lead in future to some improvement in the latter respect. But absurd results could, and regrettably still do, arise under the traditional system. For example, in the 1978 case of *American Cyanamid v Ethicon*[6] no less than 103 days were spent in trying an action on a patent involving an absorbable surgical suture (not a particularly complex subject-matter from the technological standpoint) and having as Claim 1 simply:

> 1. A sterile article for the surgical repair or replacement of living tissue, the article being readily absorbable by living tissue and being formed from a polyhydroxyacetic acid ester.

In *Minnesota Mining and Manufacturing v Rennicks (UK)*,[6a] the plaintiff's costs were apparently in excess of £2 million for a patent relating to retroreflective sheeting (as used in road signs and the like).

---

1 Sections 287 to 292.
2 *Central Electricity Generating Board v Chamberlain and Hookham* [1958] RPC 217 at page 224, line 51 to page 225, line 36.
3 *Ferro v Escol* [1990] RPC 651 at page 653, line 27.
4 [1983] RPC 395.
5 1990 c.41.
6 [1979] RPC 215.
6a [1992] RPC 331.

The immediate genesis of the Patents County Court lay in the following:

> Green Paper on 'Intellectual Property Rights and Innovation'
>   (1983)[7]
> White Paper on 'Intellectual Property and Innovation' (1986)[8]
> Oulton Committee Report (1987)

The White Paper had proposed that the primary forum for infringement/validity disputes should be the Patent Office rather than the Court, and that the Patent Office should for this purpose be given additional powers including that to grant injunctions. The proposal proved highly controversial. In the cautious language of the subsequent Oulton Committee Report:

> 6. The reaction to the White Paper has been mixed, attracting strong opposition from the legal profession and strong support from others, including the Chartered Institute of Patent Agents.

In the end, the Oulton Committee recommended the introduction of a Patents County Court.

Overview

The broad position is that the Patents County Court is constituted as a part of the county courts system generally. It therefore works under the County Court Rules as a whole, but with certain important modifications to reflect the particular intended function of the Court. These modifications include:

> (a) removal of the normal county court limit as to damages that can be awarded;
> (b) parties can be represented by a patent agent alone;
> (c) a special code of interlocutory procedure.

Jurisdiction

A patentee wishing to undertake infringement/validity proceedings can accordingly now commence either in the Patents Court or in the Patents County Court. There are provisions[9] permitting, at discretion, transfer of proceedings from the Patents County Court to the Patents Court and vice versa. The latter apply also to proceedings already in existence at the formal date of opening of the Patents County Court. In considering transfer (either way) the Court is required to have regard to the financial position of the parties.[10] Transfer to the Patents County Court, alternatively refusal of transfer

---

7   Cmnd 9117.
8   Cmnd 9712.
9   Sections 40 to 42, County Courts Act 1984.
10   Section 289(2), 1988 Act.

from the Patents County Court, may be ordered notwithstanding that the proceedings are likely to raise an important question of law or fact.[11]

Practice under the transfer provisions naturally is still in an early stage of development. But it appears that the Patents Court may be reluctant to permit transfer where the party applying for transfer (at least) is not proposing to be represented in the Patents County Court by a patent agent.[12] It is only where there is representation by the patent agent alone, to the exclusion of counsel, that the intended purpose of reduction in litigation costs is achieved.

As for the type of subject-matter coming within the jurisdiction of the Patents County Court, this is defined as being proceedings:

(a) relating to patents or designs; or
(b) ancillary to, or arising out of the same subject-matter as, proceedings relating to patents or designs.

The precise scope of 'ancillary' proceedings is at present uncertain. But it would be reasonably clear that an action involving both patent infringement and misuse of confidential information concerning the patented subject-matter is embraced.

Procedure

The special code of interlocutory procedure is outlined in new Order 48A of the County Court Rules (contained in the 'County Court Practice', the so-called Green Book). As compared to the conventional procedure of the Patents Court, as discussed in previous Chapter 7, the accent is upon speed and simplicity. To this end, the initial pleadings are required to be fuller – more akin in this respect to the requirements of Patent Office pleadings; further pleadings (for example, a request for particulars) are restricted; notices to admit (and interrogatories) require the permission of the Court; the Court may order a Patent Office report on any question of fact or opinion arising (in addition to the usual power of appointing scientific advisers); discovery also needs the permission of the Court.

The further handling of the action generally, including the issues just mentioned, is dealt with at a so-called 'preliminary consideration' following an application for directions which has to be filed by each party within 14 days of close of pleadings. The full list of matters prescribed in this connection by Rule 8(5) is:

(a) the witnesses who may be called;
(b) whether their evidence should be given orally or in writing or any combination of the two;
(c) the exchange of witness statements;
(d) the provision of Patent Office Reports;
(e) the use of assessors at the hearing;
(f) transfer to the High Court;
(g) reference to the Court of Justice of the European Communities;

11 *Ibid.*
12 *GEC-Marconi v Xyllyx View Data Terminals* [1991] FSR 319; and *Memminger-Iro GmbH v Trip-lite* [1991] FSR 322; IPD 15053 (on appeal).

(h) applications for discovery and inspection;
(i) applications for leave under rule 6 above; and
(j) written reports of the results of any experiments of which particulars have been given under rule 8 (2)(c).

It appears from early practice that the Court will have thoroughly read all the documents in advance of the oral hearing, and will expect advocacy to be both succinct and limited to the real points of substance. In this respect, the trial procedure is perhaps to be likened more to that of contested oppositions in the European Patent Office than either to that of the Patents Court or even the Patent Office. The first decision of the Court in a full-scale patent action was that in *Daily v Etablissements Fernard Berchet*[13] involving the 'Locopousse' toy push-train. In *Prout v British Gas*[14] it effectively made new law, by holding that prior experimental public user of a kind which was reasonably necessary to prove and test the patented invention did not invalidate. *APH Road Safety v Moxon Plant Hire* (Patent No. 2183276 relating to traffic bollards, unreported) was the first case in which both parties were represented by patent agents.

As for costs, these would normally be on the more restrictive county court scales, although there is power to award on the more generous High Court basis. Appeals from the Patents County Court lie to the Court of Appeal.

Although the eventual role of the Patents County Court in the adjudication of patent disputes overall is naturally still unsettled, it is submitted that the legislative experiment is intrinsically worthy of support by users of the patent system.

Bibliography

P. Ford (His Honour Judge Ford), 'Patent Litigation: A Better Deal for Litigants?' [1990] EIPR 435.
D. Gladwell, 'The Patents County Court' CIPA Volume 18 (1988–89) 422.
A. Webb, 'Patent Litigation in the UK – The New Patents County Court' [1991] EIPR 203.
Patents County Court Users' Guide 1990 (Central Office of Information).

13 [1991] RPC 587; appeal allowed at [1992] FSR 533.
14 [1992] FSR 478.

9 Employee Inventions

Introduction

One of the most radical changes introduced by the 1977 Act has been in connection with inventions made by employees. A statutory code has been enacted. In many instances the rights of the employee have been enhanced. The new provisions only apply to inventions actually made subsequent to the appointed day of 1 June 1978 for the new Act.

Generally speaking, the new regime has failed to generate as much litigation as might have been expected back in 1978. A number of factors may account for this including a lack of appreciation on the part of employees of the new regime, the often lengthy lead-time between the date of making an invention and its subsequent exploitation, and the deterrent effect of costs (even on Patent Office scales) and delay so far as the employee is concerned. But the provisions are likely to assume increasing importance in the future.

Historical Background

The new law is most easily appreciated against the backcloth of the old, which will of course continue to apply in any event to inventions made before 1 June 1978. Patents on such inventions may still persist until around the middle of the present decade.

The old law was largely (although not entirely) common law. It provided, generally speaking, that the skilled technical or scientific employee would hold any invention which he made in the regular course of his employment in trust on behalf of his employer. This was so even if there was no express provision in the employee's service contract (although there almost invariably is nowadays) to that effect. Thus, the employer was regarded as the true owner of the invention, and the Court would not hesitate to step in if necessary and compel a recalcitrant employee to come to heel; he might be compelled to execute an assignment, as in *Triplex Safety Glass v Scorah*,[1] or the documents required for obtaining foreign patent protection for the invention, as in *British Celanese v Moncrieff*.[2]

Such an attitude was not unreasonable. It was after all the employer who, in the ultimate, provided the skilled employee with the facilities (the laboratory, apparatus and problem in the first place) for making the invention; by virtue of the very nature of his job, it was quite possible that an invention would arise. In short, the making of inventions was one of the tasks which he was employed as such to do.

A similar attitude was taken by the Court towards those who, although perhaps not employed primarily in a technical or scientific capacity, nevertheless stood otherwise in a fiduciary relation to their employer. A prime example here is that of the company director, as in the case of *Fine Industrial Commodities v Powling*.[3] *Worthington Pumping*

1   55 RPC 21.
2   65 RPC 165.
3   71 RPC 254 at 283.

Engine v Moore[4] involved the general manager of the English branch of a foreign firm, with like effect.

The converse, however, applied to those employees who were not employed for their technical or scientific skill even if their contract of employment purported to transfer any inventions to the employer. Thus, in *Electrolux v Hudson*,[5] the stores man was allowed to retain his invention concerning an adaptor for vacuum cleaners, using disposable bags, which he had made in his own time at home in the evening and using his own materials, even though his employers were engaged in this field. The employer's 'Standard Conditions of Employment', which purported to transfer all rights in any invention made by any employees relating to any article manufactured or marketed by the employer, were held to be unenforceable against him. The contrast between the width of the restrictive covenant (the employer being engaged in numerous fields of activity outside vacuum cleaners) and the limited nature of the employee's position was too great.

1977 Act

The new law enshrines statutorily in section 39(1) and (2) the broad pre-existing distinction as between inventions made by skilled employees (or those in fiduciary position) and those made by the unskilled, although it is over-simplistic to regard the new merely as a codification of the former common law in this respect. Inventions of the first type enure to the employer; those of the second type remain with the employee.

A minor amendment (by way of addition of section 39(3)) was made by the 1988 Act. The effect of this is to prevent the employer holding out against the employee, in the case of an invention of the second type, any rights which the employer may separately have in associated copyright or design right. The need for the derogation arises from the wider rights accorded to the employer under the separate statutory provisions applicable to subject-matter (devised by the employee) of the latter kinds. The copyright and design right provisions of the 1988 Act contain no equivalent to section 39.

The new law also, and this is an important new point, gives the skilled employee a statutory right against the employer for compensation in respect of the invention in certain circumstances. This represents a complete departure from the old law. Previously, if the service contract of an employee of scientific or technical kind provided that he should assign his rights in any invention made in the course of his employment for even a nominal sum, say £1, that was the end of the matter for him even if the invention was worth several million pounds to the employer.

Of course, an intelligent employer might in such circumstances have made an *ex gratia* payment or other special bonus; the scientist would no doubt enjoy professional acclaim; medals and/or prizes might also follow; but often there was little by way of tangible financial reward. An attempt to use section 56(2) of the previous 1949 Act to force compensation in such circumstances failed in *Patchett v Sterling Engineering*.[6] That section, still in force in relation to 'existing' patents granted under the 1949 Act,

4   20 RPC 41.
5   [1977] FSR 312.
6   72 RPC 50.

is effectively limited to determination of disputes concerning shares (as between employer/employee) in inventions; if one party or the other is wholly entitled already, the section cannot be invoked. Thus, the employee (a skilled production engineer) failed in *Patchett* because under the common law the beneficial interest in his inventions vested in the employer and his previous negotiations with the employer had not in fact led to any countervailing formal agreement. They had just fizzled out; at most there was some kind of incomplete (and therefore unenforceable) 'understanding'.

The statutory right for compensation in respect of inventions made by unskilled employees arises only when the unskilled employee has subsequently assigned to, or licensed, the employer. Inventions are, of course, likely to be made less frequently in the first place by unskilled employees than by skilled ones; but if the unskilled employee does invent something, his employer may constitute one of the few avenues for exploitation open to him.

Dividing line

The precise location of the dividing line between section 39(1) and (2) inventions is naturally an issue of significance. The somewhat convoluted statutory phraseology is as follows:

> 39. (1) Notwithstanding anything in any rule of law, an invention made by an employee shall, as between him and his employer, be taken to belong to his employer for the purposes of this Act and all other purposes if –
> (a) it was made in the course of the *normal duties* of the employee or in the course of duties falling *outside his normal duties, but specifically assigned* to him, *and* the circumstances in either case were such that an invention *might reasonably be expected to result* from the carrying out of his duties; *or*
> (b) the invention was made in the course of the duties of the employee and, at the time of making the invention, because of the nature of his duties and the particular responsibilities arising from the nature of his duties he had a *special obligation* to further the interests of the employer's undertaking.
> (2) *Any other* invention made by an employee shall, as between him and his employer, be taken for those purposes to belong to the employee.   (*Emphasis added*)

Sub-section 1(a) incorporates a dual requirement – normal or assigned duties + expectation of invention – and hence is clearly apt to cover the standard case of a person like a research chemist or engineer working in commercial industry, even if the precise scope of his duties is never mapped, as where the scientist has an element of discretion in choice of field of research (*Secretary of State for Defence's Application*[6a]); conversely, for the factory floor-sweeper since there can hardly be any relevant expectation. Sub-section 1(b) is likewise apt to cover the case of the company director. But the precise points at which it becomes unreasonable to expect invention, and where special obligation ends, as one descends down the scientific and managerial scales respectively, are by no means clear. And unless the provisions of sub-section 1(a) or (b) are met, the invention ('Any *other* invention . . .') remains with the employee.

It may be best to approach these latter questions from a negative standpoint in the first instance. Thus, where ordinary performance of an employee's job does not as such

6a IPD 13063.

require him to supply anything by way of creative nature out of his own mind, it is hardly possible to expect invention; a draughtsman whose task was just to copy existing drawings would be excluded but one whose task was to design from scratch might well be included. Likewise on the administrative and managerial side. If the employee's obligations are no more than the ordinary good faith (to serve his employer's interests) expected of any employee, he probably keeps his invention even if he happens to have made the invention during working hours and hence literally in the course of his duties; there has to be some extra factor present to provide the special obligation also needed.

These considerations are reflected in *Harris' Patent*,[7] one of the first cases to be decided under section 39. It concerned an employee of middle rank, both scientifically and managerially. The employee had been originally employed as a fitter but had risen to become departmental manager in respect of 'Wey' valves, an important area of his employer's business; his responsibilities included both sales and after-sales service together with 'trouble-shooting' at customer installations for which he relied on his specialised knowledge of the valves and their application. He had made an improvement to the valve. It was held that neither limb of section 39(1) applied. Section 39(1)(a) failed because he had not been employed to design or invent; the employer was not as such a research-based manufacturer but normally either bought abroad from the original Swiss developers or sub-contracted out locally, and the trouble-shooting involved no more than application of known engineering practice without application of inventive ingenuity. Section 39(1)(b) failed because his responsibility could not in all the circumstances (for example, he had no power to hire or fire and never attended board meetings) be regarded as amounting to a special obligation.

Additional problems may arise with university and like personnel; are they employed just to teach or both to teach and to do research of a kind which may reasonably be expected to produce inventions? The wording of their contract of employment may be significant; this in turn may depend on when the contract was made. Attitudes of universities have changed in recent times, due to financial exigencies; many now actively seek additional research income.

Two final points are worth noting at this stage. The first is that sub-sections (1) and (2) of section 39 draw the dividing line between the employer- and employee-ownership in terms of the origin of the invention rather than simply in terms of employee qualifications or status. The professional aeronautical research engineer working for a commercial aircraft manufacturer may well be entitled to keep his valuable invention relating to dart-flights – notwithstanding that it is based on air-flow concepts comparable to those involved in his ordinary work – for the reason that improvement of darts is outside his nominated duties. The second point is that subsections (1) and (2) of section 39 only apply to inventions made by employees. If the inventor's arrangement with the company, sponsor or other party as the case may be are not such as to render him an employee at all, then the statutory provisions are excluded *in limine*. Mutual rights may then depend on other contractual arrangements (if any) or common law. Consultant scientists, in particular, need to take care that the position as regards patent rights in any invention flowing from their consultancy work is clear.

7   [1985] RPC 19.

Criteria of Compensation — Section 39(1) Inventions

The criteria are set out principally in section 40(1) and section 41(1) and (4) of the 1977 Act. The statutory language is quite new (which means that there are no precedents directly available to interpret it) and is obviously intended to provide as complete a code as possible. It may be useful to highlight the main provisions:

> (1) The patent (for the invention in question) must be of *outstanding benefit* to the employer.
> (2) The employee is to receive a *fair share* (in all the circumstances) of the benefit derived from the invention by the employer.
> (3) In assessing fair share, there must be taken into account (among other factors) the nature of the employee's duties and his *existing remuneration*; the *effort and skill* which *he* has devoted to making the invention; the effort and skill which *others (whether to the level of being co-inventors or not) have likewise devoted; any contribution made by the employer.*
> (4) An employee who makes an unsuccessful claim for compensation (say, because the benefit accrued to the employer has not yet reached the 'outstanding' level) is not thereby debarred from making a subsequent claim (when the benefit has reached that level). *(Emphasis added)*

Certain reasonable deductions can be made from the statutory language, taken with the few reported decisions so far.

> (1) It is clear that mere commercial exploitation as such is not enough to found a compensation claim; the adjective 'outstanding' does indicate a clear intention to restrict compensation to those inventions which are, to use the colloquialism, 'winners'. Such an interpretation is supported by *GEC Avionics' Patent*,[8] where the Superintending Examiner said:

> . . . it is noted that the word 'outstanding' is used rather than 'significant' or 'substantial' or other such term. It must be something out of the ordinary and not such as one would normally expect to arise from the results of the duties that the employee is paid for . . .

and by *British Steel's Patent*[9], where he said:

> . . . I would regard it as going further than [a comparative term], implying a superlative.

> (2) Only the benefit to the employer need be outstanding, not the degree of inventive ingenuity involved. It follows that an invention of modest ingenuity, but great commercial value, may be embraced whereas the invention of great ingenuity, but modest commercial value, would fall outside.
> (3) The relative degree of benefit, and hence attainment of the 'outstanding'

8 [1992] RPC 107 at 115.
9 [1992] RPC 117 at 122.

level, will depend on the employer's circumstances. A given invention may be fundamental to the success of a small firm, but yet be trivial in the context of the patent portfolio of a major corporation.

(4) The benefit need not derive from the employer's own actual use of the invention; if he sells or licenses out to others the relevant patents, the proceeds of such alternative modes of exploitation are to be taken into account also.

(5) Both the foreign and domestic benefit to the employer are included, provided of course that the foreign benefit does derive from a corresponding foreign patent(s).

(6) The benefit must in all cases be attributable to the patent involved. If the employer does not take out a patent, but relies instead on keeping the invention secret (as he might perhaps do if it were, for example, an invention concerned solely with the adjustment of the reaction conditions for a particular catalytic process), there is no basis for compensation. Likewise, if the benefit derives partly from a patent and partly from ancillary working know-how, the patent part must of itself alone meet the 'outstanding' criterion.

Criteria of Compensation – Section 39(2) Inventions

The criteria here, as specified by section 40(2) and section 41(1) and (5), are less stringent on the whole. Although some criteria are common with the case of the section 39(1) invention, the 'outstanding benefit' requirement is replaced by the requirement that the benefit received by the employee (from his assignment, licence to the employer) is 'inadequate in relation to the benefit derived by the employer from the patent' and that it be 'just' that he receive further compensation.

Naturally, an employee in possession of a section 39(2) invention who chooses to exploit entirely on his own accord (excluding his employer) has no compensation rights at all. Nor can such an employee complain if his employer refuses to take any interest at all in the invention, and declines to enter into arrangement for its exploitation.

Ancillary Aspects

Other important aspects to keep in mind in relation to the new legislation are:

(1) Invention

The new provisions are limited to inventions, but it is not entirely clear as to whether the statute is limited in section 39 strictly to patentable inventions, or whether a wider meaning is intended. Workshop improvements lacking inventive character, know-how, and subject-matters specifically excluded from the ranks of patentable invention by the prohibitions in the 1977 Act (for example, computer programs or plant varieties) may all be spoken of colloquially as 'inventions' and be of substantial commercial value.

From the standpoint of the skilled or fiduciary employee, this doubt may be of little practical significance. Since it is the patent which must be of outstanding benefit to the employer, for him to have a possible compensation claim at all, it would seem to follow that there must have been a patentable invention present. But the position for the unskilled employee may be different. If 'invention' for section 39 purposes is given a wide meaning, then he may be able to assert that his suggestions, although non-patentable, enure to him under section 39(2) notwithstanding any contrary provision in the employer's suggestion scheme or like arrangement. Some support for the wider view is provided by the decision in *Viziball's Application*;[10] it was held here that 'invention' for the purposes of section 8 (entitlement disputes) was not necessarily restricted to patentable inventions but could include alleged inventions. There is also the potential repercussive effect of section 43(4) (as amended by the 1988 Act) to be taken into account – indeed for both types of employee. This amended sub-section appears to equate 'patent', for purposes of sections 39 to 42 as a whole (not merely just sections 40 to 42), with other types of 'granted' protection, but its overall meaning is obscure.

(2) Records

'Outstanding benefit' can only be assessed from the actual commercial usage of the invention, and such commercial usage may well only become important during the latter part of the life of the patent(s) involved. It is obvious, therefore, that the compensation provisions cast heavy new record-keeping burdens on the employer. In view of the warning provided by the Act, it is, of course, likely that conflicts of evidence between the employee and employer concerning the extent of benefit achieved will be resolved by the tribunal against the employer. It is the employer who is in a unique position to keep such data. Commercial data as to level of sales, profit margins, licensing income and the like is most unlikely to be available to the research scientist in the laboratory – indeed he may be specifically precluded from such access, under the employer's corporate management structure.

(3) Unfair contracts

An employer, by virtue of his position as the provider of paid work, might be tempted to try to reduce by separate arrangement the rights of employees in their future inventions. Thus, he might introduce into the standard contract of employment of any employee whose inventions (if any) are likely to be of section 39(2) kind a restrictive general term to the effect that any invention actually so made should be assigned or licensed to the employer for a nominal amount.

Section 42(2) outlaws generally – at least on its face – such arrangements for contracting-out of the benefit of the Act. Any contract term which diminishes the employee's rights in the inventions or in the patents thereon is rendered unenforceable to the extent of such diminution. The provision is unlikely to apply, however, to any genuine compromise of a compensation claim under section 40(2) in a given case.

It is uncertain as to whether section 42(2) has any impact in the case of employees whose future inventions (if any) are likely to be of section 39(1) kind – for example, in the case where the employer inserts into the employment contract of his director of research a special provision whereby the normal compensation rights under section 40(1) are foregone. It could be argued that rights in the patents (of any such future inventions) includes compensation rights. But in any event wider legal principles suggest that such arrangements may be unenforceable. Genuine compromises of section 40(1) claims – say,

10   [1988] RPC 213 at 217.

where the director of research wishes to retire and enjoy now rather than leave to his heirs compensation in respect of an invention which will clearly be of outstanding benefit to his employer even though the precise quantum of benefit will not be known until ten years' time – on the other hand would seem permissible.

(4) Collective agreement

This is a further so far uncharted area of the new Act. It is explicitly provided by section 40(3) that the statutory compensation provisions (although not the provisions as regards ownership of the invention) can be overridden by a collective agreement within the meaning of the Trade Union and Labour Relations Act 1974.[11]

The terms of such an agreement are in no way dictated by the 1977 Act; no list of compulsory topics is presented. Rather, the 1977 Act merely lays down certain ground rules for formulation of the agreement.

Thus, section 40(3) requires that the agreement be non-discriminatory within a given group of employees, while section 40(6) requires that the employee-inventor be a member of the trade union with which the agreement is made. The employer may accordingly find himself faced with the statutory compensation provisions superseded for some inventors but not others. Such a split may, of course, cut across the other demarcation line provided between section 39 (1) and (2) in the first place.

The collective agreement may also, if desired, extend beyond inventions into matters of know-how, registered designs and the like. It would not be surprising if the union involved were to seek to enlarge its scope in this fashion. The question of enforceability of such a collective agreement lurks in the background, bearing in mind the presumption against enforceability provided by section 18(1) of the Trade Union and Labour Relations Act 1974.

Bibliography

B. Bercusson, 'The Contract of Employment and Contracting Out – The UK Patents Act 1977', [1980] EIPR 257.

W.R. Cornish, 'Rights in employees' inventions – the United Kingdom position' [1990] IIC Vol. 21, 298.

H. Davis-Ferid, 'The Employed Inventor under United Kingdom and German Law', [1981] EIPR 102.

A.N. Devereux, 'Compensation and awards to employee inventors' [1985–86] CIPA (Vol. 15) 47.

T.Z. Gold, 'Entitlement disputes: a case review' [1990] EIPR 382.

K. Hodkinson, 'Employee inventions and designs: Ownership, claims and compensation; and managing employee inventions', *The Company Lawyer* (1986) Vol. 2 146 and 183.

B. Reid, 'Chemists' Rights under the new Patents Act', *Chemistry in Britain*, April 1983 at 294.

---

11   1974 c.52.

10 Licensing and Assignment

Patent licences can be divided broadly into two types: compulsory licences and voluntary licences. Other species, licences of right and Crown rights, are akin to a compulsory licence and will be considered under that head.

Compulsory Licences

Compulsory licensing provisions have been present in the United Kingdom patent law since 1883. Originally, the emphasis was on preventing abuse of monopoly by a patentee, for example by charging excessively high prices for the patented product, or by sterilising some invention of significant public importance by maintaining the patent in force but refusing to work it. Nowadays, the emphasis is on achieving maximum utilisation of the patented invention. This is reflected in the grounds set out in section 48(3) of the 1977 Act. These apply both to 'new' patents granted under the 1977 Act and 'existing' patents already granted under the 1949 Act.

Paraphrased, the grounds now are:

(1) invention not being worked at all in the United Kingdom;
(2) invention not being worked to fullest reasonably practicable extent;
(3) demand not being met on reasonable terms;
(4) demand being met by importation;
(5) export markets not being supplied;   by refusal
(6) working of other improvement inventions being to license
hindered;   on reasonable
(7) commercial or industrial activities generally   terms or
in the United Kingdom being unfairly prejudiced; at all
(8) unacceptable licence conditions, leading to prejudice as in (7) above or unwarranted restrictions on unpatented materials.

The grounds are similar to those present in the 1949 Act and are couched, inevitably, in somewhat general terms.

It does not follow, however, that an application for a compulsory licence will be successful even if the applicant can establish a *prima facie* case under one or other of the grounds. The Patent Office has to consider all the circumstances of the case, including such statutorily prescribed factors[1] as time lapsed since the patent was granted (in any event an applicant must wait until three years from grant have elapsed), efforts already made by the patentee, ability of the applicant to work the invention himself, reasonable remuneration of the inventor (or patentee), and applicant's capital risk. Such overall consideration has to be given even if the patentee does not himself oppose the application for a compulsory licensee; normally, of course, he does oppose. In a particularly complex case, the Patent Office may refer the proceedings to an arbitrator.

---

1 Section 50(1) and (2).

There have been relatively few compulsory licence applications in recent decades, apart from those[2] under the special provisions in section 41 of the 1949 Act (now abolished) concerning compulsory licences on patents relating to foods, drugs (in the pharmaceutical sense) and surgical or curative devices. Nevertheless they have probably wielded an influence wider than might have been expected from the paucity of the case law. The background threat of a compulsory licence application is a potent lever in the hands of a person applying to a patentee for a voluntary licence on reasonable terms. In similar vein is the express statutory provision in section 48(8) that an existing licensee is always perfectly entitled in any event to apply for a compulsory licence instead.

The decisions given in such cases as have been litigated have naturally tended to hinge very much on the precise facts involved. Many of the grounds are couched in rather general terms, inviting the presentation of substantial evidence as to the commercial and economic background to the dispute. It is, therefore, difficult to extract much by way of definitive guidelines from the decisions. It is clear in particular that there is no standard norm as to what constitutes a 'reasonable' royalty, although attention is always paid to the generally prevailing level of royalty for licensing in the industry in question, if available.[3] The principles applicable in the case of licence of right cases (see later) may also be prayed in aid. A list of instructional decisions, however, follows:

Under 1949 Act

Colbourne Engineering's Application.[4] Existing exclusive licensee, very experienced in the field (water-softeners), had undertaken substantial development expenditure and was already selling, whereas applicant was just proposing to import from abroad; application refused.
Fette's Patent.[5] Unsuccessful argument by importing patentee that six and a half years constituted insufficient time period for institution of manufacture in the United Kingdom of screw thread rolling device.
Kamborian's Patent.[6] Offer of fresh licence on shoe machinery apparatus, at enhanced royalty rate of $33\frac{1}{3}$% rate, following expiration of previous licence at $7\frac{1}{2}$% held not unreasonable in absence of evidence that customers would not buy at consequential price level necessitated by $33\frac{1}{3}$% rate.
Penn Engineering & Manufacturing's Patent.[7] Emphasis on the public interest in encouraging exportation; patent relating to self-anchoring and countersinking studs. Licence to permit export granted.

Under 1977 Act

Extrude Hone Corporation's Patent.[8] Licence granted to applicant already being sued by patentee for infringement of elderly patent, relating to abrasive flow machines, under which patentee himself had marketed to date in spasmodic fashion only.

2   PLUK at 203; *Transactions* Volume LXXX at C 51 and B 29.
3   *Brownie Wireless Co.'s Application* 46 RPC 457 (1929).
4   72 RPC 169.
5   [1961] RPC 396.
6   [1961] RPC 403.
7   [1973] RPC 233.
8   [1982] RPC 359.

Enviro-Spray System's Patents.[9] Licence refused because of doubt as to ability of intended licensee to work the invention.

Halcon SD Group's Patents.[10] Evidence as to validity of the patent may be relevant, since it may go towards assessing the technical advance achieved by the patent which in turn affects the appropriate level of royalty.

Monsanto's CCP Patent.[11] Licence refused to manufacturer of solvent for use in patented carbonless copy paper; failure by applicant to show that lump sum price demanded by patentee for licence was unreasonable.

The future role of section 48(3) has also been rendered uncertain by the recent decision of the ECJ in *EC Commission v United Kingdom*,[11a] holding that the available grounds, insofar as they rely on importation, are contrary to the Treaty of Rome.

Licences of right

A licence as of right, under section 46 of the Act, is to be distinguished from a regular compulsory licence. What it means is that the official register entry of the patent has been marked 'licence of right', so that any third party is automatically entitled to a licence under the patent; there is no longer any burden on the potential licensee to show justification for the grant of a licence. The terms of such licence are settled by the Patent Office, if the parties cannot agree them mutually.

Application for such 'licence as of right' endorsement of the patent can be made by the patentee himself. The attraction for him is that henceforth the renewal fees due on the patent are halved. Endorsement is therefore a favoured approach of the solo inventor in particular; it enables him to advertise, in effect, his willingness to license, while simultaneously saving him considerable sums on renewal fees.

Alternatively, an applicant for a compulsory licence may apply instead for a licences of right endorsement (even though that would open the door to potential competition from other licensees). The Crown may also ask for endorsement in certain situations following a report of the Monopolies and Merger Commission under the Fair Trading Act 1973,[12] or under the Competition Act 1980.[13] The Commission has to conclude that a monopoly situation or merger situation qualifying for investigation subsists under the umbrella of patent protection with consequential results contrary to the public interest; alternatively that a person was engaged in an anti-competitive practice or pursuing a course of conduct against the public interest.

Another source of endorsed patents lies in the extension of term accorded to certain 'existing' patents under the transitional provisions of the 1977 Act, as mentioned in Chapter 5 above. In the period since the first edition, there has been a veritable spate of decisions involving such patents – particularly where the patent relates to a pharmaceutical since in this area the 'winners' are few and regulatory delays may mean that commercial exploitation is possible only towards the end of the patent's life.

This spate is now checked, for two reasons. First because of the inevitable decrease with passage of time of patents capable of being extended under the transitional provisions, and

9   [1986] RPC 147.
10   [1989] RPC 1.
11   [1990] FSR 1.
11a   [1993] FSR 1.
12   1973 c.41.
13   1980 c.21.

secondly because of the restriction of the licence of right possibilities for pharmaceutical (and subsequently for pesticidal) uses effected by the 1988 Act. Nevertheless, this case law retains some permanent significance (both in relation to endorsed patents generally, and perhaps also regular compulsory licences under non-endorsed patents).

The leading decision has probably been that in *Smith Kline & French Laboratories' (Cimetidine) Patents*.[14] This held that:

(i) the required reasonable royalty should be that which would be agreed between a notional willing licensor and licensee (following in this respect the earlier Crown use case of *Patchett's Patent*[15]) but that the patentee's position as manufacturer (if any) should be ignored;

(ii) royalties in comparable cases provide the best guide to such a royalty since they represented what actually willing licensors and licensees had agreed in the past;

(iii) where no comparable licence existed, then reliance could be placed instead on the so-called section 41 approach derived from the decision in *Geigy SA's*[16] patent under the 1949 Act provisions applicable to food or medicine, and the like; this in turn involves examination of patentee's expenditure on research and development, promotional expenditure, and return on capital employed;

(iv) as a last resort, a 'profits available' approach could be followed.

It is accordingly now reasonably clear that in a licence of right situation the practical realities dominate. The previously accepted rule of thumb that mechanical inventions would bear a royalty rate of around 5% is now fragile. The *Smith Kline & French* guidelines are not limited to pharmaceutical cases – see, for example, the reliance placed in *Cabot Safety Corporation's Patent*[17] (earplug) on the terms of the United States licence and the commercial value of the invention.

Crown use

The Crown has also traditionally reserved to itself the power to make use of a patented invention, where necessary in the public interest. For 'existing' patents, the applicable provisions are those of sections 46 to 49 of the 1949 Act; for 'new' patents under the 1977 Act, sections 55 to 59 control.

The powers are quite sweeping; for example, they include such matters as the supply of drugs for the National Health Service.[18] Their applicability is not limited to the subsistence of a state of war or emergency, although their scope becomes wider in such instances. Compensation for the use by the government department involved is normally payable, at a rate to be determined by the Court if agreement between the patentee and the department is not forthcoming.

14   [1990] RPC 203.
15   [1967] RPC 237.
16   [1964] RPC 391.
17   [1992] RPC 39.
18   *Pfizer v Ministry of Health* [1965] RPC 261.

Voluntary Licences

With a voluntary licence the terms are, in principle, entirely up to individual negotiation between the patentee and licensee. A patent licence can be defined as 'a right not to be sued under the patent', and it follows accordingly that a patentee can agree either to forego the totality of his rights to sue, or instead only a part of them. Thus, a licence can be limited in geographical area (for example, to make and sell only in Greater London), in time (for example, for a period of, say, five years only out of the whole life of the patent), or in proportion of the protected subject-matter (for example, if the patent relates to electric generators generally the licence can be limited to ones of less than 25 kW capacity).

A voluntary patent licence can also constitute just a part of some overall wider agreement between the parties. For example, it is quite common for a patentee to license out together both the patent and the associated confidential information (his so-called 'know-how') concerning operation of the patented invention, which he has accumulated since the time of first filing his patent application. Another common addition to the simple patent licence is that of provisions concerning future improvements. The patentee may require, as a condition of granting the licence, to receive back in return cross-licences under any future improvements to the invention made by the licensee. Likewise, he may also agree to grant licences on future improvements of his own. Another situation arises where there are patent licence provisions ancillary to some research and development contract or consultancy agreement.

From the practical standpoint, a patent licence at the drafting/negotiation stage needs to be examined by the parties in two main respects, namely:

(1) Is the licence agreement intrinsically legally adequate to express the parties' mutual intentions?

(2) Do the terms of the licence contravene any statutory requirement or other rule of law?

A similar approach is, of course, useful when the question is one of the interpretation or validity of an existing licence.

As regards respect (1) above, it is essential that the licence document define properly the agreement reached between the parties on such fundamental matters as scope of the licence grant, royalty rates, mode of payment, duration of the licence and the like; a licence agreement can fail for uncertainty just as much as any other contract can. In addition to these fundamental matters, it is normally highly desirable that the agreement deal also with other potentially contentious points which may arise during operation of the licence even though not essential to its formation. A complete checklist cannot be provided here, but the following may be useful:

(i) possible termination for cause and/or on notice, as distinct from termination on effluxion of time; the licensee may go bankrupt, or fail to provide sufficient royalties due to lack of exploitation effort;

(ii) accounting data (for example quarterly statements and their verification);

(iii) mode of payment of royalties;

(iv) minimum royalties;

(v) parties' rights on termination; this is particularly important if the licence covers associated know-how as well;

(vi) responsibility for renewal fees;

(vii) responsibility for prosecution of infringements;

(viii) definition of what constitutes an improvement (if improvements clauses are included);

(ix) quality control and/or marking;

(x) product liability;

(xi) severance (for example if certain terms are subsequently held void);

(xii) applicable law of the agreement;

(xiii) arbitration on disputes under the agreement (if so desired).

It is important also to have the fact of the licence recorded on the Patent Office Register, since a later registered licence may take priority over an earlier unregistered one. To avoid public disclosure of all the licence terms, the documentation may be split into two – namely, a formal licence (which alone is registered) making cross-reference to the comprehensive agreement (which is not). The registration rules, and the inevitable uncertainty of an oral agreement, render it strongly preferable that any patent licence agreement should be in writing – although there is nothing in theory to prevent an oral licence.

It is respect (2) which is liable to present the greater degree of difficulty, because the law is undoubtedly in a state of change. The law now shows an increasing distaste, as compared to the 'laissez-faire' and 'freedom of contract' concepts of earlier times, for the placing on the licensee of fetters which are inequitable against him personally or alternatively work contrary to the interest of the public in general.

Sections 44 and 45 of the 1977 Act (reflecting generally sections 57 and 58 of the 1949 Act) provide one group of statutory reliefs. Under section 44, a patent licence may be capable of being declared void in so far as it requires the licensee to acquire from the licensor in addition non-patented products (other than spare parts) or prohibits the licensee from using in addition products or patented processes of third parties. The provision thus effects a sharp reduction in the permissible scope of additional 'tying-in' clauses, say in respect of raw materials purchase, in a patent licence.

Section 45 provides that a patent licence can automatically be terminated by the licensee on three months' notice once the patent has expired, quite irrespective of anything to the contrary in the licence agreement itself. Thus a licensor cannot obtain for himself a perpetual royalty as a condition of granting the licence in the first place.

The Restrictive Trade Practices Act 1976[19] has some impact. Although straightforward two-party patent licences as such are outside the scope of this Act, patent pooling agreements as between three or more principal parties are not. This means that patent pooling agreements, which can often work strongly to the detriment of a newcomer to the industrial field in question (if he cannot persuade existing members of the pool to accept him into the club), are liable to be held void unless they can pass through one or other of the eight 'public interest' gateways set out in section 10 of that Act.

A further point arises in connection with the question of challenge to the validity of the licensed patent. The traditional common law rule, as adumbrated in *Crossley v Dixon*[20] in 1863, is that the licensee is estopped from making such challenge. The

19   1976 c.34.
20   32 LJ Ch. 617.

thinking behind this rule was well expressed in the 1891 case of *Wilson v Union Oil Mills*,[21] where Charles J. said:

> . . . it seems to me to be agreeable to one's ideas of common sense and of justice. A man has no right to work the patent of another without enquiry for a long time under an agreement whereby he has contracted to pay royalty, and then, when he is called upon to pay royalty, to say, 'Oh, your patent after all is an invalid patent'.

Notwithstanding its hallowed nature, the precise scope of application of the rule today is by no means clear. There are two further legal threads that also should be borne in mind. The first is that refinement of the principle in case law subsequent to 1863 led to the additional rule that the estoppel only went as far as the relationship under which it was created. For example, in *Fuel Economy v Murray*[22] in 1930 the defendant was already licensed to use the patented boiler expansion joint in Northumberland, Durham and parts of Yorkshire. He was sued in respect of separate infringements in Nottinghamshire and Berkshire. It was held that in those infringement proceedings he was not prevented from alleging invalidity of the patent; *contra*, of course, if he were being sued for back-royalties due under the licence in the limited area. Other types of licence arrangement may have comparable results – for example, if the patentee gives a positive covenant or guarantee as to validity; the precise nature of the basis on which the parties contracted and the rights granted are material.

Secondly, and perhaps more significantly, there has been in recent times the increasing impetus of anti-trust considerations. The Treaty of Rome is discussed more fully in the next section of this chapter. It suffices here to say that it appears that the legal concept of estoppel of the licensee (either inherently or by virtue of a formal 'no-challenge' clause in the licence agreement) is contrary to Articles 85 and 86 of the Treaty, for cases where the Treaty is pertinent in the first place on account of the licence having an effect on inter-state trade. Such an approach was adopted early on by the Commission in *AOIP v Beyrard*,[23] on the basis that a no-challenge clause:

> . . . constitutes a contractual restriction of competition in that it deprives the licensee of the possibility, which is available to everyone else, of removing an obstacle to his freedom of action in the commercial field by means of an action for revocation of the patents.

And a no-challenge clause is now on the 'black list' of their subsequent Regulation No. 2349/84.[24]

In the United States, the comparable rule of estoppel was upset in 1969 by the Supreme Court in the landmark decision of *Lear v Adkins*,[25] where it was said:

> Thus, although licensee estoppel may be consistent with the letter of contractual doctrine, we cannot say that it is compelled by the spirit of contract law, which seeks to balance the claims of promisor and promisee in accord with the requirements of good faith
>
> . . . . .

21   9 RPC 57 at 63.
22   47 RPC 346.
23   [1976] FSR 181 at 189.
24   Article 3.1.
25   162 USPQ 1.

> Surely the equities of the licensor do not weigh very heavily when they are balanced against the important public interest in permitting full and free competition in the use of ideas which are in reality a part of the public domain. Licensees may often be the only individuals with enough economic incentive to challenge the patentability of an inventor's discovery. If they are muzzled, the public may continually be required to pay tribute to would-be monopolists without need or justification. We think it plain that the technical requirements of contract doctrine must give way before the demands of the public interest in the typical situation involving the negotiation of a licence after a patent has issued.

in a case where the licence contract (in relation to an aviation gyroscope) had been executed after filing of the patent application but prior to grant, and the licensee had subsequently (but also prior to grant) informed the licensor that it considered the subject-matter unpatentable and would no longer pay royalties.

Treaty of Rome

The Treaty establishing the European Economic Community (EEC), the so-called 'Treaty of Rome', has already been mentioned. By virtue of section 2(1) of the European Communities Act 1972,[26] the provisions of that Treaty are rendered part of English law. In contrast to the usual technique of introducing specific domestic legislation reflecting the terms of a convention or treaty ratified by the United Kingdom – as, for example, the passing of the 1977 Act so as to incorporate into domestic patent law the provisions of the European Patent Convention as signed at Munich in 1973 – the 1972 Act incorporates Community law wholesale. As put expressively by Denning L.J. in the passing-off case of *Bulmer v Bollinger*:[27]

> But when we come to matters with a European element, the Treaty is like an incoming tide. It flows into the estuaries and up the rivers. It cannot be held back. Parliament has decreed that the Treaty is henceforth to be part of our law. It is equal in force to any statute.

For present purposes the relevant provisions of the Treaty are Articles 36 and 222 (which preserve individual national intellectual property rights generally); Articles 85(1) and (2) (which respectively prohibit anti-competitive practices within the Common Market, and nullify accordingly any agreements having that effect); and Article 86 (which prohibits abuse of dominant position). It is in the reconciliation of the inherently somewhat conflicting provisions of these Articles that much of the difficulty with EEC law has arisen. The position is certainly not eased by the variety of fora available; decisions concerning the justifiability of patent licensing arrangements may be made by the Commission of the European Communities ('the Commission'), by national courts (of the United Kingdom or other Member States), and – at the top of the pyramid – by the European Court of Justice (ECJ) following a reference under Article 177 of the Treaty from a national court of tribunal for exercise of its interpretative jurisdiction or alternatively on appeal under Article 173 from the Commission. The texts of these Articles are reproduced in Appendix 10.

26 1972 c.68. Text in 'Statutes' section.
27 [1975] RPC 321 at 336.

EEC competition law is by no means yet fully mature so far as patent licensing and infringement are concerned. It is a complex subject, and the following comments are intended to provide no more than an outline of some of the issues which commonly arise.

National effect

It is quite clear from the decision of the Court of Appeal in *Chemidus Wavin v Société pour la Transformation*[28] that patent licence provisions contrary to Article 85 will be struck down by a United Kingdom Court, although severance of the objectionable clauses will be preferred to total nullity of the agreement if at all possible. Articles 85 and 86 are only concerned *in limine*, however, with inter-state trade as distinct from intra-state trade. It is certainly arguable, therefore, both from the terms of Articles 85 and 86 and from precedents like the ECJ decision in the spare parts supply case of *Hugin Kassaregister AB v EC Commission*,[29] that a purely domestic patent licence could escape unscathed.

Thus, a licence granted by a United Kingdom patentee to a United Kingdom licensee under a United Kingdom patent (being the only patent owned by the patentee) might escape any Article 85/86 complications – provided, of course, that the licensing arrangements lacked any provision which in the circumstances might have a consequential effect on inter-state trade. An example of potential effect is provided by a licence on a patent relating to the construction of wine-making vats which purported to prohibit export to France but not to Germany of vats so manufactured. Likewise, if the licence covered a corresponding foreign patent(s) also in a country (countries) outside the Common Market, for example, the United States of America. *Contra*, however, if the licence is one granted by the United Kingdom patentee in respect of a corresponding foreign patent of his in a Common Market country; this was the kind of situation involved in the *Chemidus Wavin* case itself.

Exhaustion of rights

This paramountcy of the freedom of inter-state trade underpins also the doctrine of exhaustion of rights. Exhaustion means in effect that once a patented product (or other article embodying an invention), reaches the market-place with the patentee's consent (as expressed either by payment of a licence fee or by direct sale by the patentee himself), then his rights over the product have expired. Thus, if a patentee owns a series of patents in countries of the Common Market covering a sausage product and licenses Company A in Country X and Company B in Country Y then he cannot prevent the subsequent importation into and sale in Country Y of sausages originally put properly on the market in Country X. If there were no doctrine of exhaustion such sausages might well, in the eyes of the law of Country Y, rank as infringements; this in turn would enable the original patentee either to extract two royalties on the one article or alternatively carve up the licensing territories rigidly among his licensees. But under the exhaustion doctrine the sausage becomes a 'franked' article once first lawfully marketed.

28   [1977] FSR 181.
29   [1979] 3 CMLR 345.

One of the landmark cases here is the ECJ decision in *Centrafarm BV v Sterling Drug*[30] involving the drug nalidixic acid (Negram); drugs are, of course, particularly susceptible to movement across territorial boundaries (and hence so-called 'parallel importation') because of the low transport costs involved; many of the exhaustion cases concern them. The patentee in this case was unable to prevent the resale in Holland of nalidixic acid, lawfully marketed in the United Kingdom, at a lower price than that charged by the patentee himself in Holland. In *Merck v Stephar*[31] the principle was even extended so far as to preclude the patentee from preventing importation into Holland of a drug (Moduretic) originally sold by him in Italy not under any patent at all (since Italian law at the time prohibited the grant of patents on pharmaceutical products).

But the patentee can still succeed if the product was first put onto the market in a country outside the Common Market. This is what happened in the earlier *In re Tylosin*[32] case where the antibiotic Tylosin involved had been originally made and sold in active ingredient form in the United States of America or the United Kingdom (before the latter's accession to the EEC); the fact that the product had passed at an intermediate stage through a supplier in another Common Market country (Holland) did not suffice to enable the eventual German seller to escape liability, in the eyes of the Bundesgerichtshof (German Federal Supreme Court). Likewise, if the product was first put onto the market within the Common Market under a compulsory licence as distinct from a voluntary licence or voluntary sale, since compulsion negates the existence of consent (*Pharmon v Hoechst*[33] – drug (frusemide) made in the United Kingdom under a compulsory licence obtained under section 41 of the 1949 Act and then exported to Holland).

Articles 85(1) and (3)

Another aspect of the impact of the Treaty of Rome on patent licensing arises under Article 85(3). Article 85(3) provides in effect for possible exemption from the prohibitions of Article 85(1) (if the licensing agreement is otherwise caught by it) on various public interest-type grounds. The exemptions can be equated, very approximately, with those provided for in relation to patent pooling agreements by the Restrictive Trade Practices Act 1976[34] section 10(1), even though the actual wordings of the exemption provisions differ considerably in the two instances.

But whereas patent pooling agreements are nowadays fairly rare, licensing agreements are common. The desire for greater certainty as to exactly what kinds of provisions are likely to be acceptable, or conversely unacceptable, under Articles 85(1) and (3) taken jointly has led to considerable efforts over the years on the part of the Commission to clarify the subject. Although this is essentially a specialist topic, and the position is not yet resolved, brief reference may be made here to some of the chronology so far:

(1) Commission Notice dated 24 December 1962[35] (the so-called 'Christmas

30 [1976] FSR 164.
31 [1982] FSR 57.
32 [1977] 1 CMLR 460.
33 [1986] FSR 108.
34 [1976] c.34.
35 JO 1962, 2922.

message') and constituting Regulation No. 17/62. This was the first attempt on the part of the Commission to promulgate a policy under Article 85(1) in this context. It deals broadly with such matters as negative clearance (under Article 85(1) or 86); exemption (under Article 85(3)); making of complaints by aggrieved parties; enforcement and fines.

(2) Commission Notice dated 19 December 1977,[36] concerning possible exclusion from Article 85(1) of certain agreements (including patent licence agreements) of minor importance. A revised version of this Notice came into effect on 3 September 1986.[37] The limits are couched in terms of share occupied by the patent product in relation to the total market (within the Common Market) for products of that general type (up to 5 per cent) and turnover of the contracting parties (up to 200 million ECU);

(3) Regulation No. 2349/84 dated 23 July 1984[38] representing the so-called 'block exemption' so far as patent licences are concerned. It enumerates a list of formal exemptions to Article 85(1) (Article 1) followed by a 'white list' (Article 2) and then a 'black list' (Article 3) of types of clause. Many of these exemptions and listings represent a distillation of the earlier case law. For example, the exemption of an 'open' exclusive licence reflects the 1982 decision of the ECJ in *Nungesser v EC Commission*[39] in the related field of plant breeders' rights. By an 'open' exclusive licence is meant an exclusive licence which nevertheless does not affect the position of third parties such as parallel importers and licensees for other territories. The 'white list' provisions include, for example, minimum royalties, field of use restrictions, prohibition on sub-licensing, quality controls and most favoured nation obligations. On the 'black list' are *inter alia* no-challenge provisions, tying-in clauses, price controls, customer/distributor restrictions and obligations for the licensee to assign improvements. The above recitations are not comprehensive. Moreover, the Commission still retains a reserve power to take action if the particular circumstances of the agreement render this advisable;[40] the exemptions are not immutable.

Although not given under the Regulation itself, the decision of the ECJ in *Windsurfing International v EC Commission*[41] is of general importance on the topic of patent licensing. A tying-in provision, requiring the licensee to exploit the licensed patent only for the manufacture of sailboards using boards which had been given the patentee's prior approval (the German patent involved claimed only a rig for a sailboard) was struck down; the quality control defence failed on the facts.

(4) Regulation No. 418/85 dated 19 December 1984[42] concerning research and development agreements. This is structured similarly to the patent licensing Regulation No. 2349/84. Although primarily concerned with agreements which

36 [1977] 3 CMLR 648.
37 JO 1986, C 231/2.
38 JO 1984, L 219/15.
39 [1983] 1 CMLR 278.
40 Article 9.
41 [1986] 3 CMLR 489.
42 JO 1985 L 53/5.

may give rise to patentable inventions in the future, rather than subsisting patents, certain aspects of the Regulation may be noted here. An obligation to obtain and maintain patents arising from the research and development is on the 'white list',[43] but a provision precluding subsequent challenge to the validity of any patents arising (that is after the agreement has expired) is again on the 'black list'.[44]

(5) Regulation No. 556/89 dated 30 November 1988[45] represents the analogous 'block exemption' so far as know-how licences are concerned. Its provisions are broadly similar to those of the patent licence Regulation No. 2349/84, although not identical.

For mixed patent + know-how licensing agreements both Regulations may have to be considered. Broadly, the line of distinction is that Regulation No. 2349/84 only applies to those mixed agreements where the patents are 'necessary'[46] for achieving the objects of the licensed technology, with Regulation No. 556/89 applying to remaining agreements where the patents are 'not necessary'.[47] When it is difficult to be sure of necessity, the safer course may accordingly be to assume that Regulation No. 556/89 applies.

Article 86

Strictly as far as patent licensing is concerned, Article 86 has generally lesser impact than Articles 85(1) and (3) although it is legally quite distinct therefrom. As made clear by the ECJ in *Parke, Davis v Probel*[48] (patent infringement dispute concerning the drug chloramphenicol), it is necessary to show for an Article 86 infraction all three separate elements of:

(1) the existence of a dominant position;
(2) an improper exploitation of it; and
(3) the possibility that trade may be affected between Member States as a result.

A patent, by virtue of its very nature, may give a patentee a monopolistic and hence 'dominant' position; likewise to an exclusive licensee. But *Parke, Davis* makes it clear that presence of element (1) alone is not enough. Elements (2) (improper exploitation) and (3) (consequential effect on trade) do not necessarily follow from element (1); what matters are the precise terms on which the patentee exploits his monopoly; the terms of the licence, assuming that the patentee exploits in this manner, may (or may not) lead to elements (2) and (3) being present as well. *Parke, Davis* does not itself attempt to provide an exhaustive list of criteria whereby improper licensing exploitation and effect on trade can be gauged; at most it indicates that differential sale prices may (not necessarily must) be a relevant factor; nor is there a series of Commission Notices comparable to those just discussed in relation to Article 85. From a general standpoint,

43   Article 5(1)(c).
44   Article 6 (b).
45   JO 1989 L 61/1.
46   Recital (9).
47   Recital (2).
48   [1968] FSR 393.

however, it is not easy to visualise circumstances which give rise to objection under Article 86 but not Article 85(1).

Assignment

Under section 30 of the 1977 Act (applicable both to 'existing' patents under the 1949 Act and 'new' patents under the 1977 Act), a patent (or patent application) is declared to be personal property and can be, *inter alia*, assigned. However, in contradistinction to the position with a licence, such an assignment is void unless it is in writing and signed by or on behalf of the parties to the transaction. This greater degree of required solemnity reflects the difference between the position of a licensee and an assignee. A licensee, as mentioned before, merely acquires by his licence a right not to be sued by the patentee in respect of the acts permitted by the licence. An assignee, on the other hand, steps positively into the shoes of the original patentee. Successive assignments are, of course, possible.

No particular form of assignment document is required but it is important that the assignment, once completed, is registered on the Patent Office Register. Just as with licences, a later registered assignment may defeat an earlier unregistered assignment.

Other Dealings and Devolution

Other kinds of dealing in the patent, in particular mortgaging, are possible. The patent may also devolve by operation of law, for example on death or bankruptcy, in line with other kinds of property.

Bibliography

C. Bellamy and G.D. Child, *Competition Law of the EEC* 1987 (3rd ed.).

M. Burnside, 'Patents and Anti-Trust – The Ill-Defined Boundary', CIPA Volume 6 (1976–77) at 259.

M. Hills, 'Compulsory Licences as of Right' CIPA Volume 17 (1987–88) at 134.

V. Korah, European Competition Law Monographs – *Patent Licensing and EEC Competition Rules Regulation 2349/84* (1985); *R & D and the EEC Competition Rules Regulation 418/85* (1986); *Know-How Licensing Agreements and the EEC Competition Rules Regulation 556/89* (1989). 'The Group Exemption for Know-How Licences' [1988] EIPR 134.

K. Lewis, 'Dealings with UK Patents and Know-How', [1979] EIPR at 217.

G. Lynfield, 'Framework of Community Government and Anti-trust Laws', CIPA Volume 2 (1972–73) at 246.

A. Serjeant, 'Compulsory Licences in the United Kingdom', AIPL (1975) at 395.

11 Contest in the Patent Office

Introduction

Reference has been made in earlier chapters to various kinds of *inter partes* disputes, involving patents, over which the Patent Office has jurisdiction. These include, in relation to the 1977 Act, disputes concerning:

- amendment of specification and/or claims
- entitlement to the patent
- employee inventions
- licences as of right
- compulsory licences
- revocation of patents
- infringement of patents (only by agreement of both parties)
- declaration of non-infringement

Certain like jurisdiction still persists under the remaining powers of the 1949 Act, for example the amendment of specification and/or claims of 'existing' patents granted under the 1949 Act. It will also be recalled that in many instances the jurisdiction is not exclusive to the Patent Office; for example, proceedings for declaration of non-infringement can be brought either in the Patent Office or in the Court.

Standard Procedure

The Patent Office has evolved over the decades a reasonable standard procedure for handling disputes conducted before it. The procedure is laid down in the Rules, themselves promulgated under the authority vested in the Secretary of State (section 123(1) of the 1977 Act, and corresponding section 94(1) of the 1949 Act giving authority to the Board of Trade), and is characterised by an emphasis on written material (in contrast to the Court's traditional emphasis on oral material – although that is now changing in face of the pressure of current litigation costs) and overall flexibility.

Such standard procedure largely survives the periodic promulgation of new Patents Acts. The Rules themselves are in turn periodically revised and reissued within the lifetime of a given Patents Act. The Rules currently applicable are the Patents Rules 1990[1] (for 'new' patents under the 1977 Act) and the Patents Rules 1968[2] (for 'existing' patents under the 1949 Act).

In the typical case of an application for revocation of a patent the stages (under Rule 75 of the 1990 Rules, alternatively Rules 40 to 42, 96 and 97 of the 1968 Rules) are:

(1) Statement of case by applicant for revocation.
(2) Counterstatement by patentee.

1   1990 No. 2384.
2   SI 1968 No. 1389.

(3) Evidence-in-chief by applicant for revocation, in support of his case.
(4) Evidence-in-chief by patentee, in corresponding support of his case.
(5) Evidence-in-reply by applicant for revocation.

There are, of course, variations of the standard procedure in some instances. Thus, on an application for a compulsory licence (section 48 of the 1977 Act), the applicant has first to satisfy the Patent Office (by a statement of case and supporting evidence) that he has a *prima facie* case before it will be entertained at all, and the patentee brought in (Rule 70). The purpose of this preliminary sieving stage is no doubt to discourage frivolous applications.

The 1990 Rules introduced (belatedly) an important change in regard to licence of right procedure, by eliminating the usual initial statement of case by the applicant for the licence and requiring him instead only to file his requested draft licence at this stage (Rule 62(1)(b)). The purpose of this change was no doubt to abolish the regrettable practice on the part of patentees which had grown up since the 1985 decision of the House of Lords in *R v Comptroller-General ex parte Gist-Brocades*[3] (which held that a licence of right under section 46 of the 1977 Act in respect of a new existing patent extended in term under the transitional provisions of the 1977 Act ran only from the date of grant rather than from the date of application) of requesting further particulars of the applicant's statement (often on somewhat artificial grounds) prior to filing their own counter-statement, thereby delaying as a whole the subsequent stages and eventual Patent Office hearing and date of grant. At this point in the life of an important patent being profitably worked by the patentee, every extra day's undiluted monopoly may be financially very valuable. Lord Diplock had presciently foreseen the likely need for revision of the previous 1982 Rules in this respect,[4] and it is unfortunate that such delay in formally making the necessary change occurred; the licence of right jurisdiction in respect of new existing patents is, naturally, rapidly approaching extinction for chronological reasons.

Another variation, of a different sort, is presented by the ordinary application for amendment (section 75(1)(2)) of a 'new' patent granted under the 1977 Act. There is no express reference in applicable Rule 78 to evidence stages; but undoubtedly the Patent Office would permit evidence to be filed on both sides, if the issues raised on the application so justified, under the omnibus provision of Rule 78(3) that: 'The comptroller may give such directions as he may think fit with regard to the subsequent procedure'.

The standard procedure is exemplified by the model set of forms, for an application for revocation of a 'new' patent, provided in Appendix 11. Over and above this example, some other practically important aspects of procedure in the Patent Office will now be considered:

Amendment of pleadings

The Patent Office has in the past been reasonably generous in allowing amendment of the pleadings by an opponent both in respect of:

---

3 [1986] RPC 203.
4 At page 253, lines 18 to 23.

(1) new material in support of existing pleaded grounds; and
(2) addition of entirely new grounds.

This flexibility was of particular importance in the case of oppositions or belated oppositions (applications for revocation) under the 1949 Act, on account of the time limits (relatively brief) there provided for initiation of the proceedings in the first instance. In the leading belated opposition case of *Addressograph-Multigraph's Patent*,[5] the Patents Appeal Tribunal approved the rule that in exercising its discretion as regards new grounds, the Patent Office should take account of:

(1) the diligence of the person seeking to introduce the new grounds;
(2) the relevance of the new art;
(3) the time which has elapsed since the proceedings were launched;
(4) whether the further delay resulting from the introduction of the new grounds would be unjust to the patentee or against the public interest.

In *Addressograph-Multigraph* itself, a new ground (prior claiming – section 14(1)(c) of the 1949 Act) was allowed to be added some three years after commencement of the proceedings; but the Appeal Tribunal indicated quite clearly that such delay was at the limit of permissibility and had it been a matter for their discretion in the first place they might well have refused the introduction. Although the 1977 Act permits applications for revocation at any time during the life of the patent, so rendering unlikely any exact recurrence of the *Addressograph-Multigraph* situation itself, it is to be expected that the underlying principle will continue to apply – for example, in respect of opposition to an application for amendments (two months' time limit under Rule 78(1)).

A similar measure of generosity is naturally accorded to the patentee. In face of some new ground or material brought forward by an opponent, he may well wish, for example, to offer some amendment or further amendment to his Claim 1.

Although, notionally, permission to one party to amend a pleading may necessitate giving the other party similar permission and then a whole new round of evidence, the Patent Office in practice is reluctant to permit amendment to be used as a mere vehicle for delay; shortened terms for evidence may be set, or alternatively simultaneous filing of an amended pleading and evidence relevant thereto required.

Late evidence

The Patent Office also has power (for example, under Rule 75(6) in respect of applications for revocation) to admit additional evidence subsequent to completion of the normal evidence stages. In reality, the practice as regards additional evidence is again normally quite generous although a patentee wishing to oppose its introduction can always cite *Rohm & Haas' Application* where it was held that late evidence would be admitted only:

. . . if it were both relevant and decisive, in the sense that if it were admitted and remained uncontradicted it would tip the balance in favour of the opponents.[6]

5   [1974] RPC 264.
6   [1966] FSR 403 at 404.

The underlying reason for the reluctance of the Patent Office to exclude late evidence on part of the patentee himself probably springs from the principle of the entitlement of the patentee to the benefit of the doubt at this stage. The opponent (under the 1949 Act) or applicant for revocation (under the 1977 Act) always has a possible second bite at the cherry (by commencing proceedings in the Court) whereas the patentee does not (if the attack in the Patent Office proceedings succeeds). Thus, it would be harsh on the patentee if, for example, his evidence as to commercial success which he wishes to rely on in defending an obviousness attack, was to be excluded simply because that success had only materialised subsequent to completion of his normal evidence stage. Conversely, if the opponent wishes to bring in additional late evidence it is often tactically advantageous for the patentee to welcome it; the patentee may well be able to make play with the argument that the opponent's case fails, even when bolstered with the extra help of the late evidence.

Contents of evidence

The distinction between the pleadings and evidence stages means that the former are often rather brief documents outlining the parties' case and pointing out the areas on which evidence will be filed. They are however, like pleadings in the Patents County Court, normally more comprehensible and helpful than pleadings in the Patents Court itself.

The written evidence (given by way of Statutory Declaration or Affidavit) is usually the critical element of each party's case. This should be confined to facts and not argument. The latter will, of course, often creep in, particularly if the document has been prepared overseas in a country where it is the practice to use a composite 'brief'; but, generally speaking, it is a mistake to include it. Presentation of argument based on the evidential facts, or on any issues of law arising, is better left to the Hearing itself. The Patent Office in the United Kingdom normally allows the parties as much time as they need at the Hearing to develop such arguments. This is in sharp contrast to the procedure in certain foreign Patent Offices, where there may be a limitation as to time which renders necessary the presentation of some at least of the argument in the earlier written documents.

Thus, if revocation of a patent is being applied for on ground of obviousness, any bald assertions by experts in their evidence that they consider the invention obvious (or conversely non-obvious) are unlikely to cut very much ice with the Hearing Officer. Far from being swayed by any such assertion, he is much more likely positively to discount the evidence of such experts as representing an attempt to foreclose the very issue on which he (the Hearing Officer) alone has the power of decision. The more useful course by far for an applicant's expert to follow in such circumstances is to present such a substratum of background fact as must inexorably lead any Hearing Officer to the conclusion that the invention is obvious.

An instructive example of a successful Statutory Declaration in support of an obviousness attack is represented by the Watson Declaration in *Johns-Manville Corporation's Patent*,[7] reproduced in full at pages 480 to 483 of the report.

7   [1967] RPC 479.

Cross-examination

Cross-examination of a witness on the contents of his written evidence is permitted. In the past this procedure was fairly rare, being confined generally (apart from compulsory licence cases or other instances where assessment of complex accounting data was involved) to situations like obtaining (section 14(1)(a)) of the 1949 Act or prior user where the relevant facts may be peculiarly within the knowledge of the particular witness involved, as distinct from knowledge prevalent in the industry generally. However, Rule 103(2) under the 1977 Act effected a small but significant change on this topic. This sub-Rule provides that the Comptroller 'shall' allow any witness to be cross-examined on his affidavit or declaration, unless he directs otherwise. 'Shall' stands in contrast to the much weaker word 'may ' employed both in the corresponding provision (statutory) in the 1949 Act (section 83(1)) concerning cross-examination, and in Rule 103(2) itself as to the possibility of giving oral evidence-in-chief. In *Norris's Patent*[8] (entitlement dispute on a refractometer invention) the absence of cross-examination on the acutely conflicting written evidence of the two parties was criticised by the Patents Court on appeal.

The trend to a greater degree of cross-examination in the Patent Office is of course to be welcomed. The prospect of cross-examination curbs a witness from making extravagant statements in his written evidence. It may make him more cautious in just blindly signing some document which was drafted not by him but for him by his advisers (patent agent and/or counsel).

Discovery and the like

The Patent Office has power to order discovery at the behest of either party (Rule 103(3)), and also generally at any stage of the proceedings to direct that any document, information or evidence as may be required shall be furnished (Rule 106). Although these powers are only exercised sparingly, they represent areas in which Patent Office procedure is, at root, quite different to that of the Court.

For patent actions in the Court, discovery is a standard step. The fact that the great bulk of the documentary material so produced is often of little relevance to the issues in the action is regarded as being of little consequence. In the Patent Office, on the other hand, the party requesting discovery may have to put up a convincing case as to why it should be ordered – bearing in mind that Patent Office proceedings are intended to be relatively simple and inexpensive. Thus, in the amendment case of *Temmler-Werke's Patent*,[9] an opponent was refused discovery in respect of the patentee's files so far as knowledge by the patentee of the prior art sought to be avoided was concerned; if the opponent could have shown lack of candour in this respect by the patentee, then he might have had the amendment refused on discretionary grounds. Part of the justification for refusing discovery was said by the Appeal Tribunal to lie in the power of the Patent Office itself to require production of relevant documents – that is to say in the quasi-inquisitorial power of the Patent Office given by Rule 106 (or rather its predecessor in that case).

8   [1988] RPC 159.
9   [1966] RPC 187.

Petrie & McNaught's Application[10] represents in contrast an instance where discovery was ordered both to meet the opponent's request and to meet the Hearing Officer's own questions. Prior user by the applicants themselves, of a drier, was alleged by the opponents. Applicants denied prior use in their pleadings, but their evidence on its face contradicted to some extent their pleading. To quote from the preliminary decision:

> This evidence raises more questions than it answers. It establishes that a machine of the kind in question was supplied and erected by the applicants, but it leaves several questions unanswered which are vital to the issue of prior user. These include (1) Did the machine comprise the applicants' invention; (2) At what date was the sale completed and the machine pass into the purchaser's possession; . . .
>
> Questions (1) and (2) should, by their nature, be capable of ready answer by documents likely to be within the applicants' possession . . .
>
> I ought to accede to the opponents' request up to a point, to ensure that the applicants disclose such documents (if any) in their possession and under their control as would serve to resolve my questions (1) and (2) above.

And in the entitlement case of *Norris's Patent*, mentioned above in connection with cross-examination, the Patents Court made it clear that discovery of relevant documents would have helped. Indeed, cross-examination and discovery often go hand-in-hand since one of the purposes of cross-examination may be to expose contradictions between the witness's present and past statements.

It appears from the decision of the Divisional Court in *Fuji Photo Film's Patent*[11] that the administration of interrogatories is available in principle (at least under the Patent Office's inquisitorial power), but difficult to obtain in practice.

As for experiments, there is no procedure in the Patent Office comparable to the Court procedure of repetition in the presence of the other party. Nevertheless, presentation of experimental evidence – for example, in respect of an insufficiency attack – is by no means unusual in Patent Office proceedings. If experimental evidence is given by a declarant, the other party may well try to repeat the experiment (if it considers the experiment relevant to the issues) of its own volition. If the other party cannot obtain the same results as before, cross-examination may be called for in order to probe the possible reasons for the difference and enable the Patent Office to come to a conclusion as to its evidential weight; without cross-examination, the opponent is likely to fail on the basis that he has not discharged the onus of proof. Alternatively, if no challenge is presented, the Patent Office is likely to accept the first results as accurate.

Hearing and decision

Hearing procedure is relatively informal. Parties may appear by themselves, by their patent agents (quite common), by their solicitors (rare) or by counsel (also quite common). There is no time limit as to argument (as already mentioned), but most hearings are completed in the day they are started since the Hearing Officer will usually have familiarised himself with the documents in outline in advance. The Hearing Officer may well also have some substantial degree of expertise in the field in question, which

10 [1966] FSR 234[1] at 236[1].
11 [1974] RPC 639.

assists his assimilation of the facts; he is usually a Superintending Examiner, acting under the delegated authority of the Comptroller-General.

The patentee normally has the right to open, and to make a reply speech after the opponent has made his speech, even though he may not have been the party bringing the proceedings in the first place. 'Patentee' and 'opponent' are here used in a generic sense. The opponent might be, for example, an applicant for revocation of a 'new' patent, an applicant for a licence of right or compulsory licence, a belated opponent in the strict sense to an 'existing' patent. This practice of patentee-commencement was referred to as 'hallowed' in *Du Pont de Nemours' (Hull's) Application*,[12] where it was unsuccessfully challenged by the opponent. Whether it has survived unscathed the passing of the 1977 Act is not yet completely certain. Only in exceptional circumstances, for example in cases of 'obtaining' (section 14(1)(a) of the 1949 Act), would the practice have been reversed in the past.

The question of burden of proof is often contentious; many decisions in the 1949 to 1977 era canvass it. Two principles can broadly be extracted from the same, and are considered still applicable today under the 1977 Act, namely:

> (1) that in any case of real doubt at the end of the day the patentee will be given the benefit of that doubt;
> (2) that the precise nature of the issue(s) in dispute may influence the stringency of the Patent Office's approach.

Principle (1) derives from the fact, already mentioned, that the opponent normally has the opportunity of a second bite at the cherry (in later Court proceedings) whereas the patentee does not (if he loses now he loses for all time) combined with the relatively lesser investigatory power of the ordinary Patent Office procedure. It is supported by some strong *dicta* in the Court of Appeal, such as:

General Electric's Application[13]

> . . . in pursuance of the public policy, inherent in the adoption of a system of granting only 'examined patents', that the register shall not be cluttered up with patents which would be *certain* to be revoked by the Court in a revocation action. (*Emphasis added*)

> (By Diplock L.J.)

General Electric's (Cox's) Patent[14]

> It seems to me that the test can be stated, perhaps more simply, in these terms: Is it clear on the evidence before the Comptroller that, if the issue of obviousness (assuming that to be the ground relied on) were fought out in a full scale revocation action, the claims would be held bad for obviousness? If the answer is affirmative, then it is right that the patent should be killed in its infancy. If the answer is negative, the patentee should not be deprived of his patent without the protection of a full scale action. In other words, section 33, like section 14, is designed to clear the register of patents which

---

12 [1979] FSR 128.
13 [1964] RPC 413 at 452.
14 [1977] RPC 421 at 437.

are *manifestly untenable*. It is not intended to provide a method of disposing of truly contentious cases. *(Emphasis added)*

(By Buckley, L.J.)

Principle (2) reflects the fact that in civil litigation generally some issues may inherently need to be proven more convincingly than others. It is legitimate to expect, for example, that an applicant for revocation of a 'new' patent under section 72(1)(b) (no entitlement to grant) may need to prove his contention more strictly than one who is applying under section 72(1)(a) on the basis that the inventor's article in the learned journal, disclosing his invention in its entirety, reached the library shelves before the date of his application. The first type of objection may carry with it some taint of fraudulent behaviour which the second type of objection does not.

Again, distinction can be drawn between:

(1) issues of pure technical fact – for example, exactly what is the hardness of the alloy of composition disclosed in Example 1 of the cited prior specification? and
(2) issues which are really inferences of technical fact – for example, is it obvious to use the alloy of Example 1, in view of its hardness, as a bearing material for the shafts of steam turbines?

The Patent Office may be justified in being more cautious on the latter than the former.

The decision of the Court of Appeal in *Dunlop Holdings' Application*[15] is also noteworthy. Opposition was entered on the ground of prior user, on the basis of a commercial sale of some fifty to one hundred wheels of an experimental kind some fifteen years before the date of the patent application. The applicants tried to raise the argument that such user was secret, and hence excluded. Their attempt failed, Buckley, L.J. saying:

> As to the standard of proof, there is nothing in the statute to suggest that any standard different from the normal standard of proof required in civil litigation – that is to say, the balance of probability – should be adopted.
> . . .
> How then does the matter stand on the issues and evidence in the present case ? Evidence was adduced only on one side; that evidence was all one way; it is uncontroverted by any evidence in answer; it has not been challenged by any cross-examination . . .

This was hardly a case where deferral of a final conclusion would assist justice to be done; memories in, say, five to ten years' time as to circumstances existing many years ago already would be unlikely to have become any sharper – indeed, they might well have become more blurred.

The Patent Office has to provide a reasoned decision on the dispute heard before it. Quite apart from the fact that reasoned decisions always were the traditional practice, they are now compelled in any event by virtue of the Comptroller-General's standing as a tribunal for purposes of the Tribunal and Inquiries Act 1971.[16] Decisions are

15 [1979] RPC 523 at 543 and 545.
16 1971 c.62.

normally given in writing some weeks subsequent to the Hearing; immediate oral decisions are relatively rare, apart from those of procedural nature.

It is the practice of the Patent Office to order a 'contribution' to costs only, to be paid by the unsuccessful to the successful party. Such a contribution is not intended to compensate the successful party for his actual costs incurred. The amount of such contribution is assessed in light of the scale of costs currently applicable, as periodically published in the Official Journal (Patents).

Appeal

Apart from the few exceptions provided for by section 97(1) of the 1977 Act (for example, a requirement for omission of disparaging matter from a specification), and generally corresponding exceptions under the residual provisions of the 1949 Act, there is in all cases a right of appeal from any decision of the Patent Office to the Patents Court, newly created by the 1977 Act.

The Patents Court has therefore now taken over the previous appellate jurisdiction of the Patents Appeal Tribunal, itself specially created in 1932 under the Patents and Designs Act 1932, to take over appeals from the Patent Office. These appeals had originally gone to one of the Law Officers of the Crown (Solicitor-General, Attorney-General). That arrangement had provided difficulties, however, arising from the lack of scientific knowledge on the part of most (although not all) holders of those offices.

Parties are entitled to be represented in the Patents Court (on appeals from the Patent Office) by their patent agents, notwithstanding its High Court status. The expense of employing solicitors and counsel can thus be avoided if desired. As regards costs the current practice is to apply, absent exceptional circumstances, the Court rules. This means, today, that the successful party is normally entitled to costs on the so-called 'standard basis' of the Court. This is defined as meaning:

> a reasonable amount in respect of all costs reasonably incurred and any doubts which the taxing officer may have as to whether the costs were reasonably incurred or were reasonable in amount shall be resolved in favour of the paying party . . .[17]

This new practice is in contradistinction to that of the previous Patents Appeal Tribunal where it was the practice (following that of the Patent Office) to award a contribution only.[18]

The new approach may well turn out to be an unfortunate, albeit unintended, by-product of the 1977 Act. It can, in certain cases, give an unfair advantage to the party for whom legal costs is a minor consideration and derogates from the traditional function of the Patent Office as the small inventor's forum.

Time periods and appeal procedure generally is similar to that of ordinary civil appeals. The appeal is formally by way of a rehearing, with the same evidence as below in the Patent Office. The Court does have formal power to permit fresh evidence to be adduced; this can in practice be constituted either of fresh sworn testimony and/or, in a looser sense, fresh material of other kinds, for example, a fresh prior document. But good reason has to be brought forward in support of any such application, even if the

17   RSC O. 62 r. 12(1).
18   *Extrude Hone Corporation's Patent* [1982] RPC 361 at 385.

well-known triple test of *Ladd v Marshall*[19] (already mentioned in Chapter 7) in ordinary civil cases (previous diligence + importance + apparent credibility of the new evidence) is not always adhered to rigidly. As compared to a purely private dispute, there is often a public interest element in patent appeals; if the fresh document shows that Claim 1 of the patent in suit is necessarily bad it is obviously proper that the document be taken into account even if the applicant for revocation has shown somewhat less than perfect diligence in failing to unearth it earlier. Thus, in *Coin Sales' Application*,[20] the Appeal Tribunal allowed a fresh specification to be cited in support of a prior publication attack (but not obviousness); the circumstances in which this document came to light are not mentioned. In *Asea's Application*,[21] an earlier United Kingdom specification which had been classified in the Patent Office indices only under the title 'Alloys', whereas it should have been cross-referred to also under 'Process for obtaining coherent bodies from powdered metals', was allowed to be introduced both in respect of lack of novelty and obviousness when it eventually came to light in connection with corresponding foreign opposition proceedings. Nevertheless, the rule of thumb is that it is significantly harder to introduce fresh material at the appellate stage than belatedly in the Patent Office proceedings of first instance.

Further Appeal to Court of Appeal

The position as regards further appeal from the Patents Court to the Court of Appeal, for matters originating in the Patent Office, is now as follows:

(1) Leave is in all potentially eligible cases necessary, such leave being given either by the Patents Court or (if refused by the Patents Court) by the Court of Appeal.
(2) Potentially eligible cases are in any event of two kinds only, namely:

(a) where the decision arises under certain defined sections of the 1977 Act (or residual provisions of the 1949 Act); or
(b) where the ground of appeal is that the decision of the Patents Court is wrong in law.

For 1977 Act matters, the defined sections are set out in section 97(3). Broadly speaking, they cover questions of:

- entitlement to the patent
- examination of the patent application (strictly, *ex parte* matters only but mentioned here for completeness)
- other failure of the patent application
- employee rights and compensation
- infringement

19 [1954] 1 WLR 1489.
20 [1970] RPC 260.
21 [1978] FSR 115.

– amendment (*inter partes* or *ex parte*)
– revocation, by third party or on Patent Office initiative

For matters under the residual 1949 Act jurisdiction, the scope of the defined sections is rather less, being limited to the questions of belated opposition, disputes between co-owners and disputes as to inventions made by employees.

In both instances, the ground of error in law provides a convenient widening umbrella to the determined appellant – particularly since construction of the patent specification in suit ranks as a matter of law, not fact, and lack of novelty/obviousness has to be assessed in light of the true construction of such specification. The result in practice is that further appeal to the Court of Appeal is possible on a considerable, although not total, scale.

Appeal to House of Lords

The question of leave to appeal still further from the Court of Appeal to the House of Lords is determined by the principles already discussed in Chapter 7. It is by no means impossible for a case starting in the Patent Office to reach the House of Lords. *Bristol-Myers' (Johnson's) Application*[22] (secret prior user) and *Du Pont de Nemours' (Witsiepe's) Application*[23] (prior publication when the later invention is in a potential selection position) provided a pair of notable cases under the 1949 Act which reached this highest tribunal. In contrast, leave was refused in *Beecham Group's (Amoxycillin) Application*[24] – notwithstanding that the commercial stakes involved were fully comparable to those in the *Bristol-Myers* case, which was also involved with semi-synthetic penicillins (ampicillin trihydrate) – because only an issue of fact (obviousness of an orally administrable composition containing as active ingredient an epimeric form of a penicillin already taught) was present, and not an issue of law.

Cases under the 1977 Act have been directed more to questions of statutory interpretation of the Act and corresponding Rules, as in *E's Application*[25] (section 89(3) and Rule 85(1) – withdrawal of international application following failure to pay filing fee); *Textron Inc's Patent*[26] (section 28(3) – restoration of patent); *Asahi Kasei's Application*[27] (section 5(2)(a) – enabling disclosure in priority document).

Patent Office v Court

The relative merits of proceeding in the Patent Office and Patents Court (in cases where the choice of forum is open) are often worthy of careful consideration by a potential litigant. The discussions already provided in Chapter 7 (as to Patents Court procedure in infringement actions) and earlier in this chapter (as to Patent Office contest procedure generally) indicate to some extent the relevant factors. It may be convenient to summarise the traditional pros and cons here.

22   [1975] RPC 127.
23   [1982] FSR 303.
24   [1980] RPC 261.
25   [1983] RPC 231.
26   [1989] RPC 441.
27   [1991] RPC 485.

The Patent Office has, generally speaking, the following advantages:

- relative simplicity of procedure;
- relative cheapness;
- technical expertise;
- permissible representation by patent agents;
- written evidence normal;

but the disadvantages of:

- reluctance to grapple with purely legal issues;
- caution in favour of the patentee in any case of real doubt;
- reluctance to deal firmly at the interlocutory stage with dilatory tactics;
- excessive deference to the convenience of counsel as regards appointment of dates for hearings, thereby indirectly providing further opportunity for delay by a determined party.

The Court, on the other hand, has the following advantages:

- fuller investigatory powers;
- willingness to decide, as opposed merely to defer, issues;
- oral evidence + cross-examination normal;
- injunctive remedies available;

but the disadvantages of:

- expense;
- lesser technical expertise.

It is as a result often advantageous for there to be a preliminary run in the Patent Office; the more so if the matter involves complex technology which it is felt would be better understood by the Hearing Officer than the judge, since even if there is an appeal from the Patent Office decision to the Patents Court the judge will have in front of him the benefit of the Hearing Officer's analysis in his reasoned decision.

In the case of an application for revocation of a 'new' patent (under the 1977 Act) it is, furthermore, explicitly laid down in section 72(5) that a decision of the Patent Office (at first instance or on appeal) will not estop a party counter-claiming for revocation on the same (or different) grounds in a subsequent infringement action on the patent. That is to say, an unsuccessful applicant for revocation in the Patent Office can re-argue the question again *de novo* when he is subsequently sued; naturally, if he has already succeeded in the Patent Office in having the patent revoked, the point will not arise. Similar provision is made, so far as any fresh application for revocation of an 'existing' patent is concerned, by the amendment to section 33 of the 1949 Act effected by Schedule 1, Article 7(2) of the 1977 Act.

Judicial recognition of the ability of the Patent Office was accorded in *Hawker Siddeley Dynamics Engineering v Real Time Developments*,[28] already mentioned in

---

28 [1983] RPC 395.

Chapter 5. The defendants had previously commenced revocation and declaration of non-infringement proceedings in the Patent Office, prior to institution of infringement proceedings by the patentee in the Patents Court, and – contrary to expectation – it was the Patents Court and not the Patent Office proceedings which were stayed notwithstanding the greater standing of the Court in the overall hierarchy of tribunals. This welcome trend was unfortunately stopped dead in its tracks by the subsequent decision (by a then alternate judge of the Patents Court who candidly admitted in the course of argument that he had no direct personal experience of the Patent Office) in *Ferro Corporation v Escol Products*[29] involving a broadly similar situation.

The impact of the new Patents County Court upon the general question is still for the future. The precise extent of its jurisdiction is not yet entirely clear – although it would certainly seem to encompass the standard instance of an application for revocation of a granted patent. In many respects the Patents County Court (as discussed in Chapter 8) combines the best features of the Patent Office and Patents Court procedures. It undoubtedly represents what might be termed an intermediate forum, which may prove attractive to many litigants.

Bibliography

BB – Practice under section 72.
Manual of Office Practice (Patents), Patent Office (1988 ed.).
PLUK – Practice under section 14.
G. Tompkin, 'Patent Office Pleadings in Perspective', CIPA Volume 1 (1971–72) at 281.

29   [1990] RPC 651.

12 International Patents

Territoriality

A patent is, in principle, a creature of territorial vigour only. Thus, a United Kingdom patent provides, essentially, protection to the patentee within the United Kingdom only; a Belgian patent provides similar protection within Belgium only; a United States patent within the United States only; and so on. The few exceptions where the protection is extra-territorial arise mainly from instances when the laws of one country (generally a former colony) provide that a patent granted in some other country shall automatically extend to the former country also. For example, a Dutch patent extends to Curaçao and other Netherlands Antilles and a French patent to New Caledonia and dependencies and a United Kingdom patent to British Indian Ocean Territory.

An inventor or other person in the possession of an invention has therefore to take out separate patents in each separate country in which he desires protection. To facilitate him in this task (bearing in mind that in many countries, like the United Kingdom under the 1977 Act, prior publication or use anywhere in the world ranks as an anticipation and invalidates his patent) various international arrangements have sprung up. In recent years, the pace of development of these has increased markedly. There are now four major arrangements, or 'conventions' as they are often termed, of which the reader should be aware, as follows:

(1) Paris Convention of 1883 (as amended)
(2) Patent Co-operation Treaty 1970
(3) European Patent Convention 1973
(4) Community Patent Convention 1975

Minor arrangements, restricted either to particular groups of countries or to particular kinds of subject-matter, include the Pan-American Conventions of 1889, 1902, 1906 and 1910; the Strasbourg Convention on Unification of Patent Laws 1963; the European Convention on International Patent Classification 1954 and subsequent Strasbourg Convention of 1971; the Hague Agreement on Legalization of Documents 1961; the Budapest Treaty on Deposit of Micro-Organisms 1977; and the International Convention for the Protection of New Varieties of Plants 1961 (UPOV Convention) revised at Geneva in 1991. This list is not comprehensive. For a complete tabulation, and explanation of their functions, specialist works should be consulted.

It is important to remember, moreover, that in English law a treaty is, in principle, not self-executing but has normally to be brought into effect by suitable subsequent specific domestic legislation. Thus, the European Patent Convention, although originally signed on behalf of the United Kingdom in 1973, did not come into effect so far as the United Kingdom was concerned until 1978 when the domestic law was altered accordingly by the 1977 Act; likewise with the Plant Varieties and Seeds Act 1964[1] introduced following ratification of the UPOV Convention by the United Kingdom in 1962. The

---

1   1964 c.14.

generality of the European Communities Act 1972,[2] previously mentioned in Chapter 10, provides something of an exception in this respect.

If the relevant domestic statute is in discord with the treaty, the former not the latter prevails, as in the fountain-head case of *Californian Fig Syrup's Trade Mark*[3] involving the period of priority available from a foreign trade mark application. The Paris Convention (as it stood at the time) gave six months; the domestic United Kingdom Law (section 103 of the Patent Designs and Trade Marks Act 1883)[4] gave only four months, the necessary revision consequent to adherence of the United Kingdom to the Convention not having been carried out yet. The Court stated quite emphatically:

> . . . the Act does not afford the means of carrying out that Article [of the Convention], and it will, no doubt, be for Her Majesty's Government to consider – and seeing the Attorney-General here I have no doubt they will consider – what legislative steps ought to be taken to give effect to that Article, if necessary. But with that I have nothing to do. I have simply to consider this question; dealing as I am with, and being bound by a statute of this realm, whether I can give it a different interpretation from that which I should give it, simply because at this time – at the date of the passing of the Act – this convention had been entered into between certain foreign States, and it was within the bounds of possibility that Her Majesty might afterwards accede to it, and several years afterwards in point of fact Her Majesty did accede to it. I am of opinion that I cannot do so.

The position elsewhere is sometimes *contra*; for example, in the United States, under Article II, Section 2 of the Constitution:

> . . . and all *treaties* made, or which shall be made, under the authority of the United States, shall be the *supreme* Law of the land; and the Judges in every State shall be bound thereby, anything in the Constitution or laws of any State to the contrary notwithstanding.   (*Emphasis added*).

Paris Convention

This is the original (and in some respects still the most important) arrangement. It is often known simply as the 'International Convention'. The original version was signed between eleven countries in Paris on 20 March 1883. The number of contracting countries rapidly grew. Periodic revisions were also made at conferences in Rome (1886), Madrid (1890), Brussels (1900), Washington (1911), The Hague (1925), London (1934), Lisbon (1958) and Stockholm (1967). Around ninety countries are now members; the majority, although not all, of these have adopted the latest Stockholm version of the Convention. It is supervised by the World Intellectual Property Organization (WIPO) at Geneva.

Its main principles for purposes of the present brief overview are:

(1) national treatment; and
(2) right of priority.

2   1972 c.68.
3   6 RPC 126 (1888).
4   46 & 47 Vict. c.57.

National treatment, as defined in Article 2 of the Convention, means essentially that foreigners (that is, nationals and residents of other Member States) are treated alike to domestic citizens in so far as patent protection for their inventions is concerned – in other words, they are entitled to receive the appropriate 'national' treatment, but no more. Thus, if a foreigner from Country A with a liberal patent law (say, a law which grants patents for a twenty-year term) decides to take out a patent for his invention in Country B also which has a more restrictive law (say, a law which grants patents for a fifteen-year term only), he can only obtain in Country B the fifteen-year term; he cannot complain that Country B is failing to treat him in totally reciprocal fashion, since all that the domestic citizens of Country B are themselves entitled to is the fifteen-year term.

The right of priority means that, provided the corresponding patent application in Country B is filed within twelve months from first filing in Country A, then it can, in effect, be back-dated to the date of that first filing. Intervening disclosure or use of the invention which might perhaps otherwise (under the relevant law of Country B) invalidate the corresponding patent in Country B is thus rendered nugatory.

So far as the United Kingdom is concerned, the Paris Convention impinges therefore in two respects. First, it enables foreigners to obtain in the United Kingdom patents corresponding to original foreign applications on inventions made abroad; the maintenance of foreign priority in such cases is covered by sections 5 and 90 of the 1977 Patents Act, and has already been mentioned in Chapter 4. In 1977 itself (the last full year prior to the coming into force of the 1977 Patents Act and the opening of the European Patent Office under the European Patent Convention) some 70 per cent of all patent applications filed in the United Kingdom Patent Office were of this kind. Secondly, it enables United Kingdom inventors, conversely, to retain priority date for their own corresponding foreign applications on inventions originating here.

Apart from the fundamental questions of national treatment and right of priority, the Paris Convention also lays down a subsidiary framework of other principles to which contracting countries must adhere. These include such matters as the right to claim in a single patent multiple priorities (from one or more basic applications), the right to divide one patent application voluntarily into two or more, use of infringing devices on vessels and the like temporarily in the country, grace periods for payment of renewal fees and limits to the freedom of the state to grant compulsory licences to third parties. But in no sense are they sufficiently comprehensive to provide a universal code. There is still ample room left for a contracting country to incorporate its own quirks into its domestic law; in particular, each country may regulate the style and contents of the specification and claims.

Much of the skill of the patent agent and success (for a United Kingdom patentee) in foreign patenting depends on knowing what those quirks are and acting suitably on them. Notwithstanding the safeguards that it provides, the Paris Convention still leaves an inventor with the basic necessity of making separate patent applications in each country in which he seeks protection and of employing local professional representation in each country. This, however, is to some extent avoidable by using one of the arrangements now to be described.

Patent Co-operation Treaty

The Patent Co-operation Treaty (or PCT as it is generally known) can be regarded, in the broadest sense, as an arrangement for introducing a supra-national element into the patent system. Unlike the European Patent Convention and Community Patent Convention which are supra-national arrangements of a regional character, the PCT is of worldwide character and is administered by the International Bureau (the Secretariat of WIPO) at Geneva.

The Patent Co-operation Treaty is concerned with eliminating unnecessary effort and work, on the part of both the patentee and the individual Patent Offices, in the instance when a patent application is to be filed in a number of countries. It is, for example, *prima facie* a wasteful duplication of effort for a series of prior art searches on the same invention to be carried out by the Examiners in a corresponding series of Patent Offices.

In barest outline, what the PCT provides for is the initial filing of a single so-called 'International Patent Application' in a given Patent Office, termed the 'Receiving Office'; this is regarded as having the effect of filing the application in both the first country and also in all the other countries in which the applicant is interested. The totality of these are termed the 'Designated States'.

The International Patent Application is then transmitted to an International Searching Authority; the latter does the prior art search and transmits the results, the International Search Report, to the individual Patent Offices of the various individual Designated States. Further prosecution in each country is then in the hands of the local Patent Office, in accordance with its normal procedure; if prosecution is successful the appropriate national patent is granted, in normal manner.

In a variation (to which not all the countries that are party to the Treaty generally have acceded yet), the unitary treatment is taken one stage further. The International Search Report is forwarded to an International Preliminary Examining Authority, which advises as to the patentability of the invention in question, in light of the prior art found. This advice is communicated to the individual Patent Offices, who again handle the further prosecution of the application in its light; the advice is not necessarily binding, although in practice considerable attention is likely to be paid to it. In any case the patent application is subjected to a single check for formalities and is published centrally by the International Bureau.

In essence, therefore, the PCT represents an arrangement whereby the prosecution of an application in a number of countries can be centralised to some extent but yet a bundle of national patents are eventually granted.

The PCT is open to all countries which are members of the Paris Convention. The United Kingdom is a member, and section 89 of the Patents Act 1977 represents the legislative provisions whereby the PCT is brought into effect. Total membership, at around forty countries, is still considerably smaller than that of the Paris Convention but does include the important industrial countries of Japan and the United States which are outside the purview of the European systems to be discussed in the next section.

A simplified flow diagram of PCT procedure is provided in Appendix 4.

European Patent Convention

This is essentially a regional arrangement. The potential contracting countries are limited to those of Europe by Article 166 of the Convention, although not solely to those of the European Economic Community. The European Patent Convention is commonly known as the EPC. Current membership is composed of Austria, Belgium, Denmark, France, Germany (now including the former German Democratic Republic), Greece, Italy, Lichtenstein, Luxembourg, Monaco, the Netherlands, Portugal, Spain, Sweden, Switzerland and the United Kingdom.

The EPC is more advanced than the PCT in that both searching and examination are centralised in the newly founded (1978) European Patent Office (EPO) in Munich, Germany. It is similar to the PCT in that the applicant again has to designate the particular European countries in which he is interested to protect his invention. A so-called Euro-PCT application is also possible.

Although the applicant is granted, if prosecution is successful, a so-called 'European Patent', subsequent enforcement and general administration of that patent is handled within the courts and Patent Offices of the individual European countries concerned. Thus, again, in effect, a bundle of individual national patents is obtained but, unlike the PCT, the validity of each individual patent will be judged on grounds set out in the EPC rather than on the normal national grounds (if different) – see Article 138.

Nationals of both member and non-member countries are entitled to take advantage of the EPC. It is thus possible, say, for a United States applicant to make a European patent designating the United Kingdom, France, West Germany and Luxembourg as the countries in which protection is desired.

From the United Kingdom jurisprudential standpoint, much of the importance of the EPC springs from the fact that the domestic patent law has been altered, via the 1977 Patents Act, so as to be in accordance with the substantive (as distinct from merely purely procedural) provisions of the EPC. This has been frequently commented on in previous chapters. It is only necessary to repeat here the similarity between the criteria for patentability (Articles 52 to 54, 56 and 57 of EPC and sections 1 to 4 of the 1977 Act), for determining the scope of protection of the patent (Article 69(1) of EPC and section 125(1) and (3) of the 1977 Act), and for imparting protection in the case of chemical process inventions to the direct product only of that process (Article 64(2) of EPC and section 60(1)(c) of the 1977 Act). Section 130(7) of the 1977 Act expressly enumerates those sections of the 1977 Act which are:

> so framed as to have, as nearly as practicable, the same effects in the United Kingdom as the corresponding provisions of the European Patent Convention, the Community Patent Convention and the Patent Cooperation Treaty have in the territories to which those Conventions apply.

It is likely, therefore that the Patent Office and Courts of this country will have to pay increasing attention to European patent jurisprudence – a break with the insularity of the past. In obedience to the intention expressed in section 130(7), the Court has followed EPO jurisprudence in a number of areas in recent times – sometimes willingly as in the requirement that an anticipatory document provide an 'enabling disclosure' (for example as in *Genentech Inc's (Human Growth Hormone) Patent*),[5] and sometimes

5 [1989] RPC 613.

unwillingly as in the employment of a 'Swiss-style' use claim to protect a second pharmaceutical use (*John Wyeth & Brother's Application; Schering's Application*).[6] In *Gale's Application*[7] the endorsement (in relation to the exclusion from patentability of programs for computers) the endorsement was positive and enthusiastic – it was of the 'utmost importance' that the interpretations should be the same, and any substantial divergence would be 'disastrous'.

On a more day-to-day level, the decision for a United Kingdom inventor whether to file a European patent application or separate applications (with the benefit of the Paris Convention) in the European countries of interest to him involves a number of factors. One is that of cost; the European patent procedure is expensive but there comes a point at which it is nevertheless cheaper than the corresponding series of individual applications. The current rule of thumb places that point at around four countries, although its precise location will naturally vary in future according to the relative levels of fee movements as between the European and local Patent Offices and the professional charges made by patent agents in the various countries. Other, and perhaps more important, factors are those of quality of examination and the possibility of opposition under Article 99 of the EPC (within nine months from grant). Although the European Patent Office is still in its relative infancy, it seems clear that examination is thorough. If his patent application can survive that hurdle, and also that of possible opposition immediately after grant, a patentee is reasonably entitled to assume that his eventual patent will have a good (although not certain) chance of being subsequently upheld in the national courts. Actual practice is discussed more fully (but not comprehensively) at the end of this chapter. A simplified flow diagram of European procedure is provided in Appendix 4.

The EPO has proved to be very successful – perhaps even surpassing the most optimistic predictions at the time of its 1978 foundation. In 1990, no less than 62,778 applications (including Euro-PCT applications entering the regional phase) were filed and 24,757 patents granted (with an average of 6.6 designations per patent). Around 8% of granted patents are opposed, such oppositions resulting in revocation in about 40% of cases and maintenance of the patent (either in granted or amended form) in the remaining 60% of cases.

Community Patent Convention

This lies more in the future. Although the original Community Patent Convention was signed at Luxembourg in 1975 (and revised in 1989) it has not yet come into effect. Sections 86 to 88 of the 1977 Act, as subsequently amended, will enable it to be accommodated within the United Kingdom system when it does come into effect. It can essentially be regarded as an extension to the European Patent Convention with the difference that instead of a bundle of individual patents in European countries being granted there is obtained a single unitary patent throughout all those European countries which are also members of the European Economic Community.

A source of difficulty in its implementation generally has lain in the provisions concerning enforcement of Community patents. The original scheme of the Convention

6   [1985] RPC 545.
7   [1991] RPC 305 at 323.

provided for validity to be determined by the EPO and infringement (liable to be stayed in any event if revocation proceedings before the EPO are pending) determined by national courts. Choice of national court was to be determined by the defendant's residence. Following a further diplomatic conference at Brussels in 1985 it is now hoped to introduce instead a so-called Community Patent Court and Common Appeal Court (COPAC). Noteworthy is the formal enshrinement of the 'exhaustion of rights' principle, as regards infringement, in Article 32 of the Convention; also the manner in which section 60 of the 1977 Act reflects the provisions of Articles 29 to 31 of the Convention as regards definition of infringement.

Registration of United Kingdom Patents

One final possibility for a United Kingdom patentee, when it comes to foreign protection, is to register his United Kingdom patent once eventually granted (as distinct from merely being filed) in those former colonial dependencies which still permit protection to be obtained in this manner. Generally, only the very small dependencies now permit this, for example, the Falkland Islands, although Hong Kong is at present an important addition. Registration deadlines and procedure generally tend to vary from one dependency to another, as does also the term of protection afforded by the registration.

European Patent Office Practice

It may be useful to end this chapter with a brief discussion of European Patent Office practice, as it has developed so far in the interval since the opening of the European Patent Office in 1978.

The basic legal provisions as to patentability and procedure in the European Patent Convention (EPC), under which the European Patent Office works, are (as previously indicated) similar to those of the 1977 United Kingdom Act which was drafted (in the relevant respects) so as to reflect the EPC. There is again a five-step sequence of:

    (1) filing the application;
    (2) publication;
    (3) search;
    (4) substantive examination; and
    (5) if the prosecution is successful, grant.

The term of the patent is also twenty years from date of filing.

One significant difference lies, however, in respect of revocation. A European patent can be revoked *in toto* only during the first nine months from grant; subsequently, it can only be revoked country-by-country, by application to the appropriate national court. The grounds available are, generally, the same as those available to the European Examiner in the first instance.

On the important question of the attitude to be adopted by the EPO towards the question of inventive step there have been official Guidelines (Guidelines for Examination in the European Patent Office, Part C, Chapter IV, Section 9) issued under the powers of Article 10(2)(a) of the EPC. These provide neither an exhaustive list, nor a strait-jacket, but are indicative of the European approach to the subject. They are reprinted in Appendix 12. They are part of the full set of Guidelines covering European practice as a whole, available from the EPO.

Examination of the Guidelines as to inventive step suggests that the European Patent Office is deliberately trying to carve out a path of its own – borrowing in places concepts from the various individually different national European jurisprudences but not dictated by any one system. Paragraph B1 in Section 9.8, for example, clearly reflects the well-known United Kingdom case of *Williams v Nye*,[8] involving a sausage-making machine of this type (mere juxtaposed collocation of already known devices). The warning against unfair *ex post facto* analysis in Section 9.9 echoes the decision in *British Westinghouse v Braulik*.[9] Similar analogies can be drawn in other areas of the Guidelines.

The Guidelines generally are, however, no more than that. They are not controlling, even though in practice it is natural for them to be accorded more weight in proceedings of first instance (before the Examining Division or Opposition Division) than on appeal (either before the Legal Board of Appeal, the Technical Board of Appeal or the Enlarged Board of Appeal). It is not uncommon for a given Guideline to be amended, following criticism in a Board decision. A typical statement as to their status is to be found in the decision on *EXXON/Alumina spinel* (T42/84):[10]

> 9. The *Guidelines*, as stated in the General Introduction to them, do not have the binding authority of a legal text. Therefore a failure by the Examining Division to follow them is not to be regarded as a procedural violation within the meaning of Rule 67 unless it also constitutes a violation of a rule of principle of procedure governed by an article of the EPC or one of the Implementing Regulations.

As already mentioned, the case law of the EPO is now important both in its own right, given the popularity of the Office as a means of gaining patent protection in EPC countries, and by virtue of its consequential impact on United Kingdom domestic law. It is not feasible to review the subject comprehensively within the compass of the present work. But it is useful to mention briefly some of the highlights since 1978.

Inherent Patentability

In *EISAI/Second medical indication* (G05/83),[11] in response to the question referred to it by the Technical Board of Appeal:

> Can a patent with claims directed to the use be granted for the use of a substance or composition for the treatment of the human or animal body by therapy?

the Enlarged Board held:

> 1. A European patent with claims directed to the use may not be granted for the use

8 7 RPC 62.
9 27 RPC 209.
10 [1988] EPOR 387.
11 [1979–85] EPOR Vol.B 241.

of a substance or composition for the treatment of the human or animal body by therapy.

2. A European patent may be granted with claims directed to the use of a substance or composition for the manufacture of a medicament for a specified new and inventive therapeutic application.

Protection can thereby be effectively obtained for an inventive finding of a second pharmaceutical use.

In *HARVARD/Onco-mouse* (T19/90),[12] in the context of generic claims to:

> 1. A method for producing a transgenic non-human mammalian animal having an increased probability of developing neoplasms, said method comprising chromosomally incorporating an activated oncogene sequence into the genome of a non-human mammalian animal.

> 19. A transgenic non-human mammalian animal whose germ cells and somatic cells contain an activated oncogene sequence as a result of chromosomal incorporation into the animal genome, or into the genome of an ancestor of said animal, said oncogene optionally being further defined according to any one of Claims 3 to 10.

the Technical Board held that Article 53(b) of the EPC (corresponding to section 1(3)(b) of the 1977 Act) did not bar the patenting of animals as such. *LUBRIZOL/Hybrid plants* (T320/87)[13] represents another example of the statutory exceptions to patentability being construed narrowly.

Novelty

Three decisions may be mentioned here, *ICI/Pyridine herbicides* (T206/83),[14] *MOBIL/Friction reducing additive* (G02/88)[15] and *UNILEVER/Washing composition* (T666/89).[15a] ICI introduced the doctrine of 'enabling disclosure'. The applicant was able to overcome an Article 54(3) objection to a group of chemical compounds *per se* on the basis that the earlier cited document, although it disclosed compounds coming with that formula, nevertheless failed to show how the necessary starting materials for the process whereby those compounds were to be produced could themselves be made. The doctrine has been applied domestically in *Genentech Inc's (Human Growth Hormone) Patent*,[16] in the context of a novelty attack, and more recently in *Asahi Kasei's Application*,[17] in the context of the necessary degree of supporting disclosure in a priority document.

In *MOBIL*, the claim was of 'use' type and directed to the incorporation of a minor amount of a given additive to a lubricating oil composition for purposes of friction-reduction. The prior art showed incorporation of the same additive, but for purposes of inhibiting rust-formation instead. As such, there was novelty of purpose, but no novelty as regards means of technical realisation. Nevertheless, the Enlarged Board held:

12 [1990] EPOR 501.
13 [1990] EPOR 173.
14 [1986] EPOR 232.
15 [1990] EPOR 73.
15a [1992] EPOR 501.
16 [1989] RPC 613.
17 [1991] RPC 485.

A claim to the use of a known compound for a particular purpose, which is based on a technical effect which is described in the patent, should be interpreted as including that technical effect as a functional technical feature, and is accordingly not open to objection under Article 54(1) EPC provided that such technical feature has not previously been made available to the public.

The implications of this decision so far as infringement is concerned still remain to be worked out. *Prima facie*, considerable problems would seem to arise.

UNILEVER is significant because it enunciates in full the somewhat broader approach to lack of novelty (as compared to the United Kingdom) incipient in such earlier decisions as *BAYER/Diastereomers* (T12/81),[17a] *DU PONT/Copolymers* (T124/87).[17b] The accent is on what is made available as a whole to the public by the previous document that is its 'total information content'), rather than on what it clearly and unmistakeably teaches.

Inventive step

It is here that the conceptual differences between the EPO practice and domestic United Kingdom law and practice are most marked. A number of points can be taken.

First, as regards the state of the art against which the existence of inventive step has to be assessed. Domestic law has traditionally downgraded prior art which was not in use or otherwise not widely known to those working in the art at the relevant time. Disparaging remarks as to 'mere paper anticipations' or the like abound in early authorities. In the case of *General Tire & Rubber v Firestone Tyre & Rubber*[18] in more recent times, the Court of Appeal seized upon the alleged difficulty in locating the highly relevant wartime Semperit applications as an excuse to denigrate their teaching – notwithstanding the fact that for the synthetic rubber researcher in 1950 the records of the Continental work during World War II might, realistically, be reckoned as a most interesting source of ideas. The EPO in contrast (and correctly, it is submitted) tends to take the opposite view. If a given piece of prior art comes within the formal definition of 'state of the art' in Article 54(2) then it has to be taken into account just as much as does any other piece of art; age is no barrier. Thus, in *MITSUBOSHI/Endless power transmission belt* (T169/84)[19] an attempt by the patentee to discount an 80-year old United States Specification cited by the opponent was decisively turned down by the Board:

> 3.6.3 The appellants have put forward that, as banded belts are a recent development, it would be unrealistic to expect those skilled in this relatively new art to have, as part of their general knowledge, the teaching of a patent issued in 1893. But however new a technique may be, the man skilled in the art must be expected to see if the problems he is faced with have already been solved in other related technical fields which are confronted with the same problems. In the present case it must be considered that banded belts are an improvement of V-belts and that the skilled person for banded belts is the same as the one for V-belts or flat belts. It must be regarded as his normal activity

17a   [1979–85] EPOR Vol. B 308.
17b   [1989] EPOR 33.
18   [1972] RPC 457.
19   [1987] EPOR 120.

to apply to the manufacture of banded belts knowledge described in a document mentioning *inter alia* belting.

Another facet of this point lies in the need to take into account the totality of the teaching of a given prior document, and not merely those parts of it which have attracted most attention in the past. For example, in *BASF/Metal refining* (T24/81):[20]

> The Board does not share the applicant's view that only those embodiments described as being preferred in a citation are to be considered when assessing the inventive step – *all* previously published embodiments must be taken in consideration which offered a suggestion to the skilled practitioner for solving the problem addressed, even where the embodiments were not particularly emphasised. It is therefore *not* a matter of what was regarded as advantageous at that time in the publications constituting the prior art.[21]
>
> *(Emphasis added)*

BASF also illustrates the second point – the need for objectivity. As to this, the Board said:

> When assessing inventive step . . . it is not a question of the subjective achievement of the inventor, so that the case history of the invention presented at the oral proceedings is irrelevant. It is rather the objective achievement that has to be assessed.[21a]

This approach can be contrasted with that displayed, for example, in such typical domestic decisions as:

American Cyanamid v Ethicon[22]

> . . . the history of the matter, which is often the best evidence for or against obviousness . . .

American Cyanamid v Berk Pharmaceuticals[23]

> If a thing is obvious you go straight to it.

J. Lucas (Batteries) v Gaedor[24]

> In all these cases I am for my own part of the opinion that the question of obviousness is probably best tested, if this be possible, by the guidance given by contemporary events.

The EPO approach is accordingly more akin to the traditionally rather more incisive and demanding approach of the German, Dutch or even United States Patent Offices and Courts. There is much to be said for it.

The third point concerns problem and solution. This way of looking at the question

---

20 [1979–85] EPOR Vol.B. 354.
21 At paragraph 14.
21a At paragraph 4.
22 [1975] RPC 513 at 517.
23 [1976] RPC 231 at 257.
24 [1978] RPC 297 at 358.

of inventive step was enunciated in the fountainhead decision of the Board in *BAYER/Carbonless copying paper* (T01/80).[25] On occasion, this can lead to a degree of artificiality. There can be instances where the reality is that the skilled person in the art was already perfectly satisfied with the existing technical process or machine as the case may be. It can be difficult in such instances to regard him as having a 'problem' at all. Again, the unearthing of a piece of prior art not known to the inventor at the time, or to the draftsman of the patent specification, may necessitate a substantial revision during prosecution (or opposition) of the definition of the problem. Nevertheless, the approach has been consistently followed by the EPO.

The overall technique used by the EPO to assess inventive step is encapsulated in the following further passage from *BASF*:

> Objectivity in the assessment of inventive step is achieved by starting out from the objectively prevailing state of the art, in the light of which the problem is determined which the invention addresses and solves from an objective point of view . . . and consideration is given to the question of obviousness of the disclosed solution to this problem as seen by the man skilled in the art and having those capabilities which can be objectively expected of him.[25a]

In domestic jurisprudence the concept of the 'problem' – although not entirely alien – tends to receive a lesser degree of attention. For example, in one of the latest pronouncements of the Court of Appeal on the subject of inventive step (*Windsurfing International v Tabur Marine*)[26] the word is absent entirely, the approach being defined instead as:

> The first is to identify the inventive concept embodied in the patent in suit. Thereafter, the court has to assume the mantle of the normally skilled but unimaginative addressee in the art at the priority date and to impute to him what was, at that date, common general knowledge in the art in question. The third step is to identify what, if any, differences exist between the matter cited as being 'known or used' and the alleged invention. Finally, the court has to ask itself whether, viewed without any knowledge of the alleged invention, those differences constitute steps which would have been obvious to the skilled man or whether they require any degree of invention.

Bibliography

J. Bierman, 'US Patent Litigation – Trial or Torture', CIPA Volume 10 1980–81 at 343.
P. Braendli, 'The Dynamism of the European Patent System' IIC Volume 22 (1991) at 177.
Chartered Institute of Patent Agents, *European Patents Handbook*, Volumes 1 and 2 (1978 onwards), Oyez Longman.
S. Ladas, *Patents, Trademarks, and Related Rights – National and International Protection*, Volumes I, II and III, Harvard University Press, 1975.
Manual for the Handling of Applications for Patents, Designs and Trade Marks throughout the World, Volumes 1 to 4 (1927 onwards), Octrooibureau Los en Stigter Amsterdam (the 'Dutch Manual').

25   [1979–85] EPOR Vol.B 250.
25a   At paragraph 14.
26   [1985] RPC 59 at 73.

G. Paterson, 'Procedural Law and Practice of the Boards of Appeal of the European Patent Office' [1987] EIPR 221.

K. Pfanner, 'The Patent Co-operation Treaty – An Introduction', [1979] EIPR 98.

J. Richards, '10 Years of Substantive Law Development in the European Patent Office' JPTOS Volume 71 (1989) at 320.

J. Sinnott, 'A Comparative Analysis of some Reciprocal Patent Treaties', JPOS Volume 65 (1983) at 522.

N. Wallace, 'Practice before the European Patent Office – Examination and Opposition', [1983] EIPR 36.

13 Patents in Relation to Other Forms of Intellectual Property

Other Types of Protection — General

As mentioned in Chapter 1, patent protection has to be distinguished from the potential protection afforded to an inventor by the laws of confidential information, registered designs and copyright. The last of these heads includes the new unregistered design right introduced by the Copyright, Designs and Patents Act 1988 (1988 Act).[1]

Further distinction has to be drawn over the protection afforded by the laws of registered trade marks and passing-off. These latter laws are hardly capable of protecting an invention physically as such in any way; rather, they are concerned essentially only with protecting the name, style, get-up and the like under which goods (whether or not also protected under one or other of the earlier heads) are sold on the market. However, valuable commercial benefit can often be obtained by providing a newly invented article, or new form of a given article (say, a new form of safety-pin), with a characteristic trade mark or name also since such protection can outlast the other types of protection. Notionally, at least, a trade mark or name can subsist in perpetuity.

Many products of current household fame were in fact originally protected under patents. Thus, the manufacture of the well-known breakfast cereal bearing the name 'Shredded Wheat' was covered in earlier decades by United Kingdom Patent No. 19368/1895.

A special form of protection for certain botanical inventions is obtainable under the Plant Varieties and Seeds Act 1964,[2] and 1983,[3] referred to in Chapter 2. Protection under utility model law is not available at present in the United Kingdom, although it does subsist in certain foreign countries, again as already mentioned in Chapter 1.

This chapter is confined to comparing, in outline, patent protection with protection under confidential information, registered design and copyright law, and reviewing the three interfaces so arising.

Confidential Information

It is now well established that the law will in practice step in to protect the owner of confidential information against its unauthorised disclosure or use, even though there is, in the words of the Law Commission, 'a continuing doubt as to the ultimate legal foundation on which the whole jurisdiction rests' (Working Paper No. 58 (1974) at 40).

The modern law, at least in relation to confidential information of technological nature, is normally taken as starting with the judgment in 1948 of Lord Greene M.R. in *Saltman Engineering v Campbell Engineering*, concerning leather punches, wherein the principle was stated as:

---

1 1988 c.48.
2 1964 c.14.
3 1983 c.17.

> If a defendant is proved to have used confidential information, directly or indirectly obtained from a plaintiff, without the consent, express or implied, of the plaintiff, he will be guilty of an infringement of the plaintiff's rights.[4]

But there are numerous earlier precedents to similar effect, including *Morison v Moat*[5] (secret recipe for a medicine) and *Amber Size & Chemical v Menzel*[6] (secret process for producing a paper-making size).

The *Saltman* rule was subsequently significantly extended by the 'springboard' doctrine of *Terrapin v Builders' Supply (Hayes)*[7] (portable buildings), and the line of cases following, including *Seager v Copydex*[8] (carpet grips), *Coco v Clark (Engineers)*[9] (moped engines), *Potters Ballotini v Weston Baker* (small glass beads)[10] and *Harrison v Project and Design*[11] (domestic lifts). A more recent case is that of *Roger Bullivant v Ellis*[12] (customer card index taken by ex-employee). In the *Terrapin* decision itself it was defined as:

> . . . the essence of this branch of the law, whatever the origin of it may be, is that a person who has obtained information in confidence is not allowed to use it as a *springboard* for activities detrimental to the person who made the confidential communication, and springboard it remains even when all the features have been published or can be ascertained by actual inspection by any member of the public . . . It is, in my view, inherent in the principle upon which the *Saltman* case rests that the possessor of such information must be placed under a *special disability* in the field of competition to ensure that he does not get an *unfair* start.[13]   (*Emphasis added*)

However, the springboard does in the end lose its bounce. As pointed out in *Potters-Ballotini*:

> Although a man must not use such information as a springboard to get a start over others, nevertheless the springboard does not last for ever. If he does use it, a time may come when so much has happened that he can no longer be restrained.[14]

The confidential information may be of various kinds. Thus, it may be represented by information of inherently unpatentable or doubtfully patentable nature, for example, information relating to an animal breeding process or to computer programming. It may alternatively be information falling in principle within one or other category of patentable subject-matter but lacking a sufficient degree of novelty to be validly patentable in fact – that is, it may be just a workshop improvement. Another possibility is that it may be know-how valuable to the actual carrying-out of an already patented process. A still further possibility is that it represents information which is of patentable merit but which the possessor has deliberately decided to try and keep secret for his

4   65 RPC 203 at 213.
5   9 Hare 241.
6   30 RPC 433.
7   [1967] RPC 367.
8   [1967] RPC 349.
9   [1969] RPC 41.
10 [1977] RPC 202.
11 [1978] FSR 81.
12 [1987] FSR 172.
13 At 391.
14 At 206.

own benefit – for example, by selling the product of the secret process. Certain liqueurs, perfumes and food products are still today supposed to fall under this head.

One advantage of keeping the information secret is, of course, that it can, potentially, be enjoyed for a term longer than that of any patent taken out upon it. The other side of the coin is that the cat, once let out of the bag, may become totally loose. Thus, if a dishonest employee takes his employer's trade-secret way of making custard powder with him to a rival concern, that rival concern may well in turn confine itself just to re-using the information but without disseminating it further; to disseminate it further would open the door to use by other rivals as well. In such a case, enjoining the rival concern and/or claiming damages from it and the dishonest employee, has purpose. But if the dishonest employee has instead – perhaps for misguided moral reasons – published the trade secret to the whole world by advertising it or otherwise revealing it in the daily press, then the secret has effectively gone for good. The damages claim against the dishonest employee himself might be of trifling value relative to the value of the trade secret itself. Another advantage lies in the avoidance of the potential expenses of taking out, maintaining and enforcing any patent covering the trade secret in question.

Generally speaking, the possessor of the relevant trade secret has to opt for the one path (patenting) or the other (keeping it secret). The law has traditionally frowned on the person who tries to get the best of both worlds by using the information commercially in his own factory, for his own benefit, for some extended period of time and then, when he fears that disclosure is imminent, applying for a patent – *vide Wood v Zimmer*, [15] in 1815, where the inventor had discovered a new method of making the pigment verdigris in a brighter green colour, and had sold some of the improved pigment prior to taking out his patent. The rudimentary analytical techniques of the day were hardly capable of revealing, from the product, the process used. Yet the law was held to be:

> Some things are obvious as soon as they are made public. Of others the scientific world may possess itself by analysis. Some inventions almost baffle discovery. But to entitle a man to a patent, the invention must be new to the world. The public sale of that, which is afterwards made the subject of a patent, *though sold by the inventor only*, makes the patent void. *(Emphasis added)*

Under the 1949 Act, prior secret use was indeed denominated explicitly as a ground for revocation of the patent; it was immaterial whether the prior use was by the patentee himself or a third party. The 1977 Act lacks any such corresponding ground, no doubt because of the wholesale revision of the criteria for patentability necessary in order to bring the domestic law into accordance with the European Patent Convention; but it is thought that the Court would be slow to lose its grip on such a cherished principle. It would seem quite possible that the Court would regard such prior use (assuming it to be of process kind with subsequent sale of finished articles) as use which had in fact made the invention 'available' to the public, within the scope of section 2(2) of the 1977 Act. Section 64 of the 1977 Act, whilst it gives a right of continued user, does not go so far as to permit revocation of the patent on the ground of such earlier use.

---

15   1 WPC 44.

Registered Designs

Registration of a design under the Registered Designs Act 1949[16] provides the proprietor of the Design Registration with a species of copyright in the strict sense, even though the term 'copyright' when used in a more colloquial sense is usually taken as excluding design registration. Such exclusion can be regarded as flowing, in the ultimate, from the differing genesis of the two. Copyright generally, if it exists, arises inherently – in the case of a literary work, at the moment when the words are written down on paper. Design registration, on the other hand, requires (as the name implies) a formal act of registration.

The 1949 Act itself is the culmination of a series of earlier statutes, the first general provision being that of the Designs Act 1842[17] with subsequent revisions being made (generally speaking) contemporaneously with the periodic revision of the patent statute. The 1883 statute, for example, is formally entitled the 'Patents, Designs and Trade Marks Act, 1883'[18] with Part III (sections 47 to 61) devoted solely to the topic of registration of designs. The 1949 Act was amended in a number of significant respects by the Copyright, Designs and Patents Act 1988. The revised version as a whole is re-printed as Schedule 4 to that Act.

The complications resulting from the existence of two separate types of registered design – those granted under the original 1949 Act and those granted under the amended 1949 Act – are beyond the scope of this work. Depending upon the issue arising, the change in the law may (or may not) be relevant. The following discussion deals essentially with the position so far as new registered designs, granted under the provisions of the amended 1949 Act, are concerned. Much of the former fundamental case law is expected, however, to be of continued application, as will be seen.

In the broadest sense, design registration is limited to the protection of new appearance as distinct from new construction (for which latter patents constitute the appropriate mode of protection). 'Design' is defined in section 1(1) of the amended Act as:

> 1.—(1) In this Act 'design' means features of shape, configuration, pattern or ornament applied to an article by any industrial process, being features which in the finished article appeal to and are judged by the eye, but does not include—
>
> (a) a method or principle of construction, or
>
> (b) features of shape or configuration of an article which—
>
> > (i) are dictated solely by the function which the article has to perform, or
> >
> > (ii) are dependent upon the appearance of another article of which the article is intended by the author of the design to form an integral part.

The right given by registration is defined principally in section 7(1), in terms of:

> 7.—(1) The registration of a design under this Act gives the registered proprietor the exclusive right—

16 12, 13 & 14 Geo. 6 c.88.
17 5 & 6 Vict. c.100.
18 46 & 47 Vict. c.57.

(a) to make or import—

(i) for sale or hire, or

(ii) for use for the purposes of a trade or business, or

(b) to sell, hire or offer or expose for sale or hire,

an article in respect of which the design is registered and to which that design or a design not substantially different from it has been applied.

A design, in order to be registrable, must have novelty (section 1(2)), and novelty is defined in section 1(4) in terms of:

(4) A design shall not be regarded as new for the purposes of this Act if it is the same as a design—

(a) registered in respect of the same or any other article in pursuance of a prior application, or

(b) published in the United Kingdom in respect of the same or any other article before the date of the application,

or if it differs from such a design only in immaterial details or in features which are variants commonly used in the trade.

Generally, therefore, the requirements are analogous to those for a patent; there must be both actual novelty (in the sense that the new design cannot be an exact replication of some prior art design) and some element of inventiveness.

The prior design being relied on in an attack on the validity of the registered design (if itself not a registered design) may, of course, be one which has been published by virtue of prior use or in any other kind of document, including prior patent specifications. An example of the latter kind of attack is found in *Rosedale Associated Manufacturers v Airfix Products*[19] (design registration for a toy bucket for building a sand castle with a 'Maltese Cross' type of castellation on top held good over an older Patent Specification showing a mould insert capable of producing a generally similar six-castellated configuration). It should be noted in passing that there has been no expansion in the amended 1949 Act as regards what constitutes prior art, comparable to that enunciated by the 1977 Act so far as patents are concerned. Novelty is still assessed in relation to United Kingdom prior art only (albeit without limitation as to time, the designs legislation lacking any equivalent to the fifty-year rule of the Patents Act 1949).

A practical aspect of design registration law is that of dual patent and design protection. It will be appreciated that very often a new appearance of a given article will involve also a new mode of construction for the article (which may hence be patentable); conversely, a new mode of construction may, incidentally, lead to a new appearance providing the required eye-appeal for registration.

The older case of *Werner Motors v Gamage*[20] (motor cycle frames) established quite clearly that such dual protection was in principle obtainable, provided that the other criteria for design registration are met, and is thought still to be good law. Thus, it is not possible to apply for a patent and then, some years later when the patent has been

19 [1957] RPC 239.
20 21 RPC 621.

published, to obtain a valid design registration for the article appearance as depicted in one of its drawings. There will be an absence of the necessary novelty conversely, if both are applied for at the same time.

But the design registration may fail if it falls foul of the functional exclusion of section 1(b)(i). This is what happened in *Stenor v Whitesides*,[21] where a particular shape of fuse, intended for use as a safety measure in certain patented vulcanising machines was held *inter alia* to constitute 'a mere mechanical device'; the functional exclusion under the earlier designs legislation applicable at the time was drafted in those terms. A comparable decision was made in *Amp v Utilux*[22] concerning electric terminals for use in washing machines and the like. It was clearly indicated here by the various speeches of the Law Lords that the rule is quite strict; although if the designer had been motivated purely by functional considerations, yet nevertheless had incidentally produced an article with some degree of eye appeal, that might save him; likewise, if he had deliberately added an embellishment to an otherwise wholly functional article. According to Lord Pearson, 'dictated by' meant 'attributable to or caused or prompted by'. The 'dictated by' phraseology is preserved in the amended 1949 Act.

Cow v Cannon Rubber Manufacturers[23] was a case on the other side of the line. It concerned an ordinary domestic hot water bottle provided on both faces with overall relatively deep diagonal ribbing. The depth of the ribbing enabled heat radiation to take place without discomfort or risk to the user. But because the ribbing could have been applied to the bottle in other directions as well without any loss of functional effect, it was held that the design was not one dictated solely by purpose. Representations of the actual designs involved in these three cases are shown in Figure 13.1, at the end of this Chapter.

The maximum term of a design registration, provided the periodic renewal fees are paid, is 25 years for registrations granted under the amended 1949 Act. This represents a considerable improvement over the maximum 15-year term available under the original 1949 Act, and exceeds even the maximum 20-year term for a patent under the 1977 Act. The improvement should encourage increasing use of the design registration route.

Copyright

Over the interval between the Copyright Act 1956[24] and the Copyright, Designs and Patents Act 1988 an extensive degree of protection was obtainable so far as mechanical machines and devices or other constructional articles were concerned, under the ordinary provisions of the copyright law. The intrinsic desirability of such type of additional protection for subject-matter of a kind traditionally regarded as being reserved for patents and/or registered designs was highly controversial. The more so since copyright protection may endure much longer than patent or registered design protection (in some cases up to life of author + 50 years); the penalties for copyright infringement were much more severe than those for patent or registered design infringement, damages being assessable on the so-called 'conversion' basis; and the difficulty, in the absence

21   65 RPC 1.
22   [1972] RPC 103.
23   [1959] RPC 240.
24   4 & 5 Eliz.2 c.74.

of any formally published specification or registration document, of knowing exactly what copyright was potentially claimable by others.

The 1988 Act has introduced an essentially new regime for the future, ameliorating the harshness of the 1956–1988 era. But it is useful to have an inkling of the former position, both for sake of perspective and also because certain aspects of the old law still apply to copyright works which came into being prior to the commencement of the 1988 Act. No attempt is made in this book to trace the details of the transitional provisions. The old and the new law will accordingly be considered briefly in turn.

The extension of copyright protection to the engineering industry was almost certainly an inadvertent side effect of the Copyright Act 1956, the immediate spur being two-fold. First, the Copyright Act 1956 introduced freshly, as compared to the previous Copyright Act of 1911,[25] the proviso that copyright could exist in an artistic work 'irrespective of artistic quality'. Secondly, section 48(1) of the 1956 Act statutorily provided (following the train of the intervening *King Features Syndicate v O. & M. Kleeman*[26] 1941 decision relating to 'Popeye the Sailor' dolls and brooches), that there could be copyright infringement by the three-dimensional reproduction of a two-dimensional artistic work; only the so-called 'lay recognition' test of section 9(8) had to be surmounted as an extra hurdle in the latter respect.

The full impact of the 1956 changes was perhaps first clearly appreciated by the Court of Appeal in *Dorling v Honnor*[27] in 1964, concerning building plans for sailing dinghies. Subsequently, it became plain that even drawings of simple mechanical parts could be embraced; there was no need for there to be present on the engineering drawing any representation of that degree of complexity such as might popularly be thought necessary for an artistic work. In the 1973 decision of *British Northrop v Texteam Blackburn*, drawings of such objects as rivets, screws, studs, bars, washers and collars were held – at least at the interlocutory stage – to be capable of providing protection. To quote from the judgment of Megarry J.:

> . . . a single straight line drawn with the aid of a ruler would not seem to me a very promising subject for copyright. But apart from cases of such barren and naked simplicity as that, I should be slow to exclude drawings from copyright on the *mere score of simplicity*. I do not think that the mere fact that a drawing is of an elementary and commonplace article makes it too simple to be the subject of copyright.[28]
>
> (*Emphasis added*)

The need for a competitor to keep the copyright aspect in mind was strikingly illustrated in *L.B. (Plastics) v Swish Products*,[29] a case concerning knock-down drawers, fabricated out of plastics materials, of quite complex construction. The plaintiffs' patent applications had apparently foundered for some reason; the defendants had made searches through granted patents and registered designs, but had apparently quite overlooked the question of copyright. It was held that, in the actual circumstances of the evolution of their own design, their product ranked as an infringement of the plaintiffs' copyright in the relevant original drawings of the drawer construction.

---

25   1 & 2 Geo.5 c.46.
26   58 RPC 207.
27   [1964] RPC 160.
28   [1974] RPC 57 at 68.
29   [1979] RPC 551.

It was against this background that Whitford J. in *Catnic Components v Hill & Smith*[30] in 1978 uttered the *dictum* to the effect that a patentee, by the very act of applying for a patent, makes an election in favour of patent rather than copyright protection. He is therefore deemed to have necessarily abandoned any copyright protection potentially available in the patent drawings, or any drawings equivalent thereto, once the patent is published.

This *dictum* proved controversial. When the *Catnic* decision went to appeal, the Court of Appeal[31] specifically declined to express any concluded view on the point and in the House of Lords it was not raised at all, the argument there being directed solely to the patent infringement ('pith and marrow') issue. It has been criticised as having been uttered *per incuriam*, the already mentioned earlier decision of *Werner Motors v Gamage* (see page 174) (which established the propriety of dual patent and registered design proteciton, at least) not having been cited in argument to the judge.

Reaction abroad to the *dictum*, in countries tending otherwise to follow English law, has also been mixed. In the 1981 New Zealand case of *Wham-O Manufacturing v Lincoln Industries*[32] (flying saucers for terrestrial field games), the Court declined to follow the *dictum*, albeit only in the context of the effect of a corresponding parent United States patent application on the domestic copyright. Nor was it followed in the 1982 Australian case of *Ogden Industries v Kis (Australia)*.[33] In Hong Kong, the *dictum* was disapproved in *Interlego v Tyco Industries* (1987).[34] In contrast, the Canadian Federal Court in *Rucker v Gavel's Vulcanizing* (1985)[35] gave a strong judgment in support of the patent/copyright dichotomy.

Another problem arises in connection with what is meant by 'equivalent' drawings. One possibility is that drawings the functional equivalent to those in the patent specification are included generally. Another is that the exclusion is limited to the more detailed forms of the drawings in the patent specification; it is, of course, rare for patent drawings to be of practical engineering exactitude; moreover, only part of the entire product or machine (as the case is) may be illustrated in the patent specification, if the novelty of the invention lies just in that part. With the intervention of the 1988 Act it is now perhaps rather unlikely that the correctness (or not) of the *Catnic dictum* as to the patent/copyright interface will ever be finally settled.

The new law embodied in the 1988 Act retains the 'irrespective of artistic quality' proviso of the 1956 Act, but is reckoned (pending judicial interpretation of the complex statutory language) to abolish effectively copyright in respect of the three-dimensional reproduction of ordinary engineering drawings by section 51(1):

> (1) It is not an infringement of any copyright in a design document or model recording or embodying a design for anything other than an artistic work or a typeface to make an article to the design or to copy an article made to the design.

taken with the definitions of section 51(3) that:

30   [1982] RPC 183 at 206.
31   At 224.
32   [1982] RPC 281 at 298 and 299.
33   [1983] FSR 619 at 634 to 636.
34   [1987] FSR 409 at 457.
35   7 CPR (3d) 294.

(3) In this section—

'design' means the design of any aspect of the shape or configuration (whether internal or external) of the whole or part of an article, other than surface decoration; and

'design document' means any record of a design, whether in the form of a drawing, a written description, a photograph, data stored in a computer or otherwise.

In partial replacement, the 1988 Act creates the new *sui generis* 'unregistered design right' in original post-1988 designs, the term of protection for these being 15 years from date of first recordal of the design or creation of the corresponding article subject to the further limitation of 10 years (in the case when the articles have been put onto the market) from such date of first marketing. The contrast between these terms and the traditional normal copyright term is remarkable.

Moreover, licences as of right are to be available during the final 5 years of the term in any event, the licence terms to be settled by the Comptroller-General of Patents, Designs and Trade Marks (that is by the Patent Office) with appeal to the Registered Designs Appeal Tribunal. No statutory criteria akin to those set out in section 50 of the Patents Act 1977 for compulsory patent licences (and hence licences as of right) are provided in the 1988 Act. It is at present uncertain therefore as to how the Patent Office will approach their task in this connection. Decisions are not to be expected, having regard to the chronology of the provisions, until around the middle of the present decade.

It may finally be mentioned that the unregistered design right provisions of the 1988 Act have now also been applied, albeit with some modifications, to the protection of semiconductor topographies.[36]

Bibliography

I.C. Baillie, 'A Frustration of Good Design' [1991] EIPR 315.
E. Eder, 'Copyright in the Textile Industry' [1986] EIPR 312.
D. Glancy, 'The US Crime of Trade Secret Theft' [1979] EIPR 179.
M. Hart, 'Infringement and Remedies under the Copyright, Designs and Patents Act 1988' [1989] EPOR 113.
Law Commission Working Paper No. 58 – Breach of Confidence, HMSO, 1974.
L. Melville, Design Copyright in the United Kingdom', Part I [1982] EIPR 269, Part II [1982] EIPR 310.
M. Silverleaf, *Weir Pumps v CML Pumps* – Reverse Engineering and Spare Parts', [1983] EIPR 313.
P. Stone, *Copyright Law in the United Kingdom and the European Community*, Athlone Press, 1990.
Whitford Committee Report (Copyright and Designs Law) 1977, Cmnd. 6732 HMSO, Chapter 3 'Industrial Designs'.

36   Design Right (Semiconductor Topographies) Regulations 1989 (SI 1989 No. 1100).

Statutes

Patents Act 1977

1977 CHAPTER 37

An Act to establish a new law of patents applicable to future patents
and applications for patents; to amend the law of patents applicable
to existing patents and applications for patents; to give effect to
certain international conventions on patents; and for connected
purposes. [29th July 1977]

Be it enacted by the Queen's most Excellent Majesty, by and with
the advice and consent of the Lords Spiritual and Temporal, and
Commons, in this present Parliament assembled, and by the authority
of the same, as follows:-

PART I

NEW DOMESTIC LAW

Patentability

1.—(1) A patent may be granted only for an invention in respect of which the following conditions are satisfied, that is to say—   Patentable inventions.

    (a) the invention is new;

    (b) it involves an inventive step;

    (c) it is capable of industrial application;

    (d) the grant of a patent for it is not excluded by subsections (2) and (3) below;

and references in this Act to a patentable invention shall be construed accordingly.

(2) It is hereby declared that the following (among other things) are not inventions for the purposes of this Act, that is to say, anything which consists of—

    (a) a discovery, scientific theory or mathematical method;

    (b) a literary, dramatic, musical or artistic work or any other aesthetic creation whatsoever;

    (c) a scheme, rule or method for performing a mental act, playing a game or doing business, or a program for a computer;

    (d) the presentation of information;

but the foregoing provision shall prevent anything from being treated as an invention for the purposes of this Act only to the extent that a patent or application for a patent relates to that thing as such.

(3) A patent shall not be granted—

    (a) for an invention the publication or exploitation of which would be generally expected to encourage offensive, immoral or anti-social behaviour;

(b) for any variety of animal or plant or any essentially biological process for the production of animals or plants, not being a micro-biological process or the product of such a process.

(4) For the purposes of subsection (3) above behaviour shall not be regarded as offensive, immoral or anti-social only because it is prohibited by any law in force in the United Kingdom or any part of it.

(5) The Secretary of State may by order vary the provisions of subsection (2) above for the purpose of maintaining them in conformity with developments in science and technology; and no such order shall be made unless a draft of the order has been laid before, and approved by resolution of, each House of Parliament.

Novelty.

2.—(1) An invention shall be taken to be new if it does not form part of the state of the art.

(2) The state of the art in the case of an invention shall be taken to comprise all matter (whether a product, a process, information about either, or anything else) which has at any time before the priority date of that invention been made available to the public (whether in the United Kingdom or elsewhere) by written or oral description, by use or in any other way.

(3) The state of the art in the case of an invention to which an application for a patent or a patent relates shall be taken also to comprise matter contained in an application for another patent which was published on or after the priority date of that invention, if the following conditions are satisfied, that is to say—

(a) that matter was contained in the application for that other patent both as filed and as published; and

(b) the priority date of that matter is earlier than that of the invention.

(4) For the purposes of this section the disclosure of matter constituting an invention shall be disregarded in the case of a patent or an application for a patent if occurring later than the beginning of the period of six months immediately preceding the date of filing the application for the patent and either—

(a) the disclosure was due to, or made in consequence of, the matter having been obtained unlawfully or in breach of confidence by any person—

(i) from the inventor or from any other person to whom the matter was made available in confidence by the inventor or who obtained it from the inventor because he or the inventor believed that he was entitled to obtain it; or

(ii) from any other person to whom the matter was made available in confidence by any person mentioned in sub-paragraph (i) above or in this sub-paragraph or who obtained it from any person so mentioned because he or the person from whom he obtained it believed that he was entitled to obtain it;

(b) the disclosure was made in breach of confidence by any person who obtained the matter in confidence from the inventor or from any other person to whom it was made available, or who obtained it, from the inventor; or

(c) the disclosure was due to, or made in consequence of the inventor displaying the invention at an international exhibition and the applicant states, on filing the application, that the invention has been so displayed and also, within the prescribed period, files written evidence in support of the statement complying with any prescribed conditions.

(5) In this section references to the inventor include references to any proprietor of the invention for the time being.

(6) In the case of an invention consisting of a substance or composition for use in a method of treatment of the human or animal body by surgery or therapy or of diagnosis practised on the human or animal body, the fact that the substance or composition forms part of the state of the art shall not prevent the invention from being taken to be new if the use of the substance or composition in any such method does not form part of the state of the art.

3. An invention shall be taken to involve an inventive step if it is not obvious Inventive step. to a person skilled in the art; having regard to any matter which forms part of the state of the art by virtue only of section 2(2) above (and disregarding section 2(3) above).

4.—(1) Subject to subsection (2) below, an invention shall be taken to be capable Industrial of industrial application if it can be made or used in any kind of industry, including application. agriculture.

(2) An invention of a method of treatment of the human or animal body by surgery or therapy or of diagnosis practised on the human or animal body shall not be taken to be capable of industrial application.

(3) Subsection (2) above shall not prevent a product consisting of a substance or composition being treated as capable of industrial application merely because it is invented for use in any such method.

5.—(1) For the purposes of this Act the priority date of an invention to which Priority date. an application for a patent relates and also of any matter (whether or not the same as the invention) contained in any such application is, except as provided by the following provisions of this Act, the date of filing the application.

(2) If in or in connection with an application for a patent (the application in suit) a declaration is made, whether by the applicant or any predecessor in title of his, complying with the relevant requirements of rules and specifying one or more earlier relevant applications for the purposes of this section made by the applicant or a predecessor in title of his and each having a date of filing during the period of twelve months immediately preceding the date of filing the application in suit, then—

    (a) if an invention to which the application in suit relates is supported by matter disclosed in the earlier relevant application or applications, the priority date of that invention shall instead of being the date of filing the application in suit be the date of filing the relevant application in which that matter was disclosed or, if it was disclosed in more than one relevant application, the earliest of them;

    (b) the priority date of any matter contained in the application in suit which was also disclosed in the earlier relevant application or applications shall be the date of filing the relevant application in which that matter was disclosed or, if it was disclosed in more than one relevant application, the earliest of them.

(3) Where an invention or other matter contained in the application in suit was also disclosed in two earlier relevant applications filed by the same applicant as in the case of the application in suit or a predecessor in title of his and the second of those relevant applications was specified in or in connection with the application in suit, the second of those relevant applications shall, so far as concerns that invention or matter, be disregarded unless—

(a) it was filed in or in respect of the same country as the first; and

(b) not later than the date of filing the second, the first (whether or not so specified) was unconditionally withdrawn, or was abandoned or refused, without—

(i) having been made available to the public (whether in the United Kingdom or elsewhere);

(ii) leaving any rights outstanding; and

(iii) having served to establish a priority date in relation to another application, wherever made.

(4) The foregoing provisions of this section shall apply for determining the priority date of an invention for which a patent has been granted as they apply for determining the priority date of an invention to which an application for that patent relates.

(5) In this section "relevant application" means any of the following applications which has a date of filing, namely—

(a) an application for a patent under this Act;

(b) an application in or for a convention country (specified under section 90 below) for protection in respect of an invention or an application which, in accordance with the law of a convention country or a treaty or international convention to which a convention country is a party, is equivalent to such an application.

Disclosure of matter, etc., between earlier and later applications.

6.—(1) It is hereby declared for the avoidance of doubt that where an application (the application in suit) is made for a patent and a declaration is made in accordance with section 5(2) above or in connection with that application specifying an earlier relevant application, the application in suit and any patent granted in pursuance of it shall not be invalidated by reason only of relevant intervening acts.

(2) In this section—
"relevant application" has the same meaning as in section 5 above; and
"relevant intervening acts" means acts done in relation to matter disclosed in an earlier relevant application between the dates of the earlier relevant application and the application in suit, as for example, filing another application for the invention for which the earlier relevant application was made, making information available to the public about that invention or that matter or working that invention, but disregarding any application, or the disclosure to the public of matter contained in any application, which is itself to be disregarded for the purposes of section 5(3) above.

Right to apply for and obtain a patent and be mentioned as inventor

Right to apply for and obtain a patent.

7.—(1) Any person may make an application for a patent either alone or jointly with another.

(2) A patent for an invention may be granted—

(a) primarily to the inventor or joint inventors;

(b) in preference to the foregoing, to any person or persons who, by virtue of any enactment or rule of law, or any foreign law or treaty or international convention, or by virtue of an enforceable term of any agreement entered into with the inventor before the making of the invention, was or were at the time of the making of the invention entitled to the whole of the property in it (other than equitable interests) in the United Kingdom;

(c) in any event, to the successor or successors in title of any person or persons mentioned in paragraph (a) or (b) above or any person so mentioned and the successor or successors in title of another person so mentioned;

and to no other person.

(3) In this Act "inventor" in relation to an invention means the actual deviser of the invention and "joint inventor" shall be construed accordingly.

(4) Except so far as the contrary is established, a person who makes an application for a patent shall be taken to be the person who is entitled under subsection (2) above to be granted a patent and two or more persons who make such an application jointly shall be taken to be the persons so entitled.

8.—(1) At any time before a patent has been granted for an invention (whether or not an application has been made for it)— *Determination before grant of questions about entitlement to patents, etc.*

(a) any person may refer to the comptroller the question whether he is entitled to be granted (alone or with any other persons) a patent for that invention or has or would have any right in or under any patent so granted or any application for such a patent; or

(b) any of two or more co-proprietors of an application for a patent for that invention may so refer the question whether any right in or under the application should be transferred or granted to any other person;

and the comptroller shall determine the question and may make such order as he thinks fit to give effect to the determination.

(2) Where a person refers a question relating to an invention under subsection (1)(a) above to the comptroller after an application for a patent for the invention has been filed and before a patent is granted in pursuance of the application, then, unless the application is refused or withdrawn before the reference is disposed of by the comptroller, the comptroller may, without prejudice to the generality of subsection (1) above and subject to subsection (6) below,—

(a) order that the application shall proceed in the name of that person, either solely or jointly with that of any other applicant, instead of in the name of the applicant or any specified applicant;

(b) where the reference was made by two or more persons, order that the application shall proceed in all their names jointly;

(c) refuse to grant a patent in pursuance of the application or order the application to be amended so as to exclude any of the matter in respect of which the question was referred;

(d) make an order transferring or granting any licence or other right in or under the application and give directions to any person for carrying out the provisions of any such order.

(3) Where a question is referred to the comptroller under subsection (1)(a) above and—

(a) the comptroller orders an application for a patent for the invention to which the question relates to be so amended;

(b) any such application is refused under subsection 2(c) above before the comptroller has disposed of the reference (whether the reference was made before or after the publication of the application); or

(c) any such application is refused under any other provision of this Act or is withdrawn before the comptroller has disposed of the reference, but after the publication of the application;

the comptroller may order that any person by whom the reference was made may within the prescribed period make a new application for a patent for the whole or part of any matter comprised in the earlier application or, as the case may be, for all or any of the matter excluded from the earlier application, subject in either case to section 76 below, and in either case that, if such a new application is made, it shall be treated as having been filed on the date of filing the earlier application.

(4) Where a person refers a question under subsection (1)(b) above relating to an application, any order under subsection (1) above may contain directions to any person for transferring or granting any right in or under the application.

(5) If any person to whom directions have been given under subsection (2)(d) or (4) above fails to do anything necessary for carrying out any such directions within 14 days after the date of the directions, the comptroller may, on application made to him by any person in whose favour or on whose reference the directions were given, authorise him to do that thing on behalf of the person to whom the directions were given.

(6) Where on a reference under this section it is alleged that, by virtue of any transaction, instrument or event relating to an invention or an application for a patent, any person other than the inventor or the applicant for the patent has become entitled to be granted (whether alone or with any other persons) a patent for the invention or has or would have any right in or under any patent so granted or any application for any such patent, an order shall not be made under subsection (2)(a), (b) or (d) above on the reference unless notice of the reference is given to the applicant and any such person, except any of them who is a party to the reference.

(7) If it appears to the comptroller on a reference of a question under this section that the question involves matters which would more properly be determined by the court, he may decline to deal with it and, without prejudice to the court's jurisdiction to determine any such question and make a declaration, or any declaratory jurisdiction of the court in Scotland, the court shall have jurisdiction to do so.

(8) No directions shall be given under this section so as to affect the mutual rights or obligations of trustees or of the personal representatives of deceased persons, or their rights or obligations as such.

Determination after grant of questions referred before grant.

9. If a question with respect to a patent or application is referred by any person to the comptroller under section 8 above, whether before or after the making of an application for the patent, and is not determined before the time when the application is first in order for a grant of a patent in pursuance of the application, that fact shall not prevent the grant of a patent, but on its grant that person shall be treated as having referred to the comptroller under section 37 below any question mentioned in that section which the comptroller thinks appropriate.

Handling of application by joint applicants.

10. If any dispute arises between joint applicants for a patent whether or in what manner the application should be proceeded with, the comptroller may, on a request made by any of the parties, give such directions as he thinks fit for enabling the application to proceed in the name of one or more of the parties alone or for regulating the manner in which it shall be proceeded with, or for both those purposes, according as the case may require.

11.—(1) Where an order is made or directions are given under section 8 or 10 above that an application for a patent shall proceed in the name of one or some of the original applicants (whether or not it is also to proceed in the name of some other person), any licences or other rights in or under the application shall, subject to the provisions of the order and any directions under either of those sections, continue in force and be treated as granted by the persons in whose name the application is to proceed.

Effect of transfer of application under s. 8 or 10.

(2) Where an order is made or directions are given under section 8 above that an application for a patent shall proceed in the name of one or more persons none of whom was an original applicant (on the ground that the original applicant or applicants was or were not entitled to be granted the patent), any licences or other rights in or under the application shall, subject to the provisions of the order and any directions under that section and subject to subsection (3) below, lapse on the registration of that person or those persons as the applicant or applicants or, where the application has not been published, on the making of the order.

(3) If before registration of a reference under section 8 above resulting in the making of any order mentioned in subsection (2) above—

(a) the original applicant or any of the applicants, acting in good faith, worked the invention in question in the United Kingdom or made effective and serious preparations to do so; or

(b) a licensee of the applicant, acting in good faith, worked the invention in the United Kingdom or made effective and serious preparations to do so;

that or those original applicant or applicants or the licensee shall, on making a request within the prescribed period to the person in whose name the application is to proceed, be entitled to be granted a licence (but not an exclusive licence) to continue working or, as the case may be, to work the invention.

(4) Any such licence shall be granted for a reasonable period and on reasonable terms.

(5) Where an order is made as mentioned in subsection (2) above, the person in whose name the application is to proceed or any person claiming that he is entitled to be granted any such licence may refer to the comptroller the question whether the latter is so entitled and whether any such period is or terms are reasonable, and the comptroller shall determine the question and may, if he considers it appropriate, order the grant of such a licence.

12.—(1) At any time before a patent is granted for an invention in pursuance of an application made under the law of any country other than the United Kingdom or under any treaty or international convention (whether or not that application has been made)—

Determination of questions about entitlement to foreign and convention patents, etc.

(a) any person may refer to the comptroller the question whether he is entitled to be granted (alone or with any other persons) any such patent for that invention or has or would have any right in or under any such patent or an application for such a patent; or

(b) any of two or more co-proprietors of an application for such a patent for that invention may so refer the question whether any right in or under the application should be transferred or granted to any other person;

and the comptroller shall determine the question so far as he is able to and may make such order as he thinks fit to give effect to the determination.

(2) If it appears to the comptroller on a reference of a question under this section

that the question involves matters which would more properly be determined by the court, he may decline to deal with it and, without prejudice to the court's jurisdiction to determine any such question and make a declaration, or any declaratory jurisdiction of the court in Scotland, the court shall have jurisdiction to do so.

(3) Subsection (1) above, in its application to a European patent and an application for any such patent, shall have effect subject to section 82 below.

(4) Section 10 above, except so much of it as enables the comptroller to regulate the manner in which an application is to proceed, shall apply to disputes between joint applicants for any such patent as is mentioned in subsection (1) above as it applies to joint applicants for a patent under this Act.

(5) Section 11 above shall apply in relation to—

(a) any orders made under subsection (1) above and any directions given under section 10 above by virtue of subsection (4) above; and

(b) any orders made and directions given by the relevant convention court with respect to a question corresponding to any question which may be determined under subsection (1) above;

as it applies to orders made and directions given apart from this section under section 8 or 10 above.

(6) In the following cases, that is to say—

(a) where an application for a European patent (UK) is refused or withdrawn, or the designation of the United Kingdom in the application is withdrawn, after publication of the application but before a question relating to the right to the patent has been referred to the comptroller under subsection (1) above or before proceedings relating to that right have begun before the relevant convention court;

(b) where an application has been made for a European patent (UK) and on a reference under subsection (1) above or any such proceedings as are mentioned in paragraph (a) above the comptroller, the court or the relevant convention court determines by a final decision (whether before or after publication of the application) that a person other than the applicant has the right to the patent, but that person requests the European Patent Office that the application for the patent should be refused; or

(c) where an international application for a patent (UK) is withdrawn, or the designation of the United Kingdom in the application is withdrawn, whether before or after the making of any reference under subsection (1) above but after publication of the application;

the comptroller may order that any person (other than the applicant) appearing to him to be entitled to be granted a patent under this Act may within the prescribed period make an application for such a patent for the whole or part of any matter comprised in the earlier application (subject, however, to section 76 below) and that if the application for a patent under this Act is filed, it shall be treated as having been filed on the date of filing the earlier application.

(7) In this section—

(a) references to a patent and an application for a patent include respectively references to protection in respect of an invention and an application which, in accordance with the law of any country other than the United Kingdom or any treaty or international convention, is equivalent to an application for a patent or for such protection; and

(b) a decision shall be taken to be final for the purposes of this section when the time for appealing from it has expired without an appeal being brought or, where an appeal is brought, when it is finally disposed of.

13.—(1) The inventor or joint inventors of an invention shall have a right to be mentioned as such in any patent granted for the invention and shall also have a right to be so mentioned if possible in any published application for a patent for the invention and, if not so mentioned, a right to be so mentioned in accordance with rules in a prescribed document. Mention of inventor.

(2) Unless he has already given the Patent Office the information hereinafter mentioned, an applicant for a patent shall within the prescribed period file with the Patent Office a statement—

(a) identifying the person or persons whom he believes to be the inventor or inventors; and

(b) where the applicant is not the sole inventor or the applicants are not the joint inventors, indicating the derivation of his or their right to be granted the patent;

and, if he fails to do so, the application shall be taken to be withdrawn.

(3) Where a person has been mentioned as sole or joint inventor in pursuance of this section, any other person who alleges that the former ought not to have been so mentioned may at any time apply to the comptroller for a certificate to that effect, and the comptroller may issue such a certificate; and if he does so, he shall accordingly rectify any undistributed copies of the patent and of the documents prescribed for the purposes of subsection (1) above.

Applications

14.—(1) Every application for a patent—

(a) shall be made in the prescribed form and shall be filed at the Patent Office in the prescribed manner; and Making of application.

(b) shall be accompanied by the fee prescribed for the purposes of this subsection (hereafter in this Act referred to as the filing fee).

(2) Every application for a patent shall contain—

(a) a request for the grant of a patent;

(b) a specification containing a description of the invention, a claim or claims and any drawing referred to in the description or any claim; and

(c) an abstract;

but the foregoing provision shall not prevent an application being initiated by documents complying with section 15(1) below.

(3) The specification of an application shall disclose the invention in a manner which is clear enough and complete enough for the invention to be performed by a person skilled in the art.

(4) Without prejudice to subsection (3) above, rules may prescribe the circumstances in which the specification of an application which requires for its performance the use of a microorganism is to be treated for the purposes of this Act as complying with that subsection.

(5) The claim or claims shall—

(a) define the matter for which the applicant seeks protection;

(b) be clear and concise;

(c) be supported by the description; and

(d) relate to one invention or to a group of inventions which are so linked as to form a single inventive concept.

(6) Without prejudice to the generality of subsection (5)(d) above, rules may provide for treating two or more inventions as being so linked as to form a single inventive concept for the purposes of this Act.

(7) The purpose of the abstract is to give technical information and on publication it shall not form part of the state of the art by virtue of section 2(3) above, and the comptroller may determine whether the abstract adequately fulfils its purpose and, if it does not, may reframe it so that it does.

(8) Rules may require a person who has made an application for a patent for an invention which requires for its performance the use of a micro-organism not to impose or maintain in the prescribed circumstances any restrictions on the availability to the public of samples of the micro-organism and the uses to which they may be put, subject, however, to any prescribed exceptions, and rules may provide that in the event of a contravention of any provision included in the rules by virtue of this subsection the specification shall be treated for the purposes of this Act as not disclosing the invention in a manner required by subsection (3) above.

(9) An application for a patent may be withdrawn at any time before the patent is granted and any withdrawal of such an application may not be revoked.

15.—(1) The date of filing an application for a patent shall, subject to the following provisions of this Act, be taken to be the earliest date on which the following conditions are satisfied in relation to the application, that is to say—

(a) the documents filed at the Patent Office contain an indication that a patent is sought in pursuance of the application;

(b) those documents identify the applicant or applicants for the patent;

(c) those documents contain a description of the invention for which a patent is sought (whether or not the description complies with the other provisions of this Act and with any relevant rules); and

(d) the applicant pays the filing fee.

(2) If any drawing referred to in any such application is filed later than the date which by virtue of subsection (1) above is to be treated as the date of filing the application, but before the beginning of the preliminary examination of the application under section 17 below, the comptroller shall give the applicant an opportunity of requesting within the prescribed period that the date on which the drawing is filed shall be treated for the purposes of this Act as the date of filing the application, and—

(a) if the applicant makes any such request, the date of filing the drawing shall be so treated; but

(b) otherwise any reference to the drawing in the application shall be treated as omitted.

(3) If on the preliminary examination of an application under section 17 below it is found that any drawing referred to in the application has not been filed, then—

(a) if the drawing is subsequently filed within the prescribed period, the date on which it is filed shall be treated for the purposes of this Act as the date of filing the application; but

(b) otherwise any reference to the drawing in the application shall be treated as omitted.

(4) Where, after an application for a patent has been filed and before the patent is granted, a new application is filed by the original applicant or his successor in title in accordance with rules in respect of any part of the matter contained in the earlier application and the conditions mentioned in subsection (1) above are satisfied in relation to the new application (without the new application contravening section 76 below) the new application shall be treated as having, as its date of filing, the date of filing the earlier application.

(5) An application which has a date of filing by virtue of the foregoing provisions of this section shall be taken to be withdrawn at the end of the relevant prescribed period, unless before that end the applicant—

(a) files at the Patent Office one or more claims for the purposes of the application and also the abstract; and

(b) makes a request for the preliminary examination and search under the following provisions of this Act and pays the search fee.

16.—(1) Subject to section 22 below, where an application has a date of filing, Publication of then, as soon as possible after the end of the prescribed period, the comptroller application. shall, unless the application is withdrawn or refused before preparations for its publication have been completed by the Patent Office, publish it as filed (including not only the original claims but also any amendments of those claims and new claims subsisting immediately before the completion of those preparations) and he may, if so requested by the applicant, publish it as aforesaid during that period, and in either event shall advertise the fact and date of its publication in the journal.

(2) The comptroller may omit from the specification of a published application for a patent any matter—

(a) which in his opinion disparages any person in a way likely to damage him, or

(b) the publication or exploitation of which would in his opinion be generally expected to encourage offensive, immoral or anti-social behaviour.

Examination and search

17.—(1) Where an application for a patent has a date of filing and is not withdrawn, and before the end of the prescribed period— Preliminary
examination and
(a) a request is made by the applicant to the Patent Office in the prescribed search. form for a preliminary examination and a search; and

(b) the prescribed fee is paid for the examination and search (the search fee);

the comptroller shall refer the application to an examiner for a preliminary examination and search, except that he shall not refer the application for a search until it includes one or more claims.

(2) On a preliminary examination of an application the examiner shall determine whether the application complies with those requirements of this Act and the rules which are designated by the rules as formal requirements for the purposes of this Act and shall report his determination to the comptroller.

(3) If it is reported to the comptroller under subsection (2) above that not all the formal requirements are complied with, he shall give the applicant an opportunity to make observations on the report and to amend the application within a specified period (subject to section 15(5) above) so as to comply with those requirements (subject, however, to section 76 below), and if the applicant fails to do so the comptroller may refuse the application.

(4) Subject to subsections (5) and (6) below, on a search requested under this section, the examiner shall make such investigation as in his opinion is reasonably practicable and necessary for him to identify the documents which he thinks will be needed to decide, on a substantive examination under section 18 below, whether the invention for which a patent is sought is new and involves an inventive step.

(5) On any such search the examiner shall determine whether or not the search would serve any useful purpose on the application as for the time being constituted and—

(a) if he determines that it would serve such a purpose in relation to the whole or part of the application, he shall proceed to conduct the search so far as it would serve such a purpose and shall report on the results of the search to the comptroller; and

(b) if he determines that the search would not serve such a purpose in relation to the whole or part of the application, he shall report accordingly to the comptroller;

and in either event the applicant shall be informed of the examiner's report.

(6) If it appears to the examiner, either before or on conducting a search under this section, that an application relates to two or more inventions, but that they are not so linked as to form a single inventive concept, he shall initially only conduct a search in relation to the first invention specified in the claims of the application, but may proceed to conduct a search in relation to another invention so specified if the applicant pays the search fee in respect of the application so far as it relates to that other invention.

(7) After a search has been requested under this section for an application the comptroller may at any time refer the application to an examiner for a supplementary search, and subsection (4) above shall apply in relation to a supplementary search as it applies in relation to any other search under this section.

Substantive
examination and
grant or refusal
of patent.

18.—(1) Where the conditions imposed by section 17(1) above for the comptroller to refer an application to an examiner for a preliminary examination and search are satisfied and at the time of the request under that subsection or within the prescribed period—

(a) a request is made by the applicant to the Patent Office in the prescribed form for a substantive examination; and

(b) the prescribed fee is paid for the examination;

the comptroller shall refer the application to an examiner for a substantive examination; and if no such request is made or the prescribed fee is not paid within that period, the application shall be treated as having been withdrawn at the end of that period.

(2) On a substantive examination of an application the examiner shall investigate, to such extent as he considers necessary in view of any examination and search carried out under section 17 above, whether the application complies with the requirements of this Act and the rules and shall determine that question and report his determination to the comptroller.

(3) If the examiner reports that any of those requirements are not complied with, the comptroller shall give the applicant an opportunity within a specified period to make observations on the report and to amend the application so as to comply with those requirements (subject, however, to section 76 below), and if the applicant fails to satisfy the comptroller that those requirements are complied with, or to amend the application so as to comply with them, the comptroller may refuse the application.

(4) If the examiner reports that the application, whether as originally filed or as amended in pursuance of section 17 above, this section or section 19 below, complies with those requirements at any time before the end of the prescribed period, the comptroller shall notify the applicant of that fact and, subject to subsection (5) and sections 19 and 22 below and on payment within the prescribed period of any fee prescribed for the grant, grant him a patent.

(5) Where two or more applications for a patent for the same invention having the same priority date are filed by the same applicant or his successor in title, the comptroller may on that ground refuse to grant a patent in pursuance of more than one of the applications.

19.—(1) At any time before a patent is granted in pursuance of an application the applicant may, in accordance with the prescribed conditions and subject to section 76 below, amend the application of his own volition.

General power to amend application before grant.

(2) The comptroller may, without an application being made to him for the purpose, amend the specification and abstract contained in an application for a patent so as to acknowledge a registered trade mark.

20.—(1) If it is not determined that an application for a patent complies before the end of the prescribed period with all the requirements of this Act and the rules, the application shall be treated as having been refused by the comptroller at the end of that period, and section 97 below shall apply accordingly.

Failure of application.

(2) If at the end of that period an appeal to the court is pending in respect of the application or the time within which such an appeal could be brought has not expired, that period—

(a) where such an appeal is pending, or is brought within the said time or before the expiration of any extension of that time granted (in the case of a first extension) on an application made within that time or (in the case of a subsequent extension) on an application made before the expiration of the last previous extension, shall be extended until such date as the court may determine;

(b) where no such appeal is pending or is so brought, shall continue until the end of the said time or, if any extension of that time is so granted, until the expiration of the extension or last extension so granted.

21.—(1) Where an application for a patent has been published but a patent has not been granted to the applicant, any other person may make observations in writing to the comptroller on the question whether the invention is a patentable invention, stating reasons for the observations, and the comptroller shall consider the observations in accordance with rules.

Observations by third party on patentability.

(2) It is hereby declared that a person does not become a party to any proceedings under this Act before the comptroller by reason only that he makes observations under this section.

Security and safety

22.—(1) Where an application for a patent is filed in the Patent Office (whether under this Act or any treaty or international convention to which the United Kingdom is a party and whether before or after the appointed day) and it appears to the comptroller that the application contains information of a description notified

Information prejudicial to defence of realm or safety of public.

to him by the Secretary of State as being information the publication of which might be prejudicial to the defence of the realm, the comptroller may give directions prohibiting or restricting the publication of that information or its communication to any specified person or description of persons.

(2) If it appears to the comptroller that any application so filed contains information the publication of which might be prejudicial to the safety of the public, he may give directions prohibiting or restricting the publication of that information or its communication to any specified person or description of persons until the end of a period not exceeding three months from the end of the period prescribed for the purposes of section 16 above.

(3) While directions are in force under this section with respect to an application—

(a) if the application is made under this Act, it may proceed to the stage where it is in order for the grant of a patent, but it shall not be published and that information shall not be so communicated and no patent shall be granted in pursuance of the application;

(b) if it is an application for a European patent, it shall not be sent to the European Patent Office; and

(c) if it is an international application for a patent, a copy of it shall not be sent to the International Bureau or any international searching authority appointed under the Patent Co-operation Treaty.

(4) Subsection (3)(b) above shall not prevent the comptroller from sending the European Patent Office any information which it is his duty to send that office under the European Patent Convention.

(5) Where the comptroller gives directions under this section with respect to any application, he shall give notice of the application and of the directions to the Secretary of State, and the following provisions shall then have effect:—

(a) the Secretary of State shall, on receipt of the notice, consider whether the publication of the application or the publication or communication of the information in question would be prejudicial to the defence of the realm or the safety of the public;

(b) if the Secretary of State determines under paragraph (a) above that the publication of the application or the publication or communication of that information would be prejudicial to the safety of the public, he shall notify the comptroller who shall continue his directions under subsection (2) above until they are revoked under paragraph (e) below;

(c) if the Secretary of State determines under paragraph (a) above that the publication of the application or the publication or communication of that information would be prejudicial to the defence of the realm or the safety of the public, he shall (unless a notice under paragraph (d) below has previously been given by the Secretary of State to the comptroller) reconsider that question during the period of nine months from the date of filing the application and at least once in every subsequent period of twelve months;

(d) if on consideration of an application at any time it appears to the Secretary of State that the publication of the application or the publication or communication of the information contained in it would not, or would no longer, be prejudicial to the defence of the realm or the safety of the public, he shall give notice to the comptroller to that effect; and

(e) on receipt of such a notice the comptroller shall revoke the directions and may, subject to such conditions (if any) as he thinks fit, extend the time for doing anything required or authorised to be done by or under this Act in connection with the application, whether or not that time has previously expired.

(6) The Secretary of State may do the following for the purpose of enabling him to decide the question referred to in subsection (5)(c) above—

(a) where the application contains information relating to the production or use of atomic energy or research into matters connected with such production or use, he may at any time do one or both of the following, that is to say, inspect and authorise the United Kingdom Atomic Energy Authority to inspect the application and any documents sent to the comptroller in connection with it; and

(b) in any other case, he may at any time after (or, with the applicant's consent, before) the end of the period prescribed for the purposes of section 16 above inspect the application and any such documents;

and where that Authority are authorised under paragraph (a) above they shall as soon as practicable report on their inspection to the Secretary of State.

(7) Where directions have been given under this section in respect of an application for a patent for an invention and, before the directions are revoked, that prescribed period expires and the application is brought in order for the grant of a patent, then—

(a) if while the directions are in force the invention is worked by (or with the written authorisation of or to the order of) a government department, the provisions of sections 55 to 59 below shall apply as if—

(i) the working were use made by section 55;

(ii) the application had been published at the end of that period; and

(iii) a patent had been granted for the invention at the time the application is brought in order for the grant of a patent (taking the terms of the patent to be those of the application as it stood at the time it was so brought in order); and

(b) if it appears to the Secretary of State that the applicant for the patent has suffered hardship by reason of the continuance in force of the directions, the Secretary of State may, with the consent of the Treasury, make such payment (if any) by way of compensation to the applicant as appears to the Secretary of State and the Treasury to be reasonable having regard to the inventive merit and utility of the invention, the purpose for which it is designed and any other relevant circumstances.

(8) Where a patent is granted in pursuance of an application in respect of which directions have been given under this section, no renewal fees shall be payable in respect of any period during which those directions were in force.

(9) A person who fails to comply with any direction under this section shall be liable—

(a) on summary conviction, to a fine not exceeding £1,000; or

(b) on conviction on indictment, to imprisonment for a term not exceeding two years or a fine, or both.

23.—(1) Subject to the following provisions of this section, no person resident in the United Kingdom shall, without written authority granted by the comptroller, file or cause to be filed outside the United Kingdom an application for a patent for an invention unless— *Restrictions on applications abroad by United Kingdom residents.*

(a) an application for a patent for the same invention has been filed in the Patent Office (whether before, on or after the appointed day) not less than six weeks before the application outside the United Kingdom; and

(b) either no directions have been given under section 22 above in relation to the application in the United Kingdom or all such directions have been revoked.

(2) Subsection (1) above does not apply to an application for a patent for an invention for which an application for a patent has first been filed (whether before or after the appointed day) in a country outside the United Kingdom by a person resident outside the United Kingdom.

(3) A person who files or causes to be filed an application for the grant of a patent in contravention of this section shall be liable—

(a) on summary conviction, to a fine not exceeding £1,000; or

(b) on conviction on indictment, to imprisonment for a term not exceeding two years or a fine, or both.

(4) In this section—

(a) any reference to an application for a patent includes a reference to an application for other protection for an invention;

(b) any reference to either kind of application is a reference to an application under this Act, under the law of any country other than the United Kingdom or under any treaty or international convention to which the United Kingdom is a party.

Provisions as to patents after grant

24.—(1) As soon as practicable after a patent has been granted under this Act the comptroller shall publish in the journal a notice that it has been granted.

Publication and certificate of grant.

(2) The comptroller shall, as soon as practicable after he publishes a notice under subsection (1) above, send the proprietor of the patent a certificate in the prescribed form that the patent has been granted to the proprietor.

(3) The comptroller shall, at the same time as he publishes a notice under subsection (1) above in relation to a patent publish the specification of the patent, the names of the proprietor and (if different) the inventor and any other matters constituting or relating to the patent which in the comptroller's opinion it is desirable to publish.

25.—(1) A patent granted under this Act shall be treated for the purposes of the following provisions of this Act as having been granted, and shall take effect, on the date on which notice of its grant is published in the journal and, subject to subsection (3) below, shall continue in force until the end of the period of 20 years beginning with the date of filing the application for the patent or with such other date as may be prescribed.

Term of patent.

(2) A rule prescribing any such other date under this section shall not be made unless a draft of the rule has been laid before, and approved by resolution of, each House of Parliament.

(3) A patent shall cease to have effect at the end of the period prescribed for the payment of any renewal fee if it is not paid within that period.

(4) If during the period of six months immediately following the end of the prescribed period the renewal fee and any prescribed additional fee are paid, the patent shall be treated for the purposes of this Act as if it had never expired, and accordingly—

(a) anything done under or in relation to it during that further period shall be valid;

(b) an act which would constitute an infringement of it if it had not expired shall constitute such an infringement; and

(c) an act which would constitute the use of the patented invention for the services of the Crown if the patent had not expired shall constitute that use.

(5) Rules shall include provision requiring the comptroller to notify the registered proprietor of a patent that a renewal fee has not been received from him in the Patent Office before the end of the prescribed period and before the framing of the notification.

26. No person may in any proceeding object to a patent or to an amendment of a specification of a patent on the ground that the claims contained in the specification of the patent, as they stand or, as the case may be, as proposed to be amended, relate— Patent not to be impugned for lack of unity.

(a) to more than one invention, or

(b) to a group of inventions which are not so linked as to form a single inventive concept.

27.—(1) Subject to the following provisions of this section and to section 76 below, the comptroller may, on an application made by the proprietor of a patent, allow the specification of the patent to be amended subject to such conditions, if any, as he thinks fit. General power to amend specification after grant.

(2) No such amendment shall be allowed under this section where there are pending before the court or the comptroller proceedings in which the validity of the patent may be put in issue.

(3) An amendment of a specification of a patent under this section shall have effect and be deemed always to have had effect from the grant of the patent.

(4) The comptroller may, without an application being made to him for the purpose, amend the specification of a patent so as to acknowledge a registered trade-mark.

(5) A person may give notice to the comptroller of his opposition to an application under this section by the proprietor of a patent, and if he does so the comptroller shall notify the proprietor and consider the opposition in deciding whether to grant the application.

28.—(1) Where a patent has ceased to have effect by reason of a failure to pay any renewal fee within the prescribed period, an application for the restoration of the patent may be made to the comptroller under this section within one year from the date on which the patent ceased to have effect. Restoration of lapsed patents.

(2) An application under this section may be made by the person who was the proprietor of the patent or by any other person who would have been entitled to the patent if it had not ceased to have effect; and where the patent was held by two or more persons jointly, the application may, with the leave of the comptroller, be made by one or more of them without joining the others.

(3) If the comptroller is satisfied that—

(a) the proprietor of the patent took reasonable care to see that any renewal fee was paid within the prescribed period or that that fee and any prescribed additional fee were paid within the six months immediately following the end of that period, and

(b) those fees were not so paid because of circumstances beyond his control,

the comptroller shall by order restore the patent on payment of any unpaid renewal fee and any prescribed additional fee.

(4) An order under this section may be made subject to such conditions as the comptroller thinks fit (including a condition requiring compliance with any provisions of the rules relating to registration which have not been complied with), and if the proprietor of the patent does not comply with any condition of such an order the comptroller may revoke the order and give such directions consequential on the revocation as he thinks fit.

(5) Where an order is made under this section and, between the end of the period of six months beginning with the date when the patent concerned ceased to have effect and the date of the application under this section,—

(a) a person continued to do or did again an act which would have constituted an infringement of the patent if it had not expired and which he first did before the end of that period, that act shall constitute such an infringement; or

(b) a person began in good faith to do an act which would constitute an infringement of the patent if it had been in force or made in good faith effective and serious preparations to do such an act, he shall, after the order comes into force, have the rights conferred by subsection (6) below.

(6) Any such person shall have the right—

(a) to continue to do or, as the case may be, to do that act himself; and

(b) if it was done or preparations had been made to do it in the course of a business, to assign the right to do it or to transmit that right on his death or, in the case of a body corporate on its dissolution, to any person who acquires that part of the business in the course of which the act was done or preparations had been made to do it, or to authorise it to be done by any partners of his for the time being in that business;

and the doing of that act by virtue of this subsection shall not amount to an infringement of the patent concerned.

(7) The rights mentioned in subsection (6) above shall not include the right to grant a licence to any person to do an act so mentioned.

(8) Where a patented product is disposed of by any person to another in exercise of a right conferred by subsection (6) above, that other and any other person claiming through him shall be entitled to deal with the product in the same way as if it had been disposed of by a sole registered proprietor.

(9) Subsections (5) to (7) above shall apply in relation to an act which would constitute the use of a patented invention for the services of the Crown if the patent had been in force as they apply in relation to an act which would constitute an infringement of the patent if it had been in force, and subsection (8) above shall apply accordingly to the disposal of a patented product in the exercise of a right conferred by subsection (6) above as applied by the foregoing provision.

Surrender of patents.

29.—(1) The proprietor of a patent may at any time by notice given to the comptroller offer to surrender his patent.

(2) A person may give notice to the comptroller of his opposition to the surrender of a patent under this section, and if he does so the comptroller shall notify the proprietor of the patent and determine the question.

(3) If the comptroller is satisfied that the patent may properly be surrendered, he may accept the offer and, as from the date when notice of his acceptance is published in the journal, the patent shall cease to have effect, but no action for infringement shall lie in respect of any act done before that date and no right to compensation shall accrue for any use of the patented invention before that date for the services of the Crown.

Property in patents and applications, and registration

30.—(1) Any patent or application for a patent is personal property (without being a thing in action), and any patent or any such application and rights in or under it may be transferred, created or granted in accordance with subsections (2) to (7) below.

(2) Subject to section 36(3) below, any patent or any such application, or any right in it, may be assigned or mortgaged.

(3) Any patent or any such application or right shall vest by operation of law in the same way as any other personal property and may be vested by an assent of personal representatives.

(4) Subject to section 36(3) below, a licence may be granted under any patent or any such application for working the invention which is the subject of the patent or the application; and—

  (a) to the extent that the licence so provides, a sub-licence may be granted under any such licence and any such licence or sub-licence may be assigned or mortgaged; and

  (b) any such licence or sub-licence shall vest by operation of law in the same way as any other personal property and may be vested by an assent of personal representatives.

(5) Subsections (2) to (4) above shall have effect subject to the following provisions of this Act.

(6) Any of the following transactions, that is to say—

  (a) any assignment or mortgage of a patent or any such application, or any right in a patent or any such application;

  (b) any assent relating to any patent or any such application or right;

shall be void unless it is in writing and is signed by or on behalf of the parties to the transaction (or, in the case of an assent or other transaction by a personal representative, by or on behalf of the personal representative) or in the case of a body corporate is so signed or is under the seal of that body.

(7) An assignment of a patent or any such application or a share in it, and an exclusive licence granted under any patent or any such application, may confer on the assignee or licensee the right of the assignor or licensor to bring proceedings by virtue of section 61 or 69 below for a previous infringement or to bring proceedings under section 58 below for a previous act.

Nature of, and transactions in, patents and applications for patents.

31.—(1) Section 30 above shall not extend to Scotland, but instead the following provisions of this section shall apply there.

(2) Any patent or application for a patent, and any right in or under any patent or any such application, is incorporeal moveable property, and the provisions of the following subsections and of section 36(3) below shall apply to any grant of licences, assignations and securities in relation to such property.

Nature of, and transactions in, patents and applications for patents in Scotland.

(3) Any patent or any such application, or any right in it, may be assigned and security may be granted over a patent or any such application or right.

(4) A licence may be granted, under any patent or any application for a patent, for working the invention which is the subject of the patent or the application.

(5) To the extent that any licence granted under subsection (4) above so provides, a sub-licence may be granted under any such licence and any such licence or sub-licence may be assigned and security may be granted over it.

(6) Any assignation or grant of security under this section may be carried out only by writing probative or holograph of the parties to the transaction.

(7) An assignation of a patent or application for a patent or a share in it, and an exclusive licence granted under any patent or any such application, may confer on the assignee or licensee the right of the assignor or licensor to bring proceedings by virtue of section 61 or 69 below for a previous infringement or to bring proceedings under section 58 below for a previous act.

Register of patents, etc.

32.—(1) There shall continue to be a register kept at the Patent Office and known as the register of patents which shall comply with rules made by virtue of this section and shall be kept in accordance with such rules; and in this Act, except so far as the context otherwise requires—

> "register", as a noun, means the register of patents;

> "register", as a verb, means, in relation to any thing, to register or register particulars, or enter notice, of that thing in the register and, in relation to a person, means to enter his name in the register;

and cognate expressions shall be construed accordingly.

(2) Without prejudice to any other provision of this Act or rules, rules may make provision with respect to the following matters, including provision imposing requirements as to any of those matters, that is to say—

> (a) the registration of patents and of published applications for patents;

> (b) the registration of transactions, instruments or events affecting rights in or under patents and applications;

> (c) the furnishing to the comptroller of any prescribed documents or description of documents in connection with any matter which is required to be registered;

> (d) the correction of errors in the register and in any documents filed at the Patent Office in connection with registration;

> (e) making the register or entries or reproductions of entries in it available for inspection by the public;

> (f) supplying certified copies of any such entries or reproductions to persons requiring them; and

> (g) the publication and advertisement of anything done under this Act or rules in relation to the register.

(3) Notwithstanding anything in subsection (2)(b) above, no notice of any trust, whether express, implied or constructive, shall be entered in the register and the comptroller shall not be affected by any such notice.

Effect of registration, etc., on rights in patents.

33.—(1) Any person who claims to have acquired the property in a patent or application for a patent by virtue of any transaction, instrument or event to which this section applies shall be entitled as against any other person who claims to have acquired that property by virtue of an earlier transaction, instrument or event to which this section applies if, at the time of the later transaction, instrument or event—

 (a) the earlier transaction, instrument or event was not registered, or

 (b) in the case of any application which has not been published, notice of the earlier transaction, instrument or event had not been given to the comptroller, and

 (c) in any case, the person claiming under the later transaction, instrument or event, did not know of the earlier transaction, instrument or event.

(2) Subsection (1) above shall apply equally to the case where any person claims to have acquired any right in or under a patent or application for a patent, by virtue of a transaction, instrument or event to which this section applies, and that right is incompatible with any such right acquired by virtue of an earlier transaction, instrument or event to which this section applies.

(3) This section applies to the following transactions, instruments and events:—

 (a) the assignment or assignation of a patent or application for a patent, or a right in it;

 (b) the mortgage of a patent or application or the granting of security over it;

 (c) the grant, assignment or assignation of a licence or sub-licence, or mortgage of a licence or sub-licence, under a patent or application;

 (d) the death of the proprietor or one of the proprietors of any such patent or application or any person having a right in or under a patent or application and the vesting by an assent of personal representatives of a patent, application or any such right; and

 (e) any order or directions of a court or other competent authority—

  (i) transferring a patent or application or any right in or under it to any person; or

  (ii) that an application should proceed in the name of any person;

 and in either case the event by virtue of which the court or authority had power to make any such order or give any such directions.

(4) Where an application for the registration of a transaction, instrument or event has been made, but the transaction, instrument or event has not been registered, then, for the purposes of subsection (1)(a) above, registration of the application shall be treated as registration of the transaction, instrument or event.

34.—(1) The court may, on the application of any person aggrieved, order the register to be rectified by the making, or the variation or deletion, of any entry in it. ^{Rectification of register.}

(2) In proceedings under this section the court may determine any question which it may be necessary or expedient to decide in connection with the rectification of the register.

(3) Rules of court may provide for the notification of any application under this section to the comptroller and for his appearance on the application and for giving effect to any order of the court on the application.

35.—(1) The register shall be prima facie evidence of anything required or authorised by this Act or rules to be registered and in Scotland shall be admissible and sufficient evidence of any such thing. ^{Evidence of register, documents, etc.}

(2) A certificate purporting to be signed by the comptroller and certifying that

any entry which he is authorised by this Act or rules to make has or has not been made, or that any other thing which he is so authorised to do has or has not been done, shall be prima facie evidence, and in Scotland shall be admissible and sufficient evidence, of the matters so certified.

(3) Each of the following, that is to say—

(a) a copy of any entry in the register or of any document kept in the Patent Office, any specification of a patent or any application for a patent which has been published;

(b) a document reproducing in legible form an entry made in the register otherwise than in legible form; or

(c) an extract from the register or of any document mentioned in paragraph (a) or (b) above;

purporting to be certified by the comptroller and to be sealed with the seal of the Patent Office shall be admitted in evidence without further proof and without production of the original, and in Scotland such evidence shall be sufficient evidence.

Co-ownership of patents and applications for patents.
36.—(1) Where a patent is granted to two or more persons, each of them shall, subject to any agreement to the contrary, be entitled to an equal undivided share in the patent.

(2) Where two or more persons are proprietors of a patent, then, subject to the provisions of this section and subject to any agreement to the contrary—

(a) each of them shall be entitled, by himself or his agents, to do in respect of the invention concerned, for his own benefit and without the consent of or the need to account to the other or others, any act which would apart from this subsection and section 55 below, amount to an infringement of the patent concerned; and

(b) any such act shall not amount to an infringement of the patent concerned.

(3) Subject to the provisions of sections 8 and 12 above and section 37 below and to any agreement for the time being in force, where two or more persons are proprietors of a patent one of them shall not without the consent of the other or others grant a licence under the patent or assign or mortgage a share in the patent or in Scotland cause or permit security to be granted over it.

(4) Subject to the provisions of those sections, where two or more persons are proprietors of a patent, anyone else may supply one of those persons with the means, relating to an essential element of the invention, for putting the invention into effect, and the supply of those means by virtue of this subsection shall not amount to an infringement of the patent.

(5) Where a patented product is disposed of by any of two or more proprietors to any person, that person and any other person claiming through him shall be entitled to deal with the product in the same way as if it had been disposed of by a sole registered proprietor.

(6) Nothing in subsection (1) or (2) above shall affect the mutual rights or obligations of trustees or of the personal representatives of a deceased person, or their rights or obligations as such.

(7) The foregoing provisions of this section shall have effect in relation to an application for a patent which is filed as they have effect in relation to a patent and—

(a) references to a patent and a patent being granted shall accordingly include references respectively to any such application and to the application being filed; and

(b) the reference in subsection (5) above to a patented product shall be construed accordingly.

37.—(1) After a patent has been granted for an invention—

    (a) any person may refer to the comptroller the question whether he is the true proprietor of the patent or whether the patent should have been granted to him (in either case alone or jointly with any other persons) or whether the patent or any right in or under it should be transferred to him (alone or jointly with any other persons); and

    (b) any of two or more persons registered as joint proprietors of the patent may refer to the comptroller the question whether any right in or under the patent should be transferred or granted to any other person;

and the comptroller shall determine the question and make such order as he thinks fit to give effect to the determination.

(2) Without prejudice to the generality of subsection (1) above, an order under that subsection may contain provision—

    (a) directing that the person by whom the reference is made under that subsection shall be included (whether or not to the exclusion of any other person) among the persons registered as proprietors of the patent;

    (b) directing the registration of a transaction, instrument or event by virtue of which that person has acquired any right in or under the patent;

    (c) granting any licence or other right in or under the patent;

    (d) directing the proprietor of the patent or any person having any right in or under the patent to do anything specified in the order as necessary to carry out the other provisions of the order.

(3) If any person to whom directions have been given under subsection (2)(d) above fails to do anything necessary for carrying out any such directions within 14 days after the date of the order containing the directions, the comptroller may, on application made to him by any person in whose favour or on whose reference the order containing the directions was made, authorise him to do that thing on behalf of the person to whom the directions were given.

(4) Where the comptroller finds on a reference under subsection (1)(a) above that the patent was granted to a person not entitled to be granted that patent (whether alone or with other persons) and on an application made under section 72 below makes an order on that ground for the conditional or unconditional revocation of the patent, the comptroller may order that the person by whom the application was made or his successor in title may, subject to section 76 below, make a new application for a patent—

    (a) in the case of unconditional revocation, for the whole of the matter comprised in the specification of that patent; and

    (b) in the case of conditional revocation, for the matter which in the opinion of the comptroller should be excluded from that specification by amendment under section 75 below;

and where such a new application is made, it shall be treated as having been filed on the date of filing the application for the patent to which the reference relates.

(5) On any such reference no order shall be made under this section transferring the patent to which the reference relates on the ground that the patent was granted to a person not so entitled, and no order shall be made under subsection (4) above on that ground, if the reference was made after the end of the period of two years beginning with the date of the grant, unless it is shown that any person registered

as a proprietor of the patent knew at the time of the grant or, as the case may be, of the transfer of the patent to him that he was not entitled to the patent.

(6) An order under this section shall not be so made as to affect the mutual rights or obligations of trustees or of the personal representatives of a deceased person, or their rights or obligations as such.

(7) Where a question is referred to the comptroller under subsection (1)(a) above an order shall not be made by virtue of subsection (2) or under subsection (4) above on the reference unless notice of the reference is given to all persons registered as proprietor of the patent or as having a right in or under the patent, except those who are parties to the reference.

(8) If it appears to the comptroller on a reference under subsection (1) above that the question referred to him would more properly be determined by the court, he may decline to deal with it and, without prejudice to the court's jurisdiction to determine any such question and make a declaration, or any declaratory jurisdiction of the court in Scotland, the court shall have jurisdiction to do so.

(9) The court shall not in the exercise of any such declaratory jurisdiction determine a question whether a patent was granted to a person not entitled to be granted the patent if the proceedings in which the jurisdiction is invoked were commenced after the end of the period of two years beginning with the date of the grant of the patent, unless it is shown that any person registered as a proprietor of the patent knew at the time of the grant or, as the case may be, of the transfer of the patent to him that he was not entitled to the patent.

Effect of transfer of patent under s. 37.

38.—(1) Where an order is made under section 37 above that a patent shall be transferred from any person or persons (the old proprietor or proprietors) to one or more persons (whether or not including an old proprietor), then, except in a case falling within subsection (2) below, any licences or other rights granted or created by the old proprietor or proprietors shall, subject to section 33 above and to the provisions of the order, continue in force and be treated as granted by the person or persons to whom the patent is ordered to be transferred (the new proprietor or proprietors).

(2) Where an order is so made that a patent shall be transferred from the old proprietor or proprietors to one or more persons none of whom was an old proprietor (on the ground that the patent was granted to a person not entitled to be granted the patent), any licences or other rights in or under the patent shall, subject to the provisions of the order and subsection (3) below, lapse on the registration of that person or those persons as the new proprietor or proprietors of the patent.

(3) Where an order is so made that a patent shall be transferred as mentioned in subsection (2) above or that a person other than an old proprietor may make a new application for a patent and before the reference of the question under that section resulting in the making of any such order is registered, the old proprietor or proprietors or a licensee of the patent, acting in good faith, worked the invention in question in the United Kingdom or made effective and serious preparations to do so, the old proprietor or proprietors or the licensee shall, on making a request to the new proprietor or proprietors within the prescribed period, be entitled to be granted a licence (but not an exclusive licence) to continue working or, as the case may be, to work the invention, so far as it is the subject of the new application.

(4) Any such licence shall be granted for a reasonable period and on reasonable terms.

(5) The new proprietor or proprietors of the patent or any person claiming that

he is entitled to be granted any such licence may refer to the comptroller the question whether that person is so entitled and whether any such period is or terms are reasonable, and the comptroller shall determine the question and may, if he considers it appropriate, order the grant of such a licence.

Employees' inventions

39.—(1) Notwithstanding anything in any rule of law, an invention made by an employee shall, as between him and his employer, be taken to belong to his employer for the purposes of this Act and all other purposes if—

Right to employees' inventions.

  (a) it was made in the course of the normal duties of the employee or in the course of duties falling outside his normal duties, but specifically assigned to him, and the circumstances in either case were such that an invention might reasonably be expected to result from the carrying out of his duties; or

  (b) the invention was made in the course of the duties of the employee and, at the time of making the invention, because of the nature of his duties and the particular responsibilities arising from the nature of his duties he had a special obligation to further the interests of the employer's undertaking.

(2) Any other invention made by an employee shall, as between him and his employer, be taken for those purposes to belong to the employee.

40.—(1) Where it appears to the court or the comptroller on an application made by an employee within the prescribed period that the employee has made an invention belonging to the employer for which a patent has been granted, that the patent is (having regard among other things to the size and nature of the employer's undertaking) of outstanding benefit to the employer and that by reason of those facts it is just that the employee should be awarded compensation to be paid by the employer, the court or the comptroller may award him such compensation of an amount determined under section 41 below.

Compensation of employees for certain inventions.

(2) Where it appears to the court or the comptroller on an application made by an employee within the prescribed period that—

  (a) a patent has been granted for an invention made by and belonging to the employee;

  (b) his rights in the invention, or in any patent or application for a patent for the invention, have since the appointed day been assigned to the employer or an exclusive licence under the patent or application has since the appointed day been granted to the employer;

  (c) the benefit derived by the employee from the contract of assignment, assignation or grant or any ancillary contract ("the relevant contract") is inadequate in relation to the benefit derived by the employer from the patent; and

  (d) by reason of those facts it is just that the employee should be awarded compensation to be paid by the employer in addition to the benefit derived from the relevant contract;

the court or the comptroller may award him such compensation of an amount determined under section 41 below.

(3) Subsections (1) and (2) above shall not apply to the invention of an employee where a relevant collective agreement provides for the payment of compensation

in respect of inventions of the same description as that invention to employees of the same description as that employee.

(4) Subsection (2) above shall have effect notwithstanding anything in the relevant contract or any agreement applicable to the invention (other than any such collective agreement).

(5) If it appears to the comptroller on an application under this section that the application involves matters which would more properly be determined by the court, he may decline to deal with it.

(6) In this section—

"the prescribed period", in relation to proceedings before the court, means the period prescribed by rules of court, and

1974/c.52

"relevant collective agreement" means a collective agreement within the meaning of the Trade Union and Labour Relations Act 1974, made by or on behalf of a trade union to which the employee belongs, and by the employer or an employers' association to which the employer belongs which is in force at the time of the making of the invention.

(7) References in this section to an invention belonging to an employer or employee are references to it so belonging as between the employer and the employee.

Amount of compensation.

41.—(1) An award of compensation to an employee under section 40(1) or (2) above in relation to a patent for an invention shall be such as will secure for the employee a fair share (having regard to all the circumstances) of the benefit which the employer has derived, or may reasonably be expected to derive, from the patent or from the assignment, assignation or grant to a person connected with the employer of the property or any right in the invention or the property in, or any right in or under, an application for that patent.

(2) For the purposes of subsection (1) above the amount of any benefit derived or expected to be derived by an employer from the assignment, assignation or grant of—

(a) the property in, or any right in or under, a patent for the invention or an application for such a patent; or

(b) the property or any right in the invention;

to a person connected with him shall be taken to be the amount which could reasonably be expected to be so derived by the employer if that person had not been connected with him.

(3) Where the Crown or a Research Council in its capacity as employer assigns or grants the property in, or any right in or under, an invention, patent or application for a patent to a body having among its functions that of developing or exploiting inventions resulting from public research and does so for no consideration or only a nominal consideration, any benefit derived from the invention, patent or application by that body shall be treated for the purposes of the foregoing provisions of this section as so derived by the Crown or, as the case may be, Research Council.

1965 c. 4.

In this subsection "Research Council" means a body which is a Research Council for the purposes of the Science and Technology Act 1965.

(4) In determining the fair share of the benefit to be secured for an employee in

respect of a patent for an invention which has always belonged to an employer, the court or the comptroller shall, among other things, take the following matters into account, that is to say—

    (a) the nature of the employee's duties, his remuneration and the other advantages he derives or has derived from his employment or has derived in relation to the invention under this Act;

    (b) the effort and skill which the employee has devoted to making the invention;

    (c) the effort and skill which any other person has devoted to making the invention jointly with the employee concerned, and the advice and other assistance contributed by any other employee who is not a joint inventor of the invention; and

    (d) the contribution made by the employer to the making, developing and working of the invention by the provision of advice, facilities and other assistance, by the provision of opportunities and by his managerial and commercial skill and activities.

(5) In determining the fair share of the benefit to be secured for an employee in respect of a patent for an invention which originally belonged to him, the court or the comptroller shall, among other things, take the following matters into account, that is to say—

    (a) any conditions in a licence or licences granted under this Act or otherwise in respect of the invention or the patent;

    (b) the extent to which the invention was made jointly by the employee with any other person; and

    (c) the contribution made by the employer to the making, developing and working of the invention as mentioned in subsection (4)(d) above.

(6) Any order for the payment of compensation under section 40 above may be an order for the payment of a lump sum or for periodical payment, or both.

(7) Without prejudice to section 32 of the Interpretation Act 1889 (which 1889 c. 63. provides that a statutory power may in general be exercised from time to time), the refusal of the court or the comptroller to make any such order on an application made by an employee under section 40 above shall not prevent a further application being made under that section by him or any successor in title of his.

(8) Where the court or the comptroller has made any such order, the court or he may on the application of either the employer or the employee vary or discharge it or suspend any provision of the order and revive any provision so suspended, and section 40(5) above shall apply to the application as it applies to an application under that section.

(9) In England and Wales any sums awarded by the comptroller under section 40 above shall, if a county court so orders, be recoverable by execution issued from the county court or otherwise as if they were payable under an order of that court.

(10) In Scotland an order made under section 40 above by the comptroller for the payment of any sums may be enforced in like manner as a recorded decree arbitral.

(11) In Northern Ireland an order made under section 40 above by the comptroller for the payment of any sums may be enforced as if it were a money judgment.

42.—(1) This section applies to any contract (whenever made) relating to inventions made by an employee, being a contract entered into by him—

(a) with the employer (alone or with another); or

(b) with some other person at the request of the employer or in pursuance of the employee's contract of employment.

(2) Any term in a contract to which this section applies which diminishes the employee's rights in inventions of any description made by him after the appointed day and the date of the contract, or in or under patents for those inventions or applications for such patents, shall be unenforceable against him to the extent that it diminishes his rights in an invention of that description so made, or in or under a patent for such an invention or an application for any such patent.

(3) Subsection (2) above shall not be construed as derogating from any duty of confidentiality owed to his employer by an employee by virtue of any rule of law or otherwise.

(4) This section applies to any arrangement made with a Crown employee by or on behalf of the Crown as his employer as it applies to any contract made between an employee and an employer other than the Crown, and for the purposes of this section "Crown employee" means a person employed under or for the purposes of a government department or any officer or body exercising on behalf of the Crown functions conferred by any enactment.

43.—(1) Sections 39 to 42 above shall not apply to an invention made before the appointed day.

(2) Sections 39 to 42 above shall not apply to an invention made by an employee unless at the time he made the invention one of the following conditions was satisfied in his case, that is to say—

(a) he was mainly employed in the United Kingdom; or

(b) he was not mainly employed anywhere or his place of employment could not be determined, but his employer had a place of business in the United Kingdom to which the employee was attached, whether or not he was also attached elsewhere.

(3) In sections 39 to 42 above and this section, except so far as the context otherwise requires, references to the making of an invention by an employee are references to his making it alone or jointly with any other person, but do not include references to his merely contributing advice or other assistance in the making of an invention by another employee.

(4) Any references in sections 40 to 42 above to a patent and to a patent being granted are respectively references to a patent or other protection and to its being granted whether under the law of the United Kingdom or the law in force in any other country or under any treaty or international convention.

(5) For the purposes of sections 40 and 41 above the benefit derived or expected to be derived by an employer from a patent shall, where he dies before any award is made under section 40 above in respect of the patent, include any benefit derived or expected to be derived from the patent by his personal representatives or by any person in whom it was vested by their assent.

(6) Where an employee dies before an award is made under section 40 above in respect of a patented invention made by him, his personal representatives or their successors in title may exercise his right to make or proceed with an application for compensation under subsection (1) or (2) of that section.

(7) In sections 40 and 41 above and this section "benefit" means benefit in money or money's worth.

(8) Section 533 of the Income and Corporation Taxes Act 1970 (definition of connected persons) shall apply for determining for the purposes of section 41(2) above whether one person is connected with another as it applies for determining 1970 c. 10. that question for the purposes of the Tax Acts.

Contracts as to patented products, etc.

44.—(1) Subject to the provisions of this section, any condition or term of a contract for the supply of a patented product or of a licence to work a patented Avoidance of invention, or of a contract relating to any such supply or licence, shall be void in certain restrictive
conditions. so far it purports—

    (a) in the case of a contract for supply, to require the person supplied to acquire from the supplier, or his nominee, or prohibit him from acquiring from any specified person, or from acquiring except from the supplier or his nominee, anything other than the patented product;

    (b) in the case of a licence to work a patented invention, to require the licensee to acquire from the licensor or his nominee, or prohibit him from acquiring from any specified person, or from acquiring except from the licensor or his nominee, anything other than the product which is the patented invention or (if it is a process) other than any product obtained directly by means of the process or to which the process has been applied;

    (c) in either case, to prohibit the person supplied or licensee from using articles (whether patented products or not) which are not supplied by, or any patented process which does not belong to, the supplier or licensor, or his nominee, or to restrict the right of the person supplied or licensee to use any such articles or process.

(2) Subsection (1) above applies to contracts and licences whether made or granted before or after the appointed day, but not to those made or granted before 1st January 1950.

(3) In proceedings against any person for infringement of a patent it shall be a defence to prove that at the time of the infringement there was in force a contract relating to the patent made by or with the consent of the plaintiff or pursuer or a licence under the patent granted by him or with his consent and containing in either case a condition or term void by virtue of this section.

(4) A condition or term of a contract or licence shall not be void by virtue of this section if—

    (a) at the time of the making of the contract or granting of the licence the supplier or licensor was willing to supply the product, or grant a licence to work the invention, as the case may be, to the person supplied or licensee, on reasonable terms specified in the contract or licence and without any such condition or term as is mentioned in subsection (1) above; and

    (b) the person supplied or licensee is entitled under the contract or licence to relieve himself of his liability to observe the condition or term on giving to the other party three months' notice in writing and subject to payment to that other party of such compensation (being, in the case of a contract to supply, a lump sum or rent for the residue of the term of the contract and, in the case of a licence, a royalty for the residue of the term of the licence) as may be determined by an arbitrator or arbiter appointed by the Secretary of State.

(5) If in any proceeding it is alleged that any condition or term of a contract or

licence is void by virtue of this section it shall lie on the supplier or licensor to prove the matters set out in paragraph (a) of subsection (4) above.

(6) A condition or term of a contract or licence shall not be void by virtue of this section by reason only that it prohibits any person from selling goods other than those supplied by a specific person or, in the case of a contract for the hiring of or licence to use a patented product, that it reserves to the bailor (or, in Scotland, hirer) or licensor, or his nominee, the right to supply such new parts of the patented product as may be required to put or keep it in repair.

Determination of parts of certain contracts.

45.—(1) Any contract for the supply of a patented product or licence to work a patented invention, or contract relating to any such supply or licence, may at any time after the patent or all the patents by which the product or invention was protected at the time of the making of the contract or granting of the licence has or have ceased to be in force, and notwithstanding anything to the contrary in the contract or licence or in any other contract, be determined, to the extent (and only to the extent) that the contract or licence relates to the product or invention, by either party on giving three months' notice in writing to the other party.

(6) In subsection (1) above "patented product" and "patented invention" include respectively a product and an invention which is the subject of an application for a patent, and that subsection shall apply in relation to a patent by which any such product or invention was protected and which was granted after the time of the making of the contract or granting of the licence in question, on an application which had been filed before that time, as it applies to a patent in force at that time.

(3) If, on an application under this subsection made by either party to a contract or licence falling within subsection (1) above, the court is satisfied that, in consequence of the patent or patents concerned ceasing to be in force, it would be unjust to require the applicant to continue to comply with all the terms and conditions of the contract or licence, it may make such order varying those terms or conditions as, having regard to all the circumstances of the case, it thinks just as between the parties.

1974 c. 39.

(4) Without prejudice to any other right of recovery, nothing in subsection (1) above shall be taken to entitle any person to recover property bailed under a hire-purchase agreement (within the meaning of the Consumer Credit Act 1974).

(5) The foregoing provisions of this section apply to contracts and licences whether made before or after the appointed day.

(6) The provisions of this section shall be without prejudice to any rule of law relating to the frustration of contracts and any right of determining a contract or licence exercisable apart from this section.

Licences of right and compulsory licences

Patentee's application for entry in register that licences are available as of right.

46.—(1) At any time after the grant of a patent its proprietor may apply to the comptroller for an entry to be made in the register to the effect that licences under the patent are to be available as of right.

(2) Where such an application is made, the comptroller shall give notice of the application to any person registered as having a right in or under the patent and, if satisfied that the proprietor of the patent is not precluded by contract from granting licences under the patent, shall make that entry.

(3) Where such an entry is made in respect of a patent—

(a) any person shall, at any time after the entry is made, be entitled as of right to a licence under the patent on such terms as may be settled by agreement or, in default of agreement, by the comptroller on the application of the proprietor of the patent or the person requiring the licence;

(b) the comptroller may, on the application of the holder of any licence granted under the patent before the entry was made, order the licence to be exchanged for a licence of right on terms so settled;

(c) if in proceedings for infringement of the patent (otherwise than by the importation of any article) the defendant or defender undertakes to take a licence on such terms, no injunction or interdict shall be granted against him and the amount (if any) recoverable against him by way of damages shall not exceed double the amount which would have been payable by him as licensee if such a licence on those terms had been granted before the earliest infringement;

(d) the renewal fee payable in respect of the patent after the date of the entry shall be half the fee which would be payable if the entry had not been made.

(4) The licensee under a licence of right may (unless, in the case of a licence the terms of which are settled by agreement, the licence otherwise expressly provides) request the proprietor of the patent to take proceedings to prevent any infringement of the patent; and if the proprietor refuses or neglects to do so within two months after being so requested, the licensee may institute proceedings for the infringement in his own name as if he were proprietor, making the proprietor a defendant or defender.

(5) A proprietor so added as defendant or defender shall not be liable for any costs or expenses unless he enters an appearance and takes part in the proceedings.

47.—(1) At any time after an entry has been made under section 46 above in respect of a patent, the proprietor of the patent may apply to the comptroller for cancellation of the entry. *Cancellation of entry made under s. 46.*

(2) Where such an application is made and the balance paid of all renewal fees which would have been payable if the entry had not been made, the comptroller may cancel the entry, if satisfied that there is no existing licence under the patent or that all licensees under the patent consent to the application.

(3) Within the prescribed period after an entry has been made under section 46 above in respect of a patent, any person who claims that the proprietor of the patent is, and was at the time of the entry, precluded by a contract in which the claimant is interested from granting licences under the patent may apply to the comptroller for cancellation of the entry.

(4) Where the comptroller is satisfied, on an application under subsection (3) above, that the proprietor of the patent is and was so precluded, he shall cancel the entry; and the proprietor shall then be liable to pay, within a period specified by the comptroller, a sum equal to the balance of all renewal fees which would have been payable if the entry had not been made, and the patent shall cease to have effect at the expiration of that period if that sum is not so paid.

(5) Where an entry is cancelled under this section, the rights and liabilities of the proprietor of the patent shall afterwards be the same as if the entry had not been made.

(6) Where an application has been made under this section, then—

(a) in the case of an application under subsection (1) above, any person, and

(b) in the case of an application under subsection (3) above, the proprietor of the patent,

may within the prescribed period give notice to the comptroller of opposition to the cancellation; and the comptroller shall, in considering the application, determine whether the opposition is justified.

Compulsory licences

48.—(1) At any time after the expiration of three years, or of such other period as may be prescribed, from the date of the grant of a patent, any person may apply to the comptroller on one or more of the grounds specified in subsection (3) below—

(a) for a licence under the patent,

(b) for an entry to be made in the register to the effect that licences under the patent are to be available as of right, or

(c) where the applicant is a government department, for the grant to any person specified in the application of a licence under the patent.

(2) A rule prescribing any such other period under subsection (1) above shall not be made unless a draft of the rule has been laid before, and approved by resolution of, each House of Parliament.

(3) The grounds are:—

(a) where the patented invention is capable of being commercially worked in the United Kingdom, that it is not being so worked or is not being so worked to the fullest extent that is reasonably practicable;

(b) where the patented invention is a product, that a demand for the product in the United Kingdom—

(i) is not being met on reasonable terms, or

(ii) is being met to a substantial extent by importation;

(c) where the patented invention is capable of being commercially worked in the United Kingdom, that it is being prevented or hindered from being so worked—

(i) where the invention is a product, by the importation of the product,

(ii) where the invention is a process, by the importation of a product obtained directly by means of the process or to which the process has been applied;

(d) that by reason of the refusal of the proprietor of the patent to grant a licence or licences on reasonable terms—

(i) a market for the export of any patented product made in the United Kingdom is not being supplied, or

(ii) the working or efficient working in the United Kingdom of any other patented invention which makes a substantial contribution to the art is prevented or hindered, or

(iii) the establishment or development of commercial or industrial activities in the United Kingdom is unfairly prejudiced;

(e) that by reason of conditions imposed by the proprietor of the patent on the grant of licences under the patent, or on the disposal or use of the patented product or on the use of the patented process, the manufacture, use or disposal of materials not protected by the patent, or the establishment or development of commercial or industrial activities in the United Kingdom, is unfairly prejudiced.

(4) Subject to the provisions of subsections (5) to (7) below, if he is satisfied that any of those grounds are established, the comptroller may—

(a) where the application is under subsection (1)(a) above, order the grant of a licence to the applicant on such terms as the comptroller thinks fit;

(b) where the application is under subsection (1)(b) above, make such an entry as is there mentioned;

(c) where the application is under subsection (1)(c) above, order the grant of a licence to the person specified in the application on such terms as the comptroller thinks fit.

(5) Where the application is made on the ground that the patented invention is not being commercially worked in the United Kingdom or is not being so worked to the fullest extent that is reasonably practicable, and it appears to the comptroller that the time which has elapsed since the publication in the journal of a notice of the grant of the patent has for any reason been insufficient to enable the invention to be so worked, he may by order adjourn the application for such period as will in his opinion give sufficient time for the invention to be so worked.

(6) No entry shall be made in the register under this section on the ground mentioned in subsection (3)(d)(i) above, and any licence granted under this section on that ground shall contain such provisions as appear to the comptroller to be expedient for restricting the countries in which any product concerned may be disposed of or used by the licensee.

(7) No order or entry shall be made under this section in respect of a patent (the patent concerned) on the ground mentioned in subsection (3)(d)(ii) above unless the comptroller is satisfied that the proprietor of the patent for the other invention is able and willing to grant to the proprietor of the patent concerned and his licensees a licence under the patent for the other invention on reasonable terms.

(8) An application may be made under this section in respect of a patent notwithstanding that the applicant is already the holder of a licence under the patent; and no person shall be estopped or barred from alleging any of the matters specified in subsection (3) above by reason of any admission made by him, whether in such a licence or otherwise, or by reason of his having accepted such a licence.

49.—(1) Where the comptroller is satisfied, on an application made under section 48 above in respect of a patent, that the manufacture, use or disposal of materials not protected by the patent is unfairly prejudiced by reason of conditions imposed by the proprietor of the patent on the grant of licences under the patent, or on the disposal of use of the patented product or the use of the patented process, he may (subject to the provisions of that section) order the grant of licences under the patent to such customers of the applicant as he thinks fit as well as to the applicant.

Provisions about
licences under
s. 48.

(2) Where an application under section 48 above is made in respect of a patent by a person who holds a licence under the patent, the comptroller—

(a) may, if he orders the grant of a licence to the applicant, order the existing licence to be cancelled, or

(b) may, instead of ordering the grant of a licence to the applicant, order the existing licence to be amended.

(3) Where, on an application under section 48 above in respect of a patent, the comptroller orders the grant of a licence, he may direct that the licence shall operate—

(a) to deprive the proprietor of the patent of any right he has to work the invention concerned or grant licences under the patent;

(b) to revoke all existing licences granted under the patent.

(4) Section 46(4) and (5) above shall apply to a licence granted in pursuance of an order under section 48 above and to a licence granted by virtue of an entry under that section as it applies to a licence granted by virtue of an entry under section 46 above.

50.—(1) The powers of the comptroller on an application under section 48 above in respect of a patent shall be exercised with a view to securing the following general purposes:—

    (a) that inventions which can be worked on a commercial scale in the United Kingdom and which should in the public interest be so worked shall be worked there without undue delay and to the fullest extent that is reasonably practicable;

    (b) that the inventor or other person beneficially entitled to a patent shall receive reasonable remuneration having regard to the nature of the invention;

    (c) that the interests of any person for the time being working or developing an invention in the United Kingdom under the protection of a patent shall not be unfairly prejudiced.

(2) Subject to subsection (1) above, the comptroller shall, in determining whether to make an order or entry in pursuance of such an application, take account of the following matters, that is to say—

    (a) the nature of the invention, the time which has elapsed since the publication in the journal of a notice of the grant of the patent and the measures already taken by the proprietor of the patent or any licensee to make full use of the invention;

    (b) the ability of any person to whom a licence would be granted under the order concerned to work the invention to the public advantage; and

    (c) the risks to be undertaken by that person in providing capital and working the invention if the application for an order is granted,

but shall not be required to take account of matters subsequent to the making of the application.

Application by Crown in cases of monopoly or merger. 1973 c. 41.
51.—(1) Where, on a reference under section 50 or 51 of the Fair Trading Act 1973 (the 1973 Act), a report of the Monopolies and Mergers Commission (the Commission), as laid before Parliament, contains conclusions to the effect—

    (a) that a monopoly situation (within the meaning of the 1973 Act) exists in relation to a description of goods which consist of or include patented products or in relation to a description of services in which a patented product or process is used, and

    (b) that facts found by the Commission in pursuance of their investigations under section 49 of the 1973 Act operate, or may be expected to operate, against the public interest,

the appropriate Minister or Ministers may, subject to subsection (3) below, apply to the comptroller for relief under subsection (4) below in respect of the patent.

(2) Where, on a reference under section 64 or 75 of the 1973 Act, a report of the Commission, as laid before Parliament, contains conclusions to the effect—

    (a) that a merger situation qualifying for investigation has been created;

    (b) that one of the elements which constitute the creation of that situation is that the condition specified in section 64(2) or (3) of the 1973 Act prevails (or does so to a greater extent) in respect of a description of goods which consist of or include patented products or in respect of a description of services in which a patented product or process is used; and

(c) that the creation of that situation, or particular elements in or consequences of it specified in the report, operate, or may be expected to operate, against the public interest,

the Secretary of State may, subject to subsection (3) below, apply to the comptroller for relief under subsection (5) below in respect of the patent.

(3) Before making an application under subsection (1) or (2) above, the appropriate Minister or Ministers shall publish, in such manner as he or they think appropriate, a notice describing the nature of the proposed application, and shall consider any representations which, within the period of thirty days from the date of publication of the notice, may be made to him or them by persons whose interests appear to the appropriate Minister or Ministers to be likely to be affected by the proposed application.

(4) If on an application under subsection (1) above it appears to the comptroller that the facts specified in the Commission's report as being those which, in the Commission's opinion, operate or may be expected to operate against the public interest include—

(a) any conditions in a licence or licences granted under the patent by its proprietor restricting the use of the invention concerned by the licensee or the right of the proprietor to grant other licences under the patent, or

(b) a refusal by the proprietor to grant licences under the patent on reasonable terms,

the comptroller may by order cancel or modify any such condition or may, instead or in addition, make an entry in the register to the effect that licences under the patent are to be available as of right.

(5) If on an application under subsection (2) above it appears to the comptroller that the particular matters indicated in the Commission's report as being those which, in the Commission's opinion, operate or may be expected to operate against the public interest (whether those matters are so indicated in pursuance of a requirement imposed under section 69(4) or 75(3) of the 1973 Act or otherwise) include any such condition or refusal as is mentioned in paragraph (a) or (b) or subsection (4) above, the comptroller may by order cancel or modify any such condition or may, instead or in addition, make an entry in the register to the effect that licences under the patent are to be available as of right.

(6) In this section "the appropriate Minister or Ministers", in relation to a report of the Commission, means the Minister or Ministers to whom the report is made.

52.—(1) The proprietor of the patent concerned or any other person wishing to oppose an application under sections 48 to 51 above may, in accordance with rules, give to the comptroller notice of opposition; and the comptroller shall consider the opposition in deciding whether to grant the application. *Opposition, appeal and arbitration.*

(2) Where an appeal is brought from an order made by the comptroller in pursuance of an application under sections 48 to 51 above or from a decision of his to make an entry in the register in pursuance of such an application or from a refusal of his to make such an order or entry, the Attorney General, Lord Advocate or Attorney General for Northern Ireland, or such other counsel as any of them may appoint, shall be entitled to appear and be heard.

(3) Where an application under sections 48 to 51 above is opposed under subsection (1) above, and either—

(a) the parties consent, or

(b) the proceedings require a prolonged examination of documents or any scientific or local investigation which cannot in the opinion of the comptroller conveniently be made before him,

the comptroller may at any time order the whole proceedings, or any question or issue of fact arising in them, to be referred to an arbitrator or arbiter agreed on by the parties or, in default of agreement, appointed by the comptroller.

1950 c. 27.
1937 c. 8.
(1 Edw. 8 & 1
Geo. 6) (N.I.).
(4) Where the whole proceedings are so referred, section 21 of the Arbitration Act 1950 or, as the case may be, section 22 of the Arbitration Act (Northern Ireland) 1937 (statement of cases by arbitrators) shall not apply to the arbitration; but unless the parties otherwise agree before the award of the arbitrator or arbiter is made an appeal shall lie from the award to the court.

(5) Where a question or issue of fact is so referred, the arbitrator or arbiter shall report his findings to the comptroller.

Compulsory
licences;
supplementary
provisions.
53.—(1) Without prejudice to section 86 below (by virtue of which the Community Patent Convention has effect in the United Kingdom), sections 48 to 51 above shall have effect subject to any provision of that convention relating to the grant of compulsory licences for lack or insufficiency of exploitation as that provision applies by virtue of that section.

(2) In any proceedings on an application made in relation to a patent under sections 48 to 51 above, any statement with respect to any activity in relation to the patented invention, or with respect to the grant or refusal of licences under the patent, contained in a report of the Monopolies and Mergers Commission laid before Parliament under Part VII of the Fair Trading Act 1973 shall be prima facie evidence of the matters stated, and in Scotland shall be sufficient evidence of those matters.

(3) The comptroller may make an entry in the register under sections 48 to 51 above notwithstanding any contract which would have precluded the entry on the application of the proprietor of the patent under section 46 above.

(4) An entry made in the register under sections 48 to 51 above shall for all purposes have the same effect as an entry made under section 46 above.

(5) No order or entry shall be made in pursuance of an application under sections 48 to 51 above which would be at variance with any treaty or international convention to which the United Kingdom is a party.

Special
provisions where
patented
invention is
being worked
abroad.
54.—(1) Her Majesty may by Order in Council provide that the comptroller may not (otherwise than for purposes of the public interest) make an order or entry in respect of a patent in pursuance of an application under sections 48 to 51 above if the invention concerned is being commercially worked in any relevant country specified in the Order and demand in the United Kingdom for any patented product resulting from that working is being met by importation from that country.

(2) In subsection (1) above "relevant country" means a country other than a member state whose law in the opinion of Her Majesty in Council incorporates or will incorporate provisions treating the working of an invention in, and importation from, the United Kingdom in a similar way to that in which the Order in Council would (if made) treat the working of an invention in, and importation from, that country.

Use of patented inventions for services of the Crown

55.—(1) Notwithstanding anything in this Act, any government department and any person authorised in writing by a government department may, for the services of the Crown and in accordance with this section, do any of the following acts in the United Kingdom in relation to a patented invention without the consent of the proprietor of a patent, that is to say— Use of patented inventions for services of the Crown.

(a) where the invention is a product, may—

(i) make, use, import or keep the product, or sell or offer to sell it where to do so would be incidental or ancillary to making, using, importing or keeping it; or

(ii) in any event, sell or offer to sell it for foreign defence purposes or for the production or supply of specified drugs and medicines, or dispose or offer to dispose of it (otherwise than by selling it) for any purpose whatever;

(b) where the invention is a process, may use it or do in relation to any product obtained directly by means of the process anything mentioned in paragraph (a) above;

(c) without prejudice to the foregoing, where the invention or any product obtained directly by means of the invention is a specified drug or medicine, may sell or offer to sell the drug or medicine;

(d) may supply or offer to supply to any person any of the means, relating to an essential element of the invention, for putting the invention into effect;

(e) may dispose or offer to dispose of anything which was made, used, imported or kept in the exercise of the powers conferred by this section and which is no longer required for the purpose for which it was made, used, imported or kept (as the case may be),

and anything done by virtue of this subsection shall not amount to an infringement of the patent concerned.

(2) Any act done in relation to an invention by virtue of this section is in the following provisions of this section referred to as use of the invention; and "use", in relation to an invention, in sections 56 to 58 below shall be construed accordingly.

(3) So far as the invention has before its priority date been duly recorded by or tried by or on behalf of a government department or the United Kingdom Atomic Energy Authority otherwise than in consequence of a relevant communication made in confidence, any use of the invention by virtue of this section may be made free of any royalty or other payment to the proprietor.

(4) So far as the invention has not been so recorded or tried, any use of it made by virtue of this section at any time either—

(a) after the publication of the application for the patent for the invention; or

(b) without prejudice to paragraph (a) above, in consequence of a relevant communication made after the priority date of the invention otherwise than in confidence;

shall be made on such terms as may be agreed either before or after the use by the government department and the proprietor of the patent with the approval of the Treasury or as may in default of agreement be determined by the court on a reference under section 58 below.

(5) Where an invention is used by virtue of this section at any time after

publication of an application for a patent for the invention but before such a patent is granted, and the terms for its use agreed or determined as mentioned in subsection (4) above include terms as to payment for the use, then (notwithstanding anything in those terms) any such payment shall be recoverable only—

(a) after such a patent is granted; and

(b) if (apart from this section) the use would, if the patent had been granted on the date of the publication of the application, have infringed not only the patent but also the claims (as interpreted by the description and any drawings referred to in the description or claims) in the form in which they were contained in the application immediately before the preparations for its publication were completed by the Patent Office.

(6) The authority of a government department in respect of an invention may be given under this section either before or after the patent is granted and either before or after the use in respect of which the authority is given is made, and may be given to any person whether or not he is authorised directly or indirectly by the proprietor of the patent to do anything in relation to the invention.

(7) Where any use of an invention is made by or with the authority of a government department under this section, then, unless it appears to the department that it would be contrary to the public interest to do so, the department shall notify the proprietor of the patent as soon as practicable after the second of the following events, that is to say, the use is begun and the patent is granted, and furnish him with such information as to the extent of the use as he may from time to time require.

(8) A person acquiring anything disposed of in the exercise of powers conferred by this section, and any person claiming through him, may deal with it in the same manner as if the patent were held on behalf of the Crown.

(9) In this section "relevant communication", in relation to an invention, means a communication of the invention directly or indirectly by the proprietor of the patent or any person from whom he derives title.

(10) Subsection (4) above is without prejudice to any rule of law relating to the confidentiality of information.

(11) In the application of this section to Northern Ireland, the reference in subsection (4) above to the Treasury shall, where the government department referred to in that subsection is a department of the Government of Northern Ireland, be construed as a reference to the Department of Finance for Northern Ireland.

Interpretation, etc., of provisions about Crown use.

56.—(1) Any reference in section 55 above to a patented invention, in relation to any time, is a reference to an invention for which a patent has before that time been, or is subsequently, granted.

(2) In this Act, except so far as the context otherwise requires, "the services of the Crown" includes—

(a) the supply of anything for foreign defence purposes;

(b) the production or supply of specified drugs and medicines; and

(c) such purposes relating to the production or use of atomic energy or research into matters connected therewith as the Secretary of State thinks necessary or expedient;

and "use for the services of the Crown" shall be construed accordingly.

(3) In section 55(1)(a) above and subsection (2)(a) above, references to a sale or

supply of anything for foreign defence purposes are references to a sale or supply of the thing—

(a) to the government of any country outside the United Kingdom, in pursuance of an agreement or arrangement between Her Majesty's Government in the United Kingdom and the government of that country, where the thing is required for the defence of that country or of any other country whose government is party to any agreement or arrangement with Her Majesty's Government in respect of defence matters; or

(b) to the United Nations, or to the government of any country belonging to that organisation, in pursuance of an agreement or arrangement between Her Majesty's Government and that organisation or government, where the thing is required for any armed forces operating in pursuance of a resolution of that organisation or any organ of that organisation.

(4) For the purposes of section 55(1)(a) and (c) above and subsection (2)(b) above, specified drugs and medicines are drugs and medicines which are both—

(a) required for the provision of pharmaceutical services, general medical services or general dental services, that is to say, services of those respective kinds under Part II of the National Health Service Act 1977, Part IV of the National Health Service (Scotland) Act 1947 or the corresponding provisions of the law in force in Northern Ireland or the Isle of Man, and

1977 c. 49.
1947 c. 27.

(b) specified for the purposes of this subsection in regulations made by the Secretary of State.

57.—(1) In relation to—

Rights of third parties in respect of Crown use.

(a) any use made for the services of the Crown of an invention by a government department, or a person authorised by a government department, by virtue of section 55 above, or

(b) anything done for the services of the Crown to the order of a government department by the proprietor of a patent in respect of a patented invention or by the proprietor of an application in respect of an invention for which an application for a patent has been filed and is still pending,

the provisions of any licence, assignment, assignation or agreement to which this subsection applies shall be of no effect so far as those provisions restrict or regulate the working of the invention, or the use of any model, document or information relating to it, or provide for the making of payments in respect of, or calculated by reference to, such working or use; and the reproduction or publication of any model or document in connection with the said working or use shall not be deemed to be an infringement of any copyright subsisting in the model or document.

(2) Subsection (1) above applies to a licence, assignment, assignation or agreement which is made, whether before or after the appointed day, between (on the one hand) any person who is a proprietor of or an applicant for the patent, or anyone who derives title from any such person or from whom such person derives title, and (on the other hand) any person whatever other than a government department.

(3) Where an exclusive licence granted otherwise than for royalties or other benefits determined by reference to the working of the invention is in force under the patent or application concerned, then—

(a) in relation to anything done in respect of the invention which, but for the provisions of this section and section 55 above, would constitute an infringement of the rights of the licensee, subsection (4) of that section shall have effect as if for the reference to the proprietor of the patent there were substituted a reference to the licensee; and

(b) in relation to anything done in respect of the invention by the licensee by virtue of an authority given under that section, that section shall have effect as if the said subsection (4) were omitted.

(4) Subject to the provisions of subsection (3) above, where the patent, or the right to the grant of the patent, has been assigned to the proprietor of the patent or application in consideration of royalties or other benefits determined by reference to the working of the invention, then—

(a) in relation to any use of the invention by virtue of section 55 above, subsection (4) of that section shall have effect as if the reference to the proprietor of the patent included a reference to the assignor, and any sum payable by virtue of that subsection shall be divided between the proprietor of the patent or application and the assignor in such proportion as may be agreed on by them or as may in default of agreement be determined by the court on a reference under section 58 below; and

(b) in relation to any act done in respect of the invention for the services of the Crown by the proprietor of the patent or application to the order of a government department, section 55(4) above shall have effect as if that act were use made by virtue of an authority given under that section.

(5) Where section 55(4) above applies to any use of an invention and a person holds an exclusive licence under the patent or application concerned (other than such a licence as is mentioned in subsection (3) above) authorising him to work the invention, then subsections (7) and (8) below shall apply.

(6) In those subsections "the section 55(4)" payment means such payment (if any) as the proprietor of the patent or application and the department agree under section 55 above, or the court determines under section 58 below, should be made by the department to the proprietor in respect of the use of the invention.

(7) The licensee shall be entitled to recover from the proprietor of the patent or application such part (if any) of the section 55(4) payment as may be agreed on by them or as may in default of agreement be determined by the court under section 58 below to be just having regard to any expenditure incurred by the licensee—

(a) in developing the invention, or

(b) in making payments to the proprietor in consideration of the licence, other than royalties or other payments determined by reference to the use of the invention.

(8) Any agreement by the proprietor of the patent or application and the department under section 55(4) above as to the amount of the section 55(4) payment shall be of no effect unless the licensee consents to the agreement; and any determination by the court under section 55(4) above as to the amount of that payment shall be of no effect unless the licensee has been informed of the reference to the court and is given an opportunity to be heard.

(9) Where any models, documents or information relating to an invention are used in connection with any use of the invention which falls within subsection (1)(a) above, or with anything done in respect of the invention which falls within subsection (1)(b) above, subsection (4) of section 55 above shall (whether or not it applies to any such use of the invention) apply to the use of the models, documents or information as if for the reference in it to the proprietor of the patent there were substituted a reference to the person entitled to the benefit of any provision of an agreement which is rendered inoperative by this section in relation to that

use; and in section 58 below the references to terms for the use of an invention shall be construed accordingly.

(10) Nothing in this section shall be construed as authorising the disclosure to a government department or any other person of any model, document or information to the use of which this section applies in contravention of any such licence, assignment, assignation or agreement as is mentioned in this section.

58.—(1) Any dispute as to the exercise by a government department or a person authorised by a government department of the powers conferred by section 55 above, or as to terms for the use of an invention for the services of the Crown thereunder, or as to the right of any person to receive any part of a payment made or agreed to be made in pursuance of subsection (4) of that section or determined by the court in pursuance of that subsection and this section, may be referred to the court by either party to the dispute after a patent has been granted for the invention.

References of disputes as to Crown use.

(2) If in such proceedings any question arises whether an invention has been recorded or tried as mentioned in section 55 above, and the disclosure of any document recording the invention, or of any evidence of the trial thereof, would in the opinion of the department be prejudicial to the public interest, the disclosure may be made confidentially to counsel for the other party or to an independent expert mutually agreed upon.

(3) In determining under this section any dispute between a government department and any person as to the terms for the use of an invention for the services of the Crown, the court shall have regard—

(a) to any benefit or compensation which that person or any person from whom he derives title may have received or may be entitled to receive directly or indirectly from any government department in respect of the invention in question;

(b) to whether that person or any person from whom he derives title has in the court's opinion without reasonable cause failed to comply with a request of the department to use the invention for the services of the Crown on reasonable terms.

(4) In determining whether or not to grant any relief under this section and the nature and extent of the relief granted the court shall, subject to the following provisions of this section, apply the principles applied by the court immediately before the appointed day to the granting of relief under section 48 of the 1949 Act.

(5) On a reference under this section the court may refuse to grant relief by way of compensation in respect of the use of an invention for the services of the Crown during any further period specified under section 25(4) above, but before the payment of the renewal fee and any additional fee prescribed for the purposes of that section.

(6) Where an amendment of the specification of a patent has been allowed under any of the provisions of this Act, the court shall not grant relief by way of compensation under this section in respect of any such use before the decision to allow the amendment unless the court is satisfied that the specification of the patent as published was framed in good faith and with reasonable skill and knowledge.

(7) If the validity of a patent is put in issue in proceedings under this section and it is found that the patent is only partially valid, the court may, subject to subsection (8) below, grant relief to the proprietor of the patent in respect of that part of the patent which is found to be valid and to have been used for the services of the Crown.

(8) Where in any such proceedings it is found that a patent is only partially valid, the court shall not grant relief by way of compensation, costs or expenses except where the proprietor of the patent proves that the specification of the patent was framed in good faith and with reasonable skill and knowledge, and in that event the court may grant relief in respect of that part of the patent which is valid and has been so used, subject to the discretion of the court as to costs and expenses and as to the date from which compensation should be awarded.

(9) As a condition of any such relief the court may direct that the specification of the patent shall be amended to its satisfaction upon an application made for that purpose under section 75 below, and an application may be so made accordingly, whether or not all other issues in the proceedings have been determined.

(10) In considering the amount of any compensation for the use of an invention for the services of the Crown after publication of an application for a patent for the invention and before such a patent is granted, the court shall consider whether or not it would have been reasonable to expect, from a consideration of the application as published under section 16 above, that a patent would be granted conferring on the proprietor of the patent protection for an act of the same description as that found to constitute that use, and if the court finds that it would not have been reasonable, it shall reduce the compensation to such amount as it thinks just.

(11) Where by virtue of a transaction, instrument or event to which section 33 above applies a person becomes the proprietor or one of the proprietors or an exclusive licensee of a patent (the new proprietor or licensee) and a government department or a person authorised by a government department subsequently makes use under section 55 above of the patented invention, the new proprietor or licensee shall not be entitled to any compensation under section 55(4) above (as it stands or as modified by section 57(3) above) in respect of a subsequent use of the invention before the transaction, instrument or event is registered unless—

    (a) the transaction, instrument or event is registered within the period of six months beginning with its date; or

    (b) the court is satisfied that it was not practicable to register the transaction, instrument or event before the end of that period and that it was registered as soon as practicable thereafter.

(12) In any proceedings under this section the court may at any time order the whole proceedings or any question or issue of fact arising in them to be referred, on such terms as the court may direct, to a Circuit judge discharging the functions of an official referee or an arbitrator in England and Wales or Northern Ireland, or to an arbiter in Scotland; and references to the court in the foregoing provisions of this section shall be construed accordingly.

(13) One of two or more joint proprietors of a patent or application for a patent may without the concurrence of the others refer a dispute to the court under this section, but shall not do so unless the others are made parties to the proceedings; but any of the others made a defendant or defender shall not be liable for any costs or expenses unless he enters an appearance and takes part in the proceedings.

Special provisions as to Crown use during emergency.

59.—(1) During any period of emergency within the meaning of this section the powers exercisable in relation to an invention by a government department or a person authorised by a government department under section 55 above shall include power to use the invention for any purpose which appears to the department necessary or expedient—

    (a) for the efficient prosecution of any war in which Her Majesty may be engaged;

(b) for the maintenance of supplies and services essential to the life of the community;

(c) for securing a sufficiency of supplies and services essential to the well-being of the community;

(d) for promoting the productivity of industry, commerce and agriculture;

(e) for fostering and directing exports and reducing imports, or imports of any classes, from all or any countries and for redressing the balance of trade;

(f) generally for ensuring that the whole resources of the community are available for use, and are used, in a manner best calculated to serve the interests of the community; or

(g) for assisting the relief of suffering and the restoration and distribution of essential supplies and services in any country or territory outside the United Kingdom which is in grave distress as the result of war;

and any reference in this Act to the services of the Crown shall, as respects any period of emergency, include a reference to those purposes.

(2) In this section the use of an invention includes, in addition to any act constituting such use by virtue of section 55 above, any act which would, apart from that section and this section, amount to an infringement of the patent concerned or, as the case may be, give rise to a right under section 69 below to bring proceedings in respect of the application concerned, and any reference in this Act to "use for the services of the Crown" shall, as respects any period of emergency, be construed accordingly.

(3) In this section "period of emergency" means any period beginning with such date as may be declared by Order in Council to be the commencement, and ending with such date as may be so declared to be the termination, of a period of emergency for the purposes of this section.

(4) A draft of an Order under this section shall not be submitted to Her Majesty unless it has been laid before, and approved by resolution of, each House of Parliament.

Infringement

60.—(1) Subject to the provisions of this section, a person infringes a patent for an invention if, but only if, while the patent is in force, he does any of the following things in the United Kingdom in relation to the invention without the consent of the proprietor of the patent, that is to say— *Meaning of infringement.*

(a) where the invention is a product, he makes, disposes of, offers to dispose of, uses or imports the product or keeps it whether for disposal or otherwise;

(b) where the invention is a process, he uses the process or he offers it for use in the United Kingdom when he knows, or it is obvious to a reasonable person in the circumstances, that its use there without the consent of the proprietor would be an infringement of the patent;

(c) where the invention is a process, he disposes of, offers to dispose of, uses or imports any product obtained directly by means of that process or keeps any such product whether for disposal or otherwise.

(2) Subject to the following provisions of this section, a person (other than the proprietor of the patent) also infringes a patent for an invention if, while the patent is in force and without the consent of the proprietor, he supplies or offers to

supply in the United Kingdom a person other than a licensee or other person entitled to work the invention with any of the means, relating to an essential element of the invention, for putting the invention into effect when he knows, or it is obvious to a reasonable person in the circumstances, that those means are suitable for putting, and are intended to put, the invention into effect in the United Kingdom.

(3) Subsection (2) above shall not apply to the supply or offer of a staple commercial product unless the supply or the offer is made for the purpose of inducing the person supplied or, as the case may be, the person to whom the offer is made to do an act which constitutes an infringement of the patent by virtue of subsection (1) above.

(4) Without prejudice to section 86 below, subsections (1) and (2) above shall not apply to any act which, under any provision of the Community Patent Convention relating to the exhaustion of the rights of the proprietor of a patent, as that provision applies by virtue of that section, cannot be prevented by the proprietor of the patent.

(5) An act which, apart from this subsection, would constitute an infringement of a patent for an invention shall not do so if—

    (a) it is done privately and for purposes which are not commercial;

    (b) it is done for experimental purposes relating to the subject-matter of the invention;

    (c) it consists of the extemporaneous preparation in a pharmacy of a medicine for an individual in accordance with a prescription given by a registered medical or dental practitioner or consists of dealing with a medicine so prepared;

    (d) it consists of the use, exclusively for the needs of a relevant ship, of a product or process in the body of such a ship or in its machinery, tackle, apparatus or other accessories, in a case where the ship has temporarily or accidentally entered the internal or territorial waters of the United Kingdom;

    (e) it consists of the use of a product or process in the body or operation of a relevant aircraft, hovercraft or vehicle which has temporarily or accidentally entered or is crossing the United Kingdom (including the air space above it and its territorial waters) or the use of accessories for such a relevant aircraft, hovercraft or vehicle;

    (f) it consists of the use of an exempted aircraft which has lawfully entered or is lawfully crossing the United Kingdom as aforesaid or of the importation into the United Kingdom, or the use or storage there, of any part or accessory for such an aircraft.

(6) For the purposes of subsection (2) above a person who does an act in relation to an invention which is prevented only by virtue of paragraph (a), (b) or (c) of subsection (5) above from constituting an infringement of a patent for the invention shall not be treated as a person entitled to work the invention, but—

    (a) the reference in that subsection to a person entitled to work an invention ...cludes a reference to a person so entitled by virtue of section 55 above, and

    (b) a person who by virtue of section 28(6) above or section 64 below is entitled to do an act in relation to the invention without it constituting such an infringement shall, so far as concerns that act, be treated as a person entitled to work the invention.

(7) In this section—

"relevant ship" and "relevant aircraft, hovercraft or vehicle" mean respectively a ship and an aircraft, hovercraft or vehicle registered in, or belonging to, any country, other than the United Kingdom, which is a party to the Convention for the Protection of Industrial Property signed at Paris on 20th March 1883; and

"exempted aircraft" means an aircraft to which section 53 of the Civil Aviation Act 1949 (aircraft exempted from seizure in respect of patent claims) applies.

1949 c. 67.

61.—(1) Subject to the following provisions of this Part of this Act, civil proceedings may be brought in the court by the proprietor of a patent in respect of any act alleged to infringe the patent and (without prejudice to any other jurisdiction of the court) in those proceedings a claim may be made— *Proceedings for infringement of patent.*

(a) for an injunction or interdict restraining the defendant or defender from any apprehended act of infringement;

(b) for an order for him to deliver up or destroy any patented product in relation to which the patent is infringed or any article in which that product is inextricably comprised;

(c) for damages in respect of the infringement;

(d) for an account of the profits derived by him from the infringement;

(e) for a declaration or declarator that the patent is valid and has been infringed by him.

(2) The court shall not, in respect of the same infringement, both award the proprietor of a patent damages and order that he shall be given an account of the profits.

(3) The proprietor of a patent and any other person may by agreement with each other refer to the comptroller the question whether that other person has infringed the patent and on the reference the proprietor of the patent may make any claim mentioned in subsection (1)(c) or (e) above.

(4) Except so far as the context requires, in the following provisions of this Act—

(a) any reference to proceedings for infringement and the bringing of such proceedings includes a reference to a reference under subsection (3) above and the making of such a reference;

(b) any reference to a plaintiff or pursuer includes a reference to the proprietor of the patent; and

(c) any reference to a defendant or defender includes a reference to any other party to the reference.

(5) If it appears to the comptroller on a reference under subsection (3) above that the question referred to him would more properly be determined by the court, he may decline to deal with it and the court shall have jurisdiction to determine the question as if the reference were proceedings brought in the court.

(6) Subject to the following provisions of this Part of this Act, in determining whether or not to grant any kind of relief claimed under this section and the extent of the relief granted the court or the comptroller shall apply the principles applied by the court in relation to that kind of relief immediately before the appointed day.

62.—(1) In proceedings for infringement of a patent damages shall not be awarded, and no order shall be made for an account of profits, against a defendant or defender who proves that at the date of the infringement he was not aware, and had no reasonable grounds for supposing, that the patent existed; and a person shall not be taken to have been so aware or to have had reasonable grounds for so supposing by reason only of the application to a product of the word "patent" or "patented", or any word or words expressing or implying that a patent has been obtained for the product, unless the number of the patent accompanied the word or words in question.

(2) In proceedings for infringement of a patent the court or the comptroller may, if it or he thinks fit, refuse to award any damages or make any such order in respect of an infringement committed during any further period specified under section 25(4) above, but before the payment of the renewal fee and any additional fee prescribed for the purposes of that subsection.

(3) Where an amendment of the specification of a patent has been allowed under any of the provisions of this Act, no damages shall be awarded in proceedings for an infringement of the patent committed before the decision to allow the amendment unless the court or the comptroller is satisfied that the specification of the patent as published was framed in good faith and with reasonable skill and knowledge.

63.—(1) If the validity of a patent is put in issue in proceedings for infringement of the patent and it is found that the patent is only partially valid, the court or the comptroller may, subject to subsection (2) below, grant relief in respect of that part of the patent which is found to be valid and infringed.

(2) Where in any such proceedings it is found that a patent is only partially valid, the court or the comptroller shall not grant relief by way of damages, costs or expenses, except where the plaintiff or pursuer proves that the specification for the patent was framed in good faith and with reasonable skill and knowledge, and in that event the court or the comptroller may grant relief in respect of that part of the patent which is valid and infringed, subject to the discretion of the court or the comptroller as to costs or expenses and as to the date from which damages should be reckoned.

(3) As a condition of relief under this section the court or the comptroller may direct that the specification of the patent shall be amended to its or his satisfaction upon an application made for that purpose under section 75 below, and an application may be so made accordingly, whether or not all other issues in the proceedings have been determined.

64.—(1) Where a patent is granted for an invention, a person who in the United Kingdom before the priority date of the invention does in good faith an act which would constitute an infringement of the patent if it were in force, or makes in good faith effective and serious preparations to do such an act, shall have the rights conferred by subsection (2) below.

(2) Any such person shall have the right—

(a) to continue to do or, as the case may be, to do that act himself; and

(b) if it was done or preparations had been made to do it in the course of a business, to assign the right to do it or to transmit that right on his death or, in the case of a body corporate on its dissolution, to any person who acquires that part of the business in the course of which the act was done or preparations had been made to do it, or to authorise it to be done by any partners of his for the time being in that business;

and the doing of that act by virtue of this subsection shall not amount to an infringement of the patent concerned.

(3) The rights mentioned in subsection (2) above shall not include the right to grant a licence to any person to do an act so mentioned.

(4) Where a patented product is disposed of by any person to another in exercise of a right conferred by subsection (2) above, that other and any person claiming through him shall be entitled to deal with the product in the same way as if it had been disposed of by a sole registered proprietor.

65.—(1) If in any proceedings before the court or the comptroller the validity of a patent to any extent is contested and that patent is found by the court or the comptroller to be wholly or partially valid, the court or the comptroller may certify the finding and the fact that the validity of the patent was so contested.

Certificate of contested validity of patent.

(2) Where a certificate is granted under this section, then, if in any subsequent proceedings before the court or the comptroller for infringement of the patent concerned or for revocation of the patent a final order or judgment or interlocutor is made or given in favour of the party relying on the validity of the patent as found in the earlier proceedings, that party shall, unless the court or the comptroller otherwise directs, be entitled to his costs or expenses as between solicitor and own client (other than the costs or expenses of any appeal in the subsequent proceedings).

66.—(1) In the application of section 60 above to a patent of which there are two or more joint proprietors the reference to the proprietor shall be construed—

Proceedings infringement by a co-owner.

    (a) in relation to any act, as a reference to that proprietor or those proprietors who, by virtue of section 36 above or any agreement referred to in that section, is or are entitled to do that act without its amounting to an infringement; and

    (b) in relation to any consent, as a reference to that proprietor or those proprietors who, by virtue of section 36 above or any such agreement, is or are the proper person or persons to give the requisite consent.

(2) One of two or more joint proprietors of a patent may without the concurrence of the others bring proceedings in respect of an act alleged to infringe the patent, but shall not do so unless the others are made parties to the proceedings; but any of the others made a defendant or defender shall not be liable for any costs or expenses unless he enters an appearance and takes part in the proceedings.

67.—(1) Subject to the provisions of this section, the holder of an exclusive licence under a patent shall have the same right as the proprietor of the patent to bring proceedings in respect of any infringement of the patent committed after the date of the licence; and references to the proprietor of the patent in the provisions of this Act relating to infringement shall be construed accordingly.

Proceedings for infringement by exclusive licensee.

(2) In awarding damages or granting any other relief in any such proceedings the court or the comptroller shall take into consideration any loss suffered or likely to be suffered by the exclusive licensee as such as a result of the infringement, or, as the case may be, the profits derived from the infringement, so far as it constitutes an infringement of the rights of the exclusive licensee as such.

(3) In any proceedings taken by an exclusive licensee by virtue of this section the proprietor of the patent shall be made a party to the proceedings, but if made a defendant or defender shall not be liable for any costs or expenses unless he enters an appearance and takes part in the proceedings.

Effect of non-registration on infringement proceedings.

68. Where by virtue of a transaction, instrument or event to which section 33 above applies a person becomes the proprietor or one of the proprietors or an exclusive licensee of a patent and the patent is subsequently infringed, the court or the comptroller shall not award him damages or order that he be given an account of the profits in respect of such a subsequent infringement occurring before the transaction, instrument or event is registered unless—

(a) the transaction, instrument or event is registered within the period of six months beginning with its date; or

(b) the court or the comptroller is satisfied that it was not practicable to register the transaction, instrument or event before the end of that period and that it was registered as soon as practicable thereafter.

Infringement of rights conferred by publication of application.

69.—(1) Where an application for a patent for an invention is published, then, subject to subsections (2) and (3) below, the applicant shall have, as from the publication and until the grant of the patent, the same right as he would have had, if the patent had been granted on the date of the publication of the application, to bring proceedings in the court or before the comptroller for damages in respect of any act which would have infringed the patent; and (subject to subsections (2) and (3) below) references in sections 60 to 62 and 66 to 68 above to a patent and the proprietor of a patent shall be respectively construed as including references to any such application and the applicant, and references to a patent being in force, being granted, being valid or existing shall be construed accordingly.

(2) The applicant shall be entitled to bring proceedings by virtue of this section in respect of any act only—

(a) after the patent has been granted; and

(b) if the act would, if the patent had been granted on the date of the publication of the application, have infringed not only the patent, but also the claims (as interpreted by the description and any drawings referred to in the description or claims) in the form in which they were contained in the application immediately before the preparations for its publication were completed by the Patent Office.

(3) Section 62(2) and (3) above shall not apply to an infringement of the rights conferred by this section, but in considering the amount of any damages for such an infringement, the court or the comptroller shall consider whether or not it would have been reasonable to expect, from a consideration of the application as published under section 16 above, that a patent would be granted conferring on the proprietor of the patent protection from an act of the same description as that found to infringe those rights, and if the court or the comptroller finds it would not have been reasonable, it or he shall reduce the damages to such an amount as it or he thinks just.

Remedy for groundless threats of infringement proceedings.

70.—(1) Where a person (whether or not the proprietor of, or entitled to any right in, a patent) by circulars, advertisements or otherwise threatens another person with proceedings for any infringement of a patent, a person aggrieved by the threats (whether or not he is the person to whom the threats are made) may, subject to subsection (4) below, bring proceedings in the court against the person making the threats, claiming any relief mentioned in subsection (3) below.

(2) In any such proceedings the plaintiff or pursuer shall, if he proves that the threats were so made and satisfies the court that he is a person aggrieved by them, be entitled to the relief claimed unless—

(a) the defendant or defender proves that the acts in respect of which proceedings were threatened constitute or, if done, would constitute an infringement of a patent; and

(b) the patent alleged to be infringed is not shown by the plaintiff or pursuer to be invalid in a relevant respect.

(3) The said relief is—

(a) a declaration or declarator to the effect that the threats are unjustifiable;

(b) an injunction or interdict against the continuance of the threats; and

(c) damages in respect of any loss which the plaintiff or pursuer has sustained by the threats.

(4) Proceedings may not be brought under this section for a threat to bring proceedings for an infringement alleged to consist of making or importing a product for disposal or of using a process.

(5) It is hereby declared that a mere notification of the existence of a patent does not constitute a threat of proceedings within the meaning of this section.

71.—(1) Without prejudice to the court's jurisdiction to make a declaration or declarator apart from this section, a declaration or declarator that an act does not, or a proposed act would not, constitute an infringement of a patent may be made by the court or the comptroller in proceedings between the person doing or proposing to do the act and the proprietor of the patent, notwithstanding that no assertion to the contrary has been made by the proprietor, if it is shown— *Declaration or declarator as to non-infringement.*

(a) that that person has applied in writing to the proprietor for a written acknowledgement to the effect of the declaration or declarator claimed, and has furnished him with full particulars in writing of the act in question; and

(b) that the proprietor has refused or failed to give any such acknowledgement.

(2) Subject to section 72(5) below, a declaration made by the comptroller under this section shall have the same effect as a declaration or declarator by the court.

Revocation of patents

72.—(1) Subject to the following provisions of this Act, the court or the comptroller may on the application of any person by order revoke a patent for an invention on (but only on) any of the following grounds, that is to say— *Power to revoke patents on application.*

(a) the invention is not a patentable invention;

(b) the patent was granted to a person who was not the only person entitled under section 7(2) above to be granted that patent or to two or more persons who were not the only persons so entitled;

(c) the specification of the patent does not disclose the invention clearly enough and completely enough for it to be performed by a person skilled in the art;

(d) the matter disclosed in the specification of the patent extends beyond that disclosed in the application for the patent, as filed, or, if the patent was granted on a new application filed under section 8(3), 12 or 37(4) above or as mentioned in section 15(4) above, in the earlier application, as filed;

(e) the protection conferred by the patent has been extended by an amendment which should not have been allowed.

(2) An application for the revocation of a patent on the ground mentioned in subsection (1)(b) above—

 (a) may only be made by a person found by the court in an action for a declaration or declarator, or found by the court or the comptroller on a reference under section 37 above, to be entitled to be granted that patent or to be granted a patent for part of the matter comprised in the specification of the patent sought to be revoked; and

 (b) may not be made if that action was commenced or that reference was made after the end of the period of two years beginning with the date of the grant of the patent sought to be revoked, unless it is shown that any person registered as a proprietor of the patent knew at the time of the grant or of the transfer of the patent to him that he was not entitled to the patent.

(3) Rules under section 14(4) and (8) above shall, with any necessary modifications, apply for the purposes of subsection (1)(c) above as they apply for the purposes of section 14(3) above.

(4) An order under this section may be an order for the unconditional revocation of the patent or, where the court or the comptroller determines that one of the grounds mentioned in subsection (1) above has been established, but only so as to invalidate the patent to a limited extent, an order that the patent should be revoked unless within a specified time the specification is amended under section 75 below to the satisfaction of the court or the comptroller, as the case may be.

(5) A decision of the comptroller or on appeal from the comptroller shall not estop any party to civil proceedings in which infringement of a patent is in issue from alleging invalidity of the patent on any of the grounds referred to in subsection (1) above, whether or not any of the issues involved were decided in the said decision.

(6) Where the comptroller refuses to grant an application made to him by any person under this section, no application (otherwise than by way of appeal or by way of putting validity in issue in proceedings for infringement) may be made to the court by that person under this section in relation to the patent concerned, without the leave of the court.

(7) Where the comptroller has not disposed of an application made to him under this section, the applicant may not apply to the court under this section in respect of the patent concerned unless either—

 (a) the proprietor of the patent agrees that the applicant may so apply, or

 (b) the comptroller certifies in writing that it appears to him that the question whether the patent should be revoked is one which would more properly be determined by the court.

Comptroller's power to revoke patents on his own initiative.

73.—(1) If it appears to the comptroller that an invention for which a patent has been granted formed part of the state of the art by virtue only of section 2(3) above, he may on his own initiative by order revoke the patent, but shall not do so without giving the proprietor of the patent an opportunity of making any observations and of amending the specification of the patent so as to exclude any matter which formed part of the state of the art as aforesaid without contravening section 76 below.

(2) If it appears to the comptroller that a patent under this Act and a European patent (UK) have been granted for the same invention having the same priority date and that the applications for both patents were filed by the same applicant or his successor in title, the comptroller may, on his own initiative but only after the

relevant date, consider whether to revoke the patent granted under this Act and may, after giving the proprietor of the patent an opportunity of making any observations and of amending the specification of the patent, revoke the patent.

(3) In this section "the relevant date" means whichever of the following dates is relevant, that is to say—

(a) the date on which the period for filing an opposition to the patent under the European Patent Convention expires without an opposition being filed;

(b) the date when any opposition proceedings under that convention are finally disposed of by a decision to maintain the European patent;

(c) if later than either of the foregoing dates, the date when the patent under this Act is granted.

Putting validity in issue

74.—(1) Subject to the following provisions of this section, the validity of a patent may be put in issue—

Proceedings in which validity of patent may be put in issue.

(a) by way of defence, in proceedings for infringement of the patent under section 61 above or proceedings under section 69 above for infringement of rights conferred by the publication of an application;

(b) in proceedings under section 70 above;

(c) in proceedings in which a declaration in relation to the patent is sought under section 71 above;

(d) in proceedings before the court or the comptroller under section 72 above for the revocation of the patent;

(e) in proceedings under section 58 above.

(2) The validity of a patent may not be put in issue in any other proceedings and, in particular, no proceedings may be instituted (whether under this Act or otherwise) seeking only a declaration as to the validity or invalidity of a patent.

(3) The only grounds on which the validity of a patent may be put in issue (whether in proceedings for revocation under section 72 above or otherwise) are the grounds on which the patent may be revoked under that section.

(4) No determination shall be made in any proceedings mentioned in subsection (1) above on the validity of a patent which any person puts in issue on the ground mentioned in section 72(1)(b) above unless—

(a) it has been determined in entitlement proceedings commenced by that person or in the proceedings in which the validity of the patent is in issue that the patent should have been granted to him and not some other person; and

(b) except where it has been so determined in entitlement proceedings, the proceedings in which the validity of the patent is in issue are commenced before the end of the period of two years beginning with the date of the grant of the patent or it is shown that any person registered as a proprietor of the patent knew at the time of the grant or of the transfer of the patent to him that he was not entitled to the patent.

(5) Where the validity of a patent is put in issue by way of defence or counterclaim the court or the comptroller shall, if it or he thinks it just to do so, give the defendant an opportunity to comply with the condition in subsection (4)(a) above.

(6) In subsection (4) above "entitlement proceedings", in relation to a patent,

means a reference under section 37(1)(a) above on the ground that the patent was granted to a person not entitled to it or proceedings for a declaration or declarator that it was so granted.

(7) Where proceedings with respect to a patent are pending in the court under any provision of this Act mentioned in subsection (1) above, no proceedings may be instituted without the leave of the court before the comptroller with respect to that patent under section 61(3), 69, 71 or 72 above.

(8) It is hereby declared that for the purposes of this Act the validity of a patent is not put in issue merely because the comptroller is considering its validity in order to decide whether to revoke it under section 73 above.

General provisions as to amendment of patents and applications

Amendment of patent in infringement or revocation proceedings.

75.—(1) In any proceedings before the court or the comptroller in which the validity of a patent is put in issue the court or, as the case may be, the comptroller may, subject to section 76 below, allow the proprietor of the patent to amend the specification of the patent in such manner, and subject to such terms as to advertising the proposed amendment and as to costs, expenses or otherwise, as the court or comptroller thinks fit.

(2) A person may give notice to the court or the comptroller of his opposition to an amendment proposed by the proprietor of the patent under this section, and if he does so the court or the comptroller shall notify the proprietor and consider the opposition in deciding whether the amendment or any amendment should be allowed.

(3) An amendment of a specification of a patent under this section shall have effect and be deemed always to have had effect from the grant of the patent.

(4) Where an application for an order under this section is made to the court, the applicant shall notify the comptroller, who shall be entitled to appear and be heard and shall appear if so directed by the court.

Amendments of applications and patents not to include added matter.

76.—(1) An application for a patent (the later application) shall not be allowed to be filed under section 8(3), 12, or 37(4) above or as mentioned in section 15(4) above, in respect of any matter disclosed in an earlier application or the specification of a patent which has been granted, if the later application discloses matter which extends beyond that disclosed in the earlier application, as filed, or the application for the patent, as filed.

(2) No amendment of an application or the specification of a patent shall be allowed under any of the provisions of this Act to which this subsection applies if it—

(a) results in the application or specification disclosing any such matter, or

(b) (where a patent has been granted) extends the protection conferred by the patent.

(3) Subsection (2) above applies to the following provisions of this Act, namely, sections 17(3), 18(3), 19(1), 27(1), 73 and 75.

PART II

PROVISIONS ABOUT INTERNATIONAL CONVENTIONS

European patents and patent applications

77.—(1) Subject to the provisions of this Act, a European patent (UK) shall, as from the publication of the mention of its grant in the European Patent Bulletin, be treated for the purposes of Parts I and II of this Act as if it were a patent under this Act granted in pursuance of an application made under this Act and as if notice of the grant of the patent had, on the date of that publication, been published under section 24 above in the journal; and—

> Effect of European patent (UK).

> (a) the proprietor of a European patent (UK) shall accordingly as respects the United Kingdom have the same rights and remedies, subject to the same conditions, as the proprietor of a patent under this Act;

> (b) references in Parts I and III of this Act to a patent shall be construed accordingly; and

> (c) any statement made and any certificate filed for the purposes of the provision of the convention corresponding to section 2(4)(c) above shall be respectively treated as a statement made and written evidence filed for the purposes of the said paragraph (c).

(2) Subsection (1) above shall not affect the operation in relation to a European patent (UK) of any provisions of the European Patent Convention relating to the amendment or revocation of such a patent in proceedings before the European Patent Office.

(3) Sections 58(7) to (9) and 63 above shall apply to the case where, after proceedings for the infringement of a European patent have been commenced before the court or the comptroller but have not been finally disposed of, it is established in proceedings before the European Patent Office that the patent is only partially valid as those provisions apply to proceedings in which the validity of a patent is put in issue and in which it is found that the patent is only partially valid.

(4) Subject to subsection (6) below, where a European patent (UK) is amended or revoked in accordance with the European Patent Convention, the amendment shall be treated for the purposes of Parts I and III of this Act as if it had been made, or as the case may be the patent shall be treated for those purposes as having been revoked, under this Act.

(5) Where—

> (a) under the European Patent Convention a European patent (UK) is revoked for failure to observe a time limit and is subsequently restored; and

> (b) between the revocation and publication of the fact that it has been restored a person begins in good faith to do an act which would, apart from section 55 above, constitute an infringement of the patent or makes in good faith effective and serious preparations to do such an act;

he shall have the rights conferred by section 28(6) above, and subsections (8) and (9) of that section shall apply accordingly.

(6) While this subsection is in force—

> (a) subsection (1) above shall not apply to a European patent (UK) the specification of which was published in French or German, unless a translation of the specification into English is filed at the Patent Office and the prescribed fee is paid before the end of the prescribed period;

> (b) subsection (4) above shall not apply to an amendment made in French or

German unless a translation of the amendment into English is filed at the Patent Office and the prescribed fee is paid before the end of the prescribed period.

(7) Where a translation of a specification or amendment into English is not filed in accordance with subsection (6)(a) or (b) above, the patent shall be treated as always having been void.

(8) The comptroller shall publish any translation filed at the Patent Office under subsection (6) above.

(9) Subsection (6) above shall come into force on a day appointed for the purpose by rules and shall cease to have effect on a day so appointed, without prejudice, however, to the power to bring it into force again.

Effect of filing an application for a European patent (UK).

78.—(1) Subject to the provisions of this Act, an application for a European patent (UK) having a date of filing under the European Patent Convention shall be treated for the purposes of the provisions of this Act to which this section applies as an application for a patent under this Act having that date as its date of filing and having the other incidents listed in subsection (3) below, but subject to the modifications mentioned in the following provisions of this section.

(2) This section applies to the following provisions of this Act:—

section 2(3) and so much of section 14(7) as relates to section 2(3);

section 5;

section 6;

so much of section 13(3) as relates to an application for and issue of a certificate under that subsection;

sections 30 to 33;

section 36;

sections 55 to 69;

section 74, so far as relevant to any of the provisions mentioned above;

section 111; and

section 125.

(3) The incidents referred to in subsection (1) above in relation to an application for a European patent (UK) are as follows:—

(a) any declaration of priority made in connection with the application under the European Patent Convention shall be treated for the purposes of this Act as a declaration made under section 5(2) above;

(b) where a period of time relevant to priority is extended under that convention, the period of twelve months specified in section 5(2) above shall be so treated as altered correspondingly;

(c) where the date of filing an application is re-dated under that convention to a later date, the date shall be so treated as the date of filing the application;

(d) the application, if published in accordance with that convention, shall, subject to subsection (7) and section 79 below, be so treated as published under section 16 above;

(e) any designation of the inventor under that convention or any statement under it indicating the origin of the right to a European patent shall be treated for the purposes of section 13(3) above as a statement filed under section 13(2) above;

(f) registration of the application in the register of the European patents shall be treated as registration under this Act.

(4) Rules under section 32 above may not impose any requirements as to the registration of applications for European patents (UK) but may provide for the registration of copies of entries relating to such applications in the European register of patents.

(5) Subsections (1) to (3) above shall cease to apply to an application for a European patent (UK) when the application is refused or withdrawn or deemed to be withdrawn, or the designation of the United Kingdom in the application is withdrawn or deemed to be withdrawn, but if the rights of the applicant are re-established under the European Patent Convention, subsections (1) to (3) above shall as from the re-establishment of those rights again apply to the application.

(6) Where between those subsections ceasing to apply to any such application and the re-establishment of the rights of the applicant a person begins in good faith to do an act which would, apart from section 55 above, constitute an infringement of the application if those subsections then applied, or makes in good faith effective and serious preparations to do such an act, he shall have the rights conferred by section 28(6) above, and section 28(8) and (9) above shall apply to the exercise of any such right accordingly.

(7) While this subsection is in force, an application for a European patent (UK) published by the European Patent Office under the European Patent Convention in French or German shall be treated for the purposes of sections 55 and 69 above as published under section 16 above when a translation into English of the claims of the specification of the application has been filed at and published by the Patent Office and the prescribed fee has been paid, but an applicant—

(a) may recover a payment by virtue of section 55(5) above in respect of the use of the invention in question before publication of that translation; or

(b) may bring proceedings by virtue of section 69 above in respect of an act mentioned in that section which is done before publication of that translation;

if before that use or the doing of that act he has sent by post or delivered to the government department who made use or authorised the use of the invention or, as the case may be, to the person alleged to have done the act, a translation into English of those claims.

(8) Subsection (7) above shall come into force on a day appointed for the purpose by rules and shall cease to have effect on a day so appointed, without prejudice, however, to the power to bring it into force again.

79.—(1) Subject to the following provisions of this section, section 78 above, in its operation in relation to an international application for a patent (UK) which is treated by virtue of the European Patent Convention as an application for a European patent (UK), shall have effect as if any reference in that section to anything done in relation to the application under the European Patent Convention included a reference to the corresponding thing done under the Patent Co-operation Treaty. Operation of s. 78 in relation to certain European patent applications.

(2) Any such international application which is published under that treaty shall be treated for the purposes of section 2(3) above as published only when a copy of the application has been supplied to the European Patent Office in English, French or German and the relevant fee has been paid under that convention.

(3) Any such international application which is published under that treaty in a

language other than English, French or German shall, subject to section 78(7) above, be treated for the purposes of sections 55 and 69 above as published only when it is re-published in English, French or German by the European Patent Office under that convention.

80.—(1) Subject to subsection (2) below, the text of a European patent or application for such a patent in the language of the proceedings, that is to say, the language in which proceedings relating to the patent or the application are to be conducted before the European Patent Office, shall be the authentic text for the purposes of any domestic proceedings, that is to say, any proceedings relating to the patent or application before the comptroller or the court.

(2) Where the language of the proceedings is French or German, a translation into English of the specification of the patent under section 77 above or of the claims of the application under section 78 above shall be treated as the authentic text for the purpose of any domestic proceedings, other than proceedings for the revocation of the patent, if the patent or application as translated into English confers protection which is narrower than that conferred by it in French or German.

(3) If any such translation in a European patent or application conferring the narrower protection, the proprietor of or applicant for the patent may file a corrected translation with the Patent Office and, if he pays the prescribed fee within the prescribed period, the Patent Office shall publish it, but—

  (a) any payment for any use of the invention which (apart from section 55 above) would have infringed the patent as correctly translated, but not as originally translated, or in the case of an application would have infringed it as aforesaid if the patent had been granted, shall not be recoverable under that section,

  (b) the proprietor or applicant shall not be entitled to bring proceedings in respect of an act which infringed the patent as correctly translated, but not as originally translated, or in the case of an application would have infringed it as aforesaid if the patent had been granted,

unless before that use or the doing of the act the corrected translation has been published by the Patent Office or the proprietor or applicant has sent the corrected translation by post or delivered it to the government department who made use or authorised the use of the invention or, as the case may be, to the person alleged to have done that act.

(4) Where a correction of a translation is published under subsection (3) above and before it is so published a person begins in good faith to do an act which would not constitute an infringement of the patent or application as originally translated but would (apart from section 55 above) constitute an infringement of it under the amended translation, or makes in good faith effective and serious preparations to do such an act, he shall have the rights conferred by section 28(6) above, and section 28(8) and (9) above shall apply to the exercise of any such right accordingly.

81.—(1) The comptroller may direct that on compliance with the relevant conditions mentioned in subsection (2) below an application for a European patent (UK) shall be treated as an application for a patent under this Act in the following cases:—

  (a) where the application is deemed to be withdrawn under the provisions of the European Patent Convention relating to the restriction of the processing of applications;

(b) where under the convention the application is deemed to be withdrawn because it has not, within the period required by the convention, been received by the European Patent Office.

(2) The relevant conditions referred to above are that—

(a) in the case of an application falling within subsection (1)(a) above, the European Patent Office transmits a request of the applicant to the Patent Office that his application should be converted into an application under this Act, together with a copy of the files relating to the application;

(b) in the case of an application falling within subsection (1)(b) above,—

(i) the applicant requests the comptroller within the relevant prescribed period (where the application was filed with the Patent Office) to give a direction under this section, or

(ii) the central industry property office of a country which is party to the convention, other than the United Kingdom, with which the application was filed transmits within the relevant prescribed period a request that the application should be converted into an application under this Act, together with a copy of the application; and

(c) in either case the applicant within the relevant prescribed period pays the filing fee and if the application is in a language other than English, files a translation into English of the application and of any amendments previously made in accordance with the convention.

(3) Where an application for a European patent falls to be treated as an application for a patent under this Act by virtue of a direction under this section—

(a) the date which is the date of filing the application under the European Patent Convention shall be treated as its date of filing for the purposes of this Act, but if that date is re-dated under the convention to a later date, that later date shall be treated for those purposes as the date of filing the application;

(b) if the application satisfies a requirement of the convention corresponding to any of the requirements of this Act or rules designated as formal requirements, it shall be treated as satisfying that formal requirement;

(c) any document filed with the European Patent Office under any provision of the convention corresponding to any of the following provisions of this Act, that is to say, sections 2(4)(c), 5, 13(2) and 14, or any rule made for the purposes of any of those provisions, shall be treated as filed with the Patent Office under that provision or rule; and

(d) the comptroller shall refer the application for only so much of the examination and search required by sections 17 and 18 above as he considers appropriate in view of any examination and search carried out under the convention, and those sections shall apply with any necessary modifications accordingly.

82.—(1) The court shall not have jurisdiction to determine a question to which this section applies except in accordance with the following provisions of this section.

Jurisdiction to determine questions as to right to a paten

(2) Section 12 above shall not confer jurisdiction on the comptroller to determine a question to which this section applies except in accordance with the following provisions of this section.

(3) This section applies to a question arising before the grant of a European patent whether a person has a right to be granted a European patent, or a share in any such patent, and in this section "employer-employee question" means any

such question between an employer and an employee, or their successors in title, arising out of an application for a European patent for an invention made by the employee.

(4) The court and the comptroller shall have jurisdiction to determine any question to which this section applies, other than an employer-employee question, if either of the following conditions is satisfied, that is to say—

    (a) the applicant has his residence or principal place of business in the United Kingdom; or

    (b) the other party claims that the patent should be granted to him and he has his residence or principal place of business in the United Kingdom and the applicant does not have his residence or principal place of business in any of the relevant contracting states;

and also if in either of those cases there is no written evidence that the parties have agreed to submit to the jurisdiction of the competent authority of a relevant contracting state other than the United Kingdom.

(5) The court and the comptroller shall have jurisdiction to determine an employer-employee question if either of the following conditions is satisfied, that is to say—

    (a) the employee is mainly employed in the United Kingdom; or

    (b) the employee is not mainly employed anywhere or his place of main employment cannot be determined, but the employer has a place of business in the United Kingdom to which the employee is attached (whether or not he is also attached elsewhere);

and also if in either of those cases there is no written evidence that the parties have agreed to submit to the jurisdiction of the competent authority of a relevant contracting state other than the United Kingdom or, where there is such evidence of such an agreement, if the proper law of the contract of employment does not recognise the validity of the agreement.

(6) Without prejudice to subsections (2) to (5) above, the court and the comptroller shall have jurisdiction to determine any question to which this section applies if there is written evidence that the parties have agreed to submit to the jurisdiction of the court or the comptroller, as the case may be, and, in the case of an employer-employee question, the proper law of the contract of employment recognises the validity of the agreement.

(7) If, after proceedings to determine a question to which this section applies have been brought before the competent authority of a relevant contracting state other than the United Kingdom, proceedings are begun before the court or a reference is made to the comptroller under section 12 above to determine that question, the court or the comptroller, as the case may be, shall stay or sist the proceedings before the court or the comptroller unless or until the competent authority of that other state either—

    (a) determines to decline jurisdiction and no appeal lies from the determination or the time for appealing expires, or

    (b) makes a determination which the court or the comptroller refuses to recognise under section 83 below.

(8) References in this section to the determination of a question include respectively references to—

    (a) the making of a declaration or the grant of a declarator with respect to that question (in the case of the court); and

    (b) the making of an order under section 12 above in relation to that question

(in the case of the court or the comptroller).

(9) In this section and section 83 below "relevant contracting state" means a country which is a party to the European Patent Convention and has not exercised its right under the convention to exclude the application of the protocol to the convention known as the Protocol on Recognition.

83.—(1) A determination of a question to which section 82 above applies by the competent authority of a relevant contracting state other than the United Kingdom shall, if no appeal lies from the determination or the time of appealing has expired, be recognised in the United Kingdom as if it had been made by the court or the comptroller unless the court or he refuses to recognise it under subsection (2) below. *Effect of patent decisions of competent authorities of other states.*

(2) The court or the comptroller may refuse to recognise any such determination that the applicant for a European patent had no right to be granted the patent, or any share in it, if either—

(a) the applicant did not contest the proceedings in question because he was not notified of them at all or in the proper manner or was not notified of them in time for him to contest the proceedings; or

(b) the determination in the proceedings in question conflicts with the determination of the competent authority of any relevant contracting state in proceedings instituted earlier between the same parties as in the proceedings in question.

84.—(1) No individual shall carry on for gain in the United Kingdom, alone or in partnership with any other person, the business of acting as agent or other representative of other persons for the purpose of applying for or obtaining European patents or for the purpose of conducting proceedings in connection with such patents before the European Patent Office or the comptroller, or hold himself out or permit himself to be held out as so carrying on such a business, unless he satisfies the condition that his name and that of each of his partners appears on the European list. *Patent agents and other representatives.*

(2) Subsection (1) above shall not prohibit a barrister, advocate or solicitor of any part of the United Kingdom from conducting or otherwise taking part in any proceedings in connection with European patents before the European Patent Office or the comptroller to the same extent as he is entitled to take part in the corresponding proceedings in connection with patents under this Act before the Patent Office or the comptroller.

(3) A body corporate shall not for gain act or describe itself or hold itself out as entitled to act as agent or other representative of other persons for any purpose mentioned in subsection (1) above unless permitted to do so under the European Patent Convention.

(4) Any person who contravenes subsection (1) or (3) above shall be liable on summary conviction to a fine not exceeding £1,000.

(5) Proceedings for an offence under this section may be begun at any time within twelve months from the date of the offence.

(6) A person who does any act mentioned in subsection (1) above, but satisfies the condition mentioned in that subsection, shall not be treated as contravening section 114 below so long as he does not describe himself as a patent agent without qualification and does not hold himself out or permit himself to be held out as carrying on any business other than one mentioned in that subsection.

(7) In this section "the European list" means the list of professional representatives

maintained by the European Patent Office in pursuance of the European Patent Convention.

European patent attorneys.
1974 c. 47.
S.I. 1976/582
(N.I. 12).

85.—(1) For the avoidance of doubt, it is hereby declared that any person whose name appears on the European list shall not be guilty of an offence under section 21 of the Solicitors Act 1974 or Article 22 of the Solicitors (Northern Ireland) Order 1976 by reason only of his describing himself as a European patent attorney.

(2) A person whose name appears on the European list shall not be guilty of an offence under any of the enactments mentioned in subsection (3) below by reason only of the preparation by him of any document (other than a deed) for use in proceedings before the comptroller under this Act, in relation to a European patent or application for such a patent.

(3) The enactments referred to in subsection (2) above (which prohibit the preparation for reward of certain instruments or writs by persons not legally qualified) are—

(a) section 22 of the Solicitors Act 1974;

1933 c. 21.

(b) section 39 of the Solicitors (Scotland) Act 1933; and

(c) Article 23 of the Solicitors (Northern Ireland) Order 1976.

(4) In this section "the European list" means the list of professional representatives maintained by the European Patent Office in pursuance of the European Patent Convention.

Community patents

Implementation of Community Patent Convention.

86.—(1) All rights, powers, liabilities, obligations and restrictions from time to time created or arising by or under the Community Patent Convention and all remedies and procedures from time to time provided for by or under that convention shall by virtue of this section have legal effect in the United Kingdom and shall be used there, be recognised and available in law and be enforced, allowed and followed accordingly.

(2) The Secretary of State may by regulations make provision—

(a) for implementing any obligation imposed by that convention on a domestic institution or enabling any such obligation to be implemented or enabling any rights or powers conferred on any such institution to be exercised; and

(b) otherwise for giving effect to subsection (1) above and dealing with matters arising out of its commencement or operation.

(3) Regulations under this section may include any incidental, consequential, transitional or supplementary provision appearing to the Secretary of State to be necessary or expedient, including provision amending any enactment, whenever passed, other than an enactment contained in this Part of this Act, and provision for the application of any provision of the regulations outside the United Kingdom.

(4) Sections 12, 73(2), 77 to 80, 82 and 83 above shall not apply to any application for a European patent which under the Community Patent Convention is treated as an application for a Community patent, or to a Community patent (since any such application or patent falls within the foregoing provisions of this section).

(5) In this section "domestic institution" means the court, the comptroller or the Patent Office, as the case may require.

87.—(1) For the purposes of all legal proceedings, including proceedings before the comptroller, any question as to the meaning or effect of the Community Patent Convention, or as to the validity, meaning and effect of any instrument made under or in implementation of that convention by any relevant convention institution shall be treated as a question of law (and if not referred to the relevant convention court, be for determination as such in accordance with the principles laid down by and any relevant decision of that court).

Decisions on Community Patent Convention.

(2) In this section—

"relevant convention institution" means any institution established by or having functions under the Community Patent Convention, not being an institution of the United Kingdom or any other member state, and

"relevant convention court" does not include—
(a) the European Patent Office or any of its departments; or
(b) a court of the United Kingdom or of any other member state.

88.—(1) For the purposes of the application in the United Kingdom of Article 69 of the Community Patent Convention (residence of a party as founding jurisdiction in actions for infringement, etc.) the residence of a party shall be determined in accordance with the following provisions of this section until such date as the Secretary of State may by order appoint for the repeal of those provisions.

Jurisdiction in legal proceedings in connection with Community Patent Convention.

(2) For the purpose of determining whether a person is resident in any part of the United Kingdom the court shall apply the law of that part of the United Kingdom.

(3) A company within the meaning of the Companies Act 1948 shall be treated for the purposes of subsection (2) above as resident in that part of the United Kingdom where its registered office is situated or where it has a principal place of business.

1948 c. 38.

(4) Any other body corporate or any unincorporated body of persons shall be so treated as resident in that part of the United Kingdom where it has a principal place of business.

(5) Where any body has a principal place of business in two or more parts of the United Kingdom it shall be so treated as resident in all those parts.

(6) If the court determines that a person is not resident in the United Kingdom, then, in order to determine whether he is resident in a country which is a party to the Community Patent Convention the court shall, except in a case falling within subsection (7) below, apply the law which would be applied by the courts of that country in order to found jurisdiction under that convention.

(7) The question whether a person is to be taken for the purposes of this section as resident in the United Kingdom or any other country shall be determined in accordance with the law of that country of which he is a citizen if by that law his residence depends on that of another person or on the location of an authority.

International applications for patents

89.—(1) Subject to the provisions of this Act, an international application for a patent (UK) for which a date of filing has been accorded (whether by the Patent Office or by any other body) under the Patent Co-operation Treaty (in this section referred to as the Treaty) shall, until this subsection ceases to apply to the

Effect of filing international application for a patent.

PART II   application, be treated for the purposes of Parts I and III of this Act as an application for a patent under this Act having that date as its date of filing and—

 (a) the application, if published in accordance with the Treaty and if it satisfies relevant conditions, shall be so treated as published under section 16 above, subject, however, to subsection (7) below;

 (b) where the date of filing an application is re-dated under the Treaty to a later date, that date shall be so treated as the date of filing the application;

 (c) any declaration of priority made under the Treaty shall be so treated as a declaration made under section 5(2) above;

 (d) where a period of time relevant to priority is extended under the Treaty, the period of twelve months specified in section 5(2) above shall be treated as altered correspondingly;

 (e) any statement of the name of the inventor under the Treaty shall be so treated as a statement filed under section 13(2) above; and

 (f) an amendment of the application made in accordance with the Treaty shall, if it satisfies the relevant conditions, be so treated as made under this Act.

(2) Accordingly, until subsection (1) above ceases to apply to an application filed or published in accordance with the Treaty, the applicant shall, subject to subsection (7) below, have the same rights and remedies in relation to the application as an applicant for a patent under this Act has in relation to a filed or, as the case may be, a published application for such a patent.

(3) Notwithstanding anything in subsection (1) above, the provisions of the Treaty and not those of this Act relating to publication, search, examination and amendment shall apply to any such application until all the relevant conditions are satisfied and, if those conditions are not satisfied before the end of the prescribed period, the application shall be taken to be withdrawn.

(4) The relevant conditions—

 (a) in the case of an application, are that a copy of the application and, if it is not in English, a translation into English have been filed at the Patent Office and the filing fee has been paid to the Patent Office by the applicant; and

 (b) in the case of an amendment, are that a copy of the amendment and, if it is not in English, a translation into English have been filed at the Patent Office.

(5) The comptroller shall on payment of the prescribed fee publish any translation filed at the Patent Office under subsection (4) above.

(6) Before the relevant conditions are satisfied, subsection (1) above shall not operate so as to secure that an international application for a patent (UK) is to be treated for the purposes of section 8 above as an application for a patent under this Act and shall not affect the application of section 12 above to an invention for which an international application of a patent is made or proposed to be made, but when the relevant conditions are satisfied the international application shall be so treated and accordingly section 12 above shall not apply to it.

(7) For the purposes of sections 55 and 69 above an international application for a patent (UK) published in accordance with the Treaty—

 (a) shall, if published in English, be treated as published under section 16 above on its publication in accordance with the Treaty;

 (b) shall, if published in any other language and if the relevant conditions are satisfied, be treated as published under section 16 above on the publication of a translation of the application under subsection (5) above;

but, if the application is published in a language other than English, the applicant may recover a payment by virtue of section 55 above in respect of the use of the invention in question before publication of that translation, or may bring proceedings by virtue of section 69 above in respect of an act mentioned in that section which is done before publication of that translation, if before that use or the doing of that act he has sent by post or delivered to the government department who made use or authorised the use of the invention, or, as the case may be, to the person alleged to have done the act, a translation into English of the specification of the application.

(8) Subsection (1) above shall cease to apply to an international application for a patent (UK) if—

(a) the application is withdrawn or deemed to be withdrawn; or

(b) the designation of the United Kingdom in the application is withdrawn or deemed to be withdrawn;

except where the application or the designation of the United Kingdom in the application is deemed to be withdrawn under the Treaty because of an error or omission in the Patent Office or any other institution having functions under the Treaty or of an application not being received by the International Bureau, owing to circumstances outside the applicant's control, before the end of the time limited for that purpose by the Treaty.

(9) Where the relevant conditions are satisfied before the end of the prescribed period, the comptroller shall refer the application for so much of the examination and search as is required by sections 17 and 18 above as he considers appropriate in view of any examination and search carried out under the Treaty, and those sections shall apply with any necessary modifications accordingly.

(10) The foregoing provisions of this section shall not apply to an international application for a patent (UK) which is treated by virtue of the European Patent Convention as an application for a European patent (UK) or which contains an indication that the applicant wishes to obtain a European patent (UK).

(11) If an international application for a patent which purports to designate the United Kingdom is refused a filing date under the Treaty and the comptroller determines that the refusal was caused by an error or omission in the Patent Office or any other institution having functions under the Treaty, he may direct that the application shall be treated as an application under this Act.

Convention countries

90.—(1) Her Majesty may with a view to the fulfilment of a treaty or international convention, arrangement or engagement, by Order in Council declare that any country specified in the Order is a convention country for the purposes of section 5 above.

Orders in Council as to convention countries.

(2) Her Majesty may by Order in Council direct that any of the Channel Islands, any colony or any British protectorate or protected state shall be taken to be a convention country for those purposes.

(3) For the purposes of subsection (1) above every colony, protectorate, and territory subject to the authority or under the suzerainty of another country, and every territory administered by another country under the trusteeship system of the United Nations shall be taken to be a country in the case of which a declaration may be made under that subsection.

Miscellaneous

91.—(1) Judicial notice shall be taken of the following, that is to say—

Evidence of
conventions and
instruments
under
conventions.

(a) the European Patent Convention, the Community Patent Convention and the Patent Co-operation Treaty (each of which is hereafter in this section referred to as the relevant convention);

(b) any bulletin, journal or gazette published under the relevant convention and the register of European or Community patents kept under it; and

(c) any decision of, or expression of opinion by, the relevant convention court on any question arising under or in connection with the relevant convention.

(2) Any document mentioned in subsection (1)(b) above shall be admissible as evidence of any instrument or other act thereby communicated of any convention institution.

(3) Evidence of any instrument issued under the relevant convention by any such institution, including any judgment or order of the relevant convention court, or of any document in the custody of any such institution or reproducing in legible form any information in such custody otherwise than in legible form, or any entry in or extract from such a document, may be given in any legal proceedings by production of a copy certified as a true copy by an official of that institution; and any document purporting to be such a copy shall be received in evidence without proof of the official position or handwriting of the person signing the certificate.

(4) Evidence of any such instrument may also be given in any legal proceedings—

(a) by production of a copy purporting to be printed by the Queen's Printer;

(b) where the instrument is in the custody of a government department, by production of a copy certified on behalf of the department to be a true copy by an officer of the department generally or specially authorised to do so;

and any document purporting to be such a copy as is mentioned in paragraph (b) above of an instrument in the custody of a department shall be received in evidence without proof of the official position or handwriting of the person signing the certificate, or of his authority to do so, or of the document being in the custody of the department.

(5) In any legal proceedings in Scotland evidence of any matter given in a manner authorised by this section shall be sufficient evidence of it.

(6) In this section—

"convention institution" means an institution established by or having functions under the relevant convention;

"relevant convention court" does not include a court of the United Kingdom or of any other country which is a party to the relevant convention; and

"legal proceedings", in relation to the United Kingdom, includes proceedings before the comptroller.

Obtaining
evidence for
proceedings
under the
European Patent
Convention.
1975 c. 34.

92.—(1) Sections 1 to 3 of the Evidence (Proceedings in Other Jurisdictions) Act 1975 (provisions enabling United Kingdom courts to assist in obtaining evidence for foreign courts) shall apply for the purpose of proceedings before a relevant convention court under the European Patent Convention as they apply for the purpose of civil proceedings in a court exercising jurisdiction in a country outside the United Kingdom.

(2) In the application of those sections by virtue of this section any reference to the High Court, the Court of Session or the High Court of Justice in Northern Ireland shall include a reference to the comptroller.

(3) Rules under this Act may include provision—

(a) as to the manner in which an application under section 1 of the said Act of 1975 is to be made to the comptroller for the purpose of proceedings before a relevant convention court under the European Patent Convention; and

(b) subject to the provisions of that Act, as to the circumstances in which an order can be made under section 2 of that Act on any such application.

(4) Rules of court and rules under this Act may provide for an officer of the European Patent Office to attend the hearing of an application under section 1 of that Act before the court or the comptroller, as the case may be, and examine the witnesses or request the court or comptroller to put specified questions to the witnesses.

(5) Section 1(4) of the Perjury Act 1911 and section 1(4) of the Perjury Act (Northern Ireland) 1946 (statements made for the purposes, among others, of judicial proceedings in a tribunal of a foreign state) shall apply in relation to proceedings before a relevant convention court under the European Patent Convention as they apply to a judicial proceeding in a tribunal of a foreign state. 1911 c. 6 1946 c. 13 (N.I.).

93. If the European Patent Office orders the payment of costs in any proceedings before it— Enforcement of orders for costs.

(a) in England and Wales the costs shall, if a county court so orders, be recoverable by execution issued from the county court or otherwise as if they were payable under an order of that court;

(b) in Scotland the order may be enforced in like manner as a recorded decree arbitral.

(c) in Northern Ireland the order may be enforced as if it were a money judgment.

94. It shall not be lawful by virtue of any enactment to communicate the following information in pursuance of the European Patent Convention to the European Patent Office or the competent authority of any country which is party to the Convention, that is to say— Communcation of information to the European Patent Office, etc.

(a) information in the files of the court which, in accordance with rules of court, the court authorises to be so communicated;

(b) information in the files of the Patent Office which, in accordance with rules under this Act, the comptroller authorises to be so communicated.

95.—(1) There shall be paid out of moneys provided by Parliament any sums required by any Minister of the Crown or government department to meet any financial obligation of the United Kingdom under the European Patent Convention, the Community Patent Convention or the Patent Co-operation Treaty. Financial provisions.

(2) Any sums received by any Minister of the Crown or government department in pursuance of either of those conventions or that treaty shall be paid into the Consolidated Fund.

PART III

MISCELLANEOUS AND GENERAL

Legal Proceedings

96.—(1) There shall be constituted, as part of the Chancery Division of the High Court, a Patents Court to take such proceedings relating to patents and other matters as may be prescribed by rules of court.

(2) The judges of the Patents Court shall be such of the puisne judges of the High Court as the Lord Chancellor may from time to time nominate.

(3) The foregoing provisions of this section shall not be taken as prejudicing the provisions of the Supreme Court of Judicature (Consolidation) Act 1925 which enable the whole jurisdiction of the High Court to be exercised by any judge of that court.

(4) Rules of court shall make provisions for the appointment of scientific advisers to assist the Patents Court in proceedings under this Act and for regulating the functions of such advisers.

(5) The renumeration of any such adviser shall be determined by the Lord Chancellor with the consent of the Minister for the Civil Service and shall be defrayed out of moneys provided by Parliament.

97.—(1) Except as provided by subsection (4) below, an appeal shall lie to the Patents Court from any decision of the comptroller under this Act or rules except any of the following decisions, that is to say—

    (a) a decision falling within section 14(7) above;

    (b) a decision under section 16(2) above to omit matter from a specification;

    (c) a decision to give directions under subsection (1) or (2) of section 22 above;

    (d) a decision under rules which is excepted by rules from the right of appeal conferred by this section.

(2) For the purpose of hearing appeals under this section the Patents Court may consist of one or more judges of that court in accordance with directions given by or on behalf of the Lord Chancellor; and the Patents Court shall not be treated as a divisional court for the purposes of section 31(1)(f) of the Supreme Court of Judicature (Consolidation) Act 1925 (appeals from divisional courts).

(3) An appeal shall not lie to the Court of Appeal from a decision of the Patents Court on appeal from a decision of the comptroller under this Act or rules—

    (a) except where the comptroller's decision was given under section 8, 12, 18, 20, 27, 37, 40, 61, 72, 73 or 75 above; or

    (b) except where the ground of appeal is that the decision of the Patents Court is wrong in law;

but an appeal shall only lie to the Court of Appeal under this section if leave to appeal is given by the Patents Court or the Court of Appeal.

(4) An appeal shall lie to the Court of Session from any decision of the comptroller in proceedings which under rules are held in Scotland, except any decision mentioned in paragraphs (a) to (d) of subsection (1) above.

(5) An appeal shall not lie to the Inner House of the Court of Session from a decision of an Outer House judge on appeal from a decision of the comptroller under this Act or rules—

(a) except where the comptroller's decision was given under section 8, 12, 18, 20, 27, 37, 40, 61, 72, 73 or 75 above; or

(b) except where the ground of appeal is that the decision of the Outer House judge is wrong in law.

98.—(1) In Scotland proceedings relating primarily to patents (other than proceedings before the comptroller) shall be competent in the Court of Session only, and any jurisdiction of the sheriff court relating to patents is hereby abolished except in relation to questions which are incidental to the issue in proceedings which are otherwise competent there.

(2) The remuneration of any assessor appointed to assist the court in proceedings under this Act in the Court of Session shall be determined by the Lord President of the Court of Session with the consent of the Minister for the Civil Service and shall be defrayed out of moneys provided by Parliament.

Proceedings in Scotland.

99. The court may, for the purpose of determining any question in the exercise of its original or appellate jurisdiction under this Act or any treaty or international convention to which the United Kingdom is a party, make any order or exercise any other power which the comptroller could have made or exercised for the purpose of determining that question.

General powers of the court.

100.—(1) If the invention for which a patent is granted is a process for obtaining a new product, the same product produced by a person other than the proprietor of the patent or a licensee of his shall, unless the contrary is proved, be taken in any proceedings to have been obtained by that process.

(2) In considering whether a party has discharged the burden imposed upon him by this section, the court shall not require him to disclose any manufacturing or commercial secrets if it appears to the court that it would be unreasonable to do so.

Burden of proof in certain cases.

101. Without prejudice to any rule of law, the comptroller shall give any party to a proceeding before him an opportunity of being heard before exercising adversely to that party any discretion vested in the comptroller by this Act or rules.

Exercise of comptroller's discretionary powers.

102.—(1) Any party to any proceedings before the comptroller under this Act or any treaty or international convention to which the United Kingdom is a party may appear before the comptroller in person or be represented by counsel or a solicitor (of any part of the United Kingdom) or a patent agent or, subject to rules under section 115 below, by any other person whom he desires to represent him.

(2) Subsection (1) above, in its application to proceedings under any such treaty or convention, shall have effect subject to section 84(1) or (3) above.

(3) Without prejudice to the right of counsel to appear before the High Court, a member of the Bar of England and Wales who is not in actual practice, a solicitor of the Supreme Court and a patent agent shall each have the right to appear and be heard on behalf of any part to an appeal under this Act from the comptroller to the Patents Court.

Right of audience in patent proceedings.

Extension of privilege for communications with solicitors relating to patent proceedings.

103.—(1) It is hereby declared that the rule of law which confers privilege from disclosure in legal proceedings in respect of communications made with a solicitor or a person acting on his behalf, or in relation to information obtained or supplied for submission to a solicitor or a person acting on his behalf, for the purpose of any pending or contemplated proceedings before a court in the United Kingdom extends to such communications so made for the purpose of any pending or contemplated—

(a) proceedings before the comptroller under this Act or any of the relevant conventions, or

(b) proceedings before the relevant convention court under any of those conventions.

(2) In this section—

"legal proceedings" includes proceedings before the comptroller;

the references to legal proceedings and pending or contemplated proceedings include references to applications for a patent or a European patent and to international applications for a patent; and

"the relevant conventions" means the European Patent Convention, the Community Patent Convention and the Patent Co-operation Treaty.

(3) This section shall not extend to Scotland.

Privilege for communications with patent agents relating to patent proceedings.

104.—(1) This section applies to any communication made for the purpose of any pending or contemplated patent proceedings, being either—

(a) a communication between the patent agent of a party to those proceedings and that party or any other person; or

(b) a communication between a party to those proceedings and a person other than his patent agent made for the purpose of obtaining, or in response to a request for, information which that party is seeking for the purpose of submitting it to his patent agent.

(2) For the purposes of subsection (1) above a communication made by or to a person acting—

(i) on behalf of a patent agent; or

(ii) on behalf of a party to any pending or contemplated proceedings,

shall be treated as made by or to that patent agent or party, as the case may be.

(3) In any legal proceedings other than criminal proceedings a communication to which this section applies shall be privileged from disclosure in like manner as if any proceedings before the comptroller or the relevant convention court for the purpose of which the communication was made were proceedings before the court (within the meaning of this Act) and the patent agent in question had been the solicitor of the party concerned.

(4) In this section—

"legal proceedings" includes proceedings before the comptroller;

"patent agent" means an individual registered as a patent agent in the register of patent agents, a company lawfully practising as a patent agent in the United Kingdom or a person who satisfies the condition mentioned in section 84(1) or (3) above;

"patent proceedings" means proceedings under this Act or any of the relevant conventions before the court, the comptroller or the relevant convention court, whether contested or uncontested and including an application for a patent;

"party", in relation to any contemplated proceedings, means a prospective party to the proceedings; and

"the relevant conventions" means the European Patent Convention, the Community Patent Convention and the Patent Co-operation Treaty.

(5) This section shall not extend to Scotland.

105. It is hereby declared that in Scotland the rules of law which confer privilege from disclosure in legal proceedings in respect of communications, reports or other documents (by whomsoever made) made for the purpose of any pending or contemplated proceedings in a court in the United Kingdom extend to communications, reports or other documents made for the purpose of patent proceedings within the meaning of section 104 above.

Extension of privilege in Scotland for communications relating to patent proceedings.

106.—(1) In proceedings before the court under section 40 above (whether on an application or on appeal to the court), the court, in determining whether to award costs or expenses to any party and what costs or expenses to award, shall have regard to all the relevant circumstances, including the financial position of the parties.

Costs and expenses in proceedings before the Court under s. 40.

(2) If in any such proceedings the Patents Court directs that any costs of one party shall be paid by another party, the court may settle the amount of the costs by fixing a lump sum or may direct that the costs shall be taxed on a scale specified by the court, being a scale of costs prescribed by the Rules of the Supreme Court or by the County Court Rules.

107.—(1) The comptroller may, in proceedings before him under this Act, by order award to any party such costs or, in Scotland, such expenses as he may consider reasonable and direct how and by what parties they are to be paid.

Costs and expenses in proceedings before the comptroller.

(2) In England and Wales any costs awarded under this section shall, if a county court so orders, be recoverable by execution issued from the county court or otherwise as if they were payable under an order of that court.

(3) In Scotland any order under this section for the payment of expenses may be enforced in like manner as a recorded decree arbitral.

(4) If any of the following persons, that is to say—

(a) any person by whom a reference is made to the comptroller under section 8, 12 or 37 above;

(b) any person by whom an application is made to the comptroller for the revocation of a patent;

(c) any person by whom notice of opposition is given to the comptroller under section 27(5), 29(2), 47(6) or 52(1) above, or section 117(2) below;

neither resides nor carries on business in the United Kingdom, the comptroller may require him to give security for the costs or expenses of the proceedings and in default of such security being given may treat the reference, application or notice as abandoned.

(5) In Northern Ireland any order under this section for the payment of costs may be enforced as if it were a money judgment.

108. Any order for the grant of a licence under section 11, 38, 48 or 49 above shall, without prejudice to any other method of enforcement, have effect as if it

Licences granted by order of comptroller.

were a deed, executed by the proprietor of the patent and all other necessary parties, granting a licence in accordance with the order.

Offences

Falsification of register etc.

109. If a person makes or causes to be made a false entry in any register kept under this Act, or a writing falsely purporting to be a copy or reproduction of an entry in any such register, or produces or tenders or causes to be produced or tendered in evidence any such writing, knowing the entry or writing to be false, he shall be liable—

(a) on summary conviction, to a fine not exceeding £1,000,

(b) on conviction on indictment, to imprisonment for a term not exceeding two years or a fine, or both.

Unauthorised claim of patent rights.

110.—(1) If a person falsely represents that anything disposed of by him for value is a patented product he shall, subject to the following provisions of this section, be liable on summary conviction to a fine not exceeding £200.

(2) For the purposes of subsection (1) above a person who for value disposes of an article having stamped, engraved or impressed on it or otherwise applied to it the word "patent" or "patented" or anything expressing or implying that the article is a patented product, shall be taken to represent that the article is a patented product.

(3) Subsection (1) above does not apply where the representation is made in respect of a product after the patent for that product or, as the case may be, the process in question has expired or been revoked and before the end of a period which is reasonably sufficient to enable the accused to take steps to ensure that the representation is not made (or does not continue to be made).

(4) In proceedings for an offence under this section it shall be a defence for the accused to prove that he used due diligence to prevent the commission of the offence.

Unauthorised claim that patent has been applied for.

111.—(1) If a person represents that a patent has been applied for in respect of any article disposed of for value by him and—

(a) no such application has been made, or

(b) any such application has been refused or withdrawn,

he shall, subject to the following provisions of this section, be liable on summary conviction to a fine not exceeding £200.

(2) Subsection (1)(b) above does not apply where the representation is made (or continues to be made) before the expiry of a period which commences with the refusal or withdrawal and which is reasonably sufficient to enable the accused to take steps to ensure that the representation is not made (or does not continue to be made).

(3) For the purposes of subsection (1) above a person who for value disposes of an article having stamped, engraved or impressed on it or otherwise applied to it the words "patent applied for" or "patent pending", or anything expressing or implying that a patent has been applied for in respect of the article, shall be taken to represent that a patent has been applied for in respect of it.

(4) In any proceedings for an offence under this section it shall be a defence for

the accused to prove that he used due diligence to prevent the commission of such an offence.

112. If any person uses on his place of business, or on any document issued by him, or otherwise, the words "Patent Office" or any other words suggesting that his place of business is, or is officially connected with, the Patent Office, he shall be liable on summary conviction to a fine not exceeding £500.

Misuse of title "Patent Office".

113.—(1) Where an offence under this Act which has been committed by a body corporate is proved to have been committed with the consent or connivance of, or to be attributable to any neglect on the part of, a director, manager, secretary or other similar officer of the body corporate, or any person who was purporting to act in any such capacity, he, as well as the body corporate, shall be guilty of that offence and shall be liable to be proceeded against and punished accordingly.

Offences by corporations.

(2) Where the affairs of a body corporate are managed by its members, subsection (1) above shall apply in relation to the acts and defaults of a member in connection with his functions of management as if he were a director of the body corporate.

Patent agents

114.—(1) An individual shall not, either alone or in partnership with any other person, practise, describe himself or hold himself out as a patent agent, or permit himself to be so described or held out, unless he is registered as a patent agent in the register of patent agents or (as the case may be) unless he and all his partners are so registered.

Restrictions on practice as patent agent.

(2) A body corporate shall not practise, describe itself or hold itself out or permit itself to be described or held out as mentioned in subsection (1) above unless—

    (a) in the case of a company within the meaning of the Companies Act 1948 which began to carry on business as a patent agent before 17th November 1917, a director or the manager of the company is registered as a patent agent in the register of patent agents and the name of that director or manager is mentioned as being so registered in all professional advertisements, circulars or letters issued by or with the consent of the company in which the name of the company appears;

1948 c. 38.

    (b) in any other case, every director or, where the body's affairs are managed by its members, every member of the body and in any event, if it has a manager who is not a director or member, that manager, is so registered.

(3) Any person who contravenes the provisions of this section shall be liable on summary conviction to a fine not exceeding £1,000.

(4) Proceedings for an offence under this section may be begun at any time within twelve months from the date of the offence.

(5) This section shall not be construed as prohibiting solicitors from taking such part in proceedings relating to patents and applications for patents as has heretofore been taken by solicitors and, in particular, shall not derogate from the provisions of section 102 above as it applies to solicitors.

(6) A patent agent shall not be guilty of an offence under section 22 of the Solicitors Act 1974 or section 39 of the Solicitors (Scotland) Act 1933 (which

1974 c. 47.
1933 c. 21.

prohibit the preparation for reward of certain instruments or writs by persons not legally qualified) by reason only of the preparation by him for use in proceedings under this Act before the comptroller or on appeal under this Act to the Patents Court from the comptroller of any document other than a deed.

(7) For Article 23(2)(d) of the Solicitors (Northern Ireland) Order 1976 there shall be substituted the following paragraph—

S.I. 1976/582 (N.I. 12).

> "(d) a patent agent within the meaning of the Patents Act 1977 preparing, for use in proceedings under that Act or the Patents Act 1949 before the comptroller (as defined in the former Act) or on appeal under either of those Acts to the Patents Court from the comptroller, any document other than a deed;".

Power of comptroller to refuse to deal with certain agents.

115.—(1) Rules may authorise the controller to refuse to recognise as agent in respect of any business under this Act—

(a) any individual whose name has been erased from, and not restored to, the register of patent agents, or who is for the time being suspended from acting as a patent agent;

(b) any person who has been convicted of an offence under section 114 above or section 88 of the 1949 Act (which is replaced by section 114);

(c) any person who is found by the Secretary of State to have been convicted of any offence or to have been guilty of any such misconduct as, in the case of an individual registered in the register of patent agents, would render him liable to have his name erased from it;

(d) any person, not being registered as a patent agent, who in the opinion of the comptroller is engaged wholly or mainly in acting as agent in applying for patents in the United Kingdom or elsewhere in the name or for the benefit of a person by whom he is employed;

(e) any company or firm, if any person whom the comptroller could refuse to recognise as agent in respect of any business under this Act is acting as a director or manager of the company or is a partner in the firm.

(2) The comptroller shall refuse to recognise as agent in respect of any business under this Act any person who neither resides nor has a place of business in the United Kingdom.

(3) Rules may authorise the comptroller to refuse to recognise as agent or other representative for the purpose of applying for European patents any person who does not satisfy the condition mentioned in section 84(1) above and does not fall within the exemption in subsection (2) of that section.

Immunity of department

116. Neither the Secretary of State nor any officer of his—

Immunity of department as regards official acts.

(a) shall be taken to warrant the validity of any patent granted under this Act or any treaty or international convention to which the United Kingdom is a party; or

(b) shall incur any liability by reason of or in connection with any examination or investigation required or authorised by this Act or any such treaty or convention, or any report or other proceedings consequent on any such examination or investigation.

Administrative provisions

117.—(1) The comptroller may, subject to any provision of rules, correct any error of translation or transcription, clerical error or mistake in any specification of a patent or application for a patent or any document filed in connection with a patent or such an application.

Correction of errors in patents and applications.

(2) Where the comptroller is requested to correct such an error or mistake, any person may in accordance with rules give the comptroller notice of opposition to the request and the comptroller shall determine the matter.

118.—(1) After publication of an application for a patent in accordance with section 16 above the comptroller shall on a request being made to him in the prescribed manner and on payment of the prescribed fee (if any) give the person making the request such information, and permit him to inspect such documents, relating to the application or to any patent granted in pursuance of the application as may be specified in the request, subject, however, to any prescribed restrictions.

Information about patent applications and patents, and inspection of documents.

(2) Subject to the following provisions of this section, until an application for a patent is so published documents or information constituting or relating to the application shall not, without the consent of the applicant, be published or communicated to any person by the comptroller.

(3) Subsection (2) above shall not prevent the comptroller from—

(a) sending the European Patent Office information which it is his duty to send that office in accordance with any provision of the European Patent Convention; or

(b) publishing or communicating to others any prescribed bibliographic information about an unpublished application for a patent;

nor shall that subsection prevent the Secretary of State from inspecting or authorising the inspection of an application for a patent or any connected documents under section 22(6)(a) above.

(4) Where a person is notified that an application for a patent has been made, but not published in accordance with section 16 above, and that the applicant will, if the patent is granted, bring proceedings against that person in the event of his doing an act specified in the notification after the application is so published, that person may make a request under subsection (1) above, notwithstanding that the application has not been published, and that subsection shall apply accordingly.

(5) Where an application for a patent is filed, but not published, and a new application is filed in respect of any part of the subject-matter of the earlier application (either in accordance with rules or in pursuance of any order under section 8 above) and is published, any person may make a request under subsection (1) above relating to the earlier application and on payment of the prescribed fee the comptroller shall give him such information and permit him to inspect such documents as could have been given or inspected if the earlier application had been published.

119. Any notice required or authorised to be given by this Act or rules, and any application or other document so authorised or required to be made or filed, may be given, made or filed by post.

Service by post.

120.—(1) Rules may specify the hour at which the Patent Office shall be taken to be closed on any day for purposes of the transaction by the public of business

Hours of business and

under this Act or of any class of such business, and may specify days as excluded days for any such purposes.

(2) Any business done under this Act on any day after the hour so specified in relation to business of that class, or on a day which is an excluded day in relation to business of that class, shall be taken to have been done on the next following day not being an excluded day; and where the time for doing anything under this Act expires on an excluded day that time shall be extended to the next following day not being an excluded day.

Comptroller's annual report.

121. Before 1st June in every year the comptroller shall cause to be laid before both Houses of Parliament a report with respect to the execution of this Act and the discharge of his functions under the European Patent Convention, the Community Patent Convention and the Patent Co-operation Treaty, and every such report shall include an account of all fees, salaries and allowances, and other money received and paid by him under this Act, those conventions and that treaty during the previous year.

Supplemental

Crown's right to sell forfeited articles.

122. Nothing in this Act affects the right of the Crown or any person deriving title directly or indirectly from the Crown to dispose of or use articles forfeited under the laws relating to customs or excise.

Rules.

123.—(1) The Secretary of State may make such rules as he thinks expedient for regulating the business of the Patent Office in relation to patents and applications for patents (including European patents, application for European patents and international applications for patents) and for regulating all matters placed by this Act under the direction or control of the comptroller; and in this Act, except so far as the context otherwise requires, "prescribed" means prescribed by rules and "rules" means rules made under this section.

(2) Without prejudice to the generality of subsection (1) above, rules may make provision—

(a) prescribing the form and contents of applications for patents and other documents which may be filed at the Patent Office and requiring copies to be furnished of any such documents;

(b) regulating the procedure to be followed in connection with any proceeding or other matter before the comptroller or the Patent Office and authorising the rectification of irregularities of procedure;

(c) requiring fees to be paid in connection with any such proceeding or matter or in connection with the provision of any service by the Patent Office and providing for the remission of fees in the prescribed circumstances;

(d) regulating the mode of giving evidence in any such proceeding and empowering the comptroller to compel the attendance of witnesses and the discovery of and production of documents;

(e) requiring the comptroller to advertise any proposed amendments of patents and any other prescribed matters, including any prescribed steps in any such proceeding;

(f) requiring the comptroller to hold proceedings in Scotland in such circumstances as may be specified in the rules where there is more than one party to proceedings under section 8, 12, 37, 40(1) or (2), 41(8), 61(3), 71 or 72 above;

(g) providing for the appointment of advisers to assist the comptroller in any proceeding before him;

(h) prescribing time limits for doing anything required to be done in connection with any such proceeding by this Act or the rules and providing for the alteration of any period of time specified in this Act or the rules;

(i) giving effect to the right of an inventor of an invention to be mentioned in an application for a patent for the invention;

(j) without prejudice to any other provision of this Act, requiring and regulating the translation of documents in connection with an application for a patent or a European patent or an international application for a patent and the filing and authentication of any such translations;

(k) requiring the keeping of a register of patent agents and regulating the registration of patent agents and authorising in prescribed cases the erasure from the register of patent agents of the name of any person registered therein or the suspension of the right of any such person to act as a patent agent;

(l) providing for the publication and sale of documents in the Patent Office and of information about such documents.

(3) Rules may make different provision for different cases.

(4) Rules prescribing fees shall not be made except with the consent of the Treasury.

(5) The remuneration of any adviser appointed under rules to assist the comptroller in any proceeding shall be determined by the Secretary of State with the consent of the Minister for the Civil Service and shall be defrayed out of moneys provided by Parliament.

(6) Rules shall provide for the publication by the comptroller of a journal (in this Act referred to as "the journal") containing particulars of applications for and grants of patents, and of other proceedings under this Act.

(7) Rules shall require or authorise the comptroller to make arrangements for the publication of reports of cases relating to patents, trade marks and registered designs decided by him and of cases relating to patents (whether under this Act or otherwise) trade marks, registered designs and copyright decided by any court or body (whether in the United Kingdom or elsewhere).

124.—(1) Any power conferred on the Secretary of State by this Act to make rules, regulations or orders shall be exercisable by statutory instrument. *Rules, regulations and orders; supplementary.*

(2) Any Order in Council and any statutory instrument containing an order, rules or regulations under this Act, other than an order or rule required to be laid before Parliament in draft or an order under section 132(5) below, shall be subject to annulment in pursuance of a resolution of either House of Parliament.

(3) Any Order in Council or order under any provision of this Act may be varied or revoked by a subsequent order.

125.—(1) For the purposes of this Act an invention for a patent for which an application has been made or for which a patent has been granted shall, unless the context otherwise requires, be taken to be that specified in a claim of the specification of the application or patent, as the case may be, as interpreted by *Extent of invention.*

the description and any drawings contained in that specification, and the extent of the protection conferred by a patent or application for a patent shall be determined accordingly.

(2) It is hereby declared for the avoidance of doubt that where more than one invention is specified in any such claim, each invention may have a different priority date under section 5 above.

(3) The Protocol on the Interpretation of Article 69 of the European Patent Convention (which Article contains a provision corresponding to subsection (1) above) shall, as for the time being in force, apply for the purposes of subsection (1) above as it applies for the purposes of that Article.

Stamp duty.

126.—(1) An instrument relating to a Community patent or to an application for a European patent shall not be chargeable with stamp duty by reason only of all or any of the provisions of the Community Patent Convention mentioned in subsection (2) below.

(2) The said provisions are—

(a) Article 2.2 (Community patent and application for European patent in which the contracting states are designated to have effect throughout the territories to which the Convention applies);

(b) Article 39.1(c) (Community patent treated as national patent of contracting state in which applicant's representative has place of business);

(c) Article 39.1(c) as applied by Article 45 to an application for a European patent in which the contracting states are designated.

Existing patents and applications.

127.—(1) No application for a patent may be made under the 1949 Act on or after the appointed day.

(2) Schedule 1 to this Act shall have effect for securing that certain provisions of the 1949 Act shall continue to apply on and after the appointed day to—

(a) a patent granted before that day;

(b) an application for a patent which is filed before that day, and which is accompanied by a complete specification or in respect of which a complete specification is filed before that day;

(c) a patent granted in pursuance of such an application.

(3) Schedule 2 to this Act shall have effect for securing that (subject to the provisions of that Schedule) certain provisions of this Act shall apply on and after the appointed day to any patent and application to which subsection (2) above relates, but, except as provided by the following provisions of this Act, this Act shall not apply to any such patent or application.

(4) An application for a patent which is made before the appointed day, but which does not comply with subsection (2)(b) above, shall be taken to have been abandoned immediately before that day, but, notwithstanding anything in section 5(3) above, the application may nevertheless serve to establish a priority date in relation to a later application for a patent under this Act if the date of filing the abandoned application falls within the period of fifteen months immediately preceding the filing of the later application.

(5) Schedule 3 to this Act shall have effect for repealing certain provisions of the 1949 Act.

(6) The transitional provisions and savings in Schedule 4 to this Act shall have effect.

(7) In Schedules 1 to 4 to this Act "existing patent" means a patent mentioned in subsection (2)(a) and (c) above, "existing application" means an application mentioned in subsection (2)(b) above, and expressions used in the 1949 Act and those Schedules have the same meanings in those Schedules as in that Act.

128.—(1) The following provisions of this section shall have effect for the purpose of resolving questions of priority arising between patents and applications for patents under the 1949 Act and patents and applications for patents under this Act. *Priorities between patents and applications under 1949 Act and this Act.*

(2) A complete specification under the 1949 Act shall be treated for the purposes of sections 2(3) and 5(2) above—

>   (a) if published under that Act, as a published application for a patent under this Act;

>   (b) if it has a date of filing under that Act, as an application for a patent under this Act which has a date of filing under this Act;

and in the said section 2(3), as it applies by virtue of this subsection in relation to any such specification, the words "both as filed and" shall be omitted.

(3) In section 8(1), (2) and (4) of the 1949 Act (search for anticipation by prior claim) the references to any claim of a complete specification, other than the applicant's, published and filed as mentioned in section 8(1) shall include references to any claim contained in an application made and published under this Act or in the specification of a patent granted under this Act, being a claim in respect of an invention having a priority date earlier than the date of filing the complete specification under the 1949 Act.

(4) In section 32(1)(a) of the 1949 Act (which specifies, as one of the grounds of revoking a patent, that the invention was claimed in a valid claim of earlier priority date contained in the complete specification of another patent), the reference to such a claim shall include a reference to a claim contained in the specification of a patent granted under this Act (a new claim) which satisfies the following conditions:—

>   (a) the new claim must be in respect of an invention having an earlier priority date than that of the relevant claim of the complete specification of the patent sought to be revoked; and

>   (b) the patent containing the new claim must be wholly valid or be valid in those respects which have a bearing on that relevant claim.

(5) For the purposes of this section and the provisions of the 1949 Act mentioned in this section the date of filing an application for a patent under that Act and the priority date of a claim of a complete specification under that Act shall be determined in accordance with the provisions of that Act, and the priority date of an invention which is the subject of a patent or application for a patent under this Act shall be determined in accordance with the provisions of this Act.

129.—This Act does not affect Her Majesty in her private capacity but, subject to that, it binds the Crown. *Application of Act to Crown.*

130.—(1) In this Act, except so far as the context otherwise requires— *Interpretation*

>   "application for a European patent (UK)" and "international application for a patent (UK)" each mean an application of the relevant description which, on its date of filing, designates the United Kingdom;

>   "appointed day", in any provision of this Act, means the day appointed under section 132 below for the coming into operation of that provision";

"Community Patent Convention" means the Convention for the European Patent for the Common Market and "Community patent" means a patent granted under that convention";

"comptroller" means the Comptroller-General of Patents, Designs and Trade Marks;

"Convention on International Exhibitions" means the Convention relating to International Exhibitions signed in Paris on 22nd November 1928, as amended or supplemented by any protocol to that convention which is for the time being in force;

"court" means
(a) as respects England and Wales, the High Court;
(b) as respects Scotland, the Court of Session;
(c) as respects Northern Ireland, the High Court in Northern Ireland;

"date of filing" means—
(a) in relation to an application for a patent made under this Act, the date which is the date of filing that application by virtue of section 15 above; and
(b) in relation to any other application, the date which, under the law of the country where the application was made or in accordance with the terms of a treaty or convention to which that country is a party, is to be treated as the date of filing that application or is equivalent to the date of filing an application in that country (whatever the outcome of the application);

"designate" in relation to an application or a patent, means designate the country or countries (in pursuance of the European Patent Convention or the Patent Co-operation Treaty) in which protection is sought for the invention which is the subject of the application or patent;

"employee" means a person who works or (where the employment has ceased) worked under a contract of employment or in employment under or for the purposes of a government department;

"employer", in relation to an employee, means the person by whom the employee is or was employed;

"European Patent Convention" means the Convention on the Grant of European Patents, "European patent" means a patent granted under that convention, "European patent (UK)" means a European patent designating the United Kingdom, "European Patent Bulletin" means the bulletin of that name published under that convention, and "European Patent Office" means the office of that name established by that convention;

"exclusive licence" means a licence from the proprietor of or applicant for a patent conferring on the licensee, or on him and persons authorised by him, to the exclusion of all other persons (including the proprietor or applicant), any right in respect of the invention to which the patent or application relates, and "exclusive licensee" and "non-exclusive licence" shall be construed accordingly;

"filing fee" means the fee prescribed for the purposes of section 14 above;

"formal requirements" means those requirements designated as such by rules made for the purposes of section 17 above;

"international application for a patent" means an application made under the Patent Co-operation Treaty;

"International Bureau" means the secretariat of the World Intellectual Property Organization established by a convention signed at Stockholm on 14th July 1967;

"international exhibition" means an official or officially recognised international exhibition falling within the terms of the Convention on International Exhibitions or falling within the terms of any subsequent treaty or convention replacing that convention;

"inventor" has the meaning assigned to it by section 7 above;

"journal" has the meaning assigned to it by section 123(6) above;

"mortgage", when used as a noun, includes a charge for securing money or money's worth and, when used as a verb, shall be construed accordingly;

"1949 Act" means the Patents Act 1949;   1949 c. 87.

"patent" means a patent under this Act;

"patent agent" means a person carrying on for gain in the United Kingdom the business of acting as agent for other persons for the purpose of applying for or obtaining patents (other than European patents) in the United Kingdom or elsewhere or for the purpose of conducting proceedings in connection with such patents before the comptroller;

"Patent Co-operation Treaty" means the treaty of the name signed at Washington on 19th June 1970;

"patented invention" means an invention for which a patent is granted and "patented process" shall be construed accordingly;

"patented product" means a product which is a patented invention or, in relation to a patented process, a product obtained directly by means of the process or to which the process has been applied;

"prescribed" and "rules" have the meanings assigned to them by section 123 above;

"priority date" means the date determined as such under section 5 above;

"published" means made available to the public (whether in the United Kingdom or elsewhere) and a document shall be taken to be published under any provision of this Act if it can be inspected as of right at any place in the United Kingdom by members of the public, whether on payment of a fee or not; and "republished" shall be construed accordingly;

"register" and cognate expressions have the meanings assigned to them by section 32 above;

"relevant convention court", in relation to any proceedings under the European Patent Convention, the Community Patent Convention or the Patent Co-operation Treaty, means that court or other body which under that convention or treaty has jurisdiction over those proceedings, including (where it has such jurisdiction) any department of the European Patent Office;

"right", in relation to any patent or application, includes an interest in the patent or application and, without prejudice to the foregoing, any reference to a right in a patent includes a reference to a share in the patent;

"search fee" means the fee prescribed for the purposes of section 17 above;

"services of the Crown" and "use for the services of the Crown" have the meanings assigned to them by section 56(2) above, including, as respects any period of emergency within the meaning of section 59 above, the meanings assigned to them by the said section 59.

(2) Rules may provide for stating in the journal that an exhibition falls within

the definition of international exhibition in subsection (1) above and any such statement shall be conclusive evidence that the exhibition falls within that definition.

(3) For the purposes of this Act matter shall be taken to have been disclosed in any relevant application within the meaning of section 5 above or in the specification of a patent if it was either claimed or disclosed (otherwise than by way of disclaimer or acknowledgement of prior art) in that application or specification.

(4) References in this Act to an application for a patent, as filed, are references to such an application in the state it was on the date of filing.

(5) References in this Act to an application for a patent being published are references to its being published under section 16 above.

(6) References in this Act to any of the following conventions, that is to say—

(a) The European Patent Convention;

(b) The Community Patent Convention;

(c) The Patent Co-operation Treaty;

are references to that convention or any other international convention or agreement replacing it, as amended or supplemented by any convention or international agreement (including in either case any protocol or annex), or in accordance with the terms of any such convention or agreement, and include references to any instrument made under any such convention or agreement.

(7) Whereas by a resolution made on the signature of the Community Patent Convention the governments of the member states of the European Economic Community resolved to adjust their laws relating to patents so as (among other things) to bring those laws into conformity with the corresponding provisions of the European Patent Convention, the Community Patent Convention and the Patent Co-operation Treaty, it is hereby declared that the following provisions of this Act, that is to say, sections 1(1) to (4), 2 to 6, 14(3), (5) and (6), 37(5), 54, 60, 69, 72(1) and (2), 74(4), 82, 83, 88(6) and (7), 100 and 125, are so framed as to have, as nearly as practicable, the same effects in the United Kingdom as the corresponding provisions of the European Patent Convention, the Community Patent Convention and the Patent Co-operation Treaty have in their territories to which those conventions apply.

1950 c. 27.

(8) The Arbitration Act 1950 shall not apply to any proceedings before the comptroller under this Act.

(9) Except so far as the context otherwise requires, any reference in this Act to any enactment shall be construed as a reference to that enactment as amended or extended by or under any other enactment, including this Act.

Northern Ireland.

131. In the application of this Act to Northern Ireland—

(a) "enactment" includes an enactment of the Parliament of Northern Ireland and a Measure of the Northern Ireland Assembly;

(b) any reference to a government department includes a reference to a Department of the Government of Northern Ireland;

(c) any reference to the Crown includes a reference to the Crown in right of Her Majesty's Government in Northern Ireland;

1948 c. 38.

(d) any reference to the Companies Act 1948 includes a reference to the corresponding enactments in force in Northern Ireland; and

(e) the Arbitration Act (Northern Ireland) 1937 shall apply in relation to an 1937 c. 8 (N.I.). arbitration in pursuance of this Act as if this Act related to a matter in respect of which the Parliament of Northern Ireland had power to make laws.

132.—(1) This Act may be cited as the Patents Act 1977.

(2) This Act shall extend to the Isle of Man, subject to any modifications contained in an Order made by Her Majesty in Council, and accordingly, subject to any such order, references in this Act to the United Kingdom shall be construed as including references to the Isle of Man.

(3) For the purposes of this Act the territorial waters of the United Kingdom shall be treated as part of the United Kingdom.

(4) This Act applies to acts done in an area designated by order under section 1(7) of the Continental Shelf Act 1964, in connection with the exploration of the sea bed or subsoil or exploitation of their natural resources, as it applies to acts done in the United Kingdom.

(5) This Act (except sections 77(6), (7) and (9), 78(7) and (8), this subsection and the repeal of section 41 of the 1949 Act) shall come into operation on such day as may be appointed by the Secretary of State by order, and different days may be appointed under this subsection for different purposes.

(6) The consequential amendments in Schedule 5 shall have effect.

(7) Subject to the provisions of Schedule 4 to this Act, the enactments specified in Schedule 6 to this Act (which include certain enactments which were spent before the passing of this Act) are hereby repealed to the extent specified in column 3 of that Schedule.

Short title, extent, commencement consequential amendments and repeals.

1964 c. 29.

SCHEDULES
SCHEDULE 1

APPLICATION OF 1949 ACT TO EXISTING PATENTS AND APPLICATIONS

1.—(1) The provisions of the 1949 Act referred to in subparagraph (2) below Section 127 shall continue to apply on and after the appointed day in relation to existing patents and applications (but not in relation to patents and applications for patents under this Act).

(2) The provisions are sections 1 to 10, 11(1) and (2), 12, 13, 15 to 17, 19 to 21, 22(1) to (3), 23 to 26, 28 to 33, 46 to 53, 55, 56, 59 to 67, 69, 76, 80, 87(2), 92(1), 96, 101, 102(1) and 103 to 107.

(3) Sub-paragraph (1) above shall have effect subject to the following provisions of this Schedule, paragraph 2(b) of Schedule 3 below and the provisions of Schedule 4 below.

2.—(1) In section 6 of the 1949 Act, at the end of the proviso to subsection (3) (post-dating of application) there shall be inserted "and—

(c) no application shall, on or after the appointed day, be postdated under this subsection to a date which is that of the appointed day or which falls after it",

and there shall be inserted at the end of subsection (4) "; but no application shall on or after the appointed day be post-dated under this subsection to a date which is that of the appointed day or which falls after it".

(2) At the end of subsection (5) of that section (ante-dating) there shall be inserted "; but a fresh application or specification may not be filed on or after the appointed day in accordance with this subsection and those rules unless the comptroller agrees that he will direct that the application or specification shall be ante-dated to a date which falls before the appointed day".

3.—(1) This paragraph and paragraph 4 below shall have effect with respect to the duration of existing patents after the appointed day, and in those paragraphs—

> (a) "old existing patent" means an existing patent the date of which fell eleven years or more before the appointed day and also any patent of addition where the patent for the main invention is, or was at any time, an old existing patent by virtue of the foregoing provision;
>
> (b) "new existing patent" means any existing patent not falling within paragraph (a) above; and
>
> (c) any reference to the date of a patent shall, in relation to a patent of addition, be construed as a reference to the date of the patent for the main invention.

(2) Sections 23 to 25 of the 1949 Act (extension of patents on grounds of inadequate remuneration and war loss) shall not apply to a new existing patent.

(3) The period for which the term of an old existing patent may be extended under section 23 or 24 of that Act shall not exceed in the aggregate four years, except where an application for an order under the relevant section has been made before the appointed day and has not been disposed of before that day.

4.—(1) The term of every new existing patent under section 22(3) of the 1949 Act shall be twenty instead of sixteen years from the date of the patent, but—

> (a) the foregoing provision shall have effect subject to section 25(3) to (5) above; and
>
> (b) on and after the end of the sixteenth year from that date a patent shall not be renewed under section 25(3) to (5) above except by or with the consent of the proprietor of the patent.

(2) Where the term of a new existing patent is extended by this paragraph,—

> (a) any licence in force under the patent from immediately before the appointed day until the end of the sixteenth year from the date of the patent shall, together with any contract relating to the licence, continue in force so long as the patent remains in force (unless determined otherwise than in accordance with this sub-paragraph), but, if it is an exclusive licence, it shall after the end of that year be treated as a non-exclusive licence;
>
> (b) notwithstanding the terms of the licence, the licensee shall not be required to make any payment to the proprietor for working the invention in question after the end of that year;
>
> (c) every such patent shall after the end of that year be treated as endorsed under section 35 of the 1949 Act (licences of right).

(3) Where the term of a new existing patent is extended by this paragraph and any government department or any person authorised by a government department—

> (a) has before the appointed day, used the invention in question for the services of the Crown; and
>
> (b) continues to so use it until the end of the sixteenth year from the date of the patent,

any such use of the invention by any government department or person so authorised, after the end of that year, may be made free of any payment to the proprietor of the patent.

(4) Without prejudice to any rule of law about the frustration of contracts, where any person suffers loss or is subjected to liability by reason of the extension of the term of a patent by this paragraph, the court may on the application of that person determine how and by whom the loss or liability is to be borne and make such order as it thinks fit to give effect to the determination.

(5) No order shall be made on an application under sub-paragraph (4) above which has the effect of imposing a liability on any person other than the applicant unless notification of the application is given to that person.

5. In section 26(3) of the 1949 Act (no patent of addition unless date of filing of complete specification was the same as or later than the date of filing of complete specification in respect of main invention) after "main invention" there shall be inserted "and was earlier than the date of the appointed day".

6. Notwithstanding anything in section 32(1)(j) of the 1949 Act (ground for revocation that patent was obtained on a false suggestion or representation), it shall not be a ground of revoking a patent under that subsection that the patent was obtained on a false suggestion or representation that a claim of the complete specification of the patent had a priority date earlier than the date of filing the application for the patent, but if it is shown—

> (a) on a petition under that section or an application under section 33 of that Act; or

> (b) by way of defence or on a counterclaim on an action for infringement;

that such a suggestion or representation was falsely made, the priority date of the claim shall be taken to be the date of filing the application for that patent.

7.—(1) In section 33 of the 1949 Act (revocation of patent by comptroller), in subsection (1) for the words preceding the proviso there shall be substituted—

> "(1) Subject to the provisions of this Act, a patent may, on the application of any person interested, be revoked by the comptroller on any of the grounds set out in section 32(1) of this Act:".

(2) At the end of the said section 33 there shall be added the following subsection:—

> "(5) A decision of the comptroller or on appeal from the comptroller shall not estop any party to civil proceedings in which infringement of a patent is in issue from alleging that any claim of the specification is invalid on any of the grounds set out in section 32(1) of this Act, whether or not any of the issues involved were decided in that decision.".

8. In section 101(1) of the 1949 Act (interpretation) there shall be inserted in the appropriate place—

> "appointed day" means the day appointed under section 132 of the Patents Act 1977 for the coming into operation of Schedule 1 to that Act;".

Schedule 2

Application of this Act to Existing Patents and Applications

1.—(1) Without prejudice to those provisions of Schedule 4 below which apply (in certain circumstances) provisions of this Act in relation to existing patents and Section 127. applications, the provisions of this Act referred to in sub-paragraph (2) below shall apply in relation to existing patents and applications on and after the appointed day subject to the following provisions of this Schedule and the provisions of Schedule 4 below.

(2) The provisions are sections 22, 23, 25(3) to (5), 28 to 36, 44 to 54, 86, 96, 98, 99, 101 to 105, 107 to 111, 113 to 116, 118(1) to (3), 119 to 124, 130 and 132(2), (3) and (4).

2. In those provisions as they apply by virtue of this Schedule—

    (a) a reference to this Act includes a reference to the 1949 Act;

    (b) a reference to a specified provision of this Act other than one of those provisions shall be construed as a reference to the corresponding provision of the 1949 Act (any provision of that Act being treated as corresponding to a provision of this Act if it was enacted for purposes which are the same as or similar to that provision of this Act);

    (c) a reference to rules includes a reference to rules under the 1949 Act;

    (d) references to a patent under this Act and to an application for such a patent include respectively a reference to an existing patent and application;

    (e) references to the grant of a patent under this Act include a reference to the sealing and grant of an existing patent;

    (f) a reference to a patented product and to a patented invention include respectively a reference to a product and invention patented under an existing patent;

    (g) references to a published application for a patent under this Act, and to publication of such an application, include respectively references to a complete specification which has been published under the 1949 Act and to publication of such a specification (and a reference to an application for a patent under this Act which has not been published shall be construed accordingly);

    (h) a reference to the publication in the journal of a notice of the grant of a patent includes a reference to the date of an existing patent;

    (i) a reference to the priority date of an invention includes a reference to the priority date of the relevant claim of the complete specification.

SCHEDULE 3

REPEALS OF PROVISIONS OF 1949 ACT

1. Subject to the provisions of Schedule 4 below, the provisions of the 1949 Act referred to in paragraph 2 below (which have no counterpart in the new law of patents established by this Act in relation to future patents and applications) shall cease to have effect.

2. The provisions are:—

    (a) section 14 (opposition to grant of patent);

    (b) section 32(3) (revocation for refusal to comply with Crown request to use invention);

    (c) section 41 (inventions relating to food or medicine, etc.);

    (d) section 42 (comptroller's power to revoke patent after expiry of two years from grant of compulsory licence);

(e) section 71 (extension of time for certain convention applications);

(f) section 72 (protection of inventions communicated under international agreements).

SCHEDULE 4

TRANSITIONAL PROVISIONS

General

1. In so far as any instrument made or other thing done under any provision of Section 127. the 1949 Act which is repealed by virtue of this Act could have been made or done under a corresponding provision of this Act, it shall not be invalidated by the repeals made by virtue of this Act but shall have effect as if made or done under that corresponding provision.

Use of patented invention for services of the Crown

2.—(1) Any question whether—

(a) an act done before the appointed day by a government department or a person authorised in writing by a government department amounts to the use of an invention for the services of the Crown; or

(b) any payment falls to be made in respect of any such use (whether to a person entitled to apply for a patent for the invention, to the patentee or to an exclusive licensee);

shall be determined under sections 46 to 49 of that Act and those sections shall apply accordingly.

(2) Sections 55 to 59 above shall apply to an act so done on or after the appointed day in relation to an invention—

(a) for which an existing patent has been granted or an existing application for a patent has been made; or

(b) which was communicated before that day to a government department or any person authorised in writing by a government department by the proprietor of the patent or any person from whom he derives title;

and shall so apply subject to sub-paragraph (3) below, the modifications contained in paragraph 2 of Schedule 2 above and the further modification that sections 55(5)(b) and 58(10) above shall not apply in relation to an existing application.

(3) Where an act is commenced before the appointed day and continues to be done on or after that day, then, if it would not amount to the use of an invention for the services of the Crown under the 1949 Act, its continuance on or after that day shall not amount to such use under this Act.

Infringement

3.—(1) Any question whether an act done before the appointed day infringes an existing patent or the privileges or rights arising under a complete specification which has been published shall be determined in accordance with the law relating to infringement in force immediately before that day and, in addition to those provisions of the 1949 Act which continue to apply by virtue of Schedule 1 above, section 70 of that Act shall apply accordingly.

(2) Sections 60 to 71 above shall apply to an act done on or after the appointed day which infringes an existing patent or the privileges or rights arising under a

complete specification which has been published (whether before, on or after the appointed day) as they apply to infringements of a patent under this Act or the rights conferred by an application for such a patent, and shall so apply subject to sub-paragraph (3) below, the modifications contained in paragraph 2 of Schedule 2 above and the further modification that section 69(2) and (3) above shall not apply in relation to an existing application.

(3) Where an act is commenced before the appointed day and continues to be done on or after that day, then, if it would not, under the law in force immediately before that day, amount to an infringement of an existing patent or the privileges or rights arising under a complete specification, its continuance on or after that day shall not amount to the infringement of that patent or those privileges or rights.

Notice of opposition

4.—(1) Where notice of opposition to the grant of a patent has been given under section 14 of the 1949 Act before the appointed day, the following provisions shall apply:—

  (a) if issue has been joined on the notice before the appointed day, the opposition, any appeal from the comptroller's decision on it and any further appeal shall be prosecuted under the old law, but as if references in the 1949 Act and rules made under it to the Appeal Tribunal were references to the Patents Court;

  (b) in any other case, the notice shall be taken to have abated immediately before the appointed day.

(2) Sub-paragraph (1)(a) above shall have effect subject to paragraph 12(2) below.

Secrecy

5.—(1) Where directions given under section 18 of the 1949 Act in respect of an existing application (directions restricting publication of information about inventions) are in force immediately before the appointed day, they shall continue in force on and after that day and that section shall continue to apply accordingly.

(2) Where sub-paragraph (1) above does not apply in the case of an existing application section 18 of the 1949 Act shall not apply to the application but section 22 of this Act shall.

1946 c. 80.
(3) Where the comptroller has before the appointed day served a notice under section 12 of the Atomic Energy Act 1946 (restrictions on publication of information about atomic energy etc.) in respect of an existing application that section shall continue to apply to the application on and after that day; but where no such notice has been so served that section shall not apply to the application on and after that day.

Revocation

6.—(1) Where before the appointed day an application has been made under section 33 of the 1949 Act for the revocation of a patent (the original application), the following provisions shall apply:—

  (a) if issue has been joined on the application before the appointed day, the application, any appeal from the comptroller's decision on it and any further appeal shall be prosecuted under the old law, but as if references in the 1949 Act and rules made under it to the Appeal Tribunal were references to the Patents Court;

(b) if issue has not been so joined, the original application shall be taken to be an application under section 33 of the 1949 Act for the revocation of the patent on whichever of the grounds referred to in section 32(1) of that Act corresponds (in the comptroller's opinion) to the ground on which the original application was made, or, if there is no ground which so corresponds, shall be taken to have abated immediately before the appointed day.

(2) Sub-paragraph (1)(a) above shall have effect subject to paragraph 11(3) below.

7.—(1) This paragraph applies where an application has been made before the appointed day under section 42 of the 1949 Act for the revocation of a patent.

(2) Where the comptroller has made no order before that day for the revocation of the patent under that section, the application shall be taken to have abated immediately before that day.

(3) Where the comptroller has made such an order before that day, then, without prejudice to section 38 of the Interpretation Act 1889, section 42 shall continue to 1889 c. 63. apply to the patent concerned on and after that day as if this Act had not been enacted.

Licences of right and compulsory licences

8.—(1) Sections 35 to 41 and 43 to 45 of the 1949 Act shall continue to apply on and after the relevant day—

(a) to any endorsement or order made or licence granted under sections 35 to 41 which is in force immediately before that day; and

(b) to any application made before that day under sections 35 to 41.

(2) Any appeal from a decision or order of the comptroller instituted under sections 35 to 41 or 43 to 45 on or after the relevant day (and any further appeal) shall be prosecuted under the old law, but as if references in the 1949 Act and rules made under it to the Appeal Tribunal were references to the Patents Court.

(3) In this paragraph "the relevant day" means, in relation to section 41, the date of the passing of this Act and, in relation to sections 35 to 40 and 43 to 45, the appointed day.

Convention countries

9.—(1) Without prejudice to paragraph 1 above, an Order in Council declaring any country to be a convention country for all purposes of the 1949 Act or for the purposes of section 1(2) of that Act and in force immediately before the appointed day shall be treated as an Order in Council under section 90 above declaring that country to be a convention country for the purposes of section 5 above.

(2) Where an Order in Council declaring any country to be a convention country for all purposes of the 1949 Act or for the purposes of section 70 of that Act is in force immediately before the appointed day, a vessel registered in that country (whether before, on or after that day) shall be treated for the purposes of section 60 above, as it applies by virtue of paragraph 3(2) above to an existing patent or existing application, as a relevant ship and an aircraft so registered and a land vehicle owned by a person ordinarily resident in that country shall be so treated respectively as a relevant aircraft and a relevant vehicle.

Appeals from court on certain petitions for revocation

10. Where the court has given judgment on a petition under section 32(1)(j) of the 1949 Act before the appointed day, any appeal from the judgment (whether instituted before, on or after that day) shall be continued or instituted and be disposed of under the old law.

Appeals from comptroller under continuing provisions of 1949 Act

11.—(1) In this paragraph "the continuing 1949 Act provisions" means the provisions of the 1949 Act which continue to apply on and after the appointed day as mentioned in paragraph 1 of Schedule 1 above.

(2) This paragraph applies where—

(a) the comptroller gives a decision or direction (whether before or on or after the appointed day) under any of the continuing 1949 Act provisions, and

(b) an appeal lies under those provisions from the decision or direction;

but this paragraph applies subject to the foregoing provisions of this Schedule.

(3) Where such an appeal has been instituted before the Appeal Tribunal before the appointed day, and the hearing of the appeal has begun but has not been completed before that day, the appeal (and any further appeal) shall be continued and disposed of under the old law.

(4) Where such an appeal has been so instituted, but the hearing of it has not begun before the appointed day, it shall be transferred by virtue of this sub-paragraph to the Patents Court on that day and the appeal (and any further appeal) shall be prosecuted under the old law, but as if references in the 1949 Act and rules made under it to the Appeal Tribunal were references to the Patents Court.

(5) Any such appeal instituted on or after the appointed day shall lie to the Patents Court or, where the proceedings appealed against were held in Scotland, the Court of Session; and accordingly, the reference to the Appeal Tribunal in section 31(2) of the 1949 Act shall be taken to include a reference to the Patents Court or (as the case may be) the Court of Session.

(6) Section 97(3) of this Act shall apply to any decision of the Patents Court on an appeal instituted on or after the appointed day from a decision or direction of the comptroller under any of the continuing 1949 Act provisions as it applies to a decision of that Court referred to in that subsection, except that for references to the sections mentioned in paragraph (a) of that subsection there shall be substituted references to sections 33, 55 and 56 of the 1949 *Act*.

Appeals from comptroller under repealed provisions of 1949 Act

12.—(1) This paragraph applies where an appeal to the Appeal Tribunal has been instituted before the appointed day under any provision of the 1949 Act repealed by this Act.

(2) Where the hearing of such an appeal has begun but has not been completed before that day, the appeal (and any further appeal) shall be continued and disposed of under the old law.

(3) Where the hearing of such an appeal has not begun before that day, it shall be transferred by virtue of this sub-paragraph to the Patents Court on that day and the appeal (and any further appeal) shall be prosecuted under the old law, but as if references in the 1949 Act and rules made under it to the Appeal Tribunal were references to the Patents Court.

Appeals from Appeal Tribunal to Court of Appeal

13. Section 87(1) of the 1949 Act shall continue to apply on and after the appointed day to any decision of the Appeal Tribunal given before that day, and any appeal by virtue of this paragraph (and any further appeal) shall be prosecuted under the old law.

Rules

14. The power to make rules under section 123 of this Act shall include power to make rules for any purpose mentioned in section 94 of the 1949 Act.

Supplementary

15. Section 97(2) of this Act applies to—

(a) any appeal to the Patents Court by virtue of paragraph 4(1)(a), 6(1)(a), 8(2) or 11(5) above, and

(b) any appeal which is transferred to that Court by virtue of paragraph 11(4) or 12(3) above,

as it applies to an appeal under that section; and section 97 of this Act shall apply for the purposes of any such appeal instead of section 85 of the 1949 Act.

16. In this Schedule "the old law" means the 1949 Act, any rules made under it and any relevant rule of law as it was or they were immediately before the appointed day.

17. For the purposes of this Schedule—

(a) issue is joined on a notice of opposition to the grant of a patent under section 14 of the 1949 Act when the applicant for the patent files a counter-statement fully setting out the grounds on which the opposition is contested;

(b) issue is joined on an application for the revocation of a patent under section 33 of that Act when the patentee files a counter-statement fully setting out the grounds on which the application is contested.

18.—(1) Nothing in the repeals made by this Act in sections 23 and 24 of the 1949 Act shall have effect as respects any such application as is mentioned in paragraph 3(3) of Schedule 1 above.

(2) Nothing in the repeal by this Act of the Patents Act 1957 shall have effect 1957 c. 13. as respects existing applications.

(3) Section 69 of the 1949 Act (which is not repealed by this Act) and section 70 of that Act (which continues to have effect for certain purposes by virtue of paragraph 3 above) shall apply as if section 68 of that Act has not been repealed by this Act and as if paragraph 9 above had not been enacted.

SCHEDULE 5

Section 132.

CONSEQUENTIAL AMENDMENTS

Crown Proceedings Act 1947 (c. 44)

1. In section 3 of the Crown Proceedings Act 1947, for subsection (2) there shall be substituted:—

"(2) Nothing in the preceding subsection or in any other provision of this

Act shall affect the rights of any Government department under Schedule 1 to the Registered Designs Act 1949 or section 55 of the Patents Act 1977, or the rights of the Secretary of State under section 22 of the said Act of 1977."

Registered Designs Act 1949 (c. 88)

2. In section 32(1) of the Registered Designs Act 1949—

(a) in paragraph (a), for "the Patents Act 1949" there shall be substituted "the Patents Act 1977"; and

(b) in paragraph (c), after "1949" there shall be inserted "or section 114 of the Patents Act 1977".

3. In sections 42 and 44(1) of the Registered Designs Act 1949, for "the Patents Act 1949" there shall be substituted, in each case, "the Patents Act 1977".

Defence Contracts Act 1958 (c. 38)

4. In subsection (4) of section 4 of the Defence Contracts Act 1958, for the words from "Patents Act 1949" to the end there shall be substituted "Patents Act 1977".

Administration of Justice Act 1970 (c. 31)

5.—(1) In subsections (2) and (3) of section 10 of the Administration of Justice Act 1970 for "either" there shall be substituted, in each case, "the".

(2) In subsection (4) of the said section 10, for "(as so amended)" there shall be substituted "(as amended by section 24 of the Administration of Justice Act 1969)".

(3) For subsection (5) of the said section 10, there shall be substituted:—

"(5) In subsection (8) of the said section 28 (which confers power on the Tribunal to make rules about procedure etc.), there shall be inserted at the end of the subsection the words "including right of audience".

Atomic Energy Authority (Weapons Group) Act 1973 (c. 4)

6. In section 5(2) of the Atomic Energy Authority (Weapons Group) Act 1973—

(a) after the first "Patents Act 1949" there shall be inserted ", the Patents Act 1977"; and

(b) after the second "Patents Act 1949" there shall be inserted "section 55(4) of the Patents Act 1977".

Fair Trading Act 1973 (c. 41)

7.—(1) In paragraph 10 of Schedule 4 to the Fair Trading Act 1973 for "Patents Act 1949" there shall be substituted "Patents Act 1977".

(2) After the said paragraph 10 there shall be inserted:—

"10A. The services of persons carrying on for gain in the United Kingdom the business of acting as agents or other representatives of other persons for the purpose of applying for or obtaining European patents or for the purpose of conducting proceedings in connection with such patents before the European Patent Office or the comptroller and whose names appear on the European list (within the meaning of section 84(7) of the Patents Act 1977) in their capacity as such persons."

Restrictive Trade Practices Act 1976 (c. 34)

8.—(1) In paragraph 10 of Schedule 1 to the Restrictive Trade Practices Act 1976, for "the Patents Act 1949" there shall be substituted "the Patents Act 1977".

(2) After the said paragraph 10 there shall be inserted:—

> "10A. The services of persons carrying on for gain in the United Kingdom the business of acting as agents or other representatives of other persons for the purpose of applying for or obtaining European patents or for the purpose of conducting proceedings in connection with such patents before the European Patent Office or the comptroller and whose names appear on the European list (within the meaning of section 84(7) of the Patents Act 1977), in their capacity as such persons."

Schedule 6

Enactments Repealed

Section 132.

Chapter	Short Title	Extent of Repeal
7 Edw. 7. c. 29.	The Patents and Designs Act 1907.	Section 47(2).
9 & 10 Geo. 6. c. 80	The Atomic Energy Act 1946.	In section 12, subsections (1) to (7).
12, 13 & 14 Geo. 6. c. 87.	The Patents Act 1949.	Section 11(3). Section 14. Section 16(6). Section 18. Section 22(4) and (5). In section 23(1), the words from "(not exceeding" to "ten years)". In section 24, in subsection (1), the words "(not exceeding ten years)" and, in subsection (7), the words from "but" to the end. Section 27. In section 32, subsection (3). In section 33(3), the proviso. Sections 34 to 45. Sections 54, 57 and 58. Section 68. Sections 70 to 75. Sections 77 to 79. Sections 81 to 86. Section 87(1) and (3). Sections 88 to 91. Sections 93 to 95. Sections 97 to 100. Section 102(2). Schedule 1.

		Schedule 3, except paragraphs 1 and 26.
5 & 6 Eliz. 2. c. 13.	The Patents Act 1957.	The whole Act, except in relation to existing applications.
9 & 10 Eliz. 2. c. 25.	The Patents and Designs (Renewals, Extensions and Fees) Act 1961.	In section 1(1), the words from "subsection (5)" to "and in". Section 2.
10 & 11 Eliz. 2. c. 30.	The Northern Ireland Act 1962.	In Schedule 1, the entry relating to section 84 of the Patents Act 1949.
1967 c. 80.	The Criminal Justice Act 1967.	In Schedule 3, in Parts I and IV, the entries relating to the Patents Act 1949.
1968 c. 64.	The Civil Evidence Act 1968.	Section 15.
1969 c. 58.	The Administration of Justice Act 1969.	In section 24, in subsection (1), the words "85 of the Patents Act 1949 and section" and "each of", in subsections (2), (3) and (4) the words "of each of those sections" and in subsection (4) the words from "as subsection (11)" to "and" and the words "in the case of the said section 28".
1970 c. 31.	The Administration of Justice Act 1970.	In section 10, in subsection (1), the words "Patents Appeal Tribunal or the" and in subsection (4), the words from "the Patents Appeal" to "and".
1971 c. 23.	The Courts Act 1971.	Section 46.
1971 c. 36 (N.I.)	The Civil Evidence Act (Northern Ireland) 1971.	Section 11.
1973 c. 41.	The Fair Trading Act 1973.	Section 126. In Schedule 3, in paragraph 16(2), the words from "of section 40" to "Commission)", where first occurring. In Schedule 12, the entry relating to the Patents Act 1949.
1974 c. 47.	The Solicitors Act 1974.	In Schedule 3, paragraph 3.

Copyright, Designs and Patents Act 1988 (Excerpts)

Part V, Sections 274–281 and 285–286.
Part VI, Sections 287–295, Schedule 5.

Part V

Patent Agents and Trade Mark Agents

Patent agents

274.—(1) Any individual, partnership or body corporate may, subject to the Persons permitted to carry on business of a patent agent. following provisions of this Part, carry on the business of acting as agent for others for the purpose of—

    (a) applying for or obtaining patents, in the United Kingdom or elsewhere, or

    (b) conducting proceedings before the comptroller relating to applications for, or otherwise in connection with, patents.

(2) This does not affect any restriction under the European Patent Convention as to who may act on behalf of another for any purpose relating to European patents.

275.—(1) The Secretary of State may make rules requiring the keeping of a The register of patent agents. register of persons who act as agent for others for the purposes of applying for or obtaining patents; and in this Part a "registered patent agent" means a person whose name is entered in the register kept under this section.

(2) The rules may contain such provision as the Secretary of State thinks fit regulating the registration of persons, and may in particular—

    (a) require the payment of such fees as may be prescribed, and

    (b) authorise in prescribed cases the erasure from the register of the name of any person registered in it, or the suspension of a person's registration.

(3) The rules may delegate the keeping of the register to another person, and may confer on that person—

    (a) power to make regulations—

        (i) with respect to the payment of fees, in the cases and subject to the limits prescribed by rules, and

        (ii) with respect to any other matter which could be regulated by rules, and

    (b) such other functions, including disciplinary functions, as may be prescribed by rules.

(4) Rules under this section shall be made by statutory instrument which shall be subject to annulment in pursuance of a resolution of either House of Parliament.

276.—(1) An individual who is not a registered patent agent shall not— Persons entitled to describe themselves as patent agents.

    (a) carry on a business (otherwise than in partnership) under any name or other description which contains the words "patent agent" or "patent attorney"; or

    (b) in the course of a business otherwise describe himself, or permit himself to be described, as a "patent agent" or "patent attorney".

271

(2) A partnership shall not—

(a) carry on a business under any name or other description which contains the words "patent agent" or "patent attorney"; or

(b) in the course of a business otherwise describe itself, or permit itself to be described as, a firm of "patent agents" or "patent attorneys".

unless all the partners are registered patent agents or the partnership satisfies such conditions as may be prescribed for the purposes of this section.

(3) A body corporate shall not—

(a) carry on a business (otherwise than in partnership) under any name or other description which contains the words "patent agent" or "patent attorney"; or

(b) in the course of a business otherwise describe itself, or permit itself to be described as, a "patent agent" or "patent attorney",

unless all the directors of the body corporate are registered patent agents or the body satisfies such conditions as may be prescribed for the purposes of this section.

(4) Subsection (3) does not apply to a company which began to carry on business as a patent agent before 17th November 1917 if the name of a director or the manager of the company who is a registered patent agent is mentioned as being so registered in all professional advertisements, circulars or letters issued by or with the company's consent on which its name appears.

(5) Where this section would be contravened by the use of the words "patent agent" or "patent attorney" in reference to an individual, partnership or body corporate, it is equally contravened by the use of other expressions in reference to that person, or his business or place of business, which are likely to be understood as indicating that he is entitled to be described as a "patent agent" or "patent attorney".

(6) A person who contravenes this section commits an offence and is liable on summary conviction to a fine not exceeding level 5 on the standard scale; and proceedings for such an offence may be begun at any time within a year from the date of the offence.

(7) This section has effect subject to—

(a) section 277 (persons entitled to describe themselves as European patent attorneys, &c.), and

(b) section 278(1) (use of term "patent attorney" in reference to solicitors).

Persons entitled to describe themselves as European patent attorneys, &c.

277.—(1) The term "European patent attorney" or "European patent agent" may be used in the following cases without any contravention of section 276.

(2) An individual who is on the European list may—

(a) carry on business under a name or other description which contains the words "European patent attorney" or "European patent agent", or

(b) otherwise describe himself, or permit himself to be described, as a "European patent attorney" or "European patent agent".

(3) A partnership of which not less than the prescribed number or proportion of partners is on the European list may—

(a) carry on a business under a name of other description which contains the words "European patent attorneys" or "European patent agents", or

(b) otherwise describe itself, or permit itself to be described, as a firm which carries on the business of a "European patent attorney" or "European patent agent".

(4) A body corporate of which not less than the prescribed number or proportion of directors is on the European list may—

(a) carry on a business under a name or other description which contains the words "European patent attorney" or "European patent agent", or

(b) otherwise describe itself, or permit itself to be described as, a company which carries on the business of a "European patent attorney" or "European patent agent".

(5) Where the term "European patent attorney" or "European patent agent" may, in accordance with this section, be used in reference to an individual, partnership or body corporate, it is equally permissible to use other expressions in reference to that person, or to his business or place of business, which are likely to be understood as indicating that he is entitled to be described as a "European patent attorney" or "European patent agent".

278.—(1) The term "patent attorney" may be used in reference to a solicitor, and a firm of solicitors may be described as a firm of "patent attorneys", without any contravention of section 276.

Use of the term "patent attorney": supplementary provisions.

(2) No offence is committed under the enactments restricting the use of certain expressions in reference to persons not qualified to act as solicitors—

(a) by the use of the term "patent attorney" in reference to a registered patent agent, or

(b) by the use of the term "European patent attorney" in reference to a person on the European list.

1974 c. 30.
1980 c. 46.
S.I. 1976/582.
(N.I. 12)

(3) The enactments referred to in subsection (2) are section 21 of the Solicitors Act 1974, section 31 of the Solicitors (Scotland) Act 1980 and Article 22 of the Solicitors (Northern Ireland) Order 1976.

1974 c.37.
1980 c.46.
S.I. 1976/582.
(N.I. 12).

279.—(1) The Secretary of State may make rules—

Power to prescribe conditions, &c. for mixed partnerships and bodies corporate.

(a) prescribing the conditions to be satisfied for the purposes of section 276 (persons entitled to describe themselves as patent agents) in relation to a partnership where not all the partners are qualified persons or a body corporate where not all the directors are qualified persons, and

(b) imposing requirements to be complied with by such partnerships and bodies corporate.

(2) The rules may, in particular—

(a) prescribe conditions as to the number or proportion of partners or directors who must be qualified persons;

(b) impose requirements as to—

(i) the identification of qualified and unqualified persons in professional advertisements, circulars or letters issued by or with the consent of the partnership or body corporate and which relate to it or to its business; and

(ii) the manner in which a partnership or body corporate is to organise its affairs so as to secure that qualified persons exercise a sufficient degree of control over the activities of unqualified persons.

(3) Contravention of a requirement imposed by the rules is an offence for which a person is liable on summary conviction to a fine not exceeding level 5 on the standard scale.

(4) The Secretary of State may make rules prescribing for the purposes of section 277 the number or proportion of partners of a partnership or directors of a body corporate who must be qualified persons in order for the partnership or body to take advantage of that section.

(5) In this section "qualified person"—

    (a) in subsections (1) and (2), means a person who is a registered patent agent, and

    (b) in subsection (4), means a person who is on the European list.

(6) Rules under this section shall be made by statutory instrument which shall be subject to annulment in pursuance of a resolution of either House of Parliament.

Privilege for communications with patent agents.

280.—(1) This section applies to communications as to any matter relating to the protection of any invention, design, technical information, trade mark or service mark, or as to any matter involving passing off.

(2) Any such communication—

    (a) between a person and his patent agent, or

    (b) for the purpose of obtaining, or in response to a request for, information which a person is seeking for the purpose of instructing his patent agent,

is privileged from disclosure in legal proceedings in England, Wales or Northern Ireland in the same way as a communication between a person and his solicitor or, as the case may be, a communication for the purpose of obtaining, or in response to a request for, information which a person seeks for the purpose of instructing his solicitor.

(3) In subsection (2) "patent agent" means—

    (a) a registered patent agent or a person who is on the European list,

    (b) a partnership entitled to describe itself as a firm of patent agents or as a firm carrying on the business of a European patent attorney, or

    (c) a body corporate entitled to describe itself as a patent agent or as a company carrying on the business of a European patent attorney.

(4) It is hereby declared that in Scotland the rules of law which confer privilege from disclosure in legal proceedings in respect of communications extend to such communications as are mentioned in this section.

Power of comptroller to refuse to deal with certain agents.
1949 c.87.
1949 c.88.
1977 c.37.

281.—(1) This section applies to business under the Patents Act 1949, the Registered Designs Act 1949 or the Patents Act 1977.

(2) The Secretary of State may make rules authorising the comptroller to refuse to recognise as agent in respect of any business to which this section applies—

    (a) a person who has been convicted of an offence under section 88 of the Patents Act 1949, section 114 of the Patents Act 1977 or section 276 of this Act;

    (b) an individual whose name has been erased from and not restored to, or who is suspended from, the register of patent agents on the ground of misconduct;

    (c) a person who is found by the Secretary of State to have been guilty of such conduct as would, in the case of an individual registered in the register of patent agents, render him liable to have his name erased from the register on the ground of misconduct;

(d) a partnership or body corporate of which one of the partners or directors is a person whom the comptroller could refuse to recognise under paragraph (a), (b) or (c) above.

(3) The rules may contain such incidental and supplementary provisions as appear to the Secretary of State to be appropriate and may, in particular, prescribe circumstances in which a person is or is not to be taken to have been guilty of misconduct.

(4) Rules made under this section shall be made by statutory instrument which shall be subject to annulment in pursuance of a resolution of either House of Parliament.

(5) The comptroller shall refuse to recognise as agent in respect of any business to which this section applies a person who neither resides nor has a place of business in the United Kingdom, the Isle of Man or another member State of the European Economic Community.

✷   ✷   ✷

Supplementary

285.—(1) Proceedings for an offence under this Part alleged to have been committed by a partnership shall be brought in the name of the partnership and not in that of the partners; but without prejudice to any liability of theirs under subsection (4) below. *Offences committed by partnerships and bodies corporate.*

(2) The following provisions apply for the purposes of such proceedings as in relation to a body corporate—

(a) any rules of court relating to the service of documents;

(b) in England, Wales or Northern Ireland, Schedule 3 to the Magistrates' Courts Act 1980 or Schedule 4 to the Magistrates' Courts (Northern Ireland) Order 1981 (procedure on charge of offence). *1980 c.43 S.I. 1981/1675 (N.I. 26).*

(3) A fine imposed on a partnership on its conviction in such proceedings shall be paid out of the partnership assets. *1980 c. 43. S.I. 1981/1675 (N.I. 26).*

(4) Where a partnership is guilty of an offence under this Part, every partner, other than a partner who is proved to have been ignorant of or to have attempted to prevent the commission of the offence, is also guilty of the offence and liable to be proceeded against and punished accordingly.

(5) Where an offence under this Part committed by a body corporate is proved to have been committed with the consent or connivance of a director, manager, secretary or other similar officer of the body, or a person purporting to act in any such capacity, he as well as the body corporate is guilty of the offence and liable to be proceeded against and punished accordingly.

286.—In this Part— *Interpretation.*
    "the comptroller" means the Comptroller-General of Patents, Designs and Trade Marks;

    "director", in relation to a body corporate whose affairs are managed by its members, means any member of the body corporate;

"the European list" means the list of professional representatives maintained by the European Patent Office in pursuance of the European Patent Convention;

"registered patent agent" has the meaning given by section 275(1);

"registered trade mark agent" has the meaning given by section 282(1).

PART VI

PATENTS

Patents county courts

Patents county courts: special jurisdiction.

287.—(1) The Lord Chancellor may by order made by statutory instrument designate any county court as a patents county court and confer on it jurisdiction (its "special jurisdiction") to hear and determine such descriptions of proceedings—

(a) relating to patents or designs, or

(b) ancillary to, or arising out of the same subject matter as, proceedings relating to patents or designs,

as may be specified in the order.

(2) The special jurisdiction of a patents county court is exercisable throughout England and Wales, but rules of court may provide for a matter pending in one such court to be heard and determined in another or partly in that and partly in another.

(3) A patents county court may entertain proceedings within its special jurisdiction notwithstanding that no pecuniary remedy is sought.

(4) An order under this section providing for the discontinuance of any of the special jurisdiction of a patents county court may make provision as to proceedings pending in the court when the order comes into operation.

(5) Nothing in this section shall be construed as affecting the ordinary jurisdiction of a county court.

Financial limits in relation to proceedings within special jurisdiction of patents county court.

288.—(1) Her Majesty may by Order in Council provide for limits of amount or value in relation to any description of proceedings within the special jurisdiction of a patents county court.

(2) If a limit is imposed on the amount of a claim of any description and the plaintiff has a cause of action for more than that amount, he may abandon the excess; in which case a patents county court shall have jurisdiction to hear and determine the action, but the plaintiff may not recover more than that amount.

(3) Where the court has jurisdiction to hear and determine an action by virtue of subsection (2), the judgment of the court in the action is in full discharge of all demands in respect of the cause of action, and entry of the judgment shall be made accordingly.

(4) If the parties agree, by a memorandum signed by them or by their respective solicitors or other agents, that a patents county court shall have jurisdiction in any proceedings, that court shall have jurisdiction to hear and determine the proceedings notwithstanding any limit imposed under this section.

(5) No recommendation shall be made to Her Majesty to make an Order under this section unless a draft of the Order has been laid before and approved by a resolution of each House of Parliament.

289.—(1) No order shall be made under section 41 of the County Courts Act 1984 (power of High Court to order proceedings to be transferred from the county court) in respect of proceedings within the special jurisdiction of a patents county court.

(2) In considering in relation to proceedings within the special jurisdiction of a patents county court whether an order should be made under section 40 or 42 of the County Courts Act 1984 (transfer of proceedings from or to the High Court), the court shall have regard to the financial position of the parties and may order the transfer of the proceedings to a patents county court or, as the case may be, refrain from ordering their transfer to the High Court notwithstanding that the proceedings are likely to raise an important question of fact or law.

290.—(1) Where an action is commenced in the High Court which could have been commenced in a patents county court and in which a claim for a pecuniary remedy is made, then, subject to the provisions of this section, if the plaintiff recovers less than the prescribed amount, he is not entitled to recover any more costs than those to which he would have been entitled if the action had been brought in the county court.

(2) For this purpose a plaintiff shall be treated as recovering the full amount recoverable in respect of his claim without regard to any deduction made in respect of matters not falling to be taken into account in determining whether the action could have been commenced in a patents county court.

(3) This section does not affect any question as to costs if it appears to the High Court that there was reasonable ground for supposing the amount recoverable in respect of the plaintiff's claim to be in excess of the prescribed amount.

(4) The High Court, if satisfied that there was sufficient reason for bringing the action in the High Court, may make an order allowing the costs or any part of the costs on the High Court scale or on such one of the county court scales as it may direct.

(5) This section does not apply to proceedings brought by the Crown.

(6) In this section "the prescribed amount" means such amount as may be prescribed by Her Majesty for the purposes of this section by Order in Council.

(7) No recommendation shall be made to Her Majesty to make an Order under this section unless a draft of the Order has been laid before and approved by a resolution of each House of Parliament.

291.—(1) Where a county court is designated a patents county court, the Lord Chancellor shall nominate a person entitled to sit as a judge of that court as the patents judge.

(2) County court rules shall make provision for securing that, so far as is practicable and appropriate—

  (a) proceedings within the special jurisdiction of a patents county court are dealt with by the patents judge, and

  (b) the judge, rather than a registrar or other officer of the court, deals with interlocutory matters in the proceedings.

(3) County court rules shall make provision empowering a patents county court in proceedings within its special jurisdiction, on or without the application of any party—

(a) to appoint scientific advisers or assessors to assist the court, or

(b) to order the Patent Office to inquire into and report on any question of fact or opinion.

(4) Where the court exercises either of those powers on the application of a party, the remuneration or fees payable to the Patent Office shall be at such rate as may be determined in accordance with county court rules and shall be costs of the proceedings unless otherwise ordered by the judge.

(5) Where the court exercises either of those powers of its own motion, the remuneration or fees payable to the Patent Office shall be at such rate as may be determined by the Lord Chancellor with the approval of the Treasury and shall be paid out of money provided by Parliament.

Rights and duties of registered patent agents in relation to proceedings in patents county court.

292.—(1) A registered patent agent may do, in or in connection with proceedings in a patents county court which are within the special jurisdiction of that court, anything which a solicitor of the Supreme Court might do, other than prepare a deed.

(2) The Lord Chancellor may by regulations provide that the right conferred by subsection (1) shall be subject to such conditions and restrictions as appear to the Lord Chancellor to be necessary or expedient; and different provision may be made for different descriptions of proceedings.

(3) A patents county court has the same power to enforce an undertaking given by a registered patent agent acting in pursuance of this section as it has, by virtue of section 142 of the County Courts Act 1984, in relation to a solicitor.

1984 c. 28.

(4) Nothing in section 143 of the County Courts Act 1984 (prohibition on persons other than solicitors receiving remuneration) applies to a registered patent agent acting in pursuance of this section.

(5) The provisions of county court rules prescribing scales of costs to be paid to solicitors apply in relation to registered patent agents acting in pursuance of this section.

(6) Regulations under this section shall be made by statutory instrument which shall be subject to annulment in pursuance of a resolution of either House of Parliament.

Licences of right in respect of certain patents

Restriction of acts authorised by certain licences. 1977 c. 37.

293.—In paragraph 4(2)(c) of Schedule 1 to the Patents Act 1977 (licences to be available as of right where term of existing patent extended), at the end insert ", but subject to paragraph 4A below", and after that paragraph insert—

"**4A.**—(1) If the proprietor of a patent for an invention which is a product files a declaration with the Patent Office in accordance with this paragraph, the licences to which persons are entitled by virtue of paragraph 4(2)(c) above shall not extend to a use of the product which is excepted by or under this paragraph.

(2) Pharmaceutical use is excepted, that is—

(a) use as a medicinal product within the meaning of the Medicines Act 1968, and

(b) the doing of any other act mentioned in section 60(1)(a) above with a view to such use.

(3) The Secretary of State may by order except such other uses as he thinks fit; and an order may—

(a) specify as an excepted use any act mentioned in section 60(1)(a) above, and

(b) make different provision with respect to acts done in different circumstances or for different purposes.

(4) For the purposes of this paragraph the question what uses are excepted, so far as that depends on—

(a) orders under section 130 of the Medicines Act 1968 (meaning of "medicinal product"), or

(b) orders under sub-paragraph (3) above,

shall be determined in relation to a patent at the beginning of the sixteenth year of the patent.

(5) A declaration under this paragraph shall be in the prescribed form and shall be filed in the prescribed manner and within the prescribed time limits.

(6) A declaration may not be filed—

(a) in respect of a patent which has at the commencement of section 293 of the Copyright, Designs and Patents Act 1988 passed the end of its fifteenth year; or

(b) if at the date of filing there is—

(i) an existing licence for any description of excepted use of the product, or

(ii) an outstanding application under section 46(3)(a) or (b) above for the settlement by the comptroller of the terms of a licence for any description of excepted use of the product,

and in either case, the licence took or is to take effect at or after the end of the sixteenth year of the patent.

(7) Where a declaration has been filed under this paragraph in respect of a patent—

(a) section 46(3)(c) above (restriction of remedies for infringement where licences available as of right) does not apply to an infringement of the patent in so far as it consists of the excepted use of the product after the filing of the declaration; and

(b) section 46(3)(d) above (abatement of renewal fee if licences available as of right) does not apply to the patent.".

294.—In Schedule 1 to the Patents Act 1977, after the paragraph inserted by section 293 above, insert— *When application may be made for settlement of terms of licence. 1977 c. 37.*

"4B—(1) An application under section 46(3)(a) or (b) above for the settlement by the comptroller of the terms on which a person is entitled to a licence by virtue of paragraph 4(2)(c) above is ineffective if made before the beginning of the sixteenth year of the patent.

(2) This paragraph applies to applications made after the commencement of section 294 of the Copyright, Designs and Patents Act 1988 and to any application made before the commencement of that section in respect of a patent which has not at the commencement of that section passed the end of its fifteenth year.".

Patents: miscellaneous amendments

295.—The Patents Act 1949 and the Patents Act 1977 are amended in accordance with Schedule 5. *Patents: miscellaneous amendments. 1949 c. 87.*

*   *   *

SCHEDULE 5

PATENTS: MISCELLANEOUS AMENDMENTS

Withdrawal of application before publication of specification

1949 c. 87.
1. In section 13(2) of the Patents Act 1949 (duty of comptroller to advertise acceptance of and publish complete specification) after the word "and", in the first place where it occurs, insert ", unless the application is withdrawn,".

Correction of clerical errors

2.—(1) In section 15 of the Patents Act 1977 (filing of application), after subsection (3) insert—

1977 c. 37.

"(3A) Nothing in subsection (2) or (3) above shall be construed as affecting the power of the comptroller under section 117(1) below to correct errors or mistakes with respect to the filing of drawings.".

(2) The above amendment applies only in relation to applications filed after the commencement of this paragraph.

Supplementary searches

3.—(1) Section 17 of the Patents Act 1977 (preliminary examination and search) is amended as follows.

(2) In subsection (7) (supplementary searches) for "subsection (4) above" substitute "subsections (4) and (5) above" and for "it applies" substitute "they apply".

(3) After that subsection add—

"(8) A reference for a supplementary search in consequence of—

(a) an amendment of the application made by the applicant under section 18(3) or 19(1) below, or

(b) a correction of the application, or of a document filed in connection with the application, under section 117 below,

shall be made only on payment of the prescribed fee, unless the comptroller directs otherwise.".

4. In section 18 of the Patents Act 1977 (substantive examination and grant or refusal of patent), after subsection (1) insert—

"(1A) If the examiner forms the view that a supplementary search under section 17 above is required for which a fee is payable, he shall inform the comptroller, who may decide that the substantive examination should not proceed until the fee is paid; and if he so decides, then unless within such period as he may allow—

(a) the fee is paid, or

(b) the application is amended so as to render the supplementary search unnecessary,

he may refuse the application.".

5. In section 130(1) of the Patents Act 1977 (interpretation), in the definition of "search fee", for "section 17 above" substitute "section 17(1) above".

Application for restoration of lapsed patent

6.—(1) Section 28 of the Patents Act 1977 (restoration of lapsed patents) is amended as follows.

(2) For subsection (1) (application for restoration within period of one year) substitute—

"(1) Where a patent has ceased to have effect by reason of a failure to pay any renewal fee, an application for the restoration of the patent may be made to the comptroller within the prescribed period.

(1A) Rules prescribing that period may contain such transitional provisions and savings as appear to the Secretary of State to be necessary or expedient.".

(3) After subsection (2) insert—

"(2A) Notice of the application shall be published by the comptroller in the prescribed manner.".

(4) In subsection (3), omit paragraph (b) (requirement that failure to renew is due to circumstances beyond proprietor's control) and the word "and" preceding it.

This amendment does not apply to a patent which has ceased to have effect in ^1977 c. 37. accordance with section 25(3) of the Patents Act 1977 (failure to renew within prescribed period) and in respect of which the period referred to in subsection (4) of that section (six months' period of grace for renewal) has expired before commencement.

(5) Omit subsections (5) to (9) (effect of order for restoration).

7. After that section insert—

28A.—(1) The effect of an order for the restoration of a patent is as follows.

Effect of order for restoration of patent.

(2) Anything done under or in relation to the patent during the period between expiry and restoration shall be treated as valid.

(3) Anything done during that period which would have constituted an infringement if the patent had not expired shall be treated as an infringement—
 (a) if done at a time when it was possible for the patent to be renewed under section 25(4), or
 (b) if it was a continuation or repetition of an earlier infringing act.

(4) If after it was no longer possible for the patent to be so renewed, and before publication of notice of the application for restoration, a person—
 (a) began in good faith to do an act which would have constituted an infringement of the patent if it had not expired, or
 (b) made in good faith effective and serious preparations to do such an act.

he has the right to continue to do the act or, as the case may be, to do the act, notwithstanding the restoration of the patent; but this right does not extend to granting a licence to another person to do the act.

(5) If the act was done, or the preparations were made, in the course of a business, the person entitled to the right conferred by subsection (4) may—

> (a) authorise the doing of that act by any partners of his for the time being in that business, and
>
> (b) assign that right, or transmit it on death (or in the case of a body corporate on its dissolution), to any person who acquires that part of the business in the course of which the act was done or the preparations were made.

(6) Where a product is disposed of to another in exercise of the rights conferred by subsection (4) or (5), that other and any person claiming through him may deal with the product in the same way as if it had been disposed of by the registered proprietor of the patent.

> (7) The above provisions apply in relation to the use of a patent for the services of the Crown as they apply in relation to infringement of the patent.".

8. In consequence of the above amendments—

1977c. 37.

> (a) in section 60(6)(b) of the Patents Act 1977, for "section 28(6)" substitute "section 28A(4) or (5)"; and
>
> (b) in sections 77(5), 78(6) and 80(4) of that Act, for the words from "section 28(6)" to the end substitute "section 28A(4) and (5) above, and subsections (6) and (7) of that section shall apply accordingly.".

Determination of right to patent after grant

9.—(1) Section 37 of the Patents Act 1977 (determination of right to patent after grant) is amended as follows.

(2) For subsection (1) substitute—

> "(1) After a patent has been granted for an invention any person having or claiming a proprietary interest in or under the patent may refer to the comptroller the question—
>
> (a) who is or are the true proprietor or proprietors of the patent,
>
> (b) whether the patent should have been granted to the person or persons to whom it was granted, or
>
> (c) whether any right in or under the patent should be transferred or granted to any other person or persons;
>
> and the comptroller shall determine the question and make such order as he thinks fit to give effect to the determination.".

(3) Substitute "this section"—

> (a) in subsections (4) and (7) for "subsection (1)(a) above", and
>
> (b) in subsection (8) for "subsection (1) above".

10. In section 74(6) (meaning of "entitlement proceedings"), for "section 37(1)(a) above" substitute "section 37(1) above".

Employees' inventions

11.—(1) In section 39 of the Patents Act 1977 (right to employees' inventions), after subsection (2) add—

> "(3) Where by virtue of this section an invention belongs, as between him and his employer, to an employee, nothing done—
>
> (a) by or on behalf of the employee or any person claiming under

him for the purpose of pursuing an application for a patent, or

(b) by any person for the purpose of performing or working the invention,

shall be taken to infringe any copyright or design right to which, as between him and his employer, his employer is entitled in any model or document relating to the invention.".

(2) In section 43 of the Patents Act 1977 (supplementary provisions with respect to employees' inventions), in subsection (4) (references to patents to include other forms of protection, whether in UK or elsewhere) for "in sections 40 to 42" substitute "in sections 39 to 42.". 1977 c. 37.

Undertaking to take licence in infringement proceedings

12.—(1) Section 46 of the Patents Act 1977 (licences of right) is amended as follows.

(2) In subsection (3)(c) (undertaking to take licence in infringement proceedings) after the words "(otherwise than by the importation of any article" insert "from a country which is not a member State of the European Economic Community".

(3) After subsection (3) insert—

" (3A) An undertaking under subsection (3)(c) above may be given at any time before final order in the proceedings, without any admission of liability.".

Power of comptroller on grant of compulsory licence

13. In section 49 of the Patents Act 1977 (supplementary provisions with respect to compulsory licences), omit subsection (3) (power to order that licence has effect to revoke existing licences and deprive proprietor of power to work invention or grant licences).

Powers exercisable in consequence of report of Monopolies and Mergers Commission

14. For section 51 of the Patents Act 1977 (licences of right: application by Crown in consequence of report of Monopolies and Mergers Commission) substitute—

51.—(1) Where a report of the Monopolies and Mergers Commission has been laid before Parliament containing conclusions to the effect—

    (a) on a monopoly reference, that a monopoly situation exists and facts found by the Commission operate or may be expected to operate against the public interest,

    (b) on a merger reference, that a merger situation qualifying for investigation has been created and the creation of the situation, or particular elements in or consequences of it specified in the report, operate or may be expected to operate against the public interest,

    (c) on a competition reference, that a person was engaged in an anti-competitive practice which operated or may be expected to operate against the public interest, or

    (d) on a reference under section 11 of the Competition Act 1980 (reference of public bodies and certain other persons), that a person is pursuing a course of conduct which operates against the public interest,

"Powers exercisable in consequence of report of Monopolies and Mergers Commission.

the appropriate Minister or Ministers may apply to the comptroller to take action under this section.

(2) Before making an application the appropriate Minister or Ministers shall publish, in such manner as he or they think appropriate, a notice describing the nature of the proposed application and shall consider any representations which may be made within 30 days of such publication by persons whose interests appear to him or them to be affected.

(3) If on an application under this section it appears to the comptroller that the matters specified in the Commission's report as being those which in the Commission's opinion operate, or operated or may be expected to operate, against the public interest include—

(a) conditions in licences granted under a patent by its proprietor restricting the use of the invention by the licensee or the right of the proprietor to grant other licences, or

(b) a refusal by the proprietor of a patent to grant licences on reasonable terms

he may by order cancel or modify any such condition or may, instead or in addition, make an entry in the register to the effect that licences under the patent are to be available as of right.

(4) In this section "the appropriate Minister or Ministers" means the Minister or Ministers to whom the report of the Commission was made.".

Compulsory licensing: reliance on statements in competition report

15. In section 53(2) of the Patents Act 1977 (compulsory licensing: reliance on statements in reports of Monopolies and Mergers Commission)—

1977 c.37.

(a) for "application made in relation to a patent under sections 48 to 51 above" substitute "application made under section 48 above in respect of a patent"; and

(b) after "Part VIII of the Fair Trading Act 1973" insert "or section 17 of the Competition Act 1980".

Crown use: compensation for loss of profit

16.—(1) In the Patents Act 1977, after section 57 insert—

57A.—(1) Where use is made of an invention for the services of the Crown, the government department concerned shall pay—

(a) to the proprietor of the patent, or

(b) if there is an exclusive licence in force in respect of the patent, to the exclusive licensee,

compensation for any loss resulting from his not being awarded a contract to supply the patented product or, as the case may be, to perform the patented process or supply a thing made by means of the patented process.

(2) Compensation is payable only to the extent that such a contract could have been fulfilled from his existing manufacturing or other capacity; but is payable notwithstanding the existence of circumstances rendering him ineligible for the award of such a contract.

(3) In determining the loss, regard shall be had to the profit which would have been made on such a contract and to the extent to which any manufacturing or other capacity was under-used.

(4) No compensation is payable in respect of any failure to secure contracts to supply the patented product or, as the case may be, to perform the patented process or supply a thing made by means of the patented process, otherwise than for the services of the Crown.

(5) The amount payable shall, if not agreed between the proprietor or licensee and the government department concerned with the approval of the Treasury, be determined by the court on a reference under section 58, and is in addition to any amount payable under section 55 or 57.

(6) In this section 'the government department concerned', in relation to any use of an invention for the services of the Crown, means the government department by whom or on whose authority the use was made.

(7) In the application of this section to Northern Ireland, the reference in subsection (5) above to the Treasury shall, where the government department concerned is a department of the Government of Northern Ireland, be construed as a reference to the Department of Finance and Personnel.".

(2) In section 58 of the Patents Act 1977 (reference of disputes as to Crown use), for subsection (1) substitute— 1977 c.37.
"(1) Any dispute as to—

> (a) the exercise by a government department, or a person authorised by a government department, of the powers conferred by section 55 above,
>
> (b) terms for the use of an invention for the services of the Crown under that section,
>
> (c) the right of any person to receive any part of a payment made in pursuance of subsection (4) of that section, or
>
> (d) the right of any person to receive a payment under section 57A,

may be referred to the court by either party to the dispute after a patent has been granted for the invention.";

and in subsection (4) for "under this section" substitute "under subsection (1)(a), (b) or (c) above".

(3) In section 58(11) of the Patents Act 1977 (exclusion of right to compensation for Crown use if relevant transaction, instrument or event not registered), after "section 57(3) above)" insert ", or to any compensation under section 57A above,".

(4) The above amendments apply in relation to any use of an invention for the services of the Crown after the commencement of this section, even if the terms for such use were settled before commencement.

Right to continue use begun before priority date

17. For section 64 of the Patents Act 1977 (right to continue use begun before priority date) substitute—

64.—(1) Where a patent is granted for an invention, a person who in the United Kingdom before the priority date of the invention— "Right to continue use begun before priority date.

> (a) does in good faith an act which would constitute an infringement of the patent if it were in force, or

(b) makes in good faith effective and serious preparations to do such an act,

has the right to continue to do the act or, as the case may be, to do the act, notwithstanding the grant of the patent; but this right does not extend to granting a licence to another person to do the act.

(2) If the act was done, or the preparations were made, in the course of a business, the person entitled to the right conferred by subsection (1) may—

(a) authorise the doing of that act by any partners of his for the time being in that business, and

(b) assign that right, or transmit it on death (or in the case of a body corporate on its dissolution), to any person who acquires that part of the business in the course of which the act was done or the preparations were made.

(3) Where a product is disposed of to another in exercise of the rights conferred by subsection (1) or (2), that other and any person claiming through him may deal with the product in the same way as if it had been disposed of by the registered proprietor of the patent.".

Revocation on grounds of grant to wrong person

1977 c.37.

18. In section 72(1) of the Patents Act 1977 (grounds for revocation of patent), for paragraph (b) substitute—

"(b) that the patent was granted to a person who was not entitled to be granted that patent;".

Revocation where two patents granted for same invention

19. In section 73 of the Patents Act 1977 (revocation on initiative of comptroller), for subsections (2) and (3) (revocation of patent where European patent (UK) granted in respect of same invention) substitute—

"(2) If it appears to the comptroller that a patent under this Act and a European patent (UK) have been granted for the same invention having the same priority date, and that the applications for the patents were filed by the same applicant or his successor in title, he shall give the proprietor of the patent under this Act an opportunity of making observations and of amending the specification of the patent, and if the proprietor fails to satisfy the comptroller that there are not two patents in respect of the same invention, or to amend the specification so as to prevent there being two patents in respect of the same invention, the comptroller shall revoke the patent.

(3) The comptroller shall not take action under subsection (2) above before—

(a) the end of the period for filing an opposition to the European patent (UK) under the European Patent Convention, or

(b) if later, the date on which opposition proceedings are finally disposed of;

and he shall not then take any action if the decision is not to maintain the European patent or if it is amended so that there are not two patents in respect of the same invention.

(4) The comptroller shall not take action under subsection (2) above if the European patent (UK) has been surrendered under

section 29(1) above before the date on which by virtue of section 25(1) above the patent under this Act is to be treated as having been granted or, if proceedings for the surrender of the European patent (UK) have been begun before that date, until those proceedings are finally disposed of; and he shall not then take any action if the decision is to accept the surrender of the European patent.".

Applications and amendments not to include additional matter

20. For section 76 of the Patents Act 1977 (amendments of applications and patents not to include added matter) substitute— 1977 c. 37.

76.—(1) An application for a patent which—

(a) is made in respect of matter disclosed in an earlier application, or in the specification of a patent which has been granted, and

(b) discloses additional matter, that is, matter extending beyond that disclosed in the earlier application, as filed, or the application for the patent, as filed,

may be filed under section 8(3), 12 or 37(4) above, or as mentioned in section 15(4) above, but shall not be allowed to proceed unless it is amended so as to exclude the additional matter.

(2) No amendment of an application for a patent shall be allowed under section 17(3), 18(3) or 19(1) if it results in the application disclosing matter extending beyond that disclosed in the application as filed.

(3) No amendment of the specification of a patent shall be allowed under section 27(1), 73 or 75 if it—

(a) results in the specification disclosing additional matter, or

(b) extends the protection conferred by the patent.".

Amendments of applications and patents not to include added matter.

Effect of European patent (UK)

21.—(1) Section 77 of the Patents Act 1977 (effect of European patent (UK)) is amended as follows.

(2) For subsection (3) (effect of finding of partial validity on pending proceedings) substitute—

"(3) Where in the case of a European patent (UK)—

(a) proceedings for infringement, or proceedings under section 58 above, have been commenced before the court or the comptroller and have not been finally disposed of, and

(b) it is established in proceedings before the European Patent Office that the patent is only partially valid,

the provisions of section 63 or, as the case may be, of subsections (7) to (9) of section 58 apply as they apply to proceedings in which the validity of a patent is put in issue and in which it is found that the patent is only partially valid.".

(3) For subsection (4) (effect of amendment or revocation under European Patent Convention) substitute—

"(4) Where a European patent (UK) is amended in accordance with the European Patent Convention, the amendment shall have effect for the purposes of Parts I and III of this Act as if the specification of the patent had been amended under this Act; but subject to subsection (6)(b) below.

(4A) Where a European patent (UK) is revoked in accordance with the European Patent Convention, the patent shall be treated for the purposes of Parts I and III of this Act as having been revoked under this Act.".

(4) In subsection (6) (filing of English translation), in paragraph (b) (amendments) for "a translation of the amendment into English" substitute "a translation into English of the specification as amended".

(5) In subsection (7) (effect of failure to file translation) for the words from "a translation" to "above" substitute "such a translation is not filed".

The state of the art: material contained in patent applications

1977 c. 37.

22. In section 78 of the Patents Act 1977 (effect of filing an application for a European patent (UK)), for subsection (5) (effect of withdrawal of application, &c.) substitute—

"(5) Subsections (1) to (3) above shall cease to apply to an application for a European patent (UK), except as mentioned in subsection (5A) below, if—

(a) the application is refused or withdrawn or deemed to be withdrawn, or

(b) the designation of the United Kingdom in the application is withdrawn or deemed to be withdrawn,

but shall apply again if the rights of the applicant are re-established under the European Patent Convention, as from their re-establishment.

(5A) The occurrence of any of the events mentioned in subsection (5)(a) or (b) shall not affect the continued operation of section 2(3) above in relation to matter contained in an application for a European patent (UK) which by virtue of that provision has become part of the state of the art as regards other inventions.".

Jurisdiction in certain proceedings

23. Section 88 of the Patents Act 1977 (jurisdiction in legal proceedings in connection with Community Patent Convention) is repealed.

Effect of filing international application for patent

24.—(1) Section 89 of the Patents Act 1977 (effect of filing international application for patent) is amended as follows.

(2) After subsection (3) insert—

"(3A). If the relevant conditions are satisfied with respect to an application which is amended in accordance with the Treaty and the relevant conditions are not satisfied with respect to any amendment, that amendment shall be disregarded.".

(3) After subsection (4) insert—

"(4A). In subsection (4)(a) 'a copy of the application' includes a copy of the application published in accordance with the Treaty in a language other than that in which it was filed.".

(4) For subsection (10) (exclusion of certain applications subject to European Patent Convention) substitute—

> "(10). The foregoing provisions of this section do not apply to an application which falls to be treated as an international application for a patent (UK) by reason only of its containing an indication that the applicant wishes to obtain a European patent (UK); but without prejudice to the application of those provisions to an application which also separately designates the United Kingdom.".

(5) The amendments in this paragraph shall be deemed always to have had effect.

(6) This paragraph shall be repealed by the order bringing the following paragraph into force.

25. For section 89 of the Patents Act 1977 (effect of filing international application 1977 c. 37. for patent) substitute—

> 89.—(1) An international application for a patent (UK) for which "Effect of a date of filing has been accorded under the Patent Co-operation international Treaty shall, subject to— application for patent.
>
> section 89A (international and national phases of application), and
>
> section 89B (adaptation of provisions in relation to international application),
>
> be treated for the purposes of Parts I and III of this Act as an application for a patent under this Act.
>
> (2) If the application, or the designation of the United Kingdom in it, is withdrawn or (except as mentioned in subsection (3)) deemed to be withdrawn under the Treaty, it shall be treated as withdrawn under this Act.
>
> (3) An application shall not be treated as withdrawn under this Act if it, or the designation of the United Kingdom in it, is deemed to be withdrawn under the Treaty—
>
> > (a) because of an error or omission in an institution having functions under the Treaty, or
> >
> > (b) because, owing to circumstances outside the applicant's control, a copy of the application was not received by the International Bureau before the end of the time limited for that purpose under the Treaty,
>
> or in such other circumstances as may be prescribed.
>
> (4) For the purposes of the above provisions an application shall not be treated as an international application for a patent (UK) by reason only of its containing an indication that the applicant wishes to obtain a European patent (UK), but an application shall be so treated if it also separately designates the United Kingdom.
>
> (5) If an international application for a patent which designates the United Kingdom is refused a filing date under the Treaty and the comptroller determines that the refusal was caused by an error or omission in an institution having functions under the Treaty, he may direct that the application shall be treated as an application under this Act, having such date of filing as he may direct.

89A.—(1) The provisions of the Patent Co-operation Treaty relating to publication, search, examination and amendment, and not those of this Act, apply to an international application for a patent (UK) during the international phase of the application.

(2) The international phase of the application means the period from the filing of the application in accordance with the Treaty until the national phase of the application begins.

(3) The national phase of the application begins—

(a) when the prescribed period expires, provided any necessary translation of the application into English has been filed at the Patent Office and the prescribed fee has been paid by the applicant; or

(b) on the applicant expressly requesting the comptroller to proceed earlier with the national phase of the application, filing at the Patent Office—

(i) a copy of the application, if none has yet been sent to the Patent Office in accordance with the Treaty, and

(ii) any necessary translation of the application into English,

and paying the prescribed fee.

For this purpose a "copy of the application" includes a copy published in accordance with the Treaty in a language other than that in which it was originally filed.

(4) If the prescribed period expires without the conditions mentioned in subsection (3)(a) being satisfied, the application shall be taken to be withdrawn.

(5) Where during the international phase the application is amended in accordance with the Treaty, the amendment shall be treated as made under this Act if—

(a) when the prescribed period expires, any necessary translation of the amendment into English has been filed at the Patent Office, or

(b) where the applicant expressly requests the comptroller to proceed earlier with the national phase of the application, there is then filed at the Patent Office—

(i) a copy of the amendment, if none has yet been sent to the Patent Office in accordance with the Treaty, and

(ii) any necessary translation of the amendment into English;

otherwise the amendment shall be disregarded.

(6) The comptroller shall on payment of the prescribed fee publish any translation filed at the Patent Office under subsection (3) or (5) above.

89B.—(1) Where an international application for a patent (UK) is accorded a filing date under the Patent Co-operation Treaty—

(a) that date, or if the application is re-dated under the Treaty to a later date that later date, shall be treated as the date of filing the application under this Act,

(b) any declaration of priority made under the Treaty shall be treated as made under section 5(2) above, and where in accordance with the Treaty any extra days are allowed, the period of 12 months specified in section 5(2) shall be treated as altered accordingly, and

(c) any statement of the name of the inventor under the Treaty shall be treated as a statement filed under section 13(2) above.

(2) If the application, not having been published under this Act, is published in accordance with the Treaty it shall be treated, for purposes other than those mentioned in subsection (3), as published under section 16 above when the conditions mentioned in section 89A(3)(a) are complied with.

(3) For the purposes of section 55 (use of invention for service of the Crown) and section 69 (infringement of rights conferred by publication) the application, not having been published under this Act, shall be treated as published under section 16 above—

(a) if it is published in accordance with the Treaty in English, on its being so published; and

(b) if it is so published in a language other than English—

(i) on the publication of a translation of the application in accordance with section 89A(6) above, or

(ii) on the service by the applicant of a translation into English of the specification of the application on the government department concerned or, as the case may be, on the person committing the infringing act.

The reference in paragraph (b)(ii) to the service of a translation on a government department or other person is to its being sent by post or delivered to that department or person.

(4) During the international phase of the application, section 8 above does not apply (determination of questions of entitlement in relation to application under this Act) and section 12 above (determination of entitlement in relation to foreign and convention patents) applies notwithstanding the application; but after the end of the international phase, section 8 applies and section 12 does not.

(5) When the national phase begins the comptroller shall refer the application for so much of the examination and search under section 17 and 18 above as he considers appropriate in view of any examination or search carried out under the Treaty.".

Proceedings before the court or the comptroller

26. In the Patents Act 1977, after section 99 (general powers of the court) 1977 c. 37. insert—

99A.—(1) Rules of court shall make provision empowering the "Power of Patents Court in any proceedings before it under this Act, on or Patents Court to without the application of any party, to order the Patent Office to order report. inquire into and report on any question of fact or opinion.

(2) Where the court makes such an order on the application of a party, the fee payable to the Patent Office shall be at such rate as

may be determined in accordance with rules of court and shall be costs of the proceedings unless otherwise ordered by the court.

(3) Where the court makes such an order of its own motion, the fee payable to the Patent Office shall be at such rate as may be determined by the Lord Chancellor with the approval of the Treasury and shall be paid out of money provided by Parliament.

Power of Court
of Session to
order report.

99B.—(1) In any proceedings before the Court of Session under this Act the court may, either of its own volition or on the application of any party, order the Patent Office to inquire into and report on any question of fact or opinion.

(2) Where the court makes an order under subsection (1) above of its own volition the fee payable to the Patent Office shall be at such rate as may be determined by the Lord President of the Court of Session with the consent of the Treasury and shall be defrayed out of moneys provided by Parliament.

(3) Where the court makes an order under subsection (1) above on the application of a party, the fee payable to the Patent Office shall be at such rate as may be provided for in rules of court and shall be treated as expenses in the cause.".

1977 c. 37.

27. For section 102 of the Patents Act 1977 (right of audience in patent proceedings) substitute—

"Right of
audience, &c. in
proceedings
before
comptroller.

102.—(1) A party to proceedings before the comptroller under this Act, or under any treaty or international convention to which the United Kingdom is a party, may appear before the comptroller in person or be represented by any person whom he desires to represent him.

(2) No offence is committed under the enactments relating to the preparation of documents by persons not legally qualified by reason only of the preparation by any person of a document, other than a deed, for use in such proceedings.

(3) Subsection (1) has effect subject to rules made under section 281 of the Copyright, Designs and Patents Act 1988 (power of comptroller to refuse to recognise certain agents).

(4) In its application to proceedings in relation to applications for, or otherwise in connection with, European patents, this section has effect subject to any restrictions imposed by or under the European Patent Convention.

Right of
audience, &c. in
proceedings on
appeal from the
comptroller.

102A.—(1) A solicitor of the Supreme Court may appear and be heard on behalf of any party to an appeal under this Act from the comptroller to the Patents Court.

(2) A registered patent agent or a member of the Bar not in actual practice may do, in or in connection with proceedings on an appeal under this Act from the comptroller to the Patents Court, anything which a solicitor of the Supreme Court might do, other than prepare a deed.

(3) The Lord Chancellor may by regulations—

(a) provide that the right conferred by subsection (2) shall be subject to such conditions and restrictions as appear to the Lord Chancellor to be necessary or expedient, and

(b) apply to persons exercising that right such statutory provisions, rules of court and other rules of law and practice applying to solicitors as may be specified in the regulations;

and different provision may be made for different descriptions of proceedings.

(4) Regulations under this section shall be made by statutory instrument which shall be subject to annulment in pursuance of a resolution of either House of Parliament.

(5) This section is without prejudice to the right of counsel to appear before the High Court.".

Provision of information

28. In section 118 of the Patents Act 1977 (information about patent applications, &c.), in subsection (3) (restriction on disclosure before publication of application: exceptions) for "section 22(6)(a) above" substitute "section 22(6) above". *1977 c. 37.*

Power to extend time limits

29. In section 123 of the Patents Act 1977 (rules), after subsection (3) insert—

"(3A) It is hereby declared that rules—

(a) authorising the rectification of irregularities of procedure, or
(b) providing for the alteration of any period of time,

may authorise the comptroller to extend or further extend any period notwithstanding that the period has already expired.".

Availability of samples of micro-organisms

30. In the Patents Act 1977 after section 125 insert—

125A.—(1) Provision may be made by rules prescribing the circumstances in which the specification of an application for a patent, or of a patent, for an invention which requires for its performance the use of a micro-organism is to be treated as disclosing the invention in a manner which is clear enough and complete enough for the invention to be performed by a person skilled in the art. *"Disclosure of invention by specification: availability of samples of micro-organisms.*

(2) The rules may in particular require the applicant or patentee—

(a) to take such steps as may be prescribed for the purposes of making available to the public samples of the micro-organism, and

(b) not to impose or maintain restrictions on the uses to which such samples may be put, except as may be prescribed.

(3) The rules may provide that, in such cases as may be prescribed, samples need only be made available to such persons or descriptions of persons as may be prescribed; and the rules may identify a description of persons by reference to whether the comptroller has given his certificate as to any matter.

(4) An application for revocation of the patent under section 72(1)(c) above may be made if any of the requirements of the rules cease to be complied with.".

Patents Acts 1949 (Excerpts)

Sections 4, 7, 8, 14, 32, 33 and 101

Section 4

Contents of specification

4.—(1) Every specification whether complete or provisional, shall describe the invention, and shall begin with a title indicating the subject to which the invention relates.

(2) Subject to any rules made by the Board of Trade under this Act, drawings may, and shall if the comptroller so requires, be supplied for the purposes of any specification, whether complete or provisional; and any drawings so supplied shall, unless the comptroller otherwise directs, be deemed to form part of the specification, and references in this Act to a specification shall be construed accordingly.

(3) Every complete specification—
   (a) shall particularly describe the invention and the method by which it is to be performed;
   (b) shall disclose the best method of performing the invention which is known to the applicant and for which he is entitled to claim protection; and
   (c) shall end with a claim or claims defining the scope of the invention claimed.

(4) The claim or claims of a complete specification must relate to a single invention, must be clear and succinct, and must be fairly based on the matter disclosed in the specification.

(5) Rules made by the Board of Trade under this Act may require that in such cases as may be prescribed by the rules, a declaration as to the inventorship of the invention, in such form as may be so prescribed, shall be furnished with the complete specification or within such period as may be so prescribed after the filing of that specification.

(6) Subject to the foregoing provisions of this section a complete specification filed after a provisional specification, or filed with a convention application, may include claims in respect of developments of or additions to the invention which was described in the provisional specification or, as the case may be, the invention in respect of which the application for protection was made in a convention country, being developments or additions in respect of which the applicant would be entitled under the provisions of section one of this Act to make a separate application for a patent.

(7) Where a complete specification claims a new substance, the claim shall be construed as not extending to that substance when found in nature.

Section 7

Search for anticipation by previous publication.

7.—(1) Subject to the provisions of the last foregoing section, the examiner to whom an application for a patent is referred under this Act shall make investigation for the purpose of ascertaining whether the invention, so far as claimed in any claim of the complete specification, has been published before the date of filing of the applicant's complete specification in any specification filed in pursuance of an application for a patent made in the United Kingdom and dated within fifty years next before that date.

(2) The examiner shall, in addition, make such investigation as the comptroller may direct for the purpose of ascertaining whether the invention, so far as claimed in any claim of the complete specification, has been published in the United Kingdom before the date of filing of the applicant's complete specification in any other document (not being a document of any class described in subsection (1) of section fifty of this Act).

(3) If it appears to the comptroller that the invention, so far as claimed in any claim of the complete specification, has been published as aforesaid, he may refuse to accept the specification unless the applicant either—

    (a) shows to the satisfaction of the comptroller that the priority date of the claim of his complete specification is not later than the date on which the relevant document was published; or

    (b) amends his complete specification to the satisfaction of the comptroller.

(4) An appeal shall lie from any decision of the comptroller under this section.

SECTION 8

Search for anticipation by prior claim.

8.—(1) In addition to the investigation required by the last foregoing section, the examiner shall make investigation for the purpose of ascertaining whether the invention, so far as claimed in any claim of the complete specification is claimed in any claim of any other complete specification published on or after the date of filing the applicant's complete specification, being a specification filed—

    (a) in pursuance of an application for a patent made in the United Kingdom and dated before that date; or

    (b) in pursuance of a convention application founded upon an application for protection made in a convention country before that date.

(2) If it appears to the comptroller that the said invention is claimed in a claim of any such other specification as aforesaid, he may, subject to the provisions of this section, direct that a reference to that other specification shall be inserted by way of notice to the public in the applicant's complete specification unless within such time as may be prescribed either—

    (a) the applicant shows to the satisfaction of the comptroller that the priority date of his claim is not later than the priority date of the claim of the said other specification; or

    (b) the complete specification is amended to the satisfaction of the comptroller.

(3) If in consequence of the investigation under section seven of this Act or otherwise it appears to the comptroller—

    (a) that the invention, so far as claimed in any claim of the applicant's complete specification, has been claimed in any such specification as is mentioned in subsection (1) of that section; and

    (b) that the other specification was published on or after the priority date of the applicant's claim, then unless it has been shown to the satisfaction of the comptroller under that section that the priority date of the applicant's claim is not later than the priority date of the claim of that other specification, the provisions of subsection (2) of this section shall apply as they apply in relation to a specification published on or after the date of filing of the applicant's complete specification.

(4) The powers of the comptroller under this section to direct the insertion of a reference to another specification may be exercised either before or after a patent has been granted for the invention claimed in that other specification, but any direction given before the grant of such a patent shall be of no effect unless and until such a patent is granted.

(5) An appeal shall lie from any direction of the comptroller under this section.

Section 14

Opposition to grant of patent.

14.—(1) At any time within three months from the date of the publication of a complete specification under this Act, any person interested may give notice to the comptroller of opposition to the grant of the patent on any of the following grounds:—

(a) that the applicant for the patent, or the person described in the application as the true and first inventor, obtained the invention or any part thereof from him, or from a person of whom he is the personal representative;

(b) that the invention, so far as claimed in any claim of the complete specification, has been published in the United Kingdom, before the priority date of the claim—

(i) in any specification filed in pursuance of an application for a patent made in the United Kingdom and dated within fifty years next before the date of filing of the applicant's complete specification:

(ii) in any other document (not being a document of any class described in subsection (1) of section fifty of this Act);

(c) that the invention, so far as claimed in any claim of the complete specification, is claimed in any claim of a complete specification published on or after the priority date of the applicant's claim and filed in pursuance of an application for a patent in the United Kingdom, being a claim of which the priority date is earlier than that of the applicant's claim;

(d) that the invention, so far as claimed in any claim of the complete specification, was used in the United Kingdom before the priority date of that claim;

(e) that the invention, so far as claimed in any claim of the complete specification, is obvious and clearly does not involve any inventive step having regard to matter published as mentioned in paragraph (b) of this subsection, or having regard to what was used in the United Kingdom before the priority date of the applicant's claim;

(f) that the subject of any claim of the complete specification is not an invention within the meaning of this Act;

(g) that the complete specification does not sufficiently and fairly describe the invention or the method by which it is to be performed;

(h) that, in the case of a convention application, the application was not made within twelve months from the date of the first application for protection for the invention made in a convention country by the applicant or a person from whom he derives title,

but on no other ground.

(2) Where any such notice is given, the comptroller shall give notice of the opposition to the applicant, and shall give to the applicant and the opponent an opportunity to be heard before he decides on the case.

(3) The grant of a patent shall not be refused on the ground specified in paragraph (c) of subsection (1) of this section if no patent has been granted in pursuance of the application mentioned in that paragraph; and for the purposes of paragraph (d) or paragraph (e) of the said subsection (1) no account shall be taken of any secret use.

(4) An appeal shall lie from any decision of the comptroller under this section.

SECTION 32

Revocation of patent by court.

32.—(1) Subject to the provisions of this Act, a patent may, on the petition of any person interested, be revoked by the court on any of the following grounds, that is to say,—

(a) that the invention, so far as claimed in any claim of the complete specification, was claimed in a valid claim of earlier priority date contained in the complete specification of another patent granted in the United Kingdom;

(b) that the patent was granted on the application of a person not entitled under the provisions of this Act to apply therefor;

(c) that the patent was obtained in contravention of the rights of the petitioner or any person under or through whom he claims;

(d) that the subject of any claim of the complete specification is not an invention within the meaning of this Act;

(e) that the invention, so far as claimed in any claim of the complete specification, is not new having regard to what was known or used, before the priority date of the claim, in the United Kingdom;

(f) that the invention, so far as claimed in any claim of the complete specification, is obvious and does not involve any inventive step having regard to what was known or used, before the priority date of the claim, in the United Kingdom;

(g) that the invention, so far as claimed in any claim of the complete specification, is not useful;

(h) that the complete specification does not sufficiently and fairly describe the invention and the method by which it is to be performed, or does not disclose the best method of performing it which was known to the applicant for the patent and for which he was entitled to claim protection;

(i) that the scope of any claim of the complete specification is not sufficiently and clearly defined or that any claim of the complete specification is not fairly based on the matter disclosed in the specification;

(j) that the patent was obtained on a false suggestion or representation;

(k) that the primary or intended use or exercise of the invention is contrary to law;

(l) that the invention, so far as claimed in any claim of the complete specification, was secretly used in the United Kingdom, otherwise than as mentioned in subsection (2) of this section, before the priority date of that claim.

(2) For the purposes of paragraph (l) of subsection (1) of this section, no account shall be taken of any use of the invention—

(a) for the purpose of reasonable trial or experiment only; or

(b) by a Government department or any person authorised by a Government department, in consequence of the applicant for the patent or any person from whom he derives title having communicated or disclosed the invention directly or indirectly to a Government department or person authorised as aforesaid; or

(c) by any other person, in consequence of the applicant for the patent or any person from whom he derives title having communicated or disclosed the invention, and without the consent or acquiescence of the applicant or of any person from whom he derives title;

and for the purposes of paragraph (e) or paragraph (f) of the said subsection (1) no account shall be taken of any secret use.

(3) Without prejudice to the provisions of subsection (1) of this section, a patent may be revoked by the court on the petition of a Government department, if the court is satisfied that the patentee has without reasonable cause failed to comply with a request of the department to make, use or exercise the patented invention for the services of the Crown upon reasonable terms.

(4) Every ground on which a patent may be revoked shall be available as a ground of defence in any proceeding for the infringement of the patent.

SECTION 33*

Revocation of patent by comptroller.

33.—(1) At any time within twelve months after the sealing of a patent, any person interested who did not oppose the grant of the patent may apply to the comptroller for an order revoking the patent on any one or more of the grounds upon which the grant of the patent could have been opposed:

Provided that when an action for infringement, or proceedings for the revocation, of a patent are pending in any court, an application to the comptroller under this section shall not be made except with the leave of the court.

(2) Where an application is made under this section, the comptroller shall notify the patentee and shall give to the applicant and the patentee an opportunity to be heard before deciding the case.

(3) If on an application under this section the comptroller is satisfied that any of the grounds aforesaid are established, he may by order direct that the patent shall be revoked either unconditionally or unless within such time as may be specified in the order the complete specification is amended to his satisfaction:

Provided that the comptroller shall not make an order for the unconditional revocation of a patent under this section unless the circumstances are such as would have justified him in refusing to grant the patent in proceedings under section fourteen of this Act.

(4) An appeal shall lie from any decision of the comptroller under this section.

SECTION 101

Interpretation.

101.—(1) In this Act, except where the context otherwise requires, the following expressions have the meanings hereby respectively assigned to them, that is to say—

"Appeal Tribunal" means that Appeal Tribunal constituted and acting in accordance with section 85 of this Act as amended by the Administration of Justice Act 1969;

"applicant" includes a person in whose favour a direction has been given under section seventeen of this Act, and the personal representative of a deceased applicant;

"article" includes any substance or material, and any plant, machinery or apparatus, whether affixed to land or not;

"assignee" includes the personal representative of a deceased assignee, and references to the assignee of any person include references to the assignee of the personal representative or assignee of that person;

"comptroller" means the Comptroller-General of Patents, Designs and Trade Marks;

"convention application" has the meaning assigned to it by subsection (4) of section one of this Act;

"court" means the High Court;

"date of filing", in relation to any document filed under this Act, means the date on which the document is filed or, where it is deemed by virtue of any provision of this Act or rules made thereunder to have been filed on any different date, means the date on which it is deemed to be filed;

"exclusive licence" means a licence from a patentee which confers on the licensee, or on the licensee and persons authorised by him, to the exclusion of all other persons (including the patentee), any right in respect of the patented invention, and "exclusive licensee" shall be construed accordingly;

"invention" means any manner of new manufacture the subject of letters patent and grant of privilege within section six of the Statute of Monopolies and any new method or process of testing applicable to the improvement or control of manufacture, and includes an alleged invention;

"Journal" has the meaning assigned to it by subsection (2) of section ninety-four of this Act;

"patent" means Letters Patent for an invention;

---

*N.B. Section 33 has since been amended to a substantial extent by the Patent Act 1977, Schedule 1, Article 7(1) and (2).

"patent agent" means a person carrying on for gain in the United Kingdom the business of acting as agent for other persons for the purpose of applying for or obtaining patents in the United Kingdom or elsewhere;

"patent of addition" means a patent granted in accordance with section twenty-six of this Act;

"patentee" means the person or persons for the time being entered on the register of patents as grantee or proprietor of the patent;

"prescribed" means prescribed by rules made by the Board of Trade under this Act;

"priority date" has the meaning assigned to it by section five of this Act;

"published", except in relation to a complete specification, means made available to the public; and without prejudice to the generality of the foregoing provision a document shall be deemed for the purposes of this Act to be published if it can be inspected as of right at any place in the United Kingdom by members of the public, whether upon payment of a fee or otherwise;

"the Statute of Monopolies" means the Act of the twenty-first year of the reign of King James the First, chapter three, intituled "An Act concerning monopolies and dispensations with penal laws and the forfeiture thereof".

(2) For the purposes of subsection (3) of section one, so far as it relates to a convention application, and for the purposes of section seventy-two of this Act, the expression "personal representative" in relation to a deceased person, includes the legal representative of the deceased appointed in any country outside the United Kingdom.

European Patent Convention (Excerpts)

Articles 52–57 and 69.

ARTICLE 52

Patentable inventions

(1) European patents shall be granted for any inventions which are susceptible of industrial application, which are new and which involve an inventive step.

(2) The following in particular shall not be regarded as inventions within the meaning of paragraph 1:

    (a) discoveries, scientific theories and mathematical methods;

    (b) aesthetic creations;

    (c) schemes, rules and methods for performing mental acts, playing games or doing business, and programs for computers;

    (d) presentations of information.

(3) The provisions of paragraph 2 shall exclude patentability of the subject-matter or activities referred to in that provision only to the extent to which a European patent application or European patent relates to such subject-matter or activities as such.

(4) Methods for treatment of the human or animal body by surgery or therapy and diagnostic methods practised on the human or animal body shall not be regarded as inventions which are susceptible of industrial application within the meaning of paragraph 1. This provision shall not apply to products, in particular substances or compositions, for use in any of these methods.

ARTICLE 53

Exceptions to patentability

European patents shall not be granted in respect of:

    (a) inventions the publication or exploitation of which would be contrary to "ordre public" or morality, provided that the exploitation shall not be deemed to be so contrary merely because it is prohibited by law or regulation in some or all of the Contracting States;

    (b) plant or animal varieties or essentially biological processes for the production of plants or animals; this provision does not apply to microbiological processes or the products thereof.

ARTICLE 54

Novelty

(1) An invention shall be considered to be new if it does not form part of the state of the art.

(2) The state of the art shall be held to comprise everything made available to the public by means of a written or oral description, by use, or in any other way, before the date of filing of the European patent application.

(3) Additionally, the content of European patent applications as filed, of which the dates of filing are prior to the date referred to in paragraph 2 and which were published under Article 93 on or after that date, shall be considered as comprised in the state of the art.

(4) Paragraph 3 shall be applied only in so far as a Contracting State designated in respect of the later application, was also designated in respect of the earlier application as published.

(5) The provisions of paragraphs 1 to 4 shall not exclude the patentability of any substance or composition, comprised in the state of the art, for use in a method referred to in Article 52, paragraph 4, provided that its use for any method referred to in that paragraph is not comprised in the state of the art.

ARTICLE 55

Non-prejudicial disclosures

(1) For the application of Article 54 a disclosure of the invention shall not be taken into consideration if it occurred no earlier than six months preceding the filing of the European patent application and if it was due to, or in consequence of:

(a) an evident abuse in relation to the applicant or his legal predecessor, or

(b) the fact that the applicant or his legal predecessor has displayed the invention at an official, or officially recognised, international exhibition falling within the terms of the Convention on international exhibitions signed at Paris on 22 November 1928 and last revised on 30 November 1972.

(2) In the case of paragraph 1(b), paragraph 1 shall apply only if the applicant states, when filing the European patent application, that the invention has been so displayed and files a supporting certificate within the period and under the conditions laid down in the Implementing Regulations.

ARTICLE 56

Inventive step

An invention shall be considered as involving an inventive step if, having regard to the state of the art, it is not obvious to a person skilled in the art. If the state of the art also includes documents within the meaning of Article 54, paragraph 3, these documents are not to be considered in deciding whether there has been an inventive step.

ARTICLE 57

Industrial application

An invention shall be considered as susceptible of industrial application if it can be made or used in any kind of industry, including agriculture.

ARTICLE 69

Extent of protection

(1) The extent of the protection conferred by a European patent or a European patent application shall be determined by the terms of the claims. Nevertheless, the description and drawings shall be used to interpret the claims.

Appendices

Appendix 1

List of Patents Acts

Title of Act	Citation
Statute of Monopolies	21 Jac.1 c.3
Patent Act 1835	5 & 6 Will.4 c.83
Patent Act 1839	2 & 3 Vict. c.67
Patent Law Amendment Act 1852	15 & 16 Vict. c.83
Stamp Duties on Patents for Invention and Purchase of Indexes of Specifications Act 1852	16 Vict. c.5
Industrial Exhibitions Act 1865	28 Vict. c.3
Protection of Inventions Act 1870	33 & 34 Vict. c.27
Patents, Designs, and Trade Marks Act 1883	46 & 47 Vict. c.57
Patents Act 1886	49 & 50 Vict. c.37
Patents, Designs, and Trade Marks Act 1888	51 & 52 Vict. c.50
Patents Act 1901	1 Edw.7 c.18
Patents Act 1902	2 Edw.7 c.34
Patents and Designs (Amendment) Act 1907	7 Edw.7 c.28
Patents and Designs Act 1907	7 Edw.7 c.29
Patents and Designs Act 1908	8 Edw.7 c.4
Patents, Designs and Trade Marks (Temporary Rules) Act 1914	4 & 5 Geo.5 c.27
Patents, Designs and Trade Marks Temporary Rules (Amendment) Act 1914	4 & 5 Geo.5 c.73
Patents and Designs Act 1919	9 & 10 Geo.5 c.80
Patents and Designs (Convention) Act 1928	18 Geo.5 c.3
Patents and Designs Act 1932	22 & 23 Geo.5 c.32
Patents &c (International Conventions) Act 1938	1 & 2 Geo.6 c.29
Patents and Designs (Limits of Time) Act 1939	2 & 3 Geo.6 c.32
Patents, Designs, Copyright and Trade Marks (Emergency) Act 1939	2 & 3 Geo.6 c.107
Patents and Designs Act 1942	5 & 6 Geo.6 c.6
Patents and Designs Act 1946	9 & 10 Geo.6 c.44
Patents and Designs Act 1949	12 & 13 Geo.6 c.62
Patents Act 1949	12, 13 & 14 Geo.6 c.87
Patents Act 1957	5 & 6 Eliz.2 c.13
Patents and Designs (Renewals, Extensions and Fees) Act 1961	9 & 10 Eliz.2 c.25
Patents Act 1977	1977 c.77
Copyright, Designs and Patents Act 1988	1988 c.48

Appendix 2

Specification Example

(12) **UK Patent** (19) **GB** (11) **2 064 190 B**

(54) title of invention

Security alarm device

(51) INT CL³; G08B 7/00

(21) Application No **8037930**	(73) Proprietor **CQR Security Systems Limited, 148 Wallasey Road, Wallasey, Merseyside, L44 2AF**
(22) Date of filing **26 Nov 1980**	
(30) Priority data	
(31) **7940862**	
(32) **27 Nov 1979**	
(33) **United Kingdom (GB)**	
(43) Application published **10 Jun 1981**	(72) Inventor **Dennis Robin Solomon**
(45) Patent published **22 Jun 1983**	
(52) Domestic classification **G4N 10 5A1 5A2 5A3 5AX 5T 6B2 DD GA**	(74) Agent and/or address for service **Potts, Kerr & Co., 15 Hamilton Square, Birkenhead, Merseyside, L41 6BR**
(56) Documents cited **GB 1318891 GB 629842 GB 403024**	
(58) Field of search **G4N**	

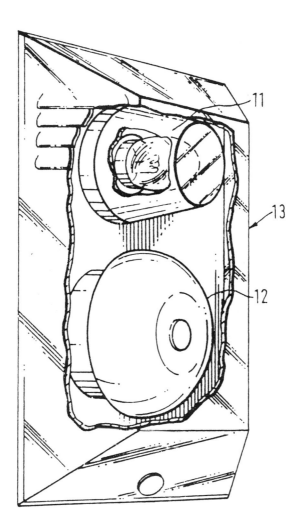

SPECIFICATION
Security alarm device

The present invention relates to a security
alarm device and more particularly is concerned
5 with so-called "bell-box'- and burglar alarm
systems.
For security of homes and commercial
premises, security alarm systems of many and
various kinds are provided. Generally, the alarm
10 bell associated with such systems is provided on
an outside wall of the home or commercial
premises. The alarm bell is normally encased in a
metal housing. Upon an intruder entering the
home or premises, the alarm device is triggered
15 off and the alarm bell rings.
A problem which arises in connection with
such devices is the noise factor associated
therewith, particularly in those cases where a
false alarm has occurred and the owner of the
20 home or premises cannot be contacted.
It is proposed to provide an arrangement
which, in addition to an alarm bell also includes a
light, the arrangement being such that, in one
embodiment, when the alarm bell is turned off
25 after a preselected period of time the light then
comes into operation. Such arrangement will
enable the police to ascertain the location of the
burglary or false alarm and to take appropriate
action, without any other persons being affected
30 by the continuous ringing of the alarm bell.
Furthermore in accordance with the invention,
and in an attempt to combat vandalism, a security
alarm device is provided in which both the alarm
bell and the light are enclosed within a housing.
35 Such housing should be formed of material which
will permit the light to be seen therethrough but
which does not permit the workings of the
security alarm device to be seen.
Such arrangements provide a compact alarm
40 device with all the integers thereof being enclosed
within a single housing.
According to the present invention there is
provided a security alarm device comprising a
housing containing an audible alarm means and a
45 visual warning means, at least a portion of said
housing being translucent, and means for
operating each of said audible alarm means and
said visual warning means.
In a preferred embodiment of the present
50 invention, the audible alarm means is in the form
of a bell alarm, the visual warning means is in the
form of a light, preferably a flashing light, and the
housing is formed of translucent plastics material.
By use of the arrangement in accordance with
55 the invention, it can be seen that a compact
arrangement is enclosed within the housing, at
least a portion of the housing being formed of
material which will permit the visual warning
means to be seen therethrough.
60 In one embodiment of the present invention,
the means for operating the audible alarm means
and the visual alarm means comprises an
electrical circuit means which includes a cut-out
arrangement for turning off the audible alarm

65 after a preselected time period, e.g. ten minutes,
and means for then bringing the visual warning
means into operation.
In an alternative embodiment, the electrical
circuit means operates both the audible alarm
70 means and the visual warning means upon
triggering off of the security alarm device and the
cut-out arrangement turns off the audible alarm
means after a preselected time period leaving the
visual warning means in operation.
75 The electrical circuit means utilised will comprise
any conventional arrangement for operating the
security alarm device in the desired sequence,
and since such description of such arrangements
are well-known in the art, no detailed circuit
80 arrangements will be given.
It is to be understood that the electrical circuit
means for operating the audible alarm means and
the visual warning means can be located either
within the housing or exterior thereof.
85 By the preferred use of a housing which is
formed completely of translucent plastics material
the security alarm device of the present invention
is rendered rust-free and covers both the audible
alarm and the visual warning means and
90 accordingly, the maintenance requirements
therefore are substantially reduced as compared
with a metal housing enclosing an audible alarm
as well as a modified arrangement wherein the
visual warning means will be provided separate
95 from the metal housing and the audible alarm.
In accordance with a particularly preferred
embodiment there is provided a burglar alarm
adapted to be attached to an outside wall of a
building, comprising a translucent housing
100 encasing a light and a bell alarm, and electrical
circuit means for operating the light and the bell
alarm.
The present invention will be further illustrated
by way of example, with reference to the
105 accompanying drawing in which the single Figure
is a perspective view of a securtiy device in
accordance with the invention, part of the housing
being cut away to show the interior of the
device.
110 As illustrated, the security alarm device
comprises a translucent plastics material housing
13, encasing an audible alarm, in the form of a
bell alarm 12, and a visual alarm, in the form of a
flashing light 11. Conventional electrical circuitry,
115 not shown, is provided to operate the bell alarm
12 and the flashing light 11.

Upon triggering off of the security alarm device
in one embodiment, the electrical circuit means
operates the bell alarm 12. After a pre-selected
120 time period, the bell alarm 12 is turned off and the
flashing light 11 then becomes operative In an
alternative embodiment both the flashinç light 11
and the bell alarm 12 become operative initially,
the bell alarm 12 being turned off after a pre-
125 selected time period, and the flashing light 11
remaining operative.

The translucent nature of the housing 13
enables the flashing light 11 to be seen, when

operative, however, the workings of the alarm device cannot be seen.

It can thus be seen that the security alarm device in accordance with the present invention
5 exhibits many substantial advantages over the prior art devices and permits an arrangement to be provided whereby the audible alarm can be turned off whilst still leaving the visual alarm operative.

10 **Claims**

1. A security alarm device comprising a housing containing an audible alarm means and a visual warning means, at least a portion of said housing being translucent, and means for
15 operating each of said audible alarm means and said visual warning means.

2. A security alarm device as claimed in claim 1, in which the audible alarm means is in the form of a bell alarm.
20   3. A security alarm device as claimed in claim 1 or 2, in which the visual warning means is in the form of a flashing light.

4. A security alarm device as claimed in claim 1, 2 or 3, in which at least a portion of the
25 housing is formed of translucent plastics material.

5. A security alarm device as claimed in any preceding claim, in which the means for operating the audible alarm means and the visual warning means comprises an electrical circuit means
30 which includes a cut-out arrangement, for turning off the audible alarm means after a pre-selected time period, and means for then bringing the visual warning means into operation.

6. A security alarm device as claimed in any
35 one of claims 1 to 4, in which the means for operating the audible alarm means and the visual warning means comprises an electrical circuit means which operates both audible alarm means and the visual warning means upon triggering off
40 the security alarm device, and including a cut-out arrangement to turn off the audible alarm means after a pre-selected time period, thereby leaving the visual warning means in operation.

7. A security alarm device, substantially as
45 hereinbefore described with reference to and as illustrated in the accompanying drawing.

8. A burgular alarm adapted to be attached to an outside wall of a building, comprising a translucent housing encasing a light and a bell
50 alarm, and electrical circuit means for operating the light and the bell alarm.

Printed for Her Majesty's Stationery Office by the Courier Press, Leamington Spa, 1983. Published by the Patent Office, 25 Southampton Buildings, London, WC2A 1AY, from which copies may be obtained

Appendix 3

Foreign Drafting

Classically, there are three ways in which a specification and claims can be drafted. They are:

(1) United Kingdom style;
(2) United States style;
(3) Germanic style.

The United Kingdom style has already been discussed in Chapter 4; this Appendix first compares, in general terms, the other styles with the United Kingdom style and, secondly, relates these to the burgeoning

(4) European style.

United States
The United States style (which naturally reflects the somewhat different statutory wording of their 1952 Patents Act, United States Code Title 35) is distinctive in respect of:

(1) the fuller degree of disclosure in the specification; and
(2) the structural definiteness of the claims.

Thus, in the case of a mechanical invention, the drawings will be more by way of a miniature version of the engineering drawings of the machine as a whole rather than just a sketch, in diagrammatic form, of the particular new element of mechanism involved; this will necessitate a correspondingly lengthier description. In the case of a chemical invention, there may be a large number of specific examples.

The requirement for structural definiteness is illustrated by the following comparative pairs of generic claims for the United Kingdom and corresponding United States patents on the same invention:

BP No.	*USP No.*
1028618	*3306867*
'1. A pressure transferable ink composition for pressure operative transfer media comprising a polymer base material, colouring matter, and a non-volatile, non-drying carrier fluid for the colouring matter and including a quarternary ammonium compound present in such an amount that the colouring matter is released from the composition more readily than from a similar composition containing none of the quarternary ammonium compound.'	'1. In a pressure transferable ink composition for pressure operative transfer media comprising *20–40* percent of a polymer base material, *10–35* percent coloring matter, and *30–60* percent of a non-volatile, non-drying carrier fluid for the coloring matter, the improvement of incorporating from *0.5–5* percent of a quarternary ammonium compound in said ink, whereby the coloring matter is more readily released.' (*Emphasis added*)

BP No.
769692

'1. A method of manufacturing flat glass in ribbon form, *characterized by forming* a ribbon of glass and then *causing* the formed ribbon to *move* along a bath of molten metal the surface of which is wider than the intended ultimate width for the ribbon, in which bath the ribbon *becomes supported* in a continuous horizontal plane of a floating element, *protecting* the surface of the molten metal in a bath against oxidation by maintaining a chemically suitable thermally regulated atmosphere thereover and *regulating* the temperature of the molten bath so that before the ribbon leaves the bath it is *chilled sufficiently* to be advanced unharmed on mechanical conveying means.' (*Emphasis added*)

USP No.
2911759

'1. A method of manufacturing flat glass in ribbon form, *comprising* the steps of *forming* a ribbon of glass to definite dimensions of width and thickness, *cooling* the ribbon to an extent sufficient to make it stiff enough to stabilize its dimensions, thereafter *directing* the stiffened ribbon onto a bath of molten metal, *floating* the ribbon thereon and *advancing* the ribbon horizontally in continuous form along the bath of molten metal, the surface of said molten metal being wider than the width of the ribbon, and while said ribbon is being advanced along said bath *protecting* the surface of the molten metal in the bath beyond the margins of said ribbon against oxidation, while *regulating* the temperature of the molten metal in the bath to first cause a surface of the advancing stiffened ribbon to be softened and then to *progressively and sufficiently cool* the softened ribbon before leaving the bath by heat exchange therewith to permit the ribbon to be advanced by mechanical conveying means without becoming damaged.'

(*Emphasis added*)

BP No.
1510483

'11. A process for coating a substrate, which comprises coating with a liquid, curable organopolysiloxane having the formula . . . . . . a powder comprising particles which are at least partially vitreous, curing said organopolysiloxane to a solid form, and electrostatically depositing the powder thus obtained onto said substrate.'

USP No.
3928668

'1. An improved process for forming a ceramic coat on a substrate by electrostatically depositing thereon a ceramic powder having an extended retention time of an electric charge, comprising:

(a) coating said ceramic powder with a liquid, curable organopolysiloxane having the formula: . . . .
(b) polymerizing the polysiloxane on said powder to a solid state to form a powder having a resistivity of at least about 10^{-12} ohm-cm in an environment having a relative humidity of about 88%.
(c) electrostatically depositing the polysiloxane coated ceramic powder substantially uniformly over a portion of said substrate substantially at ambient room temperature,

(d) subjecting said substrate to physical movement which but for the polysiloxane coating on the ceramic powder would dislodge some of said powder from the substrate, and

(e) heating the substrate to fuse the ceramic powder and form thereover a substantially uniform ceramic coat.'

In the first of these examples, the recitation of the quantitative limits (in quite wide terms) for the various ingredients in the United States Claim 1 will be noted; these are absent from the United Kingdom Claim 1.

The second example concerns the basic patent on float glass. The United States Claim 1 is of generally comparable width to the United Kingdom Claim 1, but recites more steps – so as to define the operative combination as a whole – and almost entirely in the active voice. The United Kingdom Claim 1 is substantially shorter and mingles its voices. Thus, the United Kingdom Claim calls for the sequence of 'forming' + 'causing' . . . 'to move' + 'becomes supported' whereas the United States Claim calls for 'forming' + 'directing' + 'floating' + 'advancing'. The latter is more positive language. It can also be said that the United States analysis of the invention is more fundamental. Only the margins of the molten metal bath need protection (since the glass ribbon covers the centre zone), and preliminary cooling is naturally needed to stabilise the ribbon initially formed so as to render it capable of undergoing the subsequent treatment steps; in the United Kingdom Claim 1, this is left unsaid.

The third example provides similar contrast. The physical parameter in step (b) (minimum resistivity) renders the Claim precise in respect of this quality of the ceramic powder. Additional steps (d) and (e), as compared to the United Kingdom Claim 11, essentially just specify positively the practical handling steps required for making the ceramic coating. In the result the United States Claim 1, whilst much longer and wordier than United Kingdom Claim 11, is of about the same real scope.

Germanic

The Germanic style stands at the opposite end of the spectrum. A shorter, and often sketchier, specification will suffice; the emphasis is more on placing the new invention into its appropriate context relative to the prior art; the introduction to the description often consists of a resumé of the nearest prior art, followed by a formulation of the problem left unsolved by that prior art but now triumphantly overcome by the new invention. The drawings, in a mechanical case, tend to be of diagrammatic rather than engineering kind. Claim 1 will normally be drafted in 'characterised in that' style; that is to say, it will be divided into two parts. The first part, constituting the preamble to the claim, will refer to the relevant prior art; the second part, introduced by the phrase 'characterised in that', or similar, will then recite the novel feature or features. A further point is that the definition in the characterising clause would normally be intended not so much to denote the precise boundary of the protection asserted but rather to express the new inventive idea present. The Court, in ascertaining the scope of the patent for purposes of infringement, would regard the wording of the claim as a guide and not a definition. In the jargon of patent lawyers, the Germanic style employs 'central' drafting whereas the United Kingdom and United States styles employ 'peripheral' drafting.

A typical Germanic Claim, Claim 1 of West German Patent No. 1010244, is as follows:

> 1. Method for the production of glass fibres from a tank of molten glass, which flows out of the tank over a feed chamber into a plurality of outlet orifices, from which the glass is drawn out into fibres, wherein the molten glass on transfer from the tank to the feed chamber is subjected to homogenisation and temperature comparability, *characterised in that* the glass is led on its way to the outlet orifices along a labyrinthine path. (*Emphasis added*)

The United Kingdom style of drafting will normally be adopted (at least as first choice) in countries where a patent law comparable to pre-1977 United Kingdom law is in force; these naturally include the majority of Commonwealth countries. The United States style is essentially peculiar to the United States; Canada tends to adopt something of an intermediate position between the United Kingdom and the United States. The Germanic style is adopted in the majority of European countries (as well as Germany) which have examination systems; also in Japan. In remaining countries, the style will normally follow that used in the original application (in the case of an invention emanating abroad) or be at large (in the case of a domestic invention).

European
The practice of the European Patent Office is something of a compromise. EPC Rules 29(1)(a) and (b) require that a claim should have a preamble setting out the prior art (in practice the closest piece of prior art) followed by a characterising clause setting out the new features of the invention. This of course is in accordance with traditional Germanic style. But the Rules are qualified by the proviso 'wherever appropriate', and this provides flexibility. Some recent examples of application of the proviso include:

BOSSERT KG/Two-part claim:[1] Invention consisted of a complex system of functionally interconnected parts where the inventive step lay in a change in their relation to each other.

THOMSON-CSF/Transistor structure:[2] Certain stages of the process involved were known in the prior art but carried out in a different chronological order. Hence the drawing up of a claim in two appropriately delimited parts would have been cumbersome and complicated.

THORN EMI/Discharge lamps:[3] Two documents could equally be considered to represent the nearest prior art (in the discharge lamp according to document A the electrical connections corresponded to those of the discharge lamp of Claim 1 but the gap was not defined as a spark gap, and vice versa for document B). Hence a claim in two-part form pinpointing one or other document as sole closest art might give a misleading picture of the invention.

The controlling consideration is that of Article 84 of the EPC, which requires that the claims should be clear and concise. Rule 29(1) is dominated by the Article, in accordance with the standard principle of construction that Rules made under a Convention are subordinate to the Convention itself.
   A typical European two-part Claim is represented, in contrast, by Claim 1 of EP No. 0 203 945:[4]

> 1. A dilatation catheter comprising an expandable balloon (2) through which extends a length of tubing (7) which is held on a guide element (1) and which is sealingly connected to the distal end (9) of the balloon (2) and further comprising a tube (3) for inflating the balloon (2) the tube opening into the inside (5) of the balloon while being sealed at the proximal end (11) of the balloon (2), the longitudinal axis of the tube (3) being laterally displaced with respect to the inlet opening at the proximal end of the tubing (7), which is situated near the proximal end of the balloon (2), characterized in that the tubing (7) is displaceably guided on the guide element which is formed by a flexible guide wire (1) and the tube (3) is in the longitudinal direction sufficiently stiff to transmit pushing and pulling forces so that, by moving the tube (3) forwards or rearwards, the tubing (7), together with the balloon (2) attached thereto, may be displaced on the guide wire (1) in both directions'.

Irrespective of whether a two-part or one-part Claim 1 is eventually allowed, the EPO will in any event usually require the closest prior art (at least) to be acknowledged in the introductory descriptive part of the specification.

1 [1987] EPOR 82.
2 [1987] EPOR 291.
3 [1988] EPOR 187.
4 Litigated in *Bonzel v Intervention* (No. 3) [1991] RPC 553.

Appendix 4

A: Flow Chart of the United Kingdom Patent Office Prosecution (simplified)

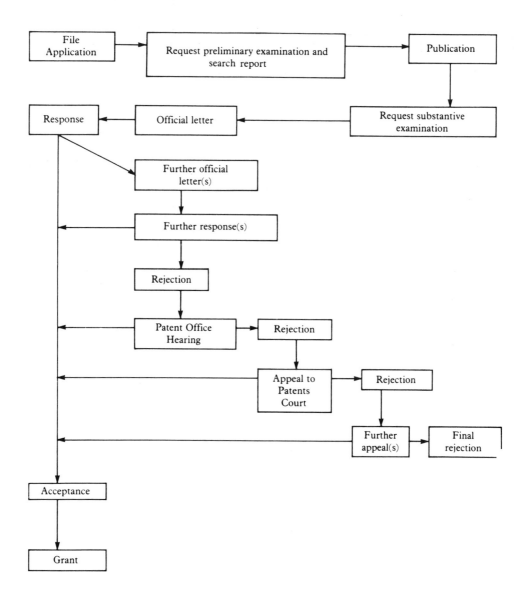

B: Flow Chart of the European Patent System Procedure (simplified)

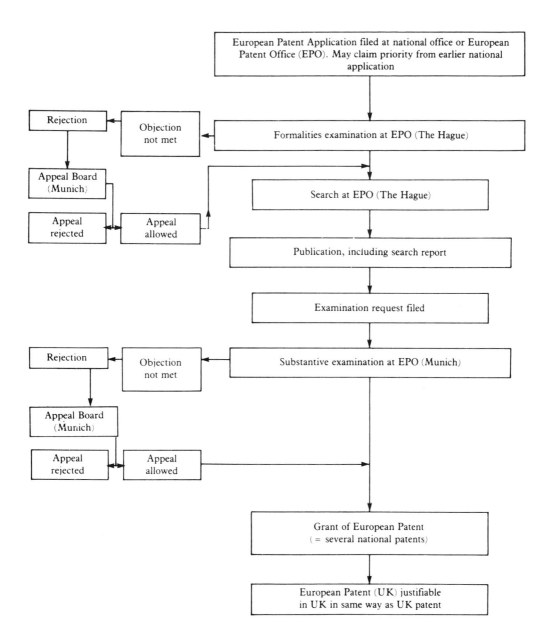

C: Flow Chart of the Patent Co-operation Treaty Procedure (simplified)

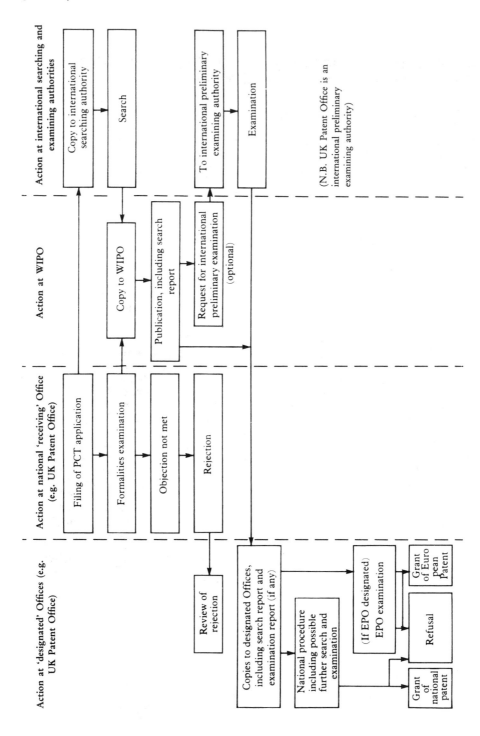

Appendix 5

Patent Rules 1968, Schedule 4 — Form of Patent (for existing patents granted under Patents Act 1949)

ELIZABETH the Second by the Grace of God of the United Kingdom of Great Britain and Northern Ireland and of Her other Realms and Territories, Queen, Head of the Commonwealth, Defender of the Faith: To all to whom these presents shall come greeting:

W H E R E A S a request for the grant of a patent has been made by

(Patentee)

for the sole use and advantage of an invention for

(Title of Invention)

A N D   W H E R E A S We, being willing to encourage all inventions which may be for the public good, are graciously pleased to condescend to the request:

K N O W   Y E ,   T H E R E F O R E, that We, of our especial grace, certain knowledge, and mere motion do by these presents, for Us, our heirs and successors, give and grant unto the person(s) above named and any successor(s), executor(s), administrator(s) and assign(s) (each and any of whom are hereinafter referred to as the patentee) our especial licence, full power, sole privilege, and authority, that the patentee or any agent or licensee of the patentee and no others, may subject to the conditions and provisions prescribed by any statute or order for the time being in force at all times hereafter during the term of years herein mentioned, make, use, exercise and vend the said invention within our United Kingdom of Great Britain and Northern Ireland, and the Isle of Man, and that the patentee shall have and enjoy the whole profit and advantage from time to time accruing by reason of the said invention during the term of sixteen years from the date hereunder written of these presents: A N D to the end that the patentee may have and enjoy the sole use and exercise and the full benefit of the said invention, We do by these presents for Us, our heirs and successors, strictly command all our subjects whatsoever within our United Kingdom of Great Britain and Northern Ireland, and the Isle of Man, that they do not at any time during the continuance of the said term either directly or indirectly make use of or put in practice the said invention, nor in anywise imitate the same, without the written consent, licence or agreement of the patentee, on pain of incurring such penalties as may be justly inflicted on such offenders for their contempt of this our Royal command, and of being answerable to the patentee according to the law for damages thereby occasioned:

P R O V I D E D   A L W A Y S that these letters patent shall be revocable on any of the grounds from time to time by law prescribed as grounds for revoking letters patent granted by Us, and the same may be revoked and made void accordingly:

P R O V I D E D   A L S O that nothing herein contained shall prevent the granting of licences in such manner and for such considerations as they may by law be granted: A N D lastly, We do by these presents for Us, our heirs and successors, grant unto the patentee that these our letters patent shall be construed in the most beneficial sense for the advantage of the patentee.

I N   W I T N E S S   whereof We have caused these our letters to be made patent as of the
. . . . day of . . . . one thousand nine hundred and . . . . and to be
sealed.

Seal of   *Comptroller-General of Patents,*
Patent Office   *Designs, and Trade Marks.*

Appendix 6

Patents Court Forms

A typical heading and termination for Court forms as used for a patent infringement action in the Patents Court is:

IN THE HIGH COURT OF JUSTICE   CH 199. . W No. . . .
CHANCERY DIVISION
PATENTS COURT

Writ issued the . . . day of . . . . 199. .

B E T W E E N:

      WHITE KNIGHT LIMITED   *Plaintiffs*

                              – and –

      RED KNAVE LIMITED   *Defendants*

                         (Body of Form)
                                                    (Signature)

SERVED the . . . day of . . . . . . 199 . . . by XYZ of (address) solicitors for the (Plaintiffs)

Forms A to O in this Appendix represent a typical set of the operative parts of the principal forms as might be used in a patent infringement action in the High Court (under the 1977 Act) between these parties involving an existing 1949 Act patent. The set is not comprehensive; nor, in a simple case, would all of Forms A to O necessarily be required, as indicated below. The formal parts of the forms (headed at beginning; signature, service details at end) are omitted in each case. For an action involving a 1977 Act patent the forms will be generally similar, although it must be borne in mind that the grounds available for an attack on validity are now more limited albeit the range of citable prior art is wider. This will affect in particular the drafting of Form E (Particulars of Objection).

The list of forms is as follows:

A   Indorsement on Writ
B   Statement of Claim
C   Particulars of Infringement
D   Defence and Counterclaim
E   Particulars of Objections
F   Reply and Defence to Counterclaim
G   Request for Further and Better Particulars of the Particulars of Objection
H   Further and Better Particulars of the Particulars of Objection
I   Plaintiffs' Request for Admissions
J   Response to Plaintiffs' Request for Admissions
K   Notice of Experiments
L   Order on Summons for Directions
M   Schedule of Interrogatories

N   Notice of Motion (Amendment of Particulars of Objection)
O   Order (On Motion to amend Particulars of Objections)

Since the titles of the forms are essentially self-explanatory, only some brief comments are made here. Further discussion is contained in Chapter 7 also. The Patents Nos. cited are of course all artificial in the context, whilst all names and addresses and other identifying indicia are fanciful.

Forms A to H represent the normal pleadings documents, although if the Particulars of Objections as they stand (Form E) are already adequate then Forms G and H are superfluous. Conversely, the defendant can ask for Further and Better Particulars of the Particulars of Infringement, if the position so warrants. Likewise the Defendant can also, and usually does, ask for Admissions by the Plaintiff (say, on some issue relevant to the validity of the Patent being sued upon) along the lines of Form I. Following admissions the parties proceed to discovery of documents (listing and categorising the documents in the manner provided for by Prescribed Form No. 26 of the Rules of the Supreme Court, not reproduced here) and experiments. Form K represents a Defendant's Notice of Experiments (here relating to validity issues) but the Plaintiff may well enter a Comparable Notice on infringement issues. The Summons for Directions, and subsequent Order thereon (Form L) should under the 1986 change in procedure now follow the successive admissions, discovery and experiments stages; previously, the Summons for Directions came earlier. However, in practice there is often an overlap and the specimen form in the White Book ('The Supreme Court Practice') on which Form L is in turn based, still retains the traditional format. There may well in any event be dispute as to the scope of discovery which needs to be resolved at this stage, or permission for interrogatories (Form M) or further experiments, and like topics, to be dealt with at this time.

Forms N and O (the latter normally being termed a *See v Scott-Paine* order after the case in which it was first introduced, at 50 RPC 36) deal with the important practical position which arises when the Defendant wishes to introduce some further prior art in support of his attack on validity, which he has encountered subsequent to the completion of the regular pleading stages. The Plaintiff is essentially given a choice either to continue, or to discontinue and have his Patent revoked but with a set-off as regards costs arising from the Defendant's omission to plead the new prior art earlier. Such amendment can of course be considered at the Summons for Directions stage, if the additional prior art has by then been uncovered.

FORM A: INDORSEMENT ON WRIT

The Plaintiffs' claim is for:
1. A Declaration that Patent No. 1234567* is valid and has been infringed by the Defendants.
2. An injunction to restrain the Defendants by their directors, officers, employees, servants or agents or otherwise howsoever from infringing the said patent.
3. An Order for the delivery up or destruction upon oath of any patented product in relation to which the said Patent is infringed and of any article containing that product as an inextricable constituent.
4. An inquiry as to damages in respect of infringement or alternatively at the Plaintiffs' option an account of the profits made by the Defendants derived by them from the infringement, and payment of all sums so found due together with interest under the provisions of section 35A of the Supreme Court Act 1981.
5. Such further or other relief as to this Honourable Court may seem meet.
6. Costs.

FORM B: STATEMENT OF CLAIM

1. The Plaintiffs are and were at all material times the proprietors of Patent No. 1234567.
2. The Patent is and was at all material times in force.
3. The Defendants have infringed and threaten and intend unless restrained by this Court to

*This Patent No. is artificial.

continue to infringe the Patent in the manner appearing in the Particulars of Infringement served herewith, whereby the Plaintiffs have suffered and will suffer damage.

AND the Plaintiffs claim:

(1) A Declaration that Patent No. 1234567 is valid and has been infringed by the Defendants:

(2) An Injunction to restrain the Defendants by their directors, officers, employees, servants o agents or otherwise howsoever from infringing the said Patent;

(3) An Order for the delivery up or destruction upon oath of any patented product in relation to which the said Patent is infringed and of any article containing that product as an inextricable constituent;

(4) An inquiry as to damages in respect of infringement or alternatively at the Plaintiffs' option an account of the profits made by the Defendants derived by them from the infringement, and payment of all sums so found due together with interest under the provisions of section 35A of the Supreme Court Act 1981;

(5) Such further or other relief as to this Honourable Court may seem meet;

(6) Costs.

FORM C: PARTICULARS OF INFRINGEMENT

The following are the Particulars of Infringement referred to in the Statement of Claim herein:

1. Subsequent to the publication of the Complete Specification of Patent No. 1234567 and prior to the issue of the Writ in this Action the Defendants have infringed Patent No. 1234567 and Claims 1 to 5, 7 to 9, and 11 in the Complete Specification thereof by doing in the United Kingdom, without the consent of the Plaintiffs, in relation to the invention the subject of the Patent the following things that is to say:

(i) insofar as the invention is a product, namely a polyurethane foam product as claimed in any one or more of Claims 1 to 5 of the Patent, by making, disposing of, offering to dispose of, using or keeping the product whether for disposal or otherwise;

(ii) insofar as the invention is a process, namely a method of making a polyurethane foam product and as claimed in any one or more Claims 7 to 9 of the Patent, by using the process and/or by disposing of, offering to dispose of, using, keeping for disposal or otherwise a product obtained directly by the process;

(iii) insofar as the invention is a process, namely a shock absorbing method employing the said polyurethane foam product as shock absorbing medium and as claimed in Claim 11 of the Patent, by supplying or offering to supply in the United Kingdom a person other than a licensee or other person entitled to work the invention with means, namely a polyurethane foam product, relating to an essential element of the invention for putting the invention into effect when the Defendants knew at all material times or it was obvious to a reasonable person in the circumstances that the said means were suitable for putting and were intended to put the invention into effect in the United Kingdom.

2. In particular the Plaintiffs complain of the following acts of the Defendants:

(i) offering the patented polyurethane foam product for sale in the United Kingdom by circulating therein around April 1992 a price list entitled 'Cumfee-Core Sheets & Slabs' (a copy whereof may be inspected at the offices of the Plaintiffs' Solicitors);

(ii) Supplying the patented polyurethane foam product to Messrs. Shadow & Son, of Shady Lane, Soulminster in the County of Essex in or around March 1992. A copy of a delivery note dated 15 March 1992 in respect of a consignment of twelve blocks of Cumfee-Core (size 6' × 4' × 6″) from the Defendants to the said Messrs. Shadow & Son may be inspected at the offices of the Plaintiffs' Solicitors.

In each case, the Defendants well knew at all material times that manufacture and/or sale and/or subsequent use of the polyurethane foam product referred to without the Plaintiffs' consent would be an infringement of Patent No. 1234567.

Particulars of Knowledge and Circumstance

Hereunder, the Plaintiffs will rely upon the following facts and matters as the best particulars which can be given before discovery:

(i) The Defendants had been sent on 14 January 1992 a letter from Messrs. Draft & Claim of 25 Southampton Buildings, London W.C.2. Chartered Patent Agents acting on behalf of the Plaintiffs, receipt of which letter was acknowledged by the Defendants in a letter dated 1st February 1992, drawing their attention to Patent No. 1234567.

3. The Plaintiffs are at present unable to give particulars of all the Defendants' infringements of the Patent but will seek relief at the trial of this Action in respect of each and every such infringement.

FORM D: DEFENCE AND COUNTERCLAIM

Defence

1. Paragraph 1 of the Statement of Claim is admitted.
2. It is admitted that Letters Patent No. 1234567 are presently subsisting, but it is averred that the same are invalid for the reasons appearing in the Particulars of Objection served herewith and in the premises paragraph 2 of the Statement of Claim is denied.
3. It is denied that the Defendants have infringed and further that they threaten or intend to infringe the said Letters Patent as alleged or at all. However the offers for sale and supply of polyurethane foam products as set out under sub-paragraphs (i) and (ii) under paragraph 2 of the Particulars of Infringement are admitted, save that it is denied that the said products or any of them were 'patented'.
4. All allegations of loss and damages are denied.
5. In the premises the Plaintiffs are not entitled to the relief claimed or any relief.

Counterclaim

6. The Defendants repeat paragraph 2 of the Defence and counterclaim for:

(i) An order that Letters Patent No. 1234567 be revoked.
(ii) Costs.

FORM E: PARTICULARS OF OBJECTIONS

The following are the Particulars of Objections referred to in the Defence and Counterclaim served herewith:
1. If, which is denied, any claim of the Complete Specification of the Patent in Suit covers any product or method of the Defendants, then the same is not new, alternatively is obvious, having regard to what was known or used before the priority date of such claim (which date is not admitted to be earlier than the date of filing the Complete Specification, namely 1st January 1976) in the United Kingdom. Hereunder the Defendants will rely upon common general knowledge and upon the publication in the United Kingdom of the following documents:

(i) Belgian Patent Specification No. 234567
(ii) Australian Patent Specification No. 12345/67
(iii) Dutch Patent Specification No. 6712345
(iv) US Patent Specification No. 2345678
(v) United Kingdom Patent Specification No. 456789*

2. The Complete Specification of the said Patent in suit does not sufficiently and fairly describe the invention and the method by which it is to be performed.
3. None of the Claims of the said Complete Specification is sufficiently and clearly defined.
4. None of the said Claims is fairly based on the matter disclosed in the said Complete Specification.

FORM F: REPLY AND DEFENCE TO COUNTERCLAIM

Reply

1. The Plaintiffs join issue with the Defendants upon their Defence save insofar as the same consists of admissions.

Defence to Counterclaim

2. The Plaintiffs deny that the Letters Patent in suit is invalid for the reasons alleged by the Defendant or at all.
3. In the premises the Defendants are not entitled to relief for which they counterclaim or to any relief.

FORM G: REQUEST FOR FURTHER AND BETTER PARTICULARS OF THE PARTICULARS OF OBJECTION

The Defendants are requested to give the following Further and Better Particulars of their Particulars of Objections.

Under Paragraph 1
A. Particulars regarding the prior user referred to, specifying:

> (i) the name and address of every person alleged to have made each and every such user;
> (ii) the earliest and latest dates of each and every such user;
> (iii) the locations at which each and every such user is alleged to have occurred;
> (iv) a description sufficient to identify each and every such user;
> (v) if any such user relates to machinery or apparatus, whether the machinery or apparatus is still in existence and where it can be inspected.

B. Particulars regarding the common general knowledge referred to, specifying:

> (i) matters in each of Defendants' cited documents (i) to (v) which are alleged to constitute common general knowledge;
> (ii) matters in any document or documents other than Defendants' cited documents (i) to (v), identifying any such document or documents and the passage or passages relied upon in each instance.

*These Patent Nos. are also artificial.

Under Paragraph 2

C. Particulars regarding the alleged lack of sufficient and fair description of the invention in the complete specification of the patent in suit.

D. Particulars regarding the alleged failure of the Complete Specification of the Patent in suit to describe the method whereby the invention is to be performed.

FORM H: FURTHER AND BETTER PARTICULARS OF THE PARTICULARS OF OBJECTION

Response to Requests under Paragraph 1

A. The Defendants are only relying on such user as was general trade practice in the art of manufacture of polyurethane foam products at the date of the Complete Specification of Patent No. 1234567.

B. It is denied that the Plaintiffs are entitled to particulars of common general knowledge.

Response to Requests under Paragraph 2

C. The Defendants do not intend to rely on this averment and will seek leave to amend their Particulars of Objection accordingly.

D. The Example in the Complete Specification fails to specify:

> (i) the order in which the various polyol and polyisocyanate and blowing agent reactants are to be mixed;
> (ii) the temperatures to be employed during the successive reaction stages.

FORM I: PLAINTIFFS' REQUEST FOR ADMISSIONS

The Plaintiffs require the Defendants to admit for the purposes of this action and counterclaim only, the following facts and each of them:

1. That subsequent to 1st January 1978 and prior to 1st June 1992 the Defendants have within the United Kingdom made, disposed of, offered to dispose of, used and kept whether for disposal or otherwise a polyurethane foam product known as 'Cumfee-Core'.

2. That the aforesaid 'Cumfee-Core' product comprised a polyurethane foam containing closed oviform cells with their ovoidal axes substantially parallel.

3. That the aforesaid 'Cumfee-Core' product contained 25–50%, by volume, of said oviform cells.

4. That the aforesaid 'Cumfee-Core' product contained oviform cells having a major axis of between 1 and 2 mms and a minor axis of between 0.75 and 1.5 mms.

5. That the aforesaid 'Cumfee-Core' product was in the form of a slab the opposite parallel faces of which were substantially parallel to the ovoidal axes.

6. That the aforesaid 'Cumfee-Core' product was in the form of a slab the opposite parallel faces of which were clad with thin unfoamed polyurethane sheet.

7. That the aforesaid 'Cumfee-Core' product had a hardness on Durometer A scale of between 5 and 35, a tensile strength of between 100 to 200 psi and a compression set of between 0 and 10%.

8. That the aforesaid 'Cumfee-Core' product was made by a process comprising forming a mixture of polyurethane foam reactants, effecting a partial foaming step at elevated temperature, cooling the partially formed foam so as to increase the viscosity thereof to a value of at least 100 poises, stretching the cooled viscous foam and finally allowing the foaming step to proceed to completion.

9. That in the aforesaid process the viscosity was allowed to increase to at least 250 poises.

10. That in the aforesaid process the cooled viscous foam was stretched by a drawing step.

11. That in the aforesaid process the foam product was subsequently cut into slabs and the slabs then clad on each side with a thin unfoamed polyurethane sheet.

FORM J: RESPONSE TO PLAINTIFFS' REQUEST FOR ADMISSIONS

For the purposes of this Action and Counterclaim only, the Defendants admit the following:
1. Each of the facts and matters set out in Paragraphs 1, 5, 6, 7, 8, 9, and 11 of the Plaintiffs' Request for Admissions.
2. Each of the facts and matters set out in Paragraphs 2, 3 and 4 of the Plaintiffs' Request for Admissions, except insofar as the ovoidal axes of the closed oviform cells are required to be substantially parallel.
3. Paragraph 10 is not admitted.

FORM K: NOTICE OF EXPERIMENTS

Take Notice that at the Trial of this Action and Counterclaim the Defendants may rely upon the following experiment:

Purpose of the Experiment
The experiment was conducted to show that it is essential to the creation of the oviform closed cells in substantially parallel arrangement that the polyol and polyisocyanate be allowed to interact first, so as to form a pre-polymer prior to introduction of the blowing agent.

Summary of Experiment
Two reactant mixes, with ingredient ratios as specified in the Example in the Complete Specification of Patent No. 1234567, were taken. In mix A, the polyol and polyisocyanate were pre-mixed, allowed to react for a short time, and blowing agent then added. In mix B, all ingredients were mixed simultaneously. After foam-formation and treatment in the manner prescribed in the Example, the product was cut open and the cross-sectional cell-structure examined microscopically.

Method
(Recite full details of the experiments)

Results
It was observed that the cell axes in the foam derived from mix A were substantially parallel whereas the cell axes in the foam derived from mix B were randomly disposed.

Conclusion
Formation of a pre-polymer prior to introduction of the blowing agent is critical to production of substantially parallel cell axes.

FORM L: ORDER ON SUMMONS FOR DIRECTIONS

UPON MOTION FOR Directions made by Counsel for the Plaintiffs
AND UPON HEARING Counsel for the Defendants
AND UPON READING the Court file
AND THE DEFENDANTS by their Counsel undertaking that it will not be less than 4 weeks before the date of the trial of this Action and Counterclaim (hereinafter called 'the trial') inform the Plaintiffs of any documents not already discovered upon which they will rely in respect of common general knowledge:
IT IS ORDERED

(1) that Paragraph C of the Request for Further and Better Particulars of Objection a copy whereof is annexed hereto be struck out and that reservice of the same be dispensed with
(2) that the following documents or legible facsimile copies thereof may be used in evidence at the trial without further proof thereof or of their contents

(a) Official Printer's copies of Specifications Nos. 1234567 456789 and of Belgium Patent Specification No. 234567 Australian Patent Specification No. 12345/67 Dutch Patent Specification No. 6712345 and US Patent Specification No. 2345678

(b) Agreed translations of Belgium Patent Specification No. 234567 and Dutch Patent Specification No. 6712345.

(3) (i) that if either party shall desire to rely at the trial of this Action and Counterclaim upon any model apparatus drawing photograph or cinematograph or video film that party shall on or before . . . give notice to the other; shall afford the other party an opportunity within . . . days of the service of such notice of inspecting the same and shall if so requested furnish the other party with copies of any such drawings or photograph and a sufficient drawing photograph or illustration of any model or apparatus

(ii) that if either party shall wish to rely upon any model apparatus drawing photograph or cinematograph or video film in reply to any matter of which notice was given under sub-paragraph (i) of this paragraph that party shall within . . . days after the inspection to be made in pursuance of the said sub-paragraph (i) give to the other party a like notice; if so requested within . . . days of the delivery of such notice shall afford like opportunities of inspection which shall take place within . . . days of such request; and shall in like manner furnish copies of any drawing or photograph and illustration of any such model or apparatus

(iii) that no further or other model apparatus drawing photograph or cinematograph or video film shall be relied upon in evidence by either party save with mutual consent or by leave of the Court

(4) If any party intends to establish any fact by means of any experiment that party shall, on or before the . . . serve a Notice in accordance with Order 104 r.12 and thereafter as soon as practicable apply to the Court for directions in relation thereto.

(5) Any party may call up to three expert witnesses in this action provided that such party:

(a) supplies the name of such expert to the opposing parties on or before . . .

(b) no later than . . . days before the date set for the hearing of this Action and Counterclaim serves upon the opposing parties a report of each such expert comprising the evidence which that expert intends to give at the trial.

(6) Each party shall, no later than . . . days before the date set for hearing this Action and Counterclaim serve upon the opposing party a signed witness statement of each witness (other than expert witnesses) which it intends to call at the trial.

(7) that any of the times mentioned herein may be enlarged by mutual consent for a period not exceeding one month or otherwise by leave of the Court

(8) that the trial of this Action and Counterclaim shall be before a Nominated Judge alone in London

(9) that any party may set down this Action and Counterclaim for a trial within 21 days after the expiry of all the times provided for in this Order

(10) that the costs of this application are to be costs in the Action and Counterclaim

(11) that the parties are to be at liberty on . . . days notice to apply for further directions and generally

FORM M: SCHEDULE OF INTERROGATORIES

Reference is made to the Defendants' Reponses dated . . . . . to the Plaintiffs' Request for Admissions herein. Paragraph 8 of the Plaintiffs' Request for Admissions was admitted, namely that the Defendants' 'Cumfee-Core' product was made by a process comprising forming a mixture of polyurethane foam reactants, effecting a partial foaming step at elevated temperature, cooling the partially formed foam so as to increase the viscosity thereof, to a value of at least 100 poises, stretching the cooled viscous foam and finally allowing the foaming step to proceed to completion.

1. In the Defendants' process for making their 'Cumfee-Core' product, was the cooled partially formed foam of viscosity at least 100 poises subsequently stretched ?

2. If so, what stretching means was employed ?

3. If so, under what physical conditions was the stretching step performed by the stretching means ?

4. If so, what degree of stretch of the cooled partially formed foam of viscosity at least 100 poises was attained ?

5. In the Defendants' process for making their 'Cumfee-Core' product, if the cooled partially formed foam of viscosity at least 100 poises, was not stretched, how was the oviform shape of the closed cells alternatively created ?

FORM N: NOTICE OF MOTION (Amendment of Particulars of Objection)

Take Notice that this Honourable Court will be moved before the Honourable Mr. Justice . . . . on . . . . at 10.30 am or so soon thereafter as Counsel can be heard by Counsel for the above-named Plaintiffs for an Order:

1. That the Particulars of Objections herein be amended in accordance with the draft amended in red and attached hereto.

FORM O: ORDER (On Motion to amend Particulars of Objections)

UPON MOTION PURSUANT to Notice of Motion dated . . . . made by Counsel for the Defendants

AND UPON HEARING Counsel for the Plaintiffs

AND UPON READING the Court file

AND THE DEFENDANTS by their Counsel undertaking that it will deliver to the Plaintiffs further amended Particulars of Objection

IT IS ORDERED that the Plaintiffs do on or before . . . . elect whether they will discontinue this Action and withdraw their Defence to the Counterclaim and consent to an Order for the revocation of Letters Patent No. 1234567

AND if the Plaintiffs shall so elect and shall give notice thereof to the Defendants within the time aforesaid

IT IS ORDERED (1) that Letters patent No. 1234567 be revoked and that it be referred to the Taxing Master to tax the costs of the Defendants of this Action down to and including the date of delivery of the Particulars of Objection and of the Counterclaim except insofar as the same have been increased by reason of the failure of the Defendants originally to deliver the Particulars of Objection in their amended or further amended form and to tax the costs of the Plaintiffs of this Action subsequent to the said . . . . down to and including this day and of the Counterclaim insofar as they have been increased by reason of the failure of the Defendants aforesaid

(2) that the Taxing Master is to set off the said costs of the Defendants and of the Plaintiffs when so taxed as aforesaid and to certify to which of them the balance after such set off is due

(3) that such balance be paid by the party from whom to the party to whom the same shall be certified to be due

AND if the Plaintiffs shall not give notice to the Defendants as aforesaid within the time aforesaid

IT IS ORDERED that the Defendants be at liberty to amend their Defence and Counterclaim and their Particulars of Objection in the manner indicated in red in the copy of the proposed further amended Defence and Counterclaim and Particulars of Objection already delivered to the Plaintiffs copies of which are on the Court File and that the Plaintiffs be at liberty to deliver on or before . . . . an amended Reply and Defence to Counterclaim

AND IT IS ORDERED that the Defendants do pay to the Plaintiffs their costs of and occasioned by the amendments aforesaid including the costs of this application to be taxed by the Taxing Master

AND the parties are to be at liberty to apply

Appendix 7

Patents County Court Forms

The following is a Statement of Case (patent infringement action) comparable to the Statement of Claim in Patents Court proceedings (Appendix 6, Form B), but formulated so as to meet the particular requirements of Order 48A Rule 4(2)(b) of the County Court Rules for 'all facts, matters and arguments relied on . . . including at least one example of each type of infringement alleged'.

It will be seen that the Statement of Case represents essentially an amalgam of the Patents Court form of pleading together with the Patent Office form of pleading (assuming that the dispute in question were capable of being heard there). The formal parts reflect the Patents Courts requirements. The argumentative parts reflect the Patent Office requirements.

The Defence and Counterclaim will in turn combine the formal parts of the Defence and Counterclaim, and associated Particulars of Objection, in Patents Court proceedings (Appendix 6, Forms D and E) together with supporting argument both as regards non-infringement and invalidity (assuming that both points are taken by the Defendants). The amalgam of Patents Court and Patent Office requirements is again present.

Similar argument may be presented in the Reply and/or Defence to Counterclaim. For these subsequent pleadings, and also the forms for use in later interlocutory stages, reference should be made to the 'County Court Practice' (the so-called 'Green Book') and also to the model forms issued under the aegis of the Patent Litigators Association.

IN THE PATENTS COUNTY COURT   Case No. 9.. PAT 00..

PLAINTIFFS

WHITE KNIGHT LIMITED

DEFENDANTS

RED KNAVE LIMITED

STATEMENT OF CASE
Under Order 48A Rule 4(2)

---

1. The Plaintiffs are and were at all material times the proprietors of Patent No. 1234567.
2. The Patent is and was at all material times in force.
3. Subsequent to the publication of the Complete Specification of Patent No. 1234567 and prior to the issue of the Writ in this Action the Defendants have infringed Patent No. 1234567 and Claims 1 to 10 in the Complete Specification thereof by doing in the United Kingdom, without the consent of the Plaintiffs, in relation to the invention the subject of the Patent the following things that is to say:

      (i) insofar as the invention is a product, namely a polyurethane foam product as claimed in any one or more of Claims 1 to 5 of the Patent, by making, disposing of, offering to dispose of, using or keeping the product whether for disposal or otherwise;

      (ii) insofar as the invention is a process, namely a method of making a polyurethane foam product and as claimed in any one or more Claims 7 to 9 of the Patent, by using the process and/or by disposing of, offering to dispose of, using, keeping for disposal or otherwise a product obtained directly by the process;

(iii) insofar as the invention is a process, namely a shock absorbing method employing the said polyurethane foam product as shock absorbing medium and as claimed in Claim 11 of the Patent, by supplying or offering to supply in the United Kingdom a person other than a licensee or other person entitled to work the invention with means, namely a polyurethane foam product, relating to an essential element of the invention for putting the invention into effect when the Defendants knew at all material times or it was obvious to a reasonable person in the circumstances that the said means were suitable for putting and were intended to put the invention into effect in the United Kingdom.

4. In particular the Plaintiffs complain of the following acts of the Defendants:

(i) offering the patented polyurethane foam product for sale in the United Kingdom by circulating therein around April 1992 a price list entitled 'Cumfee-Core Sheets & Slabs' (a copy whereof may be inspected at the offices of the Plaintiffs' Patent Agents);

(ii) Supplying the patented polyurethane foam product to Messrs. Shadow & Son, of Shady Lane, Soulminster, in the County of Essex, in or around March 1992. A copy of the delivery note dated 15 March 1992 in respect of a consignment of twelve blocks of 'Cumfee-Core' (size 6' × 4' × 6") from the Defendants to the said Messrs. Shadow & Son may be inspected at the offices of the Plaintiffs' Patent Agents.

In each case, the Defendants well knew at all material times that manufacture and/or sale and/or subsequent use of the polyurethane foam product referred to without the Plaintiffs' consent would be an infringement of Patent No. 1234567.

Particulars of Knowledge and Circumstance

Hereunder, the Plaintiffs will rely upon the following facts and matters as the best particulars which can be given before discovery:

(i) The Defendants had been sent on 14 January 1992 a letter from Messrs. Draft & Claim of 25 Southampton Buildings, London W.C.2 Chartered Patent Agents acting on behalf of the Plaintiffs, receipt of which letter was acknowledged by the Defendants in a letter dated 1st February 1992, drawing their attention to Patent No. 1234567.

5. The Plaintiffs are at present unable to give particulars of all the Defendants' infringements of the Patent but will seek relief at the trial of this Action in respect of each and every such infringement.
6. Claim 1 of Patent No. 1234567 reads:

'1. A polyurethane foam containing closed oviform cells with their ovoidal axes substantially parallel.'

7. The 'Cumfee-Core' foam blocks referred to in Paragraph 4 above are constituted of polyurethane foam. Microscopic examination of longitudinally cut sections of the blocks shows that the cells in the form are of closed form with a three-dimensional shape correspondingly essentially to that of an ellipsoid of revolution. The cells are also essentially aligned parallel to the main length of the block, the scatter of the longitudinal axes of the individual ellipsoidal cells being with 10° each side of the main longitudinal axis of the block. The Plaintiffs assert that the term 'oviform' in Claim 1 embraces profiles of elliptical shape, that is, symmetrical profiles with each end curved similarly, as well as egg-shaped profiles in the colloquial sense, that is, asymmetrical profiles with one end curved more pointedly than the other. 'Substantially parallel' is clearly apt in the context of the Patent to embrace divergence of axes of the order present in the 'Cumfee-Core' product.
8. As for Claim 2, the Plaintiffs' tests on the 'Cumfee-Core' foam blocks referred to in Paragraph 4 above show an average of 41% for cell volume.

9. As for Claim 3, the Plaintiffs' tests on the 'Cumfee-Core' foam blocks referred to in Paragraph 4 above show an average major cell axis of 1.8 mm and an average minor cell axis of 1.3 mm.

10. As for Claim 4, the 'Cumfee-Core' foam blocks referred to in Paragraph 4 above were each in the form of a rectangular parallelepiped, hence constituting a slab.

11. As for Claim 6, the Plaintiffs' tests on the 'Cumfee-Core' foam blocks referred to in Paragraph 4 above show a hardness on Durometer A scale of 27, a tensile strength of 162 psi and a compression set of 7%.

12. Claim 7 of Patent No. 1234567 reads:

> '7. A method of making a polyurethane foam according to Claim 1, comprising forming a mixture of polyurethane foam reactants, effecting a partial foaming step at elevated temperature, cooling the partially formed foam so as to increase the viscosity thereof to a value of at least 100 poises, stretching the cooled viscous foam and finally allowing the foaming step to proceed to completion.'

13. The trade journal *Polyurethane Progress*, in issue dated 30 March 1992, has a report on page 123 under the title 'Red Knave Roars Ahead' of their new 'Elliform' polyurethane foam process. It is stated to have just been put into commercial production, and to provide a foam having superior shock-absorbing effect hence rendering the foam particularly suitable for seats and upholstery in four-wheel drive vehicles intended to be driven over rough ground. The foam is to be marketed under the new name of 'Cumfee-Core', and will be available in conventional standard shapes and sizes. Certain manufacturing details are provided in the paragraph at l.h. column, lines 10–20 on page 123. These include a preliminary mixing of TDI with POPD followed by heating at 80°C with subsequent cooling to 40°C over a period of 2 hours. The cooled foam mixture is then extruded through a Dainart Type 100 rectangular nozzle extruder into the nip between successive pairs of steel rollers which elongate the loosely cohering strip and feed the same into a final curing oven.

14. The Plaintiffs accordingly assert that the manufacture of 'Cumfee-Core' is carried out by the Defendants at their Leaville factory by a process coming within the terms of Claim 7.

15. As for Claim 8, the 'Polyurethane Progress' article refers to attainment of a viscosity of 350 poises by completion of the cooling period.

16. As for Claim 9, the nip roll pairs described by 'Polyurethane Progress' will effect a drawing step.

17. Claim 11 of Patent No. 1234567 reads:

> '11. A method of reducing the transmission of vehicular ground shock to a person(s) travelling in a four-wheel type of powered vehicle over rough terrain comprising upholstering one or more seats of such vehicle with a polyurethane foam according to Claim 1.'

18. Messrs Shadow & Son as referred to in Paragraph 4 above are well-known specialist upholsterers for luxury cars of all-terrain type. The only purpose for which they would need polyurethane foam is the manufacture of such upholstery. Once they have fitted such upholstery then the benefits of that upholstery will be attained on driving the vehicle. The Plaintiffs assert that in such circumstances the requirements of Section 60(1)(c) of the Patents Act 1977 are met by the supply of infringing polyurethane foam to Messrs. Shadow & Son.

19. The Plaintiffs request, in view of the loss and damage caused to them by the activities of the Defendants hereinabove set out:

> (1) A declaration that Patent No. 1234567 is valid and has been infringed by the Defendants.
>
> (2) An injunction to restrain the Defendants by their directors, officers, employees, servants or agents or otherwise howsoever from infringing the said patent.
>
> (3) An order for the delivery up or destruction upon oath of any patented product in relation to which the said Patent is infringed and of any article containing that product as an inextricable constituent.
>
> (4) An inquiry as to damages in respect of infringement or alternatively at the Plaintiffs' option an account of the profits made by the Defendants derived by them from the

infringement, and payment of all sums so found due together with interest under the provisions of Section 69 of the County Courts Act 1984.

(5) Such further or other relief as to this Honourable Court may seem meet.

(6) Costs.

Signed: . . . .   Dated: . . . .
     XYZ
     Chartered Patent Agents for the Plaintiffs

Address for Service: XYZ
                 99 Southampton Buildings
                 London W.C.2

Appendix 8

Argument Resumés

The following were the resumés of argument presented by the parties to the Court in *American Cyanamid v Ethicon* [1979] RPC 215 on the 'best method' issue. 'Best method' denotes the requirement of the 1949 Act, applicable to existing patents (those granted under the 1949 Act), that the patentee disclose in his specification not merely a practicable method for performing the invention but the best method (section 4(3)(b)). The corresponding ground of revocation (section 32(1)(h)) is couched in terms of:

> (h) that the complete specification does not sufficiently and fairly describe the invention and the method by which it is to be performed, *or* does not disclose the *best method* of performing it which was known to the applicant for the patent and for which he was entitled to claim protection . . .

(Emphasis added)

Plaintiffs' argument
'Best Method'

1. The apparatus of Schmitt and/or Chirgwin was an apparatus for use in a research laboratory with small quantities of material. It could not be used in any substantial production of polymer which would have to be protected from moisture by other means known in the field and/or dried prior to extrusion.

2. α glycolide was not known to be better than the β glycolide for making PHAE fibres prior to October 1964, and in fact it was not. The highest it can be put against the plaintiffs is that it was thought it might be.

3. The difference between the α and β glycolide was that while both were moisture sensitive the latter reverted to the linear dimer on picking up moisture while the former did not. It was common knowledge that the glycolide monomer should be kept dry at all times and if this was done the difference between α and β would not matter.

4. The drying temperature for the glycolide was 40–50°C. Above 42°C. in a mixture of α and β glycolide, the β tends to convert to α so that any advantage of the α over the β was created in any event by the use of normal drying temperatures.

5. The date at which 'best method' is to be tested is the date of the convention application in America. If this is correct the plaintiffs could not have disclosed the use of α glycolide because it had not even been thought of by the plaintiffs by that date.'

Defendants' argument
'Best method'

1. In or about January 1964, Dr. Schmitt discovered that, if he conducted polymerisation in a vessel directly connected to extrusion means, he could avoid the problems which arose as a result of cooling the polymer, grinding it and remelting it; and could produce strong fibres. From then on for some $2\frac{1}{2}$ years all experimental fibres were made by this method using Schmitt's apparatus or Chirgwin's developments of it.

2. In about August 1964, significant discoveries and advances were made in respect of glycolide and its purity and its alpha form.

3. None of these matters was put into the complete specification filed in U.K. in October 1964 which was identical to that filed in U.S.A. in October 1963.'

The full resumés, on all points in issue (both on validity and infringement), are reported at pages 227 to 240. The documents as filed with the Court would, of course, carry formal heading and termination, as shown at the beginning of Appendix 6.

Appendix 9

Court Order

The order of the High Court, the Court of first instance, in *Ransburg v Aerostyle* ([1967] RPC 30) read in material parts as follows:

THIS COURT DOTH DECLARE that the Defendants and each of them have infringed Claims 1, 4, 5, 6, 8, 13 and 14 of Letters Patent No. 710,852 prior to the expiry of the said Letters Patent
AND THIS COURT DOTH ORDER that the following inquiry be made that is to say

> (1) An Inquiry what damages have been sustained by the Plaintiffs by reason of the infringement of the said Letters Patent by the Defendants and each of them up to the date of expiry of the said Letters Patent

AND IT IS ORDERED that the Counterclaim of the Defendants and each of them for revocation of Letters Patent No. 710,852 do stand dismissed out of this Court
AND IT IS ORDERED that the said Action insofar as it alleges infringement of Letters Patent No. 710,920 do stand dismissed out of this Court
AND IT IS ORDERED that Letters Patent No. 710,920 be revoked
AND THIS COURT DOTH HEREBY CERTIFY that upon the Trial of the said Action and the said Counterclaim the validity of all the Claims of the Specification of Letters Patent No. 710, 852 was contested and that the Particulars of Breaches pleaded by the Plaintiffs were reasonable and proper
AND in case the Plaintiffs shall obtain a regrant of Letters Patent corresponding to Letters Patent No. 710,852 under the provisions of the Patents and Designs Act 1949 the Plaintiffs are to be at liberty to apply for an Injunction and such other relief as is appropriate and generally
AND IT IS ORDERED that it be referred to the Taxing Master to tax the costs of the Plaintiffs of the said Action and of the said Counterclaim
AND IT IS ORDERED that the Defendants and each of them do pay to the Plaintiffs four fifths of the said costs when taxed
The costs of the said Inquiry are reserved

Although this order is largely self-explanatory, some points are worth noting as follows:

> (1) Two patents were involved; one (Patent No. 710852) was held valid and infringed; the other (Patent No. 710920) was held invalid, hence infringement was immaterial.
> (2) Certificate of validity was granted in respect of Patent No. 710852.
> (3) Since Patent No. 710852 had already expired at date of judgment, no injunction could be granted (but instead only an inquiry as to damages); but the Plaintiffs were given leave to return to the Court to ask for an injunction, in case their application for extension of term of the Patent should prove successful.
> (4) Since each party had been successful in part, costs were ordered to be apportioned (Plaintiffs receiving only four fifths of their normal taxed costs).

Appendix 10

European Economic Community Treaty
(Treaty of Rome) — Selected Articles

ARTICLE 36

The provisions of Articles 30 to 34 shall not preclude prohibitions or restrictions on imports, exports or goods in transit justified on grounds of public morality, public policy or public security; the protection of health and life of humans, animals or plants; the protection of national treasures possessing artistic, historic or archaeological value; or the protection of industrial and commercial property. Such prohibitions or restrictions shall not, however, constitute a means of arbitrary discrimination or a disguised restriction on trade between Member States.

ARTICLE 85

1. The following shall be prohibited as incompatible with the common market: all agreements between undertakings, decisions by associations of undertakings and concerted practices which may affect trade between Member States and which have as their object or effect the prevention, restriction or distortion of competition within the common market, and in particular those which:

   (a) directly or indirectly fix purchase or selling prices or any other trading conditions;

   (b) limit or control production, markets, technical development, or investment;

   (c) share markets or sources of supply;

   (d) apply dissimilar conditions to equivalent transactions with other trading parties, thereby placing them at a competitive disadvantage;

   (e) make the conclusion of contracts subject to acceptance by the other parties of supplementary obligations which, by their nature or according to commercial usage, have no connection with the subject of such contracts.

2. Any agreements or decisions prohibited pursuant to this Article shall be automatically void.

3. The provisions of paragraph 1 may, however, be declared inapplicable in the case of:

   –any agreement or category of agreements between undertakings;

   –any decision or category or decisions by associations of undertakings;

   –any concerted practice or category of concerted practices;

which contributes to improving the production or distribution of goods or to promoting technical or economical progress, while allowing consumers a fair share of the resulting benefit, and which does not:

   (a) impose on the undertakings concerned restrictions which are not indispensable to the attainment of these objectives;

   (b) afford such undertakings the possibility of eliminating competition in respect of a substantial part of the products in question.

ARTICLE 86

Any abuse by one or more undertakings of a dominant position within the common market or in a substantial part of it shall be prohibited as incompatible with the common market in so far as it may affect trade between Member States. Such abuse may, in particular, consist in:

   (a) directly or indirectly imposing unfair purchase or selling prices or other unfair trading conditions;

(b) limiting production, markets or technical development to the prejudice of consumers;

(c) applying dissimilar conditions to equivalent transactions with other trading parties, thereby placing them at a competitive disadvantage;

(d) making the conclusion of contracts subject to acceptance by the other parties of supplementary obligations which, by their nature or according to commercial usage, have no connection with the subject of such contracts.

ARTICLE 173

The Court of Justice shall review the legality of acts of the Council and the Commission other than recommendations or opinions. It shall for this purpose have jurisdiction in actions brought by a Member State, the Council or the Commission on grounds of lack of competence, infringement of an essential procedural requirement, infringement of this Treaty or of any rule of law relating to its application, or misuse of powers.

Any natural or legal person may, under the same conditions, institute proceedings against a decision addressed to that person or against a decision which, although in the form of a regulation or a decision addressed to another person, is of direct and individual concern to the former.

The proceedings provided for in this Article shall be instituted within two months of the publication of the measure, or of its notification to the plaintiff, or, in the absence thereof, of the day on which it came to the knowledge of the latter, as the case may be.

ARTICLE 177

THE COURT OF JUSTICE SHALL HAVE JURISDICTION TO GIVE PRELIMINARY RULINGS CONCERNING:

(a) the interpretation of this Treaty;

(b) the validity and interpretation of acts of the institutions of the Community;

(c) the interpretation of the statutes of bodies established by an act of the Council, where those statutes so provide.

Where such a question is raised before any court or tribunal of a Member State, that court or tribunal may, if it considers that a decision on the question is necessary to enable it to give judgment, request the Court of Justice to give a ruling thereon.

Where any such question is raised in a case pending before a court or tribunal of a Member State, against whose decisions there is no judicial remedy under national law, that court or tribunal shall bring the matter before the Court of Justice.

ARTICLE 222

This Treaty shall in no way prejudice the rules in Member States governing the system of property ownership.

Appendix 11

Revocation in the Patent Office of a 'new' patent granted under Patents Act 1977

Forms A to F in this Appendix (together with Specification No. 2345678* and the Livingstone citation) represent a typical set of documents such as might be filed in connection with an application for revocation in the Patent Office of a 1977 Act patent ('new' patent). Formal headings and terminations are given only for Forms A and B; headings for Forms C to F follow Form B. The full form of attestation for the Statutory Declarations used for the parties' evidence is provided for Form D(i) only.

The pleadings (Forms A to C) are, in the very broadest sense, comparable to pleadings in the High Court (Appendix 6). They are intended to set out the assertions which the parties anticipate to be able to prove, with the assistance if necessary of the evidence; this latter is normally written (Forms D to F).

Correct preparation of the written evidence is, especially for the attacking party, the virtual *sine qua non* to success in the Patent Office (as already discussed in Chapter 11). It can be a mistake to present a document which is too perfect a model of logic and conciseness. The aim of the written evidence is to provide the Hearing Officer on paper with the facts which the experts would otherwise give orally (if the proceedings were in the Court); and in real life, such evidence may well be repetitive in part and drift off into side-issues as well.

In the absence of any 'warts' at all, the Hearing Officer may conclude that the evidence has been drafted by the party's adviser(s) rather than his expert and, in the absence of cross-examination, to that extent discount its weight.

The principal points at issue in this model case are:

(1) Obviousness of the patented necklace in face of the prior art acknowledged in the Specification.
(2) Availability of the Livingstone citation as prior art.
(3) Obviousness in face of both the acknowledged prior art and the Livingstone citation.
(4) Insufficiency.

SPECIFICATION NO. 2345678 (Dated 1st June 1979)

This invention relates to necklaces. Traditional natural gemstone necklaces are now increasingly impractical for the average person, because of the increasing scarcity of suitable natural stones; this is the more so since necklaces are usually composed of stones of comparable or suitably carefully gradated size. To meet this demand, other materials (wood, glass, plastics, artificial stone) have been increasingly used in recent years, and have proved increasingly popular with younger women.

Various forms of plastics decorative elements for making multi-unit necklaces are already known. One well-known kind consists of a generally spherical body formed with a projecting necked flat fin at one pole shaped to fit, on slight deformation of the head of the fin, loosely into a corresponding shaped slot at the other pole. To assemble the necklace, the spherical bodies

---

* This Specification No. is of course an artificial one in the context.

(as many as required) simply have to be push-fitted into each other head-to-tail. The looseness of the connection provides the necessary flexibility for the eventual necklace.

It is an object of the present invention to provide a new necklace construction whereby the length and decorative appearance of the necklace can be altered as desired by the wearer.

According to the present invention, a unit for the production of necklaces and the like comprises a cylindrical block of polygonal cross-section but with a pair of substantially flat end-faces, at least one of the end-faces being formed with an undercut circular recess and a cylindrical connector at the opposite end-face formed with a necked annular collar capable of engaging loosely within the undercut recess of an adjacent like unit.

In the simplest version of the unit, the connector is made integral with the block at the end-face remote from that in which the recess is formed. In an alternative version, enabling greater play (both axial and transverse) between adjacent units, the connector is a separate element and is formed with a collar at each end. This in turn will necessitate a recess being provided in each end-face of the block.

Push-fitting is used in both instances to assemble the blocks and connectors into a necklace.

In both versions, adjacent blocks can twist relative to each other by rotation of the connector(s) in its associated recess(es). This rotatability, coupled with the polygonal cross-section of the blocks, permits contrasting visual effects to be obtained as between blocks or block multiples via suitable coloration or other decoration, e.g. by application of bright metal particles, of polygonal surfaces.

In the drawings, Fig. 1 shows an element 1 of octagonal cross-section, made of suitable plastics material (e.g. polyvinyl chloride) and with polygonal faces 2 all separately and differently coloured. Fig. 4 is a cross-sectional view of Fig. 1. One end-face 3 is formed with a circular recess 4 of undercut generally semi-circular profile. The opposite end-face is formed with a necked protruberance incorporating an annular collar 5 of generally semi-circular profile and width both slightly smaller than that of the recess 4.

Fig. 2 shows an element of generally similar design but with a circular recess in each end-face, and intended for use with separate connectors as shown in Fig. 3. The Fig. 3 connector is formed with a waisted central portion 6 and an annular collar, akin to that of Fig. 1, at each end.

All the figures are drawn to an enlarged scale. Normally the elements would be only 10 mm–25 mm long, with correspondingly smaller transverse and connector dimensions, so as to enable necklaces having a suitable multiplicity of elements (say 20–30) to be constructed.

Claims:
1. A unit for the production of necklaces comprising a cylindrical block of polygonal cross-section but with a pair of substantially flat end-faces, at least one of the end-faces being formed with an undercut circular recess and a cylindrical connector at the opposite end-face formed with a necked annular collar capable of engaging loosely within the undercut recess of an adjacent like unit.
2. A unit according to Claim 1 in which the cylindrical block has on one end-face an integral connector protruding therefrom, and a recess in the opposed end-face.
3. A unit according to Claim 1 in which the cylindrical block contains an undercut recess in each end-face.

Patent No. 2345678

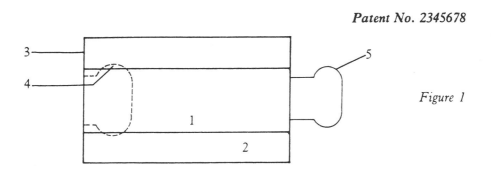

Figure 1

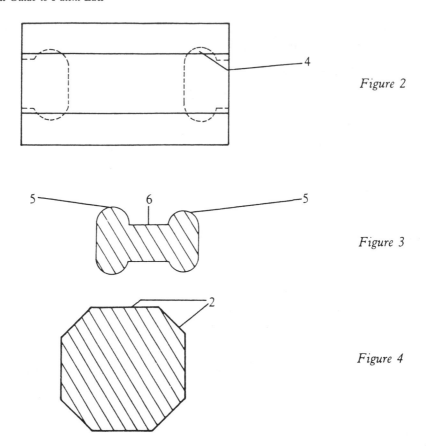

Figure 2

Figure 3

Figure 4

EXTRACT FROM Ph.D THESIS OF J. LIVINGSTONE ON 'LIFE AND CUSTOMS OF THE TIMBUCCA TRIBE IN WEST GRIQUALAND', PRESENTED TO THE UNIVERSITY OF BARKING IN 1956.

In the course of my travels up to the source of the Stanley river, I noticed the unusual form and shape of the decorative neckwear worn by the younger females.

This neckwear was made from a local tree of the *Leitneriaceae* family, the branches of which were pith-centred and grew with an unusual concave ribbed appearance. Sections would be cut, with a diameter of around 1″ and length 3–4″, and their insides hollowed out. The external surfaces would be coloured white/black, yellow/black or red/black, using local coloured earths, in length-wise halves. It was the custom for unmarried females to wear just one white/black section, strung around the neck by a suitable fibrous thong passing through the central bore. Married females would wear an additional section for each successive child (yellow/black for a boy and red/black for a girl); striking colour contrasts would thus sometimes be observed, for multiparous females.

Normally the white or coloured (yellow, red) half or halves only of each section would be exposed. But when one of the elders of the tribe died each section would be turned around, on the supporting thong, so as to show black as a sign of mourning. The generally biconcave configuration of the sections, combined with their substantial weight, prevented rotation in normal everyday wear; occasionally, however, when running or dancing accidental flipping-over of a section (or sections) might occur and a black half (or halves) be exposed as a result. Black/yellow, black/red and black/yellow/red combinations might then be seen. Some rough sketches of a typical section are shown.

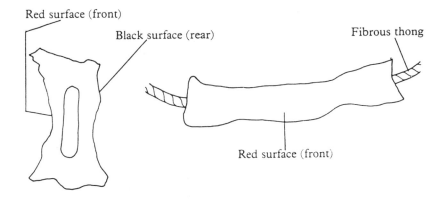

Forms A to F are as follows:

A   Application for Revocation
B   Statement of Case
C   Counterstatement
D1 and D2   Applicants' Evidence-in-chief (two Declarations)
E   Patentees' Evidence-in-chief
F   Applicants' Evidence-in-reply

(Written Exhibits DEF.1,2 and 3 forming parts of Forms D, F are not included, for sake of brevity, but drawn Exhibit GHI.1, forming part of Form E, is. All names and addresses given in Forms A to F are of course fanciful, as are also the documents discussed.)

FORM A
PATENTS ACT 1977
PATENTS FORM NO. 38/77
APPLICATION FOR THE REVOCATION OF A PATENT (SECTION 72)

We, Ethnic Jewellery Designs Inc. of 7 West 47th Street, New York, N.Y. 10234, United States of America, apply for revocation of Patent No. 2345678 standing in the name of Modern Necklaces Ltd.

(Signature)
(Agents and Address for Service)

FORM B
PATENTS ACT 1977

In the matter of
Patent No. 2345678 of
Modern Necklaces Ltd.
     – and –
In the matter of an
Application for
Revocation thereof by
Ethnic Jewellery
Designs Inc.

STATEMENT UNDER RULE 75(1)

1.   The Applicants apply for revocation of Patent No. 2345678 upon the grounds:

(a) that the invention of Patent No. 2345678 is not a patentable invention;
(b) that the Specification of Patent No. 2345678 does not disclose the invention clearly enough and completely enough for it to be performed by a person skilled in the art.

2.   Under ground (a) the Applicants contend that the invention of Patent No. 2345678 is obvious, and accordingly fails to involve any inventive step, having regard to the following matters which formed part of the state of the art at the priority date of the invention:

(i) the prior knowledge and prior use of multi-unit necklaces acknowledged in Patent No. 2345678 at page 1, lines 9–17 of the Specification.
(ii) the 1956 PhD thesis of Dr J. Livingstone (University of Barking) entitled 'Life and Customs of the Timbucca tribe in West Griqualand'

3.   Under ground (b) the Applicants contend that the Specification fails to disclose, in so far as the invention relates to elements of mineral or other incompressible materials, how such elements can be joined together. In all the embodiments described in the Specification resilient deformation is essential in order that the collar of the connector may pass through the mouth of the recess and then expand into the undercut in order to be engaged firmly therein; similarly, when it is desired to pull the connector out of the recess.
4.   Revocation of Patent No. 2345678 is requested. Alternatively, such amendment as may be capable of meeting the objections raised. An award of costs is also requested.

Dated this 1st day of January 1992

(Signature)
(Agents and Address)

FORM C
COUNTERSTATEMENT UNDER RULE 75(3)

1.   The Applicants' allegations as to absence of inventive step in the invention of Patent No. 2345678 are denied.
2.   So far as the prior art acknowledged in the Specification of Patent No. 2345678 is concerned, the Patentees point out these elements were non-rotatable; the generally rectangular cross-section of the fin, and associated slot, positively prevent any rotation. The whole purpose of the invention of Patent No. 2345678 is thus the converse of this prior art.
3.   So far as the Livingstone thesis is concerned, the Patentees deny that this was made available to the public prior to the priority date of the invention, 1 June 1979. Livingstone's pioneering anthropological work on the Timbucca tribe was only published posthumously in his book *The Timbucca Tribe* (1982, Barking University Press).
4.   The practices to which he refers as having taken place in West Griqualand around 1956 were not public knowledge in themselves. Entry to the Timbucca homelands was hazardous during the 1950s; it was well known that strangers were liable to be harmed; Livingstone was one of the first to live among them and return unscathed.
5.   Even if the PhD thesis and/or the West Griqualand practices did constitute public knowledge by 1979, it is denied that the skilled jewellery designer would have had any cause or incentive to combine such knowledge with the knowledge concerning plastic elements. The materials used in the two cases are totally different. Trees of the *Leitneriaceae* family do not commonly grow in the United Kingdom, although there may be an occasional specimen in specialist botanic gardens. Nor is the wood a commonly imported item.

6.   The Applicants' allegations as to insufficiency of disclosure are denied. They are asserting too wide a construction for Section 72(1)(c) (and consequentially also section 14(3) upon which it is founded) of the Act. The Patentees deny that they are required to disclose how all embodiments of the invention are to be performed. Disclosure as to performance of one embodiment alone is adequate. The Applicants have made no complaint as to the adequacy of the instructions given in relation to the specific embodiments of Figs. 1 to 4 of the Specification.
7.   Refusal of the Application for Revocation, and an award of costs, are requested.

Dated this 1st day of March 1992

(Signature)
(Agents and Address)

FORM D1 (APPLICANTS' EVIDENCE-IN-CHIEF UNDER RULE 75(4)) STATUTORY DECLARATION

I, Arthur Bolingbroke Curieuse of 888 Mottingham Lane, Mottingham, London S.E.9 do hereby solemnly and sincerely declare as follows:

1.   I am a technical assistant in the firm of Draft & Claim, 25 Southampton Buildings, London W.C.2, Chartered Patent Agents acting on behalf of the Applicants for Revocation in this matter
2.   On February 1st 1992 I travelled to Barking, Essex to visit the Library at the University there. I went to the reception desk in the Library and asked to see the PhD thesis of Dr. J. Livingstone in issue here. I was initially refused access, for the reason that I was not a member of Barking University. I then asked to see the University Librarian, and explained to him my reason for asking to inspect the thesis, and as to why the publication of the information in Livingstone's posthumous book was not enough. The Librarian in reply pointed out that under the Regulations of the University of Barking, a PhD candidate is required to present his thesis solely for the purpose of showing to the Board of Examiners the nature and extent of his research work. The latter would themselves naturally keep the subject-matter of thesis confidential; the Examiners were aware, particularly in respect of scientific work, of the possible danger of premature publication. Nevertheless the thesis had been catalogued and present in the Library since 1956 and would no doubt have been produced to any member of the University who might have asked to see it. At this time, there were no records of any such inspection ever having taken place; he had no personal recollection himself on the point, and had moreover only been appointed to the post in 1976. Permission to take the thesis out of the Library for study elsewhere would definitely have been refused, in accordance with long-standing University policy. The Library has never provided copying facilities for readers, on account of potential copyright problems. There are office-copying facilities for the staff, but the rule is that these can only be used for administrative purposes.
3.   At the conclusion of our discussion he agreed to show me the thesis. I accordingly saw the thesis, checked that it contained the passage at page 99 relied on by the Applicants for revocation. The thesis was dated June 1st 1956, signed 'J. Livingstone' and bore a catalogue stamp of August 1st 1956.

AND I MAKE this solemn Declaration conscientiously believing the same to be true and by virtue of the provisions of the Statutory Declarations Act 1835
Declared at 1 Old Square, Lincoln's Inn, London W.C.2 this 15th day of April 1992

Before me A. Tulkinghorne

(Arthur Bolingbroke Curieuse)
(Signature)

A Commissioner for Oaths

FORM D2 (APPLICANTS' EVIDENCE-IN-CHIEF UNDER RULE 75(4)) STATUTORY DECLARATION

I, Dempster Elihu Fachmann of 999 Skunk's Misery Lane, Sunningfield, Surrey do hereby solemnly and sincerely declare as follows:

1.   I have 38 years' experience in the jeweller industry. I am a graduate of Washington Heights High School, New York N.Y. and Cantitoe College, Bedford N.Y. where I studied Fine Arts. I joined Ethnic Jewellery Designs Inc. as management trainee in 1945, rising successively to designer (1949), chief designer (1959), works departmental manager (1964) and executive vice-president (1970). Since 1975 I have been resident managing director of Ethnic Jewellery Designs (UK) Ltd, the United Kingdom subsidiary of Ethnic Jewellery Designs Inc. I am the author of Manual of Modern Jewellery Manufacture (published by Trinket Press N.Y., in 1971) and of numerous articles in the jewellery trade press. I also received the Aurora Gold Medal of the American Jewellery Society in 1974 for services to jewellery design.

2.   I have read the Specification of Patent No. 2345678 the Application for Revocation with Statement, Counterstatement as well as the cited Livingstone publication.

3.   The acknowledgement in the Specification as regards prior multi-unit necklaces made of plastics materials is essentially correct. The sphere/fin type of unit was in fact first sold by my Company in the United Kingdom around 1970, following successful introduction in the United States in 1968. Sales grew rapidly in the early 1970s, reaching a peak of around 100, 000 sets of units (i.e. around 100,000 necklaces) in 1974. Since then, sales have gradually tailed off until today they are only around 5,000 per year. The sets were all made in our factory at Worthsville, Kentucky, U.S.A., whence they were exported to the United Kingdom and the twelve further European countries in which we have local subsidiaries.

4.   Certain circumstances of the jewellery trade are highly significant in the present matter. These include:

(i) The fickle nature of the market. One is essentially catering, so far as plastics multi-unit necklaces are concerned, for a younger market; most buyers are teenagers or younger women in their 20s. These tend to follow slavishly fashion trends, which may change overnight. Older women tend to be more conservative in their jewellery taste, preferring natural stones to plastics or like materials and being less concerned with ability to alter necklace length.

(ii) The increasing public interest in recent times in 'ethnic' products – that is, products and styles derived from under-developed countries, in particular those in S. America and in the African and Indian sub-continents.

5.   My Company specialised, in particular, in necklaces with designs emanating from Africa. Some of our most popular designs pre-1979 were those based on ivory cubes (originating with the Sanduru tribe in Sierra Leone), cowrie shells (originating in Micronesia) and monazite pebbles (originating in the Andaman Islands).

6.   In the course of my duties with my Company I travelled a great deal in under-developed countries seeking out ideas which might be adapted for a Western market. I became familiar with many anthropologists since I was particularly interested in the art and designs of tribes and peoples which were relatively little known to Western eyes.

7.   Specifically, I was aware of Dr. Livingstone's work with the Timbucca. Around 1962 I had discussions with Professor Darkin (at that time head of the Department of Archaeology and Anthropology in the University of Barking) whilst attending the XIXth triennial Congress of the World Anthropological Union in Rangitanga, W. Samoa. He was very excited about the work being done by one of his research students, Dr. J. Livingstone, in the hitherto rarely studied Timbucca tribe. The use of the contrasting colour sections as between nulliparous/multiparous females, and sex of progeny, in their neck adornments had never been previously encountered in Africa (although known in certain parts of S. America). This might have great significance as regards the history of peoples' migration in earlier millenia. The change to black in times of mourning was also highly unusual; up to then, use of black decoration at such times had been considered to be an exclusively Christian practice.

8.   He invited me to visit him at Barking University when travelling home from W. Samoa, in order that I could look at Livingstone's sketches myself. I accepted the invitation but unfortunately was unable to fulfil it on account of a strike in our Worthsville factory, necessitating an urgent return to the United States. At no time did he imply that Dr. Livingstone's work was secret or to be kept confidential. On the contrary, he seemed anxious to disseminate news of Dr. Livingstone's work and was encouraging him to write a book concerning it (this is the book which eventually came out much later in 1982). I had the distinct impression that he was grooming Dr. Livingstone for succession to his own professional chair; and indeed this happened in 1968. Although I am unaware of exactly how far knowledge of the work was distributed in anthropological circles during the 1960s and 1970s, I can hardly imagine that I was the only recipient. My relationship with Professor Darkin was one of casual acquaintance rather than trusted friend.

9.   Around 1977–78 there was a sharp change in market demand in the United Kingdom. Young women now started to want multicoloured necklaces. The well-established sphere/fin sets of units (25 elements per set normally) were in one colour only (cream, yellow, red and the like). We could of course meet this demand by providing in each set a great number of individually separated coloured elements (say, 10 cream + 10 yellow + 10 red + 10 black). But this would have led to a substantial increase in price, and our customers were in principle those with little purchasing power. An urgent need therefore arose for a new design, utilising the essentially cheap form of plastics element but permitting colour contrasts to be simply obtained.

10.   I immediately recalled at this point the Timbucca-type of necklace. Now produced as Exhibit DEF.1 is a copy of my memorandum dated 1 March 1978 to the Technical Director of Ethnic Jewellery Inc. at head office. I pointed out in this memorandum that a separate supporting string such as used in Africa would probably be unacceptable to the Western market. Tying/untying of the knot each time the necklace was put on/taken off, or altered in length, would be too troublesome for the average wearer. It was necessary instead for the plastics beads to be capable of being rotated relative to each other and the obvious way of doing this was by replacement of the fin-shaped projection, and corresponding slot, of the standard element by an arrangement of spigot/recess type.

11.   It never occurred to me that it could be suggested that there was anything inventive in employing an arrangement of this type in the necklace. The cylindrical spigot/undercut recess is one of the oldest forms of male/female fastener known; it is used in a wide range of industries. I produce as Exhibit DEF.2 pages 100–110 (constituting Chapter VIII) of *Manual of Fastening Devices* (Shufflebottom) published by Engineering Press, Manchester, England, 1972, as indicative of well-established common knowledge in this respect.

12.   Where real difficulty lay was in the development of suitable moulding machinery for the mass-production of elements bearing different colours and/or decorative effect surfaces on successive surfaces of the polygonal elements. Subsequent application of colour, sparkling or twinkling frit or the like, after the element had been initially moulded and had cooled down, would be expensive. It was desirable to combine the decoration steps into the formation steps. Suitable machinery for this was eventually developed and United States Patent Application Serial No. 234567 (now granted as United States Patent No. 3999999)* was filed on 1st July 1979. Figs. 19 and 20 of this Application show an eventual element almost identical to that of Figs. 1 and 4 of Patent No. 2345678.

13.   I note that no attempt is made in Patent No. 2345678 to explain how the differential coloration of successive polygonal surfaces is to be achieved. In the context of manufacturing plastics multi-element necklaces for a mass market, hand painting or the like of each surface is – whilst a theoretical possibility – an absurdity in commercial practice. This is possibly the reason why Modern Necklaces have quite failed so far to put any commercial product according to Patent No. 2345678 onto the United Kingdom so far. The key contribution to a necklace of this kind has been provided by the Applicants' development of their combined moulding/decorating machinery; yet exploitation of that contribution in the United Kingdom is precluded so long as Patent No. 2345678 subsists.

---

*This Patent No. is artificial in the context.

AND I MAKE this solemn Declaration conscientiously believing the same to be true and by virtue of the provisions of the Statutory Declarations Act 1835
Declared at 1 Old Square, Lincoln's Inn, London W.C.2 this 15th day of April 1992

Before me A. Tulkinghorne

(Dempster Elihu Fachmann)
(Signature)

A Commissioner for Oaths

FORM E (PATENTEES' EVIDENCE-IN-CHIEF UNDER RULE 75(5)) STATUTORY DECLARATION

I, George Herbert Inkpen of 777 Sweeting Road, Silvertown, London E.16 do hereby solemnly and sincerely declare as follows:

1.   I have 27 years' experience in the jewellery industry. After leaving school at age 16 in 1956 I was apprenticed to Messrs Solder & Braze of Sufferance Street, London E.C.1 as trainee craftsman. I subsequently attended Goldsmith's College on a part-time day release basis and gained my Higher National Certificate in 1963. I remained with Messrs. Solder & Braze as craftsman, and later as designer, until 1975 when I left to found Modern Necklaces Ltd. I have spent the whole of my working life in the Hatton Garden area and have a wide knowledge of jewellery manufacture. I am a co-inventor of the subject-matter of Patent No. 2345678.
2.   I have read all the papers in these proceedings.
3.   I have never visited Africa; nor had I ever heard of the Timbucca tribe or Dr. Livingstone until these proceedings. In pursuit of my career as jewellery manufacturer and designer I had never any reason to cultivate the acquaintance of those in anthropological circles. My knowledge and experience are rooted in the United Kingdom jewellery trade as actually practised.
4.   I agree of course with Mr Fachmann that fashion in the jewellery trade, particularly at the cheap end of the market, is fickle. I also agree that towards the end of the 1970s there were signs of consumer resistance to the conventional single-colour multiple element plastics necklace. There seemed to be a demand for brighter and more colourful necklaces – perhaps in response to the deepening recession in trade and business generally.
5.   Myself and my co-inventor John Kenneth Lamprey derived no assistance from the Timbucca neck adornments, or from such items as the press-stud and allied fasteners shown in Exhibit DEF.2, when making the invention of Patent No. 2345678. I suddenly had the idea, when discussing possible new lines for the summer 1979 season with my co-director John Kenneth Lamprey in the Plain & Syrup café, Fetter Lane, E.C.4 one tea-time in the autumn of 1978, of making the elements polygonal; this would provide a sharper and more decisive appearance. My co-director (named as co-inventor) immediately pointed out that by colouring the successive angular surfaces of the polygon differently we could get colour contrast. It was a further step from there to use a circular collar in place of the conventional flat fin, so as to give personally adjustable colour contrast.
6.   In retrospect, the subject-matter of Patent No. 2345678 may well appear to have been obvious but the fact is that the jewellery market in the United Kingdom is (at the cheap end) extremely competitive. It is rather like ladies' fashion-wear; everyone is constantly looking for fresh ideas. Yet in the intervening 8–9 years between introduction of the sphere/fin type of element and our invention no third party has evolved a similar element.
7.   Patent No. 2345678 has the further advantage that retailers can hold lower stocks and hence reduce tied-up working capital. Previously they had to hold sets of single-coloured elements for making single-colour necklaces in all popular colours. With Patent No. 2345678 not only can contrasting colours be obtained but also there is the possibility of providing single-colour appearance, depending to some extent on the shape and size of the polygonal faces. To take an example, if the polygonal elements possess a cross-section in the form of

an isosceles triangle with low vertex angle and faces coloured purple, yellow (over the two sides) and black (over the base) one can create an overall purple or overall yellow appearance as well as purple/yellow/black contrasts. The monochrome appearance, say, purple appearance, is achieved by having all the vertex edges of the individual elements arranged on the inner arc of the necklace so that the purple faces are exposed and the yellow faces are disposed inwardly (against the wearer's dress or skin) and hence hidden. The base faces, which are relatively small in any event because of the acute triangle cross-section will point downwardly towards the ground (at least in the front) and hence be largely concealed.

8.   Mr Fachmann is wrong in suggesting that no product according to Patent No. 2345678 has yet been commercially successful. The sketches (scale × 2) now produced and shown to me marked GHI.1 are of my Company's 'Perpular' necklace, introduced in spring 1981 and with sales of over 10,000 sets of elements since.

9.   The 'Perpular' necklace is an adaptation of that illustrated by Figs. 2 and 3 of Patent No. 2345678. The connector is made out of crude amethyst rock (of purple coloration but not up to gem quality); large quantities of this are available, as a by-product of gem amethyst mining in W. Africa. The central body of the connector is considerably lengthened and cut so as to provide hexagonal faces; the ends are rounded and of enlarged diameter. The block on the other hand is considerably shortened and made out of suitable plastics material, again hexagonally faced. This is normally coloured black. In wear, the necklace thus presents an appearance of purple translucent rod-like prisms separated by opaque prismatic black beads.

10.   Use of plastic for the block (or separate connector) is of course the self-evident way to carry out the invention when incompressible starting material is desired to be used. It is only necessary for one half of the fastening arrangement (collar or undercut recess) to be deformable; it is not necessary for them both to be.

AND I MAKE this solemn Declaration conscientiously believing the same to be true and by virtue of the provisions of the Statutory Declarations Act 1835
Declared at 11 Old Square, Lincoln's Inn, London W.C.2 this 15th day of June 1992

Before me A. Postinghorne

(George Herbert Inkpen)
(Signature)

A Commissioner for Oaths

Sketch   GHI.1

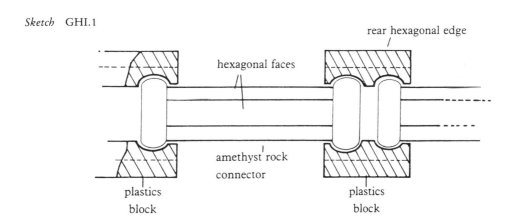

FORM F (APPLICANTS' EVIDENCE-IN-REPLY UNDER RULE 75(5)) STATUTORY DECLARATION

I, Dempster Elihu Fachmann of 999 Skunk's Misery Lane, Sunningfield, Surrey do hereby solemnly and sincerely declare as follows:

1.   I am the Dempster Elihu Fachmann who has previously made a Statutory Declaration on 15th day of April 1992 in these proceedings. I have read the Statutory Declaration dated 15th June 1992 of George Herbert Inkpen on behalf of the Patentees.

2.   As for the 'Perpular' necklace, this is well known to me. But this necklace is very different to anything suggested in Patent No. 2345678. The roles of the block and connector seem, so far as visual effect is concerned, to have been reversed. In the embodiments described in the Specification of Patent No. 2345678 the connector is much shorter than the block; the dominant (if not entire) visual effect is provided by the block, the connector being concealed in each case, in the assembled necklace, within the associated undercut recess. Additionally, there is no colour contrast as between successive polygonal faces of each block; each face carries the characteristic purple colour of the amethyst rock. It would seem to me doubtful as to whether the 'Perpular' necklace comes within the scope of the claims of Patent No. 2345678.

3.   Mr Inkpen disclaims any earlier acquaintanceship with the Timbucca tribe or anthropologists. That may well be so. But I cannot accept that he was entirely unaware of the influence of design from Third World countries. I produce as Exhibit DEF.3 a copy of a speech given by Mr Inkpen before the Annual Dinner of the United Kingdom Association of Jewellery Designers and Manufacturers (the principal domestic jewellery trade body) on 28 February 1970 entitled 'Challenges to the jewellery trade in the new decade', as reported in *Jewellery Business Monthly* Volume 99 pages 9–11 (1970). He said here, for example, at page 11:

> . . . it is clear from the recent slowing-down of trade that the British public is not satisfied with our present standard of design. New sources of design must be found. The younger market is looking for something fresh and unconventional. The vitality and colour of Africa, especially, has much to offer us in this respect. I anticipate a resurgence of interest in ethnic designs in the forthcoming years . . .

AND I MAKE this solemn Declaration conscientiously believing the same to be true and by virtue of the provisions of the Statutory Declarations Act 1835

Declared at 1 Old Square, Lincoln's Inn, London W.C.2 this 15th day of August 1992

Before me A. Tulkinghorne

(Dempster Elihu Fachmann)
(Signature)

A Commissioner for Oaths

Appendix 12

Guidelines (Selection) for Examination in the European Patent Office

Part C, Chapter IV, Section 9

9. Inventive step

9.1 *An invention shall be considered as involving an inventive step if, having regard to the state of the art, it is not obvious to a person skilled in the art.* Novelty and inventive step are different criteria. Novelty exists if there is any difference between the invention and the known art. The question – Is there inventive step ? – only arises if there is novelty.

9.2 The '*state of the art*' for the purposes of considering inventive step is as defined in Article 54, paragraph 2 (see IV, 5); it does not include later published European applications referred to in Article 54, paragraph 3. As mentioned in IV, 5.3, '*date of filing*' in Article 54, paragraph 2 means date of priority where appropriate (see Chapter V).

9.3 Thus the question to consider, in relation to any claim defining the invention, is whether at the priority date of that claim, having regard to the art known at that time, it would have been obvious to the person skilled in the art to arrive at something falling within the terms of the claim. If so, the claim is bad for lack of inventive step. The term '*obvious*' means that which does not go beyond the normal progress of technology but merely follows plainly or logically from the prior art, i.e. something which does not involve the exercise of any skill or ability beyond that to be expected of the person skilled in the art. In considering inventive step, as distinct from novelty (see IV, 7.3), it is fair to construe any published document in the light of subsequent knowledge and to have regard to all the knowledge generally available to the person skilled in the art at the priority date of the claim.

9.3a The invention claimed must normally be considered as a whole. Thus it is not correct as a general rule, in the case of a combination claim, to argue that the separate features of the combination taken by themselves are known or obvious and that 'therefore' the whole subject-matter claimed is obvious. The only exception to this rule is where there is no functional relationship between the features of the combination i.e. where the claim is merely for a juxtaposition of features and not a true combination (see the example at IV, 9.8 B1).

9.4 While the claim should in each case be directed to technical features (and not, for example, merely to an idea), in order to assess whether an inventive step is present it is important for the examiner to bear in mind that there are various ways in which the skilled person may arrive at an invention. An invention may, for example, be based on the following:

(i) The formulation of an idea or of a problem to be solved (the solution being obvious once the problem is clearly stated).

Example: the problem of indicating to the driver of a motor vehicle at night the line of the road ahead by using the light from the vehicle itself. As soon as the problem is stated in this form the technical solution, viz. the provision of reflective markings along the road surface, appears simple and obvious.

(ii) The devising of a solution to a known problem.

Example: the problem of permanently marking farm animals such as cows without causing pain to the animals or damage to the hide has existed since farming began. The solution ('freeze-branding') consists in applying the discovery that the hide can be permanently depigmented by freezing.

(iii) The arrival at an insight into the cause of an observed phenomenon (the practical use of this phenomenon then being obvious).

Example: the agreeable flavour of butter is found to be caused by minute quantities of a particular compound. As soon as this insight has been arrived at, the technical application comprising adding this compound to margarine is immediately obvious.

Many inventions are of course based on a combination of the above possibilities – e.g. the arrival at an insight and the technical application of that insight may both involve the use of the inventive faculty.

9.5   In identifying the contribution any particular invention makes to the art in order to determine whether there is an inventive step, account should be taken first of what the applicant himself acknowledges in his description and claims to be known; any such acknowledgement of known art should be regarded by the examiner as being correct unless the applicant states he has made a mistake (see VI, 8.5). However, the further prior art contained in the search report may put the invention in an entirely different perspective from that apparent from reading the applicant's specification by itself (and indeed this cited prior art may cause the applicant voluntarily to amend his claims to redefine his invention before his application comes up for examination). In order to reach a final conclusion as to whether any claim includes an inventive step it is necessary to determine the difference between the subject-matter of that claim and the whole of the known art and, in considering this matter, the examiner should not proceed solely from the point of view suggested by the form of claim (prior art plus characterising portion – see III, 2).

9.5a   If an independent claim is new and non-obvious, there is no need to investigate the obviousness or non-obviousness of any claims dependent thereon. Similarly, if a claim to a product is new and non-obvious there is no need to investigate the obviousness of any claims for a process which inevitably results in the manufacture of that product or any claims for a use of that product, in spite of the fact that claims in different categories are referred to in Rule 30 as 'independent' claims. In particular, analogy processes are patentable insofar as they provide a novel and inventive product (see Technical Board of Appeal Decision T119/82, OJ 5/1984, p. 217).

9.6   The person skilled in the art should be presumed to be an ordinary practitioner aware of what was common general knowledge in the art at the relevant date. He should also be presumed to have had access to everything in the *'state of the art'*, in particular the documents cited in the search report, and to have had at his disposal the normal means and capacity for routine work and experimentation. If the problem prompts the person skilled in the art to seek its solution in another technical field, the specialist in that field is the person qualified to solve the problem. The assessment of whether the solution involves an inventive step must therefore be based on that specialist's knowledge and ability (see Technical Board of Appeal Decision T32/81, OJ 6/1982, p. 225). There may be instances where it is more appropriate to think in terms of a group of persons, e.g. a research or production team, than a single person. This may apply e.g. in certain advanced technologies such as computers or telephone systems and in highly specialised processes such as the commercial production of integrated circuits or of complex chemical substances.

9.7   In considering whether there is inventive step (as distinct from novelty (see IV, 7)), it is permissible to combine together the disclosures of two or more documents or parts of documents, different parts of the same document or other pieces of prior art, but only where such combination would have been obvious to the person skilled in the art at the effective priority date of the claim under examination (see Decision of the Technical Board of Appeal T2/83, OJ 6/1984, p. 265). In determining whether it would be obvious to combine two or more distinct documents, the examiner should have regard to the following:

(i) Whether the content of the documents is such as to make it likely or unlikely that the person skilled in the art, when concerned with the problem solved by the invention, would combine them – for example, if two disclosures considered as a whole could not in practice be readily combined because of inherent incompatibility in disclosed features essential to the invention, the combining of these disclosures should not normally be regarded as obvious.

(ii) Whether the documents come from similar, neighbouring or remote technical fields.

(iii) The number of documents which need to be combined.

The combining of two or more parts of the same document would be obvious if it would be natural for the skilled person to associate these parts with one another. It would normally be obvious to combine with other prior documents a well-known textbook or standard dictionary; this is only a special case of the general proposition that it is obvious to combine the teaching of one or more documents with the common general knowledge in the art. It would, generally speaking, also be obvious to combine two documents one of which contains a clear and unmistakable reference to the other. In determining whether it is permissible to combine a document with an item of prior art made public in some other way, e.g. by use, similar considerations apply.

9.8 The following list gives examples for guidance of circumstances where an invention should be regarded as obvious or where it involves an inventive step. It is to be stressed that these examples are only guides and that the applicable principle in each case is 'was it obvious to a person skilled in the art?' Examiners should avoid attempts to fit a particular case into one of these examples where the latter is not clearly applicable. Also, the list is not exhaustive.

(A1) Inventions involving the application of known measures in an obvious way and in respect of which an inventive step is therefore to be ruled out:

> (i) The teaching of a prior document is incomplete and at least one of the possible ways of 'filling the gap' which would naturally or readily occur to the skilled person results in the invention.
>
> *Example*: The invention relates to a building structure made from aluminium. A prior document discloses the same structure and says that it is of light-weight material but fails to mention the use of aluminium.

> (ii) The invention differs from the known art merely in the use of well-known equivalents (mechanical, electrical or chemical).
>
> *Example*: The invention relates to a pump which differs from a known pump solely in that its motive power is provided by a hydraulic motor instead of an electric motor.

> (iii) The invention consists merely in a new use of a well-known material employing the known properties of that material.
>
> *Example*: Washing composition containing as detergent a known compound having the known property of lowering the surface tension of water, this property being known to be an essential one for detergents.

> (iv) The invention consists in the substitution in a known device of a recently developed material whose properties make it plainly suitable for that use.
>
> *Example*: An electric cable comprises a polyethylene sheath bonded to a metallic shield by an adhesive. The invention lies in the use of a particularly newly developed adhesive known to be suitable for polymer-metal bonding.

> (v) The invention consists merely in the use of a known technique in a loosely analogous situation.
>
> *Example*: The invention resides in the application of a pulse control technique to the electric motor driving the auxiliary mechanisms of an industrial truck, such as a fork-lift truck, the use of this technique to control the electric propulsion motor of the truck being already known.

(A2) Inventions involving the application of known measures in a non-obvious way and in respect of which an inventive step is therefore to be recognised:

(i) A known working method or means when used for a different purpose involves a new, surprising effect.

Example: It is known that high frequency power can be used in inductive butt welding. It should therefore be obvious that high-frequency power could also be used in conductive butt welding with similar effect; an inventive step would exist in this case, however, if high-frequency power were used for the continuous conductive butt welding of coiled strip but without removing scale (such scale removal being on the face of it necessary in order to avoid arcing between the welding contact and the strip). The unexpected additional effect is that scale removal is found to be unnecessary because at high frequency the current is supplied in a predominantly capacitative manner via the scale which forms a dielectric.

(ii) A new use of a known device or material involves overcoming technical difficulties not resolvable by routine techniques.

Example: The invention relates to a device for supporting and controlling the rise and fall of gas holders, enabling the previously employed external guiding framework to be dispensed with. A similar device was known for supporting floating docks or pontoons but practical difficulties not encountered in the known applications needed to be overcome in applying the device to a gas holder.

(B1) Obvious and consequently non-inventive combination of features:

The invention consists merely in the juxtaposition or association of known devices or processes functioning in their normal way and not producing any non-obvious working inter-relationship.

Example: Machine for producing sausages consists of a known mincing machine and a known filling machine disposed side by side.

(B2) Not obvious and consequently inventive combination of features:

The combined features mutually support each other in their effects to such an extent that a new technical result is achieved. It is irrelevant whether each individual feature is fully or partly known by itself.

Example: A mixture of medicines consists of a painkiller (analgesic) and a tranquilliser (sedative). It was found that through the addition of the tranquilliser, which intrinsically appeared to have no pain-killing effect, the analgesic effect of the pain-killer was intensified in a way which could not have been predicted from the known properties of the active substances.

(C1) Obvious and consequently non-inventive selection among a number of known possibilities:

(i) The invention consists merely in choosing from a number of equally likely alternatives.

Example: The invention relates to a known chemical process in which it is known to supply heat electrically to the reaction mixture. There are a number of well-known alternative ways of so supplying the heat, and the invention resides merely in the choice of one alternative.

(ii) The invention resides in the choice of particular dimensions, temperature ranges or other parameters from a limited range of possibilities, and it is clear that these parameters could be arrived at by routine trial and error or by the application of normal design procedures.

Example: The invention relates to a process for carrying out a known reaction and is characterised by a specified rate of flow of an inert gas. The prescribed rates are merely those which would necessarily be arrived at by the skilled practitioner.

(iii) The invention can be arrived at merely by a simple extrapolation in a straightforward way from the known art.

Example: The invention is characterised by the use of a specified minimum content of a substance X in a preparation Y in order to improve its thermal stability, and this characterising feature can be derived merely by extrapolation on a straight-line graph, obtainable from the known art, relating thermal stability to the content of substance X.

(iv) The invention consists merely in selecting particular chemical compounds or compositions (including alloys) from a broad field.

Example: The prior art includes disclosure of a chemical compound characterised by a specified structure including a substituent group designated 'R'. This substituent 'R' is defined so as to embrace entire ranges of broadly-defined radical groups such as all alkyl or aryl radicals either unsubstituted or substituted by halogen and/or hydroxy, although for practical reasons only a very small number of specific examples are given. The invention consists in the selection of a particular radical or particular group of radicals from amongst those referred to, as the substituent 'R' (the selected radical or group of radicals not being specifically disclosed in the prior art document since the question would then be one of lack of novelty rather than obviousness). The resulting compounds

(a) are not described as having, nor shown to possess, any advantageous properties not possessed by the prior art examples; or

(b) are described as possessing advantageous properties compared with the compounds specifically referred to in the prior art but these properties are ones which the person skilled in the art would expect such compounds to possess, so that he is likely to be led to make this selection.

(C2) Not obvious and consequently inventive selection among a number of known possibilities:

(i) The invention involves special selection in a process of particular operating conditions (e.g. temperature and pressure) within a known range, such selection producing unexpected effects in the operation of the process or the properties of the resulting product.

Example: In a process where substance A and substance B are transformed at high temperature into substance C, it was known that there is in general a constantly increased yield of substance C as the temperature increases in the range between 50 and 130° C. It is now found that in the temperature range from 63 to 65° C, which previously had not been explored, the yield of substance C was considerably higher than expected.

(ii) The invention consists in selecting particular chemical compounds or compositions (including alloys) from a broad field, such compounds or compositions having unexpected advantages.

Example: In the example of a substituted chemical compound given at (iv) under (C1) above, the invention again resides in the selection of the substituent radical 'R' from the total field of possibilities defined in the prior disclosure. In this case, however, not only does the selection embrace a particular area of the possible field, and result in compounds that can be shown to possess advantageous properties (see VI, 5.7a) but there are no indications which would lead the person skilled in the art to this particular selection rather than any other in order to achieve the advantageous properties.

(D) Overcoming a technical prejudice:

As a general rule, there is an inventive step if the prior art leads the person skilled in the art away from the procedure proposed by the invention. This applies in particular when the skilled person would not even consider carrying out experiments to determine whether these were alternatives to the known way of overcoming a real or imagined technical obstacle.

Example: Drinks containing carbon dioxide are, after being sterilised, bottled while hot in sterilised bottles. The general opinion is that immediately after withdrawal of the bottle from the filling device the bottled drink must be automatically shielded from the outside air so as to prevent the bottled drink from spurting out. A process involving the same steps but in which no precautions are taken to shield the drink from the outside air (because none are in fact necessary) would therefore be inventive.

9.9 It should be remembered that an invention which at first sight appears obvious might in fact involve an inventive step. Once a new idea has been formulated it can often be shown theoretically how it might be arrived at, starting from something known, by a series of apparently easy steps. The examiner should be wary of *ex post facto* analysis of this kind. He should always bear in mind that the documents produced in the search have, of necessity, been obtained with foreknowledge of what matter constitutes the alleged invention. In all cases he should attempt to visualise the overall state of the art confronting the skilled man before the applicant's contribution and he should seek to make a 'real life' assessment of this and other relevant factors. He should take into account all that is known concerning the background of the invention and give fair weight to relevant arguments or evidence submitted by the applicant. If, for example, an invention is shown to be of considerable technical value, and particularly if it provides a technical advantage which is new and surprising, and this can convincingly be related to one or more of the features included in the claim defining the invention, the examiner should be hesitant in pursuing an objection that such a claim lacks inventive step. The same applies where the invention solves a technical problem which workers in the art have been attempting to solve for a long time, or otherwise fulfils a long-felt need. Commercial success alone is not to be regarded as indicative of inventive step, but evidence of immediate commercial success when coupled with evidence of a long-felt want is of relevance provided the examiner is satisfied that the success derives from the technical features of the invention and not from other influences (e.g. selling techniques or advertising).

9.10   The relevant arguments and evidence to be considered by the examiner for assessing inventive step may be taken either from the originally filed patent application, or be submitted by the applicant during the subsequent proceedings (see C-VI, 5.7*a*).

Glossary

Ambiguity. A ground of objection to an 'existing' patent (patent granted under the 1949 Act) only, defined statutorily as: 'that the scope of any claim of the complete specification is not sufficiently and clearly defined'.

Anticipation. In principle, a somewhat imprecise term; often used as a synonym for lack of novelty. More common in earlier patent jurisprudence, where it would sometimes cover obviousness also to a limited extent, on account of lack of novelty being then regarded more widely than today; a distinction was sometimes drawn between formal novelty and true novelty.

Best method. A requirement of the 1949 Act that a patentee should disclose in his specification the best method of performing the invention; the corresponding ground of objection, to an 'existing' patent (patent granted under the 1949 Act) only, is defined statutorily as: 'that the complete specification . . . does not disclose the best method of performing it which was known to the applicant for the patent and for which he was entitled to claim protection'.

Claim. That part of a patent which defines (at least at first instance) the boundary of the monopoly granted for the invention.

Community Patent Convention. The Convention, signed at Luxembourg in 1975, whereby a single unitary patent effective throughout the countries of the European Economic Community will be obtainable; not yet effective.

Complete Specification. The term used up to the 1977 Act to denote the final Specification of the Patent; it had, under the 1949 Act, to 'particularly describe the invention and the method by which it is to be performed' (as well as disclosing the best method) and was to be distinguished from the Provisional Specification, in the two-specification procedure available under that Act (and its predecessor Acts) right up to the passing of the 1977 Act.

Comptroller-General. Titular head of the Patent Office.

Compulsory licence. A patent licence compulsorily granted by the Patent Office on application of a third party; the special compulsory licence provisions of the 1949 Act in respect of inventions relating to food, medicine, surgical or curative devices have been repealed by the 1977 Act.

Cripps question. A reference to the test of obviousness formulated by the late Sir Stafford Cripps K.C in 1928 in *Sharpe & Dohme v Boots Pure Drug*. Now generally discarded since it has become appreciated that the formulation merely re-states the question rather than providing any useful separate definition or approach.

De minimis. Shortened form of *De minimis non curat lex*, a legal Latin expression meaning 'the law does not concern itself with trifles'.

De novo. Legal Latin expression meaning 'anew'.

Disclaimer. A reduction in the scope of a patent claim; sometimes also used to describe a retraction from an assertion in the patent specification.

Enabling disclosure. A concept of United States origin, but more recently accentuated in United Kingdom and European Patent Office jurisprudence. A prior documentary disclosure is said to be 'enabling' (or conversely, 'non-enabling') if the instructions are sufficient (or conversely, insufficient) to enable the skilled person to replicate its teaching. In the field of prior use the doctrine is controversial.

Equivalents. A controversial doctrine of patent law to the effect that a patent can be infringed even though the alleged infringement falls outside the strict scope of the patent claims provided that the alleged infringement is 'equivalent' to the claimed invention; also known as infringement by 'pith and marrow'.

European Patent Application. See **European Patent Convention**.

European Patent Convention. The Convention, signed at Munich in 1973, under which the European Patent Office was set up and the European patent system, involving filing of a European Patent Application, created.

Exhaustion of rights. A term developed in EEC intellectual property jurisprudence. As applied to patents, it means that once a patented article has been put onto the market in an EEC country by the patentee or his voluntary licensee then subsequent importation into and sale in another EEC country cannot be prevented. Sometimes also used in connection with purely national legal provisions.

Existing patent. The statutory term in the 1977 Act for a patent granted under the 1949 Act, sub-divided further in the 1977 Act into 'old existing patents' (to denote patents dated on or before 1 June 1967) and 'new existing patents' (to denote patents dated after 1 June 1967); existing patents are commonly (but imprecisely) denominated as 'old' patents in ordinary parlance, the statutory phraseology being intrinsically somewhat confusing.

Expressio unius est exclusio alterius. Legal Latin expression meaning 'the mention of one is the exclusion of another'.

Fair basis. This term refers primarily to the requirement of the 1949 Act that a claim be 'fairly based' on the disclosure in the specification; it is thus a ground of objection to an 'existing' patent (patent granted under the 1949 Act) that 'any claim is not fairly based on the matter disclosed in the specification'.

False suggestion. A ground of objection to an 'existing' patent (patent granted under the 1949 Act) only, defined statutorily as: 'that the patent was obtained on a false suggestion or representation'.

Gillette defence. As originally enunciated in 1913 in *Gillette Safety Razor v Anglo American Trading*, the defence that the infringement is not novel; a shorthand way of pleading either that the patent is too broad in face of the prior art (and hence invalid) or, if construed more narrowly so as to be valid in face of the prior art, then there is no infringement by the defendant; the defence should today be rephrased as 'the alleged infringement is obvious', in view of the change in the meaning of the word 'novel' in patent law during the interval since 1913. The modern enunciation is contained in *Windsurfing v Tabur Marine* (1985).

In limine. Legal Latin expression meaning 'on the threshold'.

Insufficiency. A ground of objection to a patent, on the basis that the specification fails to describe properly how the invention is to be carried out; defined statutorily in the 1977 Act as: 'the specification of the patent does not disclose the invention clearly enough and completely enough for it to be performed by a person skilled in the art'.

Interlocutory injunction. A temporary injunction granted in advance of trial.

International Convention. The Convention, originally signed at Paris in 1883, whereby an inventor may within twelve months of filing his domestic patent application file a corresponding foreign patent application(s) with a priority date of the original filing. The great majority of countries now adhere to the Convention.

International Patent Application. See **Patent Co-operation Treaty**.

Inutility. A ground of objection to an 'old' patent (patent granted under the 1949 Act) only, defined statutorily as: 'that the invention, so far as claimed in any claim of the complete specification, is not useful'.

Letters Patent. The formal mode of grant of a patent, under the Seal of the Patent Office, employed up to the passing of the 1977 Act; under the 1977 Act a Certificate of Grant is issued instead.

Licence as of right. When a patent is endorsed 'licence as of right', either on application of the patentee or a third party, licences are freely available on terms to be settled by the Patent Office if not otherwise agreed.

Manner of new manufacture. The definition contained in the Statute of Monopolies 1624 as to what could still be the subject of the grant of Letters Patent; remained as the definition of 'invention' in patent law up to the passing of the 1977 Act.

'New' patent. A patent granted under the 1977 Act; see also **Existing patent**.

Novelty. An essential requirement for patentability is that an invention possess novelty, that is, 'newness', as a whole even if some of its constituent parts are individually already known.

Obiter dictum. Legal Latin expression meaning a remark of the judge on a point not directly in issue before him. Often abbreviated to *dictum* (plural, *dicta*).

Obviousness. Derived from the Latin (*ob* + *via*) meaning 'in the way of'; in order that a valid patent may be granted the subject-matter of a given invention must not only be new but also non-obvious – that is to say, it must represent something more than a mere routine improvement; usually the most common ground of objection to a patent.

'Old' patent. A patent granted under the 1949 Act; see also **Existing patent**.

Omnibus claim. Essentially, a narrow form of claim directed to the machine (or process, product) substantially as described in the patent specification with reference to the drawings and/or specific examples. Often present as the final claim of a set of claims.

Patent of addition. Under the 1949 Act, but not the 1977 Act, a patentee who made an improvement in, or modification of, his parent invention could apply for a patent of addition on the fresh subject-matter. Advantages were that novelty only was required (not non-obviousness also), and no renewal fees were payable; a disadvantage was that the term of the patent of addition was limited to that of the parent patent.

Patentability. A generic term, denoting the sum of the conditions which a given invention must fulfil if a valid patent is to be granted for it.

Patent Co-operation Treaty. The Treaty, signed at Washington in 1970, providing for simplification of the procedure for obtaining patent protection in multiple countries by filing of an International Patent Application.

Patents Appeal Tribunal. From 1932 to 1978 the tribunal, normally a High Court judge, which heard appeals from decisions of the Patent Office.

'Pith and marrow'. See **Equivalents**.

Prior claiming. A ground of objection to an 'existing' patent (patent granted under the 1949 Act) only, defined statutorily as: 'that the invention, so far as claimed in any claim of the complete specification, was claimed in a valid claim of earlier priority date contained in the complete specification of another patent granted in the United Kingdom'. It was intended to deal with the problem of contemporaneous similar inventions leading in turn to conflicting, but chronologically overlapping, patents. The 1977 Act adopts the alternative 'whole contents' approach to the resolution of this problem.

Priority date. A term used in both the 1949 and 1977 Acts to denote the chronological date to which a claim and an invention respectively, are entitled.

Provisional Specification. The term used up to the 1977 Act to denote the initial form of the specification of the Patent, in the case of an original domestic Patent Application; it had, under the 1949 Act, merely to 'describe the invention'; to be distinguished from the subsequent Complete Specification, normally required under the 1949 Act to be filed within the succeeding twelve months.

Purposive construction. An approach to construction (interpretation) of a patent specification which is at present in vogue. It derives from Lord Diplock's judgment in 1982 in *Catnic v Hill & Smith*.

Quia timet. Legal Latin expression meaning 'because he fears'; thus, application may be made *quia timet* for an interlocutory injunction if a patentee fears forthcoming (but not yet extant) infringement.

Ratio decidendi. Legal Latin expression meaning the 'true rule' of a legal decision. Often abbreviated to 'ratio' or 'rationale'.

Register. The register, kept at the Patent Office, on which are recorded details of the grant, renewal, assignment, licensing, other dealings, and orders concerning the patent.

Selection patent. A patent directed to subject-matter constituting a fraction (usually small) of an existing class or field already known in general terms; the selected subject-matter fraction must itself be new, and possess an unexpected advantage; important in the area of chemical patenting, although not restricted thereto.

Specification. That part of a patent which teaches the reader how to carry out the invention in respect of which the patent is granted.

Stare decisis. Legal Latin expression meaning the doctrine of precedent.

State of the art. A term used in the 1977 Act to denote the totality of existing prior matter in the public domain, for the field to which the invention relates.

Statute of Monopolies. The Act, passed in 1624 to deal with Elizabethan-era abuses of the system of Crown grants of monopoly, which constitutes the foundation-stone of United Kingdom patent law.

Subject-matter. A term sometimes found in older judgments as a synonym for non-obviousness.

Treaty of Rome. The Treaty establishing the European Economic Community, signed at Rome in 1957.

Verification. Refers to the *dictum* of Astbury, J. in *Sharp & Dohme v Boots Pure Drug*, viz. 'you cannot take a patent out for verifying a prior statement'.

Whole contents. A term used to denote the approach taken by the 1977 Act to resolution of the problem which arises when similar inventions are made contemporaneously leading in turn to conflicting, but chronologically overlapping, patents; whereas under the 1949 Act it was permitted to cite just the claims of the earlier patent against the claims of the later patent, under the 1977 Act the whole of the contents of the earlier patent (that is, Specification and Claims) can be so relied on; a limitation is that such contents cannot be relied on to show obviousness, but instead solely lack of novelty.

General Bibliography

T. Blanco White, *Patents for Inventions*, Stevens and Sons, 1974 (4th ed.) and 1983 (5th ed.).

CIPA, *European Patents Source Finder*, Longman, 1988 onwards.

CIPA, *Guide to the Patents Acts*, Sweet & Maxwell, 1990 (3rd ed.).

W. Cornish, *Intellectual Property – Patents, Copyright, Trade Marks and Allied Rights*, Sweet & Maxwell, 1989 (2nd ed.).

W. Cornish, *Materials on Intellectual Property*, ESC Publishing, 1990.

R. Crespi, *Patents: A Basic Guide to Patenting in Biotechnology*, Cambridge University Press, 1988.

L. Melville, *Forms and Agreements on Intellectual Property and International Licensing*, Clark Boardman and Sweet & Maxwell, 1979 onwards (3rd ed.).

J. Pagenberg, *License Agreements – Patents, Utility Models, Know-how, Computer Software*, Carl Heymanns Verlag, 1991.

G. Paterson, *The European Patent System*, Sweet & Maxwell, 1992.

B. Reid, *Cases on Patents*, Waterlow Publishers, 1988.

Terrell on the Law of Patents, Sweet & Maxwell, 1982 (13th ed.).

M. Vitoria *et al.*, *Encyclopaedia of United Kingdom and European Patent Law*, Sweet & Maxwell, 1978 onwards.

Index